George Jones

Life Scenes from the Four Gospels

George Jones

Life Scenes from the Four Gospels

ISBN/EAN: 9783337280154

Printed in Europe, USA, Canada, Australia, Japan

Cover: Foto ©Lupo / pixelio.de

More available books at **www.hansebooks.com**

MAP OF
PALESTINE
in the time of
CHRIST.

Scale of Miles

LIFE-SCENES

FROM THE

FOUR GOSPELS.

THIRD EDITION,

WITH MAPS AND ILLUSTRATIONS.

BY

Rev. GEORGE JONES, M. A.,

CHAPLAIN UNITED STATES NAVY.

PHILADELPHIA:

J. C. GARRIGUES & CO.,

No. 148 SOUTH FOURTH STREET.

1868.

PREFACE.

THE object in this book is to give a *fulness* to the scenes in the Gospels by means of the various knowledge which modern research has placed within reach; and also to add *freshness* to them in our minds so much accustomed to see them in one point of view. How far this is regarded as having been accomplished will appear in the following notice which the first edition has elicited in the "Sunday School Times," Philadelphia, from one of its correspondents.

"This volume, by the Rev. George Jones, of the United States Navy, is replete with information and truly dramatic interest. Every statement in it has been subjected to severest tests, and been found to consist with the simple truth.

"It is a graceful and captivating harmony of the gospels, in which the reader is carried along from one scene to another with true historic accuracy, and yet with an interest rivalling that excited by fable or romance; while the careful sketches of the country and the customs of those days, introduce the sacred narrative to the mind as a new history, full of a reality never before so vividly seen and felt.

*   ·   *   *   *   *   *   *   *

"The exciting narrative of the whole life of our Lord is never interrupted, excepting where it is important to give descriptions of the country or its customs, and the reader moves along with the story, with a perception of its reality, as if he were himself an observer or an actor in its scenes.

"The author has personally visited the land he describes, and with profound reverence for his subject, apparent on every page, writes with such singleness of purpose, simplicity and vividness, as to make the work truly '*life scenes* from the four gospels.'

"Pastors, Sabbath-school teachers and Christians generally will find the book very valuable. It has in it a great deal of information sought out and selected with indefatigable labor, judgment and integrity, and of undisputed **authority. It is** peculiarly calculated to impart a realizing and **unwonted perception** of our Lord Jesus Christ."

The author must be allowed to acknowledge the great satisfaction afforded him by such testimonials received from **all parts of the country** and from persons **of** all conditions **of life; for never before did he put** such severe and earnest **labor, or so much heart into any undertaking as in this.**

While preparing the **work he** felt greatly encouraged by **meeting with** the following in the writings of others, calling **it is true, for** much **more than he could hope** to effect; yet **showing how much a work in this line of effort** was needed.

From Canon Stanley's book on Sinai and Palestine.

"So to delineate the outward **events of the Old and New** Testa**ment,** as that they should come **home** with **a new** power to those who, by long familiarity, have almost ceased to regard them **as** historical **truth at** all—so to bring **out** their inward **spirit** that a **more** com**plete** realization of **their outward** form should not degrade but exalt **the faith** of which **they are** the vehicle—this would indeed be an object worthy of all labor which travellers and theologians have ever **bestowed on** the East."

From the N. Y. "Christian Advocate and Journal" (Methodist) of June 1st, 1865.

"We **have** never met **with a book in** which the life of Christ **has been** adequately delineated from the modern point of view. . . . . **The** materials for illustration are abundantly at hand, and we trust **one day to see** them graphically and vividly employed for that pur**pose. The book, if** properly executed, would **vie in** interest with **any romance; for the** tragedy culminating at **Calvary is** without a **parallel in all the elements of** pathos and sublime **incident."**

From a Critique on Renan's "Life of Jesus," by a Professor in Theology.

"This life of Jesus, so **fascinating to the lovers of** romance, may also lead Christian thinkers **to depict the living** Christ more vividly in all his human endowments, relations, **and** sympathies. We are, perhaps, too apt to dwell upon **him as the** centre of doctrines; to substitute the abstract dogma for **the living** person. The success of Renan's **book** is, doubtless, in **part, to be** attributed to the graphic beauty **with which he depicts the scenes in** the midst **of** which the youth of our Lord was spent; to the air of living interest he throws around the personal narratives and the records of events; to his use of a prolific and cultivated imagination in making resurrection of the past, so that it often seems like a present reality. How much more perfectly, without inconsistencies and contradictions, might this be done by the reverent Christian scholar, imbibing the full spirit of the evangelists, and using all the resources of thought and scholarship to illustrate the wondrous story of Jesus of Nazareth! Let this but be written in a book, as it is inscribed on every loving and believing heart; let the radiant person of our Lord appear in visible majesty and grace, and such poor fictions as that of Renan will quickly vanish, as do the phantoms of a rayless night before the brightness of a rising sun."

Any one attempting what is required in the above, will probably find the result to be far short of his wishes; but if only a small portion is accomplished, still the importance of the subjects can make that small part worth the attempt.

In a work like this, it is of the highest consequence to guard against a too free use of the imagination. When a certain amount of sure data are allowed in any circumstances of human action or feeling, we may know that certain other things will be the accompaniments: and so far the author has gone in filling up these life pictures; taking, in connection with this, all that can be gained from history, topography, and criticism respecting that country and the usages of those times. There is always in such efforts, a temptation to let the fancy have too much liberty; but the sacredness of the subjects here was too great to allow of such indulgence; and the author has endeavored to be constantly on his guard so as to keep to the truth in every case. Though wishing to place full and vivid life-scenes before the reader, he has felt it to be more important to be truthful than to be graphic.

A scene which he once witnessed himself, has helped in the attempt to represent the listening multitudes in those ancient days in Palestine. It is not often that any one has an opportunity of seeing a person of mature intellect and

1 *

candid mind listening for the first time in his life to the
Gospel of Christ; but the author saw this once in the missionary church in the centre of Shanghae, in China; and
the scene was a singularly interesting one. The missionary
was preaching in the native language; very soon, a man
apparently about forty-five years of age and with an open
and intelligent countenance, rose in the congregation, as if
unable longer to keep his seat. He stood during the rest of the
discourse seemingly unconscious of everything but what he
was listening to, his hands grasping the back of the seat before him, his features lighted up and showing deep attention, and his eyes never once removed from the speaker's
face, a slight nod of the head frequently giving assent to
what was said. After the services were over, he followed
the missionary to his room; mentioned that he came to the
city on business from a distant town in the interior; that a
friend belonging to the same place had once heard the mis-
sionaries, and had told him of them; and that he had come,
on this occasion, to hear for himself.

It is true that no man can ever approximate to the power
over an audience by him, of whom his enemies themselves
declared that "never man spake like this man;" but yet
that sight showed in some slight degree, what may have been
the scenes in Palestine when the crowds were following the
Messiah, and listening to his preaching. It has been with
the author constantly, while writing this book;—that intent face, that rapt attention, those glistening eyes, that surprised and pleased look, and those nods of assent.

As respects the order of events in this work, that in Robinson's Harmony of the Gospels has been followed after com-
paring it with works of a similar kind. For the purpose
of enabling the reader to form a judgment for himself respecting the truthfulness of the scenes depicted, references
are given throughout to authorities, especially in the Scriptures themselves.

The first edition of this book **was in a cheap** form, as it was but an experiment, and the author could not tell **how** the effort would be received : but the commendations from every direction lead him now to reproduce the volume somewhat enlarged **and** in better style of publication, **and with** pictorial **illustrations of places and** modes of **life.** These last have been **prepared with great** care, and in accordance with only the **best authorities ancient and** modern : **they are** it **is** believed correct representations: nothing **has been introduced in them merely for** the **sake of** pictorial **effect.** GEORGE JONES.

UNITED STATES **NAVAL** ASYLUM,
PHILADELPHIA, *May 27th*, 1867.

Among the numerous books referred to as authorities in addition to the Scriptures it may be well to give here the following titles more in detail:—

H. S. Alford: "The Greek Testament, with a critically revised text and a critical commentary."

S. T. Bloomfield: "The Greek Testament, with English notes, critical, **philo**logical, and exegetical."

Adam Clarke: Commentary on the Scriptures.

Horne: Introduction to the Critical Study and Knowledge of the Holy Scriptures, by Thos. Hartwell Horne, M. A.

Jahn: Introduction to the Old Testament from the Latin and Greek works of John Jahn, with additional references and notes by S. H. Turner D. D. and W. R. Whittingham, D. D.

Jahn: **Biblical Archæology, translated by T. C.** Upham.

Josephus: **W**orks of Flavius Josephus, translated by William Whiston, A. M.

Lightfoot: The whole works of Rev. John Lightfoot. (9 vols.) Edited by J. R. Pitman.

Olin: Travels in Egypt, Arabia, Petrea and the Holy Land, by Rev. Stephen Olin, D. D.

F. A. D. Olshausen: Biblical Commentary on the Gospels.

Robinson & Smith: Biblical Researches in Palestine, &c.

F. A. D. Tholuck: **Commentary on the Gospel of Saint John.**

W. H. Thomson: **The Land and the Book.**

Van de Velde: **Narrative of a Journey** through **Syria** and Palestine.

ILLUSTRATIONS.

CONTENTS.

CHAPTER I.

AT THE JORDAN.

CHAPTER II.

AT THE JORDAN.

CHAPTER III.

THE WILDERNESS OF JUDEA.

CHAPTER IV.

AT THE JORDAN.

CHAPTER V.

CONDITION OF PALESTINE.

CHAPTER VI.

JEWISH MANNERS AND CUSTOMS.

CHAPTER VII.

JEWISH FESTIVALS.

CHAPTER VIII.

OVERCLOUDING OF THE JEWISH MIND.

CHAPTER IX.

JOST, A MODERN JEWISH HISTORIAN.

CHAPTER X.

AT THE JORDAN.

CHAPTER XI.

AT CANA IN GALILEE.

CHAPTER XII.

THE TEMPLE.

CHAPTER XIII.

THE TEMPLE CLEANSED.

CHAPTER XIV.

NICODEMUS.

CHAPTER XV.

IN SAMARIA AND GALILEE.

CHAPTER XVI.

AT NAZARETH.

CHAPTER XVII.

THE LAKE OF GALILEE, CAPERNAUM.

CHAPTER XVIII.

AT CAPERNAUM AND THROUGH GALILEE.

CHAPTER XIX.

AT CAPERNAUM—THE PARALYTIC HEALED.

CHAPTER XX.

AT JERUSALEM; ALSO AT CAPERNAUM.

CHAPTER XXI.

SERMON ON THE MOUNT.

CHAPTER XXII.

AT NAIN.

CHAPTER XXIII.

CASTLE OF MACHERUS—JOHN'S DEATH.

CHAPTER XXIV.

THE TWO DINNERS.

CHAPTER XXV.

"LET US MAKE HIM A KING."

CHAPTER XXVI.

THE TRANSFIGURATION.

CHAPTER XXVII.

DISPUTE AMONG THE APOSTLES ON THE WAY BACK TO GALILEE.

CHAPTER XXVIII.

JERUSALEM—FEAST OF TABERNACLES.

CHAPTER XXIX.

THE MESSIAH AT THE FEAST OF TABERNACLES.

CHAPTER XXX.

BETHANY AND THE ROAD TO JERICHO.

CHAPTER XXXI.

THE MAN BORN BLIND.

CHAPTER XXXII.

THE FEAST OF DEDICATION.

CHAPTER XXXIII.

RAISING OF LAZARUS.

CHAPTER XXXIV.

IN EPHRAIM AND PEREA.

CHAPTER XXXV.

JERICHO.

CHAPTER XXXVI.

THE MESSIAH AT JERICHO—BLIND MEN HEALED.

CHAPTER XXXVII.

JERUSALEM DESCRIBED.

CHAPTER XXXVIII.

THE PUBLIC ENTRY.

CHAPTER XXXIX.

AT THE TEMPLE—WOES DENOUNCED.

CHAPTER XL.

THE PLOT.

CHAPTER XLI.

SUPPER AT BETHANY—JUDAS.

CHAPTER XLII.

THE PASSOVER FEAST.

CHAPTER XLIII.

GETHSEMANE.

CHAPTER XLIV.

HALL OF CAIAPHAS.

CHAPTER XLV.

THE TRIAL BEFORE PILATE.

CHAPTER XLVI.

THE CRUCIFIXION.

CHAPTER XLVII.

THE BURIAL.

CHAPTER XLVIII.

THE RESURRECTION.

CHAPTER XLIX.

AFTER THE RESURRECTION—THE ASCENSION.

CHAPTER L.

" WHAT THINK YE OF CHRIST ?"

LIFE-SCENES.

CHAPTER I.

AT THE JORDAN.

THERE was a very strange scene at the banks of the Jordan. The time of which we are writing was about eighteen hundred and thirty-seven years ago; and the scene referred to was a large gathering of excited people around a man of singular appearance, who was making a most wonderful announcement, and was engaging in a baptismal rite of startling significance. He was a gaunt ascetic; in his dress and manner, and in his authoritative language, reminding all who saw and heard him of the old prophets; and, indeed, in his appearance so much resembling Elijah, that the query was immediately started in every man's mind, whether he was not actually that prophet risen from the dead. The idea of such a resurrection of Elijah was familiar to the minds of the Jews; for the belief had long been universal among them that, restored to life, he would be the precursor of their expected Messiah. This man was proclaiming, "Repent ye, *for the kingdom of heaven is at hand.*" It was believed by the Jews that, at the appearing of the Messiah, they were to be initiated by baptism into the new dispensation of his kingdom;[1] and here, now, they

---

[1] Bloomfield on Matt. iii. 1.

were called to come and to be baptized; and numbers, after confessing their sins, were led down into the Jordan for that rite.

The scenery all around was in character with the strange performer in this ceremony;—a desert spot, represented by a modern traveller to that region as a dreary waste, "weird, and singularly wild and impressive." The Jordan is a very peculiar stream. After issuing from the Lake of Tiberias, which is itself 652 feet below the level of the Mediterranean, its course is southwardly, in a valley called by the present natives El Ghor, or "the depression," five or six miles wide, and sunk from 1000 to 1200 feet below the adjacent country. Running lengthwise in the Ghor is a second valley, depressed below it to a depth of fifty feet, and with a width of 400 yards; and then, sunk again in this, and winding about in a most tortuous manner, is the channel of the river. The stream has an average width of fifty-six yards, with commonly a depth of from three to five feet. The current is usually rapid, for the distance between the Lake of Tiberias and the Dead Sea is, in a straight line, sixty miles, and the descent between them is 660 feet. Sometimes the stream presents cataracts, at others it expands and has a gentle flow. Where it is rapid, the bottom consists of rock or sand. The channel is fringed at its immediate sides with rushes or cane, and also with willows and similar trees, which, in the utter barrenness around, are a pleasant relief to the eye. Such is the stream so often referred to in our hymnology, and so dear, by its associations, to every Christian heart. Its channel being so far below the level of the Ghor that its water never overflows into the latter; and this wide valley having no springs, the region is mostly a scene of desolation, and appears to have been so in the earliest times.[1] The soil at the spot we have now under

---

[1] See Josephus *De bello*, iii. 10, § 7.

consideration is described by modern travellers as "unfertile, and in many places encrusted with salt, and having small heaps of white powder, like sulphur, scattered at short intervals over its surface."[1] The hills bounding the Ghor are generally abrupt and broken, and are always naked and painful to the eye. **On the east** they are soon succeeded by ranges 2000 or 2500 feet in height; and, back of these, is finally the very **lofty** range of Mount Nebo, its summit forming a horizontal line smooth and unbroken, **as if an** immense wall had **there been built up against the sky.**

This will give us an idea **of** the wildness and desolation of the spot **called in the Scriptures** "the Wilderness of Judea," where this strange man was now proclaiming his startling doctrines, and was administering baptism in the Jordan. His cry that the kingdom of heaven was at hand, quickly repeated throughout Judea, and also in the regions bordering eastwardly on the river valley, sent a thrill through every Jewish heart, and met there a ready response: for there had been an expectancy of this kind universally cherished by the Jews (a temporal kingdom however), and indeed, not confined to them alone. PERCREBUERAT, **says** the Roman historian, Suetonius, ORIENTE TOTO, VETUS ET CONSTANS OPINIO ESSE IN FATIS, UT EO TEMPORE JUDEA PROFECTI RERUM POTIRENTUR: *There had been greatly multiplied through all the East an old uninterrupted opinion, originating in the decree of the Fates, that, at this time, persons coming from Judea should obtain universal dominion.*[2] Tacitus informs us that *the multitude* [*in Judea*] *relied upon an ancient prophecy, contained, as they believed, in books kept by the priests, in which it was foretold that, at this time, the power of the East would prevail over the nations, and a race of men*

---

[1] Robinson's Bib. Researches. This Description **of** the Ghor and Jordan **is drawn from Robinson,** Van de Velde, and the Dead Sea Expedition.

[2] In Vespas.

should go forth from Judea to extend their dominion over all the rest of the world.[1]   Josephus says: *But now what did most elevate them [the Jews] in this war was an ambiguous oracle that was also found in their sacred writings, how, about that time, one from their country should become governor of the habitable world.*[2]

These expectations, it is evident, had reference only to an earthly sovereignty; but as such they met even a heartier response among the Jews than any of a more spiritual character would have done; for the nation was just beginning to feel the full terrors of the Roman power, which had enclosed them in its iron embrace, and from which they knew there was no escape by human aid.   Their independence may be said to have been fully bartered away for Roman favor by Herod the Great.   Archelaus, his successor to part of his kingdom, was deposed by Augustus Cæsar, and banished to Gaul; and Roman governors were appointed to Judea; the sceptre having clearly, to every perception, departed, and their country now become only a Roman province, from which successive rulers tried who could exact the most.   Roman soldiers were scattered, in garrison, in various parts; tax-gatherers ("publicans") were to be seen everywhere, and were constantly, to the eyes of the oppressed inhabitants, reminders of their subjection to foreign power, and were hated, not only for this, but for their unjust exactions; and most alarming of all, an act of their present governor, Pontius Pilate, had shown them how insecure were their religious observances, and how exposed they were to the violation of the most cherished feelings of their nation. ' Their law forbade their paying any homage to images; and the former governors, when ordering the Roman soldiers to Jerusalem, had directed them to come without the standards surmounted by the emperor's effigies, to which,

---

[1] Hist. lib v. 12.   [2] De bello, vi. 5, § 4.

when seen, honors were always required to be paid. Pilate, aware of this hostility to images, had recently directed his soldiers to be introduced into the city by night;[1] and morning disclosed the hated effigies in Jerusalem, and in the castle of Antonia adjoining the temple enclosure itself. Horror seized upon all the people, and a deputation hastened with remonstrances to the governor at Cæsarea. He treated their act as an insult to the emperor, and had the **deputies** surrounded by his soldiers; but the effort to overawe them was futile; they fell to the ground and offered their necks to the sword, rather than yield; and, finally, the obnoxious emblems were withdrawn. Afterwards, when the governor, seizing on some of the revenues of the temple, employed them in bringing water to the city, the inhabitants shocked at such use of the sacred treasures, rose in tumult; a collision with the soldiers was the consequence, and great havoc among the unarmed multitudes ensued.

CHAPTER II.

AT THE JORDAN.

IT is not wonderful therefore, that just at this time the national heart was ready to be acted upon by such a scene as that at the Jordan, where the prophet-like man stood calling people to the cleansing of their hearts as a preparation for the new, significant rite connected with the coming of their expected great Deliverer; **and that multitudes flocked to him from regions far and near.** He had

---

[1] Jos. Antiq. xviii. **3,** § **1.**

selected a spot called Bethabara, or *the house of the ford*,[1] seemingly a thoroughfare, while also a place remote from such complications as might arise from crowded neighborhoods: and there, where all nature in its sternness harmonized with him and with the severe simplicity of his call and his act, he was soon surrounded by crowds "from Jerusalem and all Judea and all the region round about Jordan." They saw a man with only a garment of rough camel's hair such as was worn by the poorest, fastened by a leathern girdle;—locusts and wild honey for his food. Locusts are still eaten in Syria, chiefly, however, by the Bedawîn on the extreme frontiers of the desert, where after being semi-boiled and salted and dried, they are packed up and kept for use. They may be seen in the Syrian shops for sale, but are always considered as an inferior food, and are eaten only by persons of the poorest class.[2] This man had been brought up in the desert, and he still adhered to this abstemious food.

Baptism was not unknown to the Jews, for it is generally admitted to have been a rite in use among them for the admission of proselytes,[3] and it was practiced by the Persians and other oriental nations. Josephus informs us of the Essenes,—a noted sect in his nation,—that "when a proselyte hath given evidence during that time of trial [a year] that he can observe their continence, he approaches nearer to their way of living, and is made a partaker of the waters of purification."[4] But the Essenes were a sect few in number and living in retired places; and these baptismal

---

[1] Van de Velde supposes Bethabara to have been at the present ford on the way from Nablûs (Sychem) to Es Salt, about twenty miles above the Pilgrims' bathing-place near Jericho. He bases this opinion on the time (two days and a half) allowed in John ii. 1, in going from the baptismal scene, to Cana in Galilee. The width of the Jordan at this spot is 56 yards; the depth about four feet.

[2] Thompson's Land and the Book.   [3] Bloomfield.

[4] De Bello, ii. 8, § 7.

scenes at the Jordan had evidently a significance different from anything which the nation had previously known. The prophet-like man gave them their significance, corresponding to the general belief of the dispensation to be inaugurated by the Messiah.

That desert was now solitary no more. **Crowds were** flocking to it; for the cry of the Baptist **that the** kingdom **of heaven was at** hand, repeated over all the country, had startled the people out of the lethargy wrought **by oppressions,** or by a fear that God **had** withdrawn from them; for, during a period of 400 years, there **had been no prophet in** Israel.

John the Baptist looked as if he might well **be** Elijah himself;—so like him in this hairy dress, in his manner, in his authoritative proclamation; and yet he was speaking of himself humbly, saying that one was coming immeasurably greater than he.

What might the nation not expect? What hopes could be too extravagant to be indulged? **We must** not think them insane in their expectation of an universal **dominion;** for they believed that it had been promised by Jehovah, **and** almost every spot in their land bore testimony **to God's** former **powerful action in** their behalf. **Just below this place, where** John was baptizing, **God had divided the deep** waters of **the Jordan in its** rapid **flow, and had kept them** divided **till his people had** passed **over** dry-shod; **there,** Jericho had fallen simply by his almighty will; their history was **full of** his direct interpositions for their advantage,— what would he not do for them now, if the Messiah himself, the Prince, were to appear?

Those eastern people are excitable and **demonstrative, and,** in their common moods, seem **often to strangers to be wildly** emotional; and **we may imagine the scene, as** people hurried **to the river and gazed on John with an** intensity of feeling that had never before been raised in **them** by any man; and listened to his call to repentance and the reasons for it, and witnessed his baptisms;—saw the penitents descend, with the sadness of grief in their faces; and saw them come up from the river, comforted and cheerful. Such feelings are contagious; and every new-comer felt in himself the need of penitence, and longings for relief that could be bestowed only by a power not of earth.

The teachings of John were plain and simple. As a proof of penitence and of changed feelings in those applying to him, he inculcated benevolence and kind acts: "He that hath two coats, let him impart to him that hath none; and he that hath meat let him do likewise."

The crowd around him was a mixed one;—men among them shunned by their neighbors, looked down upon with dislike by almost every one in the nation, and yet with human feelings, and with the same longings as others to shake off the load of guilt and to be comforted. Such were the "publicans" who presented themselves before the Baptist. We can almost see their hesitating manner, their subdued look, and their timid approach. They were not repelled. No harshness shown,—simply the injunction given, in order to prove the truth of their penitence: "Exact no more than is appointed you."

Soldiers also came, with that old question of the human heart wanting relief, "What shall we do?" The Roman garrisons in Judea were drawn partly from Italy, but were chiefly composed of Syrians from the north of Palestine, or of foreign wanderers who had strayed into the country; and generally there was no good will between them and the Jews. But there were exceptions, such as we may see shortly after this, in the case of Cornelius of the Italian band. The soldiers at the Jordan pressed on towards the Baptist;—for the powerful sympathies of the place had seized on them, and had changed their bold, fierce nature into one of humble inquiry. The crowds gazed earnestly, as they advanced. How would these men, famed for rapacity and violence, be received? Some looked on them with indignation at their presumption in intruding on such scenes; some with the cordiality begot by the new feelings at the baptism; all with deep interest as the Baptist addressed them. His words had a latent reproof, and yet **were** gentle. "Do violence **to no man, neither accuse any falsely,** and be content with your wages." The rite was open to all coming in penitence.

But there was suddenly **a change in the character of this** scene. **A sensation was created among the multitudes by** the approach of men of rank and power, who came on proudly in the consciousness **of their** position,—Pharisees with high pretensions to sanctity which they carried ostentatiously in the large phylacteries on their foreheads and arms, and in the width of the borders to their garments drawing attention to their unusual observance of the Mosaic law (see Numbers xv. 37–41);—also Sadducees **proud** of their wealth and assumed superior **intelligence.** Both undisguisedly despised the **ranks inferior to them.** The multitudes drew back as **this newly arrived party swept** haughtily **on;** and presently **these caught the eye of the** Baptist.

What a change there was in him! How his eyes lighted up; how indignant the expression of his face; how changed was **his voice from its former gentleness!** And **his words** were **stunning. "O brood of vipers, who** hath warned you to flee from the wrath **to come? Bring** forth therefore fruits meet for repentance: and think not to say within yourselves, We have Abraham to our father: for I say unto you, that God is able of these **stones** to raise up children unto Abraham. And now **also the axe is** laid unto the **root of the trees;** therefore **every tree** which **bringeth not forth good fruit** is hewn down and cast **into the fire.** I indeed baptize you with water unto repentance; but he that cometh after me is mightier than I, whose shoes I am not worthy to bear: he shall baptize you with the Holy Ghost, and with fire; whose fan is in his hand, and he will thoroughly purge his floor, and gather his wheat into the garner; but he will burn up the chaff with unquenchable fire."

The whole scene by the Jordan was becoming more and more confounding to people's apprehensions; for, not only had the bold ascetic stigmatized these Jewish leaders in a manner that must excite their wrath, but he had even seemed to cast disrespect on all claims arising from Abrahamic descent. He had ended also with words of terrific import respecting approaching events, when all false pretensions would be scattered to the winds, and those who held them would be fearfully and eternally punished. Fear, awe, and a new sense of shrinking respect for the Baptist, crept through the hearts of the multitudes, while yet they continued to be attracted by his general mildness and forbearance, and his gentleness to the truly penitent coming forward for the baptismal rite.

The news of these scenes still continued to spread over the country, and crowds were still hurrying from all parts of it to that wild, dreary region, already filled with excited, wondering throngs.

But who was this man, whose fame was now filling the land? People were asking the question everywhere, and the results of inquiry disclosed some very interesting facts.

John's birth had been in the old age of his parents, and had been heralded by an angel. His father, a priest, while administering at the altar of incense in the temple, had seen the heavenly visitant who announced the approaching birth of the child, and said that he should be great in the sight of the Lord, and should be filled with the Holy Ghost. "And," continued the angel, "many of the children of Israel shall be turned to the Lord their God. And he shall go before him in the spirit and power of Elias, to turn the hearts of the fathers to the children, and the disobedient to the wisdom of the just; to make ready a people prepared for the Lord." The father was struck dumb, at the time, on account of his unbelief; but recovered speech when the child, eight **days** after **its birth,** was brought to the temple, where, contrary to the expectations of relatives, he named his son John, according to **the direction of** the angel. These incidents were widely known at the time "throughout all the hill country of Judea," and produced dread as well as astonishment in the minds of the people.[1] He was, according to the direction of the angel, to "drink neither wine nor strong drink;" and his training is believed to have been in that most desolate region called the "Wilderness of Judea," where probably he associated much with the Essenes, a singular people, living chiefly at the only verdant spot in that desert—the fountain and ravine of En-Gedi, on the borders of the Dead Sea. In this desert[2] he "grew strong in spirit," and was prepared for his present work of teaching and baptizing. He was now about thirty years old, the age at which the Jewish priests entered upon the temple duties according to their law.

Josephus says of him, that he "was a good man, and commanded the Jews to exercise virtue, both as to righteousness towards one another, and piety towards God, and so to come to baptism; for that the washing would be acceptable to him, if they made use of it, not in order to the putting away of some sins only, but for the purification of the body; supposing still that the soul was thoroughly purified beforehand by righteousness."[3]

---

[1] His birth is supposed by Robinson and Reland to have been at **Juttah** (Joshua xxi. 16,) a town about five miles **south** of Hebron, and twenty-five **miles** south of Jerusalem.

[2] Luke i. 80.

[3] Antiq. xviii. 5, § 2. Josephus gives John's popularity as the cause for Herod's putting him to death, "since," as he says, "they came in

His exhortations were various;[1] but they all pointed clearly to the Messiah as now about to appear; he asked no honors for himself; they were all to be given to one yet to come. In his recent address to the Pharisees and Sadducees, he spoke of himself as immeasurably inferior to him whose appearance he was heralding; for to bear the shoes of a master in that country was the task assigned to the meanest of servants, and yet the Baptist declared himself not even worthy of such an office as that. Therefore, while curiosity with regard to John was stimulated among this demonstrative people to the highest degree, it took a still more intense form as regarded the tenor of his predictions. The excitement among all classes was great. Their Rabbis searched the Scriptures, and especially the prophecies, with an interest suited to their wonderful expectations of earthly glory and power to come with the Messiah, to their hatred of the Roman government, and to their felt position among all the nations of the earth: for the Jews were everywhere a slighted and despised people; while, on the other hand, " towards the rest of mankind," says Tacitus, " they nourished a sullen and inveterate hatred of strangers."[2]

The dying words of their great progenitor, Jacob, had been, ever since his time, dwelling as a perpetual hope in the national heart—"The sceptre shall not depart from Judah, nor a lawgiver from between his feet until Shiloh come; and unto him shall the gathering of the people be."[3]

The sceptre had departed: was Shiloh now there, as John declared? There was also a passage in Daniel pointing with peculiar significancy to the present time; and every-

---

crowds about him, for they were greatly moved by hearing his words;" and "they seemed to do anything he should advise;" and the king "thought it best, by putting him to death, to prevent any mischief he might cause, and not bring himself into difficulties by sparing a man who might make him repent of it when it should be too late."

[1] Luke iii. 18.   [2] Hist. v. 5.   [3] Gen. xlix. 10.

where people were now searching, with new interest, into his prophetic words. "Seventy weeks," says that prophet, "are determined upon thy people and upon thy holy city, to finish the transgression, and to make an end of sins, and to make reconciliation for iniquity, and to bring in everlasting righteousness, and to seal up the vision and prophecy, and to anoint the Most Holy. Know, therefore, and understand that from the going forth of the commandment to restore and to build Jerusalem unto the Messiah, the Prince, shall be seven weeks and three score and two weeks."[1] Allowing years for days, the seventy weeks or four hundred and ninety years from the edict of Artaxerxes for rebuilding the city (B. C. 458) would bring the time for the appearing of the "Messiah the Prince" exactly to this period.

Thus all prophecy and all history were in harmony with John's annunciations respecting the Messiah; even foreign nations were expecting the advent of the Jewish Deliverer. How would he appear? How spread his worldly conquests? How flash over the earth the glory of his reign? —were questions that had long been discussed in the Jewish schools; all with results tending to make the Jewish mind earthly and selfish. The whole nation was in a state of intense expectancy.

The Messiah came.

But how different he was from what the excited Jewish anticipations had pictured of his appearing!

Their favorite prophet had declared of him 780 years before, "When we shall see him, there is no beauty that we should desire him. He is despised and rejected of men; a man of sorrows, and acquainted with grief; and we hid as it were our faces from him; he was despised, and we esteemed him not."[2] For the purpose of our redemption God saw fit that it should be so; but, notwithstanding that this pro-

---

[1] Dan. ix. 24, 25.   [2] Isaiah liii. 2 and 3.

3 *

phecy was familiar to the Jews, still what a chasm between this actual appearing and that which they expected the appearing of the Messiah would be!

One day, amid those crowds at the Jordan, a stranger from Galilee presented himself for baptism; but John drew back—

"I have need," he said, "to be baptized of thee, and comest thou to me?" The answer was simply:

"Suffer it to be so now: for thus it becometh us to fulfill all righteousness."

They descended to the stream, and Jesus received baptism of John.

They appear not to have met before;[1] for their previous lives had been near the opposite extremes of Palestine,— one in Galilee, the other in the desert region in the south of Palestine;—but the Divine power, under which John was acting, had given him admonition that the Messiah, whom he had been preaching, was before him; and the stern, lofty-toned man felt awed before this higher Presence. The Messiah was there!

Of his personal appearance we have no authentic record;[2] but never yet did a great thought take strong hold of any human being and not stamp itself for the time upon his face, and manifest itself in his eyes. Never yet was any grand emotion in the human heart, without impressing itself upon the features, and drawing there its unmistakable lines. Never yet was any true, permanent greatness in man, without having, for itself, a *presence*, felt and known and recognized by all as such. God has not made all men great in form, or fair to look upon; but he does make grandeur of soul stamp itself upon the face; and he makes it heard in the intonations of the voice, and felt

---

[1] John i. 33.

[2] The description attributed to Lentulus is universally considered to be spurious.

in the manner; a something, often undefinable, and yet making clear demonstration of itself. Sometimes these things are fleeting; and they pass with the heavenlike nobility of soul;—the lines of care and our lower nature resuming their place: but sometimes, even in man, benevolence, and gentleness, and love, and nobility and power of thought, are so habitual as to impress themselves permanently on his looks; and we are drawn towards him by an attraction which our hearts cannot, and we do not wish to, resist. And if this is so in man, earthy, dark in intellect, uncertain in judgment, compelled so often to grieve over sin, *what must have been Christ the sinless*, through whose face the Divinity looked out upon the universe which was his, and through whose eyes shone that love unutterable which brought him to our earth, here to die for us? What a Being there was, then, before John and the multitudes, at Jordan! a face, where Divine greatness, not fleeting but constant, had drawn the lines and sat constantly enthroned; where gentleness, and meekness, and conscious omnipotence were harmonized; and where every glance of the eye, every intonation of the voice, every lineament in the features, while showing the Divine supremacy within, were those also of one who had come in humility to seek and to save them that are lost. Who can wonder then, that when, even in the violence at Gethsemane, Jesus turned and looked upon his persecutors, they fell to the earth? Who can wonder that, in the same night, a single look upon Peter turned that recreant's heart into a fountain of tears? Or, that Pilate, drawn by that majesty of *Presence* in Christ during the trial, sought with such determination to let him go?

As the Messiah and John ascended from the baptism, a sign was given by which the latter, at the time he received his own Divine mission, had been informed,[1] that he should

---

[1] John i. 33.

recognize Him whom he was to preach, and might know that the "kingdom of heaven" had now come. He saw the heavens opened, and the Spirit of God descend and light like a dove upon Christ, while a voice came down from the supernal glory: "This is my beloved Son, in whom I am well pleased."[1]

The mission of the Messiah had thus its heavenly endorsement, and here its beginning. It began in the waters of the Jordan: it was to be sealed in blood. It began with the opening glory of heaven poured down: it was to end with the sun hidden at mid-day, and a supernatural darkness, as of night, over the earth. The heavens then opened once again, to receive him from mortal sight.

CHAPTER III.

THE DESERT.

AMONG the mountains which, near the lower end of the Jordan, sweep in a semi-circular curve westwardly from the river and form a space for the great plain of Jericho, is one midway along called Quarantana, which rises almost perpendicularly from the edge of the plain to a height of twelve or fifteen hundred feet.[2] Of Jericho scarcely any vestiges can be found: the last solitary palm tree remaining from the forests of palms, for which the place was once famous, has lately disappeared: the plain, except a spot occupied by a few wretched dwellings, is desolate: the mountains bordering it have always been a scene of desolation, and the whole region is given up to lawless bands: yet, through the long

----

[1] Matt. iii. 16, 17.   [2] Robinson.

hours of the night, a light may be seen far up among the crags of Quarantana, showing that some pilgrim is doing penance in these wild solitudes. The front of the mountain is indeed honey-combed with hermits' cells; for in ancient times the place was a favorite one for anchorites, and the mountain takes its name from a tradition that to it the Messiah, after the baptism in the Jordan, was "led up by the Spirit," and that he there spent the forty days of his temptations in the wilderness. It is not probable that a spot looking down over a wide scene of what was then busy life—the great city and its surroundings—would have been chosen for such an occasion: but back of it, that is, to the westward and southward, is a region harmonizing with all that we can conceive of those forty days of fasting and of the temptations. There, a great extent of country about 60 miles from north to south, and 15 wide, bordered on the east by the precincts of the Jordan, and the Dead Sea and reaching on the west to within a few miles of Jerusalem itself, is one of singular barrenness and dreariness; looking, says the traveller Maundrell, "so torn and disordered, as if the earth had suffered some great convulsion, in which the very bowels had been turned outward." It is, indeed, a region of utter barrenness and of constant gloom. The country is all broken into hills generally of steep ascent; and both hills and ravines are bare alike. The surface is a gray mouldering rock, or a gray earth, on which no vegetation will thrive; and the whole, from century to century, has laid quite bare to the baking sun and unfertilizing rains. Travellers through the deserts of Arabia tell us that the prevailing impression on their minds there is of antiquity, and with regard to that country, the exclamation is forced from them, "how old it is!" but this region in Judea looks as if it had never been young, but had been a blasted and an accursed place from the beginning. All avoid it who can. In the days of our Saviour, robbers haunted its thoroughfares; and, in our time, the few paths crossing it are made by the feet of marauders; and he who sees a human being moving on its hills, however distant, expects violence, and prepares for defence. Deep chasms intersect it here and there, at the sides of which the rocks almost meet, hundreds of feet above, and shut out the day; and in their faces are the mouths of caverns, such as gave refuge to David and his pursued band.[1] A recent traveller in noticing the more southern portion of this region, says the prospect before him was "indescribably stern and desolate:" and speaks of "the fantastic forms of the rocks on the foreground, a medley of gray limestones, yellowish gravel, and fragments of lava, here piled up in perpendicular cliffs, there laid one above the other in flat strata, and yonder rent asunder in frightful chasms; between these, a plain covered with a number of conical hills, white, gray and yellow, all the product of subterranean fire:"[2]—this at the close of March, when vegetation in Judea is in its highest perfection. Of the more northern portions, equally desolate, we shall have a future occasion to speak more in detail.

To this "Wilderness of Judea," as it was called, the Messiah, after his baptism, was "led of the Spirit to be tempted;" and there he remained forty days.

We are now at one of those events in Christ's earthly ministry, where the supernatural is blended so greatly with the natural that, with our limited capacities, we have to be content with ignorance, and to gaze, though wonderingly yet silently, at the little which has been revealed. How can we understand, or expect to understand, where the spiritual and the material come thus mingled in joint action; and where the mysteries of the unseen world, which our intellects in vain strive to penetrate, and which they could not com-

---

[1] 1 Samuel xxiv.
[2] Van de Velde's "Journey through Syria and Palestine."

prehend if seen, are so imperfectly developed that we catch
but a glimpse here and there as they flit before our minds?
We must remember that the times we are now considering
were those when the most wonderful event of all ages was
having its scene of action on our earth; when the Divinity
took our nature, and in a union incomprehensible to us,
was in great humility among men.—Incomprehensible; for
how can we understand this, when the union of our own
souls and bodies is a mystery beyond our comprehension,—
an every-day mystery, and familiar, but yet never once
penetrated by human science? How can we understand,
then, the Divine and human in one, or hope in the least
degree to understand? We may gather from the Inspired
Word that in those days, when heaven came down to earth,
and the two were blended as never before, and never to be
again,—that then a *general agitation* occurred, and spirits
gave demonstrations of presence and power, in demoniacs
and the possessed, to which the world at other times had
been a stranger, and which have never been repeated since.
The Scriptures tell us of a time yet to be, when the powers
of heaven *shall be shaken;* Christ coming to judge; a time
far less mysterious than this period when he was on earth,
God manifest, but in humility for man's redemption to be
effected in the cross. Who shall object in these matters?
Who dare gainsay concerning things beyond our comprehension, when we cannot understand ourselves? Men are
indeed but children—the oldest and wisest in the world, but
children—when put in comparison with the supernatural
world, where, with God, "a thousand years are but as
yesterday;" and where, among the infinites, our imaginations
strive in vain for a resting-place for observation; and so
turn quickly back to earth, wearied and overwhelmed.

Therefore, humility is now our rational and our better
part; and, with such a sense of our condition we have
repeatedly to gaze on the scenes recorded in the Gospels, not

comprehending them, and compelled to be satisfied with present ignorance. It was a time, we may believe, when " the powers of heaven" and of hell " were shaken ;" as they never otherwise had been ; and our earth, the scene of action, had to witness unusual sights.

Consequently, when these scenes of the temptation in the wilderness of Judea pass in those strange, shadowy forms before us, half revealed in the Gospels, half hidden,—we gaze in wonder, but we acquiesce in not understanding more. How could we fully understand ?

Saint Paul, through the power of inspiration, tells us, " In all things it behooved Him to be made like unto his brethren, that he might be a merciful and faithful high priest ;" and that " We have not a high-priest which cannot be touched with the feeling of our infirmities ; but was in all points tempted as we are yet without sin ;"[1] and the temptations in the wilderness appear to have been suited to the higher spiritual character of the tempted. There were three of them, applied to those feelings which are the most powerful in our own nature,—to ambition, to vanity, and to bodily want; each applied in this case in a concentrated form ; but each in vain. But we cease to argue in matters so evidently above our reason ; we will wait patiently, till we may ourselves merge into the supernatural, and no longer see " through a glass darkly," but " shall know even as we are known."

---

[1] Hebrews ii. 17 ; iv. 15.

CHAPTER IV.

AT THE JORDAN—THE DEPUTATION.

JOHN was still baptizing at the Jordan, still uttering his call to repent, "for the kingdom of heaven is at hand;" and still the excitement concerning him was continuing: the public wonder and curiosity indeed were on the increase. The Sanhedrim at Jerusalem was presently stirred up to take official action in his case.

This body, συνέδριον, *assembly,* consisted of seventy persons, with the addition of the high-priest as president; and were from the following classes of persons: 1. Officiating high-priest; 2. Ex-high-priests, and heads of the twenty-four classes of high-priests, called, by way of honor, *chief-priests;* 3. Such of the elders, i. e., princes of the tribes, heads of family associations, as were elected to this place, or put there by a nomination from the ruling executive authority; and 4. Appointments in a similar way from the scribes and learned men.[1] "It was required of these men that they should be religious, and learned in the arts and language; that they should have some skill in physic, arithmetic, astronomy and astrology; also to know what belonged to magic, sorcery and idolatry, so as to know how to judge them. They were to be without maim or blemish of body; men of years but not extremely old; and to be fathers of families, that they might be acquainted with tenderness and compassion. Their times for sitting were from the end of the morning service to the beginning of the evening service, but might be prolonged till the night, if necessary for con-

---

[1] Jahn's Archæology.

cluding any business commenced during the day; but no new business could be undertaken in the night. Their place of assembling was in a room by the courts of the Temple, and was so arranged that a portion of it projected into the priests' court, in order that it might partake of the sanctity of the place; and part was outside of it, so that the members could *sit* in the council, which no one could do in the court of the priests, except a king."[1] The first mention of the Sanhedrim is about the year B. C. 69; its origin is supposed to have been in the Council of 70 Elders appointed by Moses at Sinai, (Numbers xi. 16–24.) It had the power to judge all persons and all matters not left to inferior courts, a whole tribe, a prophet, the high-priest, and even the king himself if there were occasion.[2]

In every city there was a smaller tribunal of the judges and Levites for slighter cases: also a tribunal of 23 judges (synagogue tribunals, John xvi. 2,) which tried questions of a religious nature.

The Sanhedrim felt now, that it had become of the highest consequence to settle the important questions concerning John, which were agitating the public mind. Although the ascetic had not put himself forward as a leader, and good order had been maintained at the Jordan, yet the people were in an inflammable condition, and tumults might arise, in which case the Roman power would interfere, with vengeance upon the whole nation. A wonderful prophet, too, this seemed to be, and the excitement was the greater from the lapse of centuries since a prophet had appeared. His annunciation of the kingdom of heaven as at hand was thrilling to every expectant heart: he was introducing a great revolution by initiating the crowds flocking to him, into a new religion; and this without authority given, or asked of the rulers. He had offended also the two leading

---

[1] Lightfoot *on the Temple.*   [2] Jahn's Archæology.

sects in Judea, by his invective hurled upon them as a brood of vipers, yet the people were quiescent, though admiring his boldness. The impression was growing, everywhere, that he was something beyond a mortal like themselves;— that he was Elias (Elijah), or Jeremiah, risen from the dead; and, among some—misinterpreting his declarations to the contrary,—that he was the Messiah himself. The Pharisees believed that the power of baptizing Jews, and thereby forming a new religion, was to be confined to the Messiah and his precursors, the prophets, who they supposed would return to life for this purpose; and although it was true that John's ancestry did not fully agree with the requirements of their ancient prophets respecting the Christ, yet his mother was of the lineage of David; and although in addition his place of birth had not been at Bethlehem, still it was not fully determined among the doctors that the Messiah must be born there.[1] So there was room for discussion among the Sanhedrim, even on the question whether John might not be the Messiah himself.

Therefore, this national council, taking Pharisees, who were also priests and Levites,[2] for their deputation, sent them to John.[3] The Jewish rulers were almost exclusively

---

[1] See Bloomfield *in loco.*   [2] John i. 19; i. 24.

[3] John i. 19. It is well to remark here on a circumstance in St. John's Gospel, of which I have seen no notice among critics, except Alford, although it is an important one. It is the distinction which this Evangelist appears to make between "the Jews" and "the people." By the former he seems to mean *the leaders;* by the latter, *the masses.* There is a striking example of this in ch. vii. v. 13, when the *people* (v. 12) were secretly querying about Christ, "but no man spake openly of him for fear of *the Jews.*" The same distinction seems to be kept up uniformly in John, except where the term Jew is used as a distinctive national one.

We have something like it when we use the words, "the English," and the "English people," meaning by the former a kind of abstraction of the rulers, or the sentiment seen in their government, and by the latter, the masses.

Pharisees, or persons professing to be such; and that sect was more particularly interested in the proceedings at the Jordan: for their power lay in their influence over the masses of the people, the only instrument they could oppose to their rivals, the smaller but wealthier sect of the Sadducees; and the masses were drawn powerfully to this prophet at the Jordan.

The origin of both these leading sects is unknown, and we have no distinct traces of them previous to the Ptolemies, (B. C. 332), about which time the *oral* or *traditional law* also comes before our notice. The Pharisees were the advocates and conservators of this; the Sadducees opposed it, adhering only to the *written law*. The Pharisees believed " that souls have an immortal vigor in them, and that under the earth there will be rewards and punishments, accordingly as they have lived virtuously or viciously, in this life; and the latter are to be detained in an everlasting prison, but that the former shall have the power to revive and live again."[1] The Sadducees asserted " that souls die with the bodies:" and in this opposition of belief on vital points, we have at once the groundwork of endless disputes between these sects. The Sadducees, however, were content to keep their cold philosophy to themselves, and seldom attempted to make proselytes; but they were the wealthy men, and prided themselves on their superior wisdom and higher philosophy; to which the Pharisees opposed an affected sanctimoniousness, which drew to them the multitudes, over whom they had great influence, and by whom they more than counterbalanced the power in wealth belonging to their opponents. So domineering, indeed, was their influence in the nation in consequence of their successful zeal in making and keeping proselytes among the masses, that when a Sadducee had to take office, (which that sect did unwillingly),

---

[1] Jahn's Archæology.

he was often compelled, for his own comfort, to assume the character and pretend to the belief of the Pharisees. The latter had in the *unwritten* law, as we shall see by-and-by, an immense power, capable of bearing down any adversary who might oppose them, especially among the ignorant. With all this courting of popular favor, they however, thoroughly despised the populace, and called them in their writings "worms," "people of the earth ;" and with other opprobrious epithets, refused heaven to them, declaring that " he who has not studied is never pious."[1] They affected a great outward show of religion, ostentatiously standing while at prayer, (standing was the usual Jewish posture in prayer), at the corners of the streets, so as to be seen in two directions ; and sometimes commencing a prayer at one place and going to finish it at another. They made broad their phylacteries (written passages of Scripture, folded up and bound to the forehead and arm), and in their dress had an ostentation of a similar kind. They were so fearful of contamination that they would not eat with their own people, if holding the unpopular office of tax-gatherers ; and were disposed to spurn from their presence all who were not of their own sect ;[2] nor would they drink until the water had been strained, lest they might inadvertently swallow some unclean animalcules. With all this, they enjoined no internal righteousness, substituting externals for it: forms took the place of holiness : an omission to wash the hands before meat was considered worthy of death, no matter what iniquity might be in the heart ; and they had brought the Jewish people into disrepute abroad as a nation of perjurers,[3] by teaching that an oath by the altar, temple, heaven, earth, sacrifices, etc., etc., was of small if any obligation, unless in it the name of God had been used. They were divided into several subordinate sects; and the Jewish official books, the

---

[1] Lightfoot. [2] Jahn's Archæology. [3] Martial's Epigrams, xi. 95.

4 *

Talmuds, mention several distinct classes, under characters which show them to have been deeply immersed in the idlest and most ridiculous superstitions. Among them were the *Truncated Pharisee*, who, that he might appear in profound meditation, as if destitute of feet, scarcely lifted them from the ground; the *Mortar Pharisee*, who, that his meditations might not be disturbed, wore a deep cap in the shape of a mortar, that would only permit him to look on the ground at his feet; and the *Striking Pharisee*, who shutting his eyes as he walked to avoid the sight of women, often struck his head against the wall.[1]

Such were the men who came now, in the authority of office, to settle the questions which had been discussed for weeks with deepest earnestness in Jerusalem and throughout all Judea and the regions beyond;—questions of momentous interest, but to which no one could yet give a satisfactory reply. It was known that John had made disclaimers of any high position; but still the public mind was agitated; for with these disclaimers, he was yet performing a rite belonging only to the old prophets risen again, or to the Messiah: so, at least, they always believed.

The crowds saw the officials approaching, and could easily surmise who they were, and why they came. All knew that it was among the duties of the Sanhedrim to inquire officially into the pretensions of any one setting himself up as a prophet; and here were the inquisitors come now to do that work. The important queries which had so agitated the multitudes there, but which they had shrunk from putting to the Baptist would, they thought perhaps, be answered at last.

The crowds gave way. Probably, in those haughty looks of the Pharisees they could read their own condemnation for being captivated by one not officially recognized, and not a

---

[1] Bloomfield.

Rabbi; their old reverence for priest and Levite, and additionally for Pharisees, conservators of the unwritten law with its mysterious, undefined power, crept through their hearts again, as they saw these men approach,—perhaps there to overwhelm all the Baptist's claims, and to hurl on his proselytes objurgations or even excommunications for having submitted to the new rite. The deputation came in a manner to make impression of their authority, and to procure full and ready answers to their questions; bearing the phylacteries upon their brows and arms, and the wide fringes to their robes, as became Pharisees and men of rank. We must give attention to them; and we notice first the phylacteries, an awkward appendage, but which habit made less so to them. To construct a phylactery four pieces of parchment were taken, on which, with ink specially prepared for this purpose, were written four passages from the law, Ex. xiii. 3–10; Ex. xiii. 11–16; Deut. vi. 4–9; Deut. xi. 13–21. These four pieces were folded together in a square form, and inserted in a leather case, from which proceeded thongs of the same material. Such a case was laid on the forehead between the eye-brows; and the thongs, being passed behind the head, were tied there in a particular manner, and then came round so as to fall over the chest. Another was laid on the inside of the left arm, at the elbow, and fastened there by thongs, one of which was wound spirally along the arm, and so, crossing the palm of the hand, was fastened to the fingers. This usage was founded on Ex. xiii. 9.

The name phylactery is from the Greek, and signifies observatory, because it put them in mind of the law. In process of time the phylacteries came to be considered as a protection against evil spirits, or charms, and the Talmud says, "It is necessary that the phylacteries should be repeated at home at nights to drive away devils."[1] It is not certain

---

[1] Lightfoot.

PHYLACTERIES.

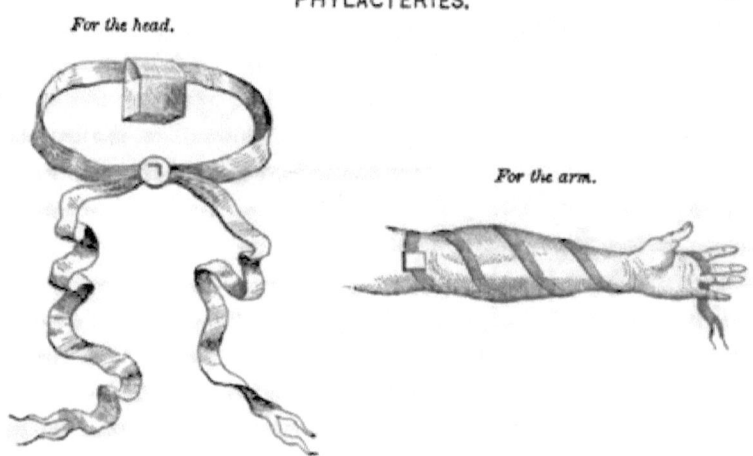

For the head.

For the arm.

whether all the Jewish people wore them, or only those who were called scholars, and who pretended to more knowledge and devotion and study than the common people;[1] but all, both learned and unlearned, were bound alike to say over the phylactery sentences morning and evening, every day, no matter where they were. The time for this was at earliest dawn, and in the evenings some time before the first watch.[2] Our Saviour condemns the width of the phylacteries, made for ostentation and vanity. The modern Jews, it is said, wear them at morning and evening prayers.

This deputation approached, not over-confident of a favorable reception, knowing as they did the Baptist's address to their Pharisee brethren on the former occasion: and now there was a striking scene;—that gaunt, sunburnt man, in his coarse dress of camel's hair bound by a leathern girdle; his unabashed manner before the officers, and his fiery eyes seeming to pierce them through;—their own stateliness and effort at ease and assurance, while their pretension to sanctity and the authoritativeness of office were impressing the

---

[1] Lightfoot.   [2] Ib.

crowd;—the multitudes glancing from the new, admired favorite to their old, feared masters; and back again to the fearless John.

" Who art thou?" the rulers asked.

The words were authoritative and abrupt. He answered, not to their question, but to what he knew was in every person's mind.

" I am not the Christ."

" What then? art thou Elias?"

" I am **not**."

" Art **thou that prophet?"** [1]

" **No**."

" Who art thou?—that we may give an answer to them that sent us. What sayest thou of thyself?"

" I am the voice of one crying in the wilderness, Make straight the way of the Lord, as said the prophet Esaias:" (the reply having allusion to a custom prevailing in those eastern countries, when a monarch was about to make a journey; at which times men were sent before to remove obstructions and to make level the roads).

" Why baptizest thou then, if thou be **not that Christ,** nor Elias, neither that prophet?"

" I baptize with **water: but there standeth one among you, whom ye know not; he it is, who coming after me is** preferred **before me, whose shoe's latchet I am not worthy to unloose**."

Among them!! **And all** interest in the officials and in John himself must have been lost, as men started and turned inquiring glances among the crowd, making scrutiny for him about whom the astounding announcement had been **made**. No one could doubt that **John** meant by this, *The Christ,* the great Messiah that had been promised to the

---

[1] It is supposed that they referred to Jeremiah. (See Deut. xviii. 15–19 and Matt. xvi. 14.)

world. That was their answer, and such the intelligence that the emissaries were to carry back to Jerusalem, and to the Sanhedrim.

Curiosity was at its utmost tension now: and the next day, as the crowds were watching John with a closeness of observation which they had never exercised before, they heard from him a sudden announcement—

"Behold the Lamb of God, which taketh away the sin of the world!"

The multitudes turned quickly ;—   .

Was that the Christ!

He came with no pomp, but quietly among them: no earthly parade of power, no attendance; not even with scholastic state, and disciples following him: but alone, in simplicity of dress and simplicity of manner.—His kingdom was not of this world.

But the multitudes might have noticed the wonderful dignity and majesty on that brow ; the quiet composure of manner, where conscious omnipotence calmly rested ; the winningness of features, where unbounded love drew the lines, and fully impressed itself; and when he spake, the modulations of his voice, where gentleness and benevolence ruled, although at times that voice could take the impressive tones of command.

John described to the earnest listeners how the demonstration of the Messiahship had been made to himself, including the announcement from heaven, "The same is he which baptizeth with the Holy Ghost." He ended with proclaiming to the gazing, earnest, wondering multitude, thrilled with so many hopes, "And I saw and bare record, that THIS IS THE SON OF GOD."

CHAPTER V.

CONDITION OF PALESTINE.

THE Messiah had come: but before following him in his
wonderful ministry, we must endeavor to familiarize ourselves with the country where this ministry was to be exercised, and the people who were to be its immediate recipients.
The reader will excuse interruptions, for such purposes, in
the narrative portions of this book. They will be as brief
as possible: but without them we cannot understand the
narratives themselves.

The two ranges of mountains, Lebanon and Anti-Lebanon,
keep parallel with each other and with the eastern coast of
the Mediterranean, for a distance of 150 miles, when finally,
Anti-Lebanon shoots up into the majestic Hermon, rising to
9376[1] feet above the level of the sea, its summit covered
nearly all the year with snow. The region having for
its northern boundary the southern extremities of these
ranges (lat. 33° 30′ N.), and on its south, the border of the
Arabian Desert (31° 10′); with the Jordan and its line of
lakes on the east, and the Mediterranean on the west, is in
modern times usually designated as Palestine; and such in
this book will be the use of the word. It forms an extent
of 170 statute miles from north to south, by a mean width
of about 50 miles: and is generally a hilly country, with
large plains interspersed however,—among which that of
Esdraelon (lat. 32° 40′) is of great dimensions; while, just
south-west of this commences the plain of Sharon, which
thence onward southwardly, forms a wide and fertile border

---

[1] Survey by Majors Scott and Pope.

along the Mediterranean.   The region of abrupt hills between this plain and Jerusalem forms what was called " The
Hill country of Judea :" the utterly barren and blasted country east of the latter, extending to the Dead Sea, has been
already described.   A cross section, from west to east in the
latitude of Jerusalem, would give: 1st, The plain of Sharon,
17 miles wide; 2d, The Hill country, 20 miles; and 3d,
The wilderness, 15 in width; and then, the great depression
of the valley of the Jordan.[1]   Jerusalem is about 2610 above,
and the Dead Sea 1312 *below* the level of the Mediterranean.
If leaving Palestine we continue across the river eastwardly
at this latitude, we come immediately to the very lofty wall-
like range of Nebo beyond which is a hilly pastoral region,
soon succeeded by immense wastes of sand.

*Profile, Section of Palestine E. and W. from the mountains of Moab to the
Mediterranean in the latitude of Jerusalem.*

The horizontal distances are on a scale of 20 miles to an inch.   The heights
and depressions on a scale of 4000 feet to an inch.   In such a profile the
same scale for heights and distances cannot be preserved.   The horizontal
line shows the level of the Mediterranean.

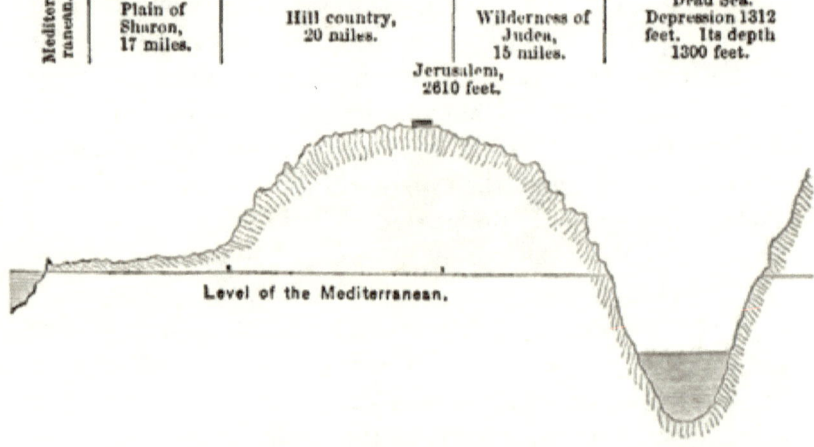

| Mediterranean. | Plain of Sharon, 17 miles. | Hill country, 20 miles. | Wilderness of Judea, 15 miles. | Dead Sea. Depression 1312 feet. Its depth 1300 feet. |

Jerusalem, 2610 feet.

Level of the Mediterranean.

---

[1] These measurements are from Van de Velde's trigonometrical sur-
veys in Syria and Palestine.   Capt. Lynch gives 2610 feet for the elevation of Jerusalem: the aneroid 2749.

Profile, Section of Palestine N. and S., from the Dead Sea towards Mount Hermon, along the line of the Jordan.

The horizontal distances are on a scale of 35 miles to an inch: the elevations 15,000 feet to an inch. The line marked *a a a* shows the level of the Mediterranean.

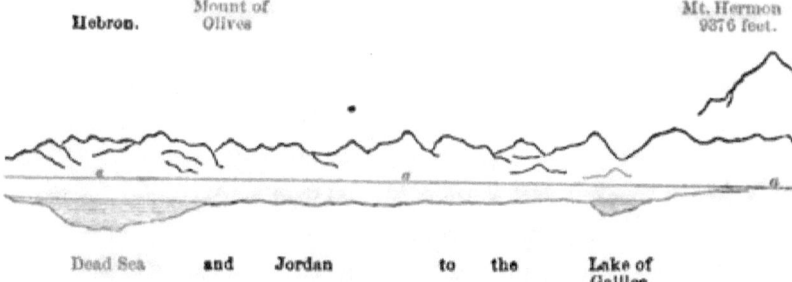

Palestine was thus a country of small extent, and singularly situated ; quite central to what was the civilized world in those ancient times, and therefore well adapted to be a radiating point of divine knowledge ; and yet, by these northern mountains, by the Arabian desert, by the western sea, and by the sand on the east, almost isolated, and little open to corrupting influences from heathen neighbors. It had no safe harbor on its whole extent of coast, until Herod the Great, at immense cost, formed one midway along ; building there also, his political capital, Cæsarea, named after his patron, Augustus Cæsar.   This latter was settled immediately by a motley population of Syrians and Greeks chiefly, as well as Jews : and from this mixture sprang finally the troubles which eventuated in the destruction of Jerusalem itself.[1]

At the time of which we are now writing, Palestine was divided into three nearly equal portions : the northern called Galilee ; the central, Samaria ; and the southern, Judea ; each with its distinctive and peculiar people, although those of Galilee and Judea went under the general appellation of Jews. A full understanding of the New Testament history requires that we should take some notice of the history of each.

---

[1] See Jos. Antiq. xx. 8, § 9.

5

When Canaan was first parceled out among the twelve tribes, the large tribe of **Judah** had assigned to it the chief portion of what afterwards became Judea: while Ephraim had **most of** what was subsequently Samaria, the two being separated by the small tribe of Benjamin wedged between then at the east, and by the equally diminutive region of Dan **at the west.** Benjamin **however, though small,** was composed **of a bold** and energetic set of **people:** it gave Saul as the first king of Israel; and afterwards Paul, the greatest of the Christian leaders and among the earliest martyrs for Christ.

Judah and **Ephraim, from their superior** size and their **position,** soon took **the lead among** the tribes, and also became **jealous of each** other:[1] and finally (B. C. 975), their rivalship culminated in a **separation of the tribes;** Benjamin alone adhering to Judah, while all the **others went** off and **became a kingdom by themselves,** Ephraim **in this** taking **the lead.   Its main city, Shechem, in the valley of** Samaria unsurpassed in fertility and **loveliness, became the** capital of its new king.   Among **these people** a semi-idolatrous religion soon took the place **of the old** Mosaic faith.   **Two** hundred and fifty-four **years after this** (B. C. 721) the **ten** tribes were carried **into captivity by** Shalmanezer, king of Assyria; and their **existence became** eventually blotted out from history.   The exceedingly fertile **plain of** Ephraim and its borders on the north, being rapidly covered with jungle, **was becoming overrun with wild-beasts, when** Shalmanezer **sent colonists from Babylonia and other parts of** his eastern **dominions to occupy it, with whom a few of the** former in-**habitants who had been left behind, united: and** thus was **formed the distinct and very peculiar race of** the Samaritans, retaining in part **their eastern heathenism, and** partly im-**bued with the** questionable religion of the ten tribes.

One hundred and thirty-three years after the captivity of the

---

[1] See also Isaiah xi. 13.

ten tribes (B. C. 588) Judah and Benjamin were also led captive to the east, Jerusalem having been taken by Nebuchadnezzar, and their temple destroyed. Chaldea, now the ruling power in the east, had become the possessor of all Palestine. But this captivity did not long continue; for Cyrus, the Persian, having taken Babylon, (B. C. 538) gave **these two tribes** permission to **return to Palestine and to rebuild their temple**, the sacred vessels of which he also restored. Some of the Jews remained in Babylon, while the others hastened back to their country : but during this time of their absence changes of importance among **themselves** had occurred. *Their original language had ceased to* **be a** *spoken one.*

The Hebrew had for a long time been declining in purity. The period about the time of Moses is called by critics its *golden age ;* that between David and Hezekiah, its *silver age.* From Hezekiah to the captivity it deteriorated so much by the further introduction of foreign terms, that its *iron age* is placed in that period; **and during the** captivity it ceased to **be a spoken language at all.**[1] Not that the transition had been very great. The dialects **spoken all** over the East had a general similitude, so great that **the** designation used by the Hebrews for *very remote* nations was that these did not understand their **language.**[2] **But still the change, during this stay in Babylon, was such that, gene-** rally, they **could not any longer understand the Hebrew** Scriptures when read in their religious assemblies; and although the original was still used in public worship, properly qualified persons had to be employed to give immediately a translation into the vernacular.[3] The new dialect which the people brought home with them was the Aramaic—sometimes called Syro-Chaldaic—and **was the language of Palestine in our Saviour's time.**

---

[1] Jahn's Introduction to the Old Testament, § 69.
[2] Deut. xxviii. 49, and Jer. v. 15.   [3] See Nehemiah viii. 8.

But there were differences also in this dialect. The places of captivity had stretched along the Euphrates, where the Chaldee and Syriac dialects were in use. On their **return,** those using the former settled in Judea, the others in Galilee ;[1] and hence existed a difference of speech, by which **a** Galilean was speedily recognized as such by the dwellers further south.

The Jews had permission from Cyrus to rebuild also the wall around their city ; and they came back with hearts full of zeal and of joy at the royal favor, in both of which the Samaritans would have gladly shared. But these people were repelled as a half-heathenish race; and immediately a **settled feud began, which has continued** down to the present **time.** The Samaritans endeavored to excite jealousies in the **Persian monarch respecting the repairs** in the city walls, and for some time with success ; but they finally ceased from such opposition, and established rival services, building **also a** rival temple on the mount Gerizim, which rises immediately above their capital city, Shechem, and which, with its opposite mountain, Ebal, had been the scene of a most singular event in the ancient times of Israel. There, after Canaan had been conquered, had been gathered the twelve tribes, one-half placed on **Gerizim** to bless, and **half** on Ebal to curse ;—indeed, **what region is there in all** the country of Palestine that **has not witnessed** strange and wonderful events? **To us, also, there is** a standing miracle in the fulfillment of the words of Moses when, after commanding the **full assemblage to take** place on Ebal and Gerizim, he added **that if they and their** posterity would **not** observe God's commandment they should become **"an** astonishment, a proverb, and a by-word among all **nations,"** whither the Lord should lead them.[2] The Maccabean, Hyrcanus, destroyed this temple (B. C. **108), and** annexed the whole

---

[1] Jahn's Introduction.   [2] See Deut. xi. 29; xxvii. 12–26; xxviii.

Samaritan country to the Jewish nation; and the bitterness from subjugation was then added to the former hatred and jealousies. The Samaritans, while receiving the Pentateuch, rejected all the other Jewish Scriptures; and were, therefore, still considered by the Jews as only a more dangerous set of heathen. What a Samaritan ate as food became, from that fact, as swine's flesh in the eyes of a Jew; no Samaritan might be made a proselyte; no one of them could by any possibility, in Jewish estimation, attain to everlasting life.

This was the country lying between the two Jewish districts of Galilee and Judea, and which had to be traversed in the frequent journeys between the two, unless a large *detour* was made across the Jordan and along its eastern banks.

The two tribes of Judah and Benjamin, after their return from captivity, still formed a part of the Persian kingdom, and were heavily taxed for its support. Their temple had been rebuilt, (commenced B. C. 535), but Jerusalem remained without walls, until the increase of the Greek power made it necessary to oppose obstacles to the extension of that nation. Then Nehemiah was empowered by the Persian government to fortify the city; but he had to do it by stealth, and at night, as the jealousies of the neighboring states, particularly Samaria, were ever throwing obstacles in the way. The Persian nation finally succumbed before Alexander, and the Jews passed quietly into the power of that universal conqueror (B. C. 332), and through him, afterwards, of the Ptolemies. They lived under successive kings of that race, generally oppressed, and often treated with great cruelty, till Antiochus Epiphanes, the *Illustrious* or the *Madman*,—for he had both these surnames,—fearing (B. C. 167) that they might seek relief from his tyranny in the increasing power of Rome already triumphant in Egypt, determined to wipe out their distinc-

5 *

tive character, and entirely destroy their individuality as a nation. He let loose his soldiers on the Sabbath, upon the unresisting Jewish people, and encouraged a general massacre: the streets of Jerusalem ran with blood: the women were carried off into slavery: he ordered a general uniformity of religion in all his dominions; forced the people to profane the Sabbath, and to eat swine's flesh, and forbade the national rite of circumcision. He dedicated their temples to Jupiter, placed an image of that god on their high altar, and ordered **sacrifices** to be there made to the Olympian deity; and, finally, substituted the Bacchanalian rites for their great feast of tabernacles. Resistance only led to slaughter: barbarities and outrage had full possession of the land.

The Maccabean family[1] **now rose into eminence,** first by slight resistance; then, after gathering strength, by heading a **general** revolt; and, finally, (B. C. 144), by establishing **the** complete independence of the Jewish nation. The alliance of Rome was sought for, and secured; and, finally, under Hyrcanus, Samaria, as already stated, and Galilee on the north, and Idumea on the south, were (B. C. 108) brought into subjection to the triumphant kingdom of Judea. But a new power—the **Roman**—**was** spreading around, soon to absorb the **Judean kingdom, as it did** the rest of the world. **In the case of** Judea, Rome followed its usual successful policy of insinuating itself into nations through **their intestine disputes.** Two competitors for the Jewish throne, **Hyrcanus** and Aristobolus, both of the Maccabean family, **asserted** their claims, and appealed to Pompey (B. C. 64) as **the** umpire; he ended by seizing on the kingdom; and from that time, although for twenty years there were resistances, and various bloody revolutions, Judea was under

---

[1] "Asmonean family" properly, but better known by the name of Maccabean, supposed to be derived from a standard which they bore.

control of the Roman empire. Antipater, an Idumean of noble birth, profiting adroitly by these dissensions, had, as the supporter of Hyrcanus, risen into distinction; and at last, having procured from Rome the High Priesthood for his favorite, he was himself made Procurator of Judea. He was the father of Herod the Great, and appointed this son as governor of Galilee. The latter, after various reverses subsequently to his father's death, had the **crown of Judea** conferred **upon** himself by Augustus and Antony (B. C. 39;) and having, with the assistance of **the Romans, rid that** country and Samaria of all competitors, and freed Galilee from the bands of robbers that had infested it, he found himself, though still subordinate to Rome, firmly seated on the throne of Palestine.

Herod was a man of extraordinary energies of mind and body. He rebuilt the walls of Jerusalem, strengthened them with towers of great size and beauty, made for himself, on Mount Zion, a palace of vast extent and architectural magnificence, and completed the walls around Moriah, producing on that eminence **a level** platform of great elevation;[1] thus making it a vast mountainous substructure for supporting the cloisters and temple with which he proposed to crown its heights. The temple erected by Zerubbabel **500 years before, had** suffered greatly from wars and **the** lapse of time; but the Jews looked with keen jealousy **on** any plans for its demolition; and it was only by making large preparations of materials ready for the new edifice, previous to commencing any changes, that Herod could keep their apprehensions within bounds. The new temple and cloisters, built by Herod will be noticed in a future chapter of this book. The amazing sums necessary for his outlays **for architectural** and warlike purposes were procured partly

---

[1] Josephus says 450 feet at the spot of the smallest elevation; 600 feet at the greatest, i. e., at the eastern side; but this is considered an exaggeration.

by heavy extortions from his people; and came partly by contributions from Jews, scattered now over nearly the whole civilized world. The constant drain of wealth always tending towards Jerusalem was the cause of serious apprehensions, even at Rome. Pompey found 2,000 talents[1] in the treasury of the temple at the time of his visit: Crassus plundered it of 10,000 talents; and both these incidents occurred at times when Jerusalem was also constantly subjected to visits from plundering hordes.

But, while indulging the national feeling in thus ornamenting the city and its sacred mountain, Herod was trying to undermine the national faith by foreign usages and amusements. "He built a theatre within the walls of Jerusalem, and an amphitheatre of immense size without. He celebrated quinquennial games on a scale of unrivalled splendor; invited the most distinguished proficients in every kind of gymnastic exercise, in chariot racing, boxing, and every kind of musical and poetic art; offered the most costly prizes; and even introduced the barbarous spectacles of the Romans, fights of wild beasts, and also combats of wild beasts with gladiators. The zealous Jews looked on in amazement, and with praiseworthy though silent abhorrence, at those strange exhibitions, so contrary to the mild genius of the great law-giver's institutions."[2]

Herod was, as already stated, from Idumea. When that country was added by Hyrcanus to Judea, the inhabitants were compelled to adopt the Jewish faith. But such a forced proselytism left the Idumeans still semi-pagan in belief; and hence we see the doubtful Judaism in Herod. He married, both from policy and affection, the beautiful Mariamne, a princess of the Maccabean family; but he failed still to secure the confidence of the Jews.

---

[1] A talent of silver was worth $1,505; of gold, $24,000.
[2] Millman's History of the Jews.

Judea was, even during Herod's magnificent reign, fast becoming a Roman province; its independence and the glory of the Maccabean dynasty had departed. Herod, after a life of daring and successful ambition, and of domestic wretchedness, died, leaving by will his kingdom divided **between his** two sons, Herod Antipas and Archelaus; to the former, Galilee and Perea; to the latter, Samaria, Judea, and Idumea. Archelaus went immediately to Rome to have his limited kingship confirmed; and there met Herod Antipas, preferring a counter-claim under a former will of their father, made it was asserted, when **he was in a saner** state of mind. While they were absent contesting their claims, both regions of country fell into confusion; and the Prefect of Syria residing at Antioch, had to interfere; the wretched people being plundered and abused on every side. A deputation of five hundred Jews went to Rome to petition for the total abolition of the kingly government and the restitution of their ancient constitution; and were joined in this by eight thousand **of their** countrymen **resident** in that city. Herod's will was, however, **confirmed by** the imperial edict, and Archelaus **took possession of his** government: but his sovereignty, marked by injustice **and cruelty, after continuing for nine years,** was suddenly brought **to** a conclusion by a summons to Rome: his brothers and subjects were his accusers; he was condemned and banished to Vienne, **in Gaul,** and his kingdom (A. D. 12) reduced to a Roman province. P. Sulpicius Quirinius was now made Prefect, or governor-general of Syria, all Palestine coming under his jurisdiction; and Coponius, a man of equestrian rank, was appointed governor of Judea. To the latter, two years afterwards, succeeded M. Ambivius; **then came Annius Rufus:** next (A. D. 16) Valerius Gratus, **and finally (A. D. 27) Pontius Pilate.** Jerusalem itself had sunk, during the rule of these governors, into secondary political consequence, the residence of the governors being at Cæsarea; but the people, since the time of Archelaus, had enjoyed an unusual state of **rest**.   This history, necessarily brief, can give the reader scarcely any conception of the disorders, tumults, exactions, and cruelties—often barbarities, to which the people of Palestine had been subjected, through nearly the whole of this long period of time.

The government was now unequivocally Roman: Pilate was over Judea as Procurator, and Herod Antipas Tetrarch of Galilee and Perea;—both subject to the Proconsul of Syria; the Jewish laws and institutions, so far as they did not conflict with the Roman, were still left in force, the power of inflicting capital punishment being the only exception; that being reserved for the representatives of Rome. Such was the political condition of Palestine when our Saviour's **public ministry commenced**.

CHAPTER VI.

JEWISH MANNERS AND CUSTOMS.

THE captivity had wrought one very remarkable change in the Jewish character:—it had cured them of their disposition **towards idolatry**.   It may seem strange that there **should ever have existed** such inclinations among a people **distinguished, as they had been, by signal** manifestations of God's power for them; who had his law in their hands; and who knew both the sternness of his prohibitions against this wickedness, and his **irrevocable purposes** for punishing it.   But the whole world around them was given to idolatry: and they found it difficult to spiritualize even their own grand and wonderful system; while, among all other nations religion **was** *sensuous,* that is, directed to the outer senses, which could more easily comprehend the nature and demands of such belief. To look inward and bind the soul to God, making it while on earth a part of the kingdom which is not of this world, is the highest act of our being; and the Jews had not only not attained to this, but had a **very** imperfect idea of what it could mean. When just released from Egypt they were ignorant **and they had** for long years been brutalized by slavery. God, **compassionating their ignorance** and weakness, allowed them a religious system in some respects sensuous, but in every item typifying the unseen; that is the tabernacle, the ark, the table of show-bread, the candlestick, the altar of incense, the mercy-seat, the cherubim, the golden ornaments, the purple hangings, the Urim and Thummim in which he condescended to make himself especially known and felt. So afterwards, also with the temple on Mount Moriah, honored as no other temple has ever been. But they regarded only the exterior; and by their own want of effort and by their worldliness, that which was meant to guide them to look within and then up to God, led them to the further sensuousness of **their** neighbors, often of the grossest kind.

Temple, altar, cherubim, Urim and Thummim,—all were swept away by the Assyrian conqueror; **and only blackened ruins** remained behind in their stead.

In their captivity the Jews had to look more directly to God; **and they did it in** mournings and humiliations, such as well befitted them, after so many vile apostasies in their own land.

When they returned there was soon evident a great change and great improvement in these outward things. They had now the *proseuchæ* and synagogues all over the country. The proseucha was a place of prayer, **a simple, open space without ostentation or ornament, but generally in a spot outside of their** cities or towns, shaded by trees. Here the traveller or the resident could bow in soul, in God's

great temple not made with hands; and feeling that Jehovah was present, could lift up his voice and heart to him.
The synagogues were places of more formal worship, and
were soon in general use: there being, it is said, in Jerusalem alone, **not less** than four hundred and eighty during its
later times.   The worship in these was doubtless more **of a**
spiritual nature than that in the temple itself; and what
was also of consequence, oral instruction was here largely
combined with singing, reading, and prayers.   The Jewish people, in all this, had evidently taken a most important
step in improvement; but still there were counteracting circumstances, (to be noticed presently, **p. 81–88**), terribly cor-
rupting their hearts.

The synagogues were of various sizes, but generally not
large.   As far as possible they were built in imitation of the
temple at Jerusalem with an open court and corridors surrounding the court.   In this was a chapel, or small building, ornamented with four columns; and in the chapel, on
an elevated place, were the books of the law kept ready for
use.   The "uppermost seats in the synagogue" were those
nearest this chapel, and these were the most honorable.   In
addition, there was erected in the court a large hall or ves-
try, into which people could retire when the weather happened to be unfavorable, and where each family had its own
particular seat.   To each building there were officers:—1st.
The Ruler of the Synagogue, who presided over the assembly and invited readers and speakers, unless some persons
who were acceptable, voluntarily offered themselves, (Luke
viii. 41, and xiii. 14, 15).   2d. The Elders of the synagogue—
πρεσβύτεροι, or presbyters; they appear to have been counsellors of the head or ruler, and were chosen from among the
most powerful and learned of the people.   The council of
the elders not only took part in the management of the internal concerns of the synagogue, but also punished transgressors of the public laws, either by turning them out of

the synagogue or decreeing the punishment of thirty-nine stripes, (John xii. 42; xvi. 2; 2 Cor. xi. 24). 3d. The Collector of alms; and, 4th. Servants of the synagogue.

When the people were collected together for worship **the** services began, after the usual greeting, with a doxology. A selection was then read from the Mosaic law, (Acts **xv. 21**). Then followed, after singing of **a second** doxology, the reading **of a portion from the Prophets.** (Luke iv. 17). **The** person **whose duty** it was to perform **the** reading **placed upon his head, as** is done **at the present day, a covering** called *Talith.* (See 2 Cor. iii. 15). **The sections which had** been read in the Hebrew **were** rendered by an interpreter into the vernacular tongue; and the reader, or some one else, then addressed the people. (Acts xiii. 15).

It was on occasions such as this that Jesus and afterwards the Apostles, taught the people. The meeting, as far as religion was concerned, was ended with prayer, to which the people responded, *Amen;* after which a collection was taken for the poor.

Such was the synagogue worship **of that period, often sanctioned by** our Saviour's presence, **and by his taking a part himself** in the services.

The modern Jewish synagogues **are, as far as possible, imitations of those ancient ones;** and a visit to them is recommended to **any one who** may **desire to look far back into the remote times. We may also** gain in them some idea of the adaptation to music **of the** language in which David wrote: for in these services the Hebrew is still almost exclusively used. It is desirable, however, to select a synagogue of the higher order: for in the inferior ones, both the language and the service are often repulsive, seeming to **be a discordant** jargon **with but little appearance of devotion.**

On entering **we** notice that the **heads of** the men, as well **as of** the women, are all kept covered as in the ancient usages: also that the *standing* posture is that of prayer, as was the case in those former days. The eye too is caught immediately by a white garment, a simple, rectangular piece of cloth, six or eight feet long by three or four wide, which each male worshipper puts on as he takes his place, and leaves behind when he retires. In the wealthier synagogues it is of silk, in others of woollen stuff; but it is always white, with blue stripes across at the ends; sometimes, but not uniformly, a fringe at each end; and in every case it has a number of cords a foot or so in length, of the same stuff, appended to each of the corners. In viewing this garment we are carried at once into the remotest antiquity: for these blue stripes at the end are "the ribbon of blue," and the cords at the corners represent the fringes commanded by Moses (Numbers xv. 32–41, but more especially Deut. xxii. 12) to be worn as a reminder of the penalty for trans- gressing the Sabbath: "and it shall be unto you for a fringe, that ye may look upon it and remember all the com- mandments of the Lord and do them." The garment is called *Talith*, and is sometimes made to cover also the head of the persons officiating in their religious service. It is worn by the congregation mostly over the shoulders, but also in a variety of ways across the back; and forms not an ungraceful drapery. I have seen, in a country church in Scotland, every man with his plaid across the shoulder, making a very picturesque congregation; but although the plaid is of the same size and shape as this garment, it wants the sacred associations of the *Talith:* the latter is always white.

The language is deeply guttural; and to my own ear, traveller as I have been among the Turks, and also the Ger- mans, it has, as chanted in these synagogues, a familiar and very far from unmusical sound; for it has both richness and power. Especially at the close of the worship, when the whole assembly unite in the singing, may we have some idea of the rich music as it floated in the old times from the heights of Moriah in the daily sacrifices; or from their companies to and from the festivals, as they travelled over hill and valley, singing on their way their great hymns **to** God.

Those ancient synagogues, and the **nature of the worship** offered there, in a large portion of which the whole assembly **united,** and also the address and instructions on those occasions, must **have had a** powerful influence in keeping the Jews, **after the captivity,** from the idolatrous tendencies so striking in the national character previous to that time.

Of education there seems **to have** been little in our full meaning of that word. The sons remained at home under the care of the mother until five years of age, when the father took them in charge and taught them in the arts and the duties of life, and more especially in the Mosaic law, and all other things connected with their religion, (Deut. vi. 20–25; vii. 19; xi. 19). For further instruction, private teachers were provided; or they were sent to **a priest or Le-**vite, who sometimes had numbers under his care. **We may** infer from Samuel, (1 Samuel i. 24–28), that **there was at** that time near the **tabernacle, a school for the instruction** of youth; but the instruction, except in **religious matters,** **was very** limited. **Astronomy in those days was apt to** **run into astrology, which was forbidden to the Jews: a lit-**tle **knowledge of mathematics sufficed for** their wants: the sciences, in all nations **at that** period were few in number. The whole bent of the Jewish scholars was towards the study of their written and their traditional law, and the questions to which these gave rise. Their teachers enjoined on all parents to have their children taught some art **or handicraft:** and **the Talmuds particularize many learned men who were** engaged **in manual labor.** "What is commanded," says a Talmudic **writer, "of a father toward** his son? To circumcise him; to **teach him** the law; to teach him a trade."

Their great cabalist, Rabbi Judah, "Our Holy Rabbi," as he was called, wrote, "He that teacheth not his son a trade, does the same as if he taught him to be a thief;" and Gamaliel (Saul's teacher) said, "He that hath a trade in his hand, to what is he like? He is like a vineyard that is fenced."

"There prevailed among the Hebrews no little propriety and refinement of manners. The Orientals would be thought by Europeans to be excessive in their gestures and expressions of good-will, when in truth they mean no more than very moderate ones among us.

"In the time of Christ the ancient mode of addressing those who were worthy of being honored, viz., *My lord*, or words to that effect, was in a measure superseded, and the more extravagant address of Rabbi, i. e., *the great mighty*, which originated in the schools, had become common among the people.

"The salutation between friends was an occurrence which consumed much time: for this reason it was anciently inculcated upon messengers who were sent upon business which required despatch, not to salute any one by the way, (2 Kings iv. 29; Luke x. 4).

"The ancient Hebrew in particular rarely used any term of reproach more severe than those of *adversary* or *opposer*, raca, *contemptible*, nabal, *fool;* an expression which means wicked man or atheist. When anything was said which was not acceptable, the dissatisfied person replied, *It is enough*, (Deut. iii. 26). The formula of assent was, *Thou hast said*, or *thou hast said rightly*. This is the form of expressing assent or an affirmative to this day." [1]

Their dress, unchanged from century to century, was generally simple and plain. It consisted of a tunic (also worn by the Romans, as we see in their sculptures), which was a loose garment encircling the body, with short sleeves,

---

[1] Jahn's Archæology.

and reaching nearly to the knees. The Babylonians, Egyptians and Persians wore another and outer tunic of more costly material, a custom also adopted by the Jews, and referred to in Matthew x. 10 and Luke ix. 3. The tunic being loose and bound by a girdle at the middle, made something like drapery, as we see in the ancient sculptures of Greece and Rome. The girdle was of leather, or flax, or silk, and was a hand's breadth in width. Over this was worn the *Simlah* or upper garment (the *Talith*), simply a rectangular piece of cloth, eight or nine feet long by five or six in width, and thrown over the shoulders, or over one shoulder with the corners tied under the other, or wrapped around the body, or in any other manner that the wearer might choose. However worn, it was always a becoming drapery. Thrown over the head and held there by a fillet, as by the Arabs of the present day, it formed a protection from the sun. It was so large that burdens could be carried in it, (Exodus xii. 34; 2 Kings iv. 39), and one end thrown over the shoulder in front and tied could be made a convenient receptacle or pocket, as in Luke vi. 38. At night the Hebrew wrapped himself in this simlah, and if travelling, his girdle unclasped and laid on a stone for a pillow made all the preparations necessary for his repose. This is seen in those countries at the present time. So necessary was this simlah to the Jew that Moses enacted a law that when given as a pledge it should be returned before night. (Exodus xxii. 25–27; Deut. xxiv. 13).

These simple garments,—the drawers, tunic and *simlah*, formed the usual costume of the Jew, a convenient and appropriate one in that southern climate: in winter the legs were often bound in cloth for warmth, and cloaks were worn also as a shelter from the weather. The cloak referred to in 2 Tim. iv. 13, was a Roman garment worn as a protection from the rain, or on journeys. Long garments were worn by those affecting particular sanctity or wisdom. The Talmud says, "Rabbi Jochanon asked Rabbi Baruaah, what kind of garment is the inner garment of the disciple of the wise man? It is such an one that the flesh may not be seen underneath him." The glossis is, "It is to reach to the very soles of the feet."[1]

White was esteemed the most appropriate color for cotton cloths, and purple for others; black was used for common wear and particularly for mourners. On festival days, the rich and powerful robed themselves in white cotton, and the fullers had discovered a method of giving it a dazzling brilliancy, which was very highly esteemed. Scarlet was much admired. The tunics of the women were longer than those of the men, and their dress was usually of finer quality of cloth; they always wore veils, even at home, except in the presence of servants and of those relatives with whom nuptials were interdicted: their hair was also dressed differently from that of the men.

Add to the sandals, tunic, and simlah, a beard and sometimes a turban or covering for the head, and we have an idea of the outward appearance of the Jew of those ancient times. The face which we call *Jewish* is by no means universal: any one who will now, look around in a Jewish synagogue of the better kind, will see many faces of our own type, which would be not at all distinguishable in the street; and doubtless in those remote periods the Jewish features generally were of a cast superior to these seen now, after the long centuries, during which these people have been as the Pariahs of mankind. That universal traveller, Bayard Taylor, says of the Jews whom he met in Palestine, "The native Jewish families in Jerusalem, as well as those in other parts of Palestine, present a marked difference from the Jews of Europe and America. They possess the same physical characteristics in the dark, oblong eye, the prominent nose, the strongly

---

[1] Lightfoot.

marked cheek and jaw; but in the latter these traits have become harsh and coarse. Centuries devoted to the lowest and most debasing forms of traffic, with the endurance of persecutions and contumely, have greatly changed and vulgarized the appearance of the race. But the Jews of the Holy City still retain a noble beauty, which proved to my mind their descent from the ancient princely house of Israel. The forehead is loftier, the eye larger and more frank in its expression, the nose more delicate in its prominence, and the face of a purer oval. I have remarked the same distinction in the countenance of those Jewish families of Europe whose members have devoted themselves to art or literature. Mendelssohn's was a face that must have belonged to the house of David."[1]

Miss Martineau remarks on the same subject: "The idlers who hung about us [at Hebron] were a very handsome set of people; and in the town we were yet more struck with the beauty of those we passed. Among all the Jews we saw, I observed only one who had what we call the Jewish cast of countenance. Here and at Jerusalem and elsewhere we saw many Jews with fair complexions, blue eyes, and light hair. Such eyes I never saw as both the blue and the brown; soft, noble eyes, such as bring tears into one's own, one knows not why. The form of the face was unusually fine, and the complexion clear brown or fair; the hair beautiful."[2]

That singular addition to their costume,—the phylacteries, has already been described. When a Jew wished to make a profession of unusual strictness in observing the law, he enlarged their size, so as to make them a more striking object to the public eye.

Mezuza was a name given to an appendage of a similar kind designed for the door-posts of their houses, both the

---

[1] "The Land of the Saracen."   [2] "Eastern Life."

outer doors and their chambers, and attached also to the knockers of doors on the right side. They wrote on parchment with a peculiar kind of ink, Deut. vi. 4–9, and xi. 13: the parchment was rolled up and put in a case on the outside of which was inscribed שׁדי *Shadai*, one of the names of God, and the case was nailed to the door-post. As often as they passed this they touched the name of the Deity with a finger which they afterwards kissed. The Mezuza are still used in Jewish houses, and may sometimes be seen in our own country.

The Mezuza.[1]

CHAPTER VII.

JEWISH FESTIVALS.

THRICE in the year every adult male was bound to appear at Jerusalem; namely, at the feasts of Passover, of Pentecost, and of Tabernacles. This seems to have been a great demand on their time and means; but religious observances were to the Jews no simple pastime, but the main business of life; as their Sabbath, Sabbatical years, their tithes, sacri-

---

[1] This affords a good opportunity for elucidating Matt. v. 18: "Till heaven and earth pass, one jot or one tittle shall in no wise pass from the law, till all be fulfilled." The small letter on the left, the least in the Jewish alphabet is *Yod*, (Yot, Jot,) and the tips at the upper part of the letter on the right is what is meant by *tittle* (in the Greek of this passage κεραία, *tip* or *horn*). "Not the smallest letter or least part of a letter shall be dropped from the words of the law," &c.

fices, and feasts and festivals may testify. Their whole polity was a great religious system. God, according to this, was their owner as well as king. Their means, and they themselves, were his. He had a right to their first-born of children: the firstlings of their flocks had to be offered to him; so also the first of their fruits: nay more; of the remainder, one-tenth was still to be taken to the temple; or to be changed into money if the owner was too remote to offer the substance; the money to be given for religious uses. There were also numerous other offerings which we will not stop here to particularize.

In lieu of taking the first-born child, (due to God because he had saved the first-born of Israel from the destroying angel in Egypt), he had accepted for himself a tribe,—that of Levi,—and had set it aside for his service. Of this tribe he had then taken a portion—the distinguished family of Aaron—for the priesthood; the remainder being reserved for the other offices of the tabernacle and temple. But even after this, the first-born of all children had to be brought to the temple, and had to be there redeemed with money, according to the estimate of the priest, which was never to exceed five shekels ($2,50) in amount. The first-born of cattle could not be redeemed, but had to be offered to God: so also the first-fruits of the earth.

These three journeys to Jerusalem, made each year, were not the inconvenient, laborious tasks which they may perhaps seem to us to have been. The two extremes of Palestine were only 170 of our statute miles apart: from the most remote portions of it a good pedestrian could reach Jerusalem in about four days; travelling as they did, with families and cattle, this distance would take about six; the nearer places, of course, less in proportion. Their word for feast, גח *chag*, means *rejoicing;*[1] and such was doubtless the feeling

---

[1] From חגג to dance, to celebrate a feast by dancing.

strongest in the heart of old and young in their families, while making preparations for such a journey, and while they were on the way.

The writer of this work is the more able to picture to himself this act of going up to their festivals from having once travelled a day and a half with companies of German pilgrims on their way to a celebrated shrine, that of Maria Zell, (the Virgin of Zell), lying about forty miles to the southward of Vienna. The circumstances were all so peculiar and marked with the picturesque, and were so illustrative of what may have been in Judea, in those ancient times, that he will briefly describe them, speaking in the first person for the sake of convenience.

I was making a pedestrian tour through Europe, and was at this time (August, 1833), proceeding from Trieste to Vienna. Having stopped at a wayside inn for refreshment one day, after dinner, I was dozing on the porch when I was roused up by three women travellers standing there bargaining for some soup. They had great loaves of brown bread on their heads, and were soon, by such aid, engaged in making a hearty meal. I asked them where they were going, and they said, "to Maria Zell." My informant, pointing to one of the company added, "This woman is becoming blind, and wanted to go there and pray; for Maria of Zell is powerful to help; this other is quite blind already." "But surely you cannot expect *her* to be restored." "No, but she would not stay at home." The person speaking could see, and was their guide; their whole journey to the shrine would occupy nine days.

On the second day after this, while travelling on, I was passed by a young man, a long staff in his hand, and going like the wind; and he soon left me behind. In answer to my inquiry, as he lingered a minute with me, he said that he was going to Maria Zell.

That evening I crossed a small stream, and followed a

winding road from it to the village of Fronleiten, on its bank, where I stopped to spend the next day, the Sabbath. At the tavern they gave me a bed in a large music room, as was often the case in the villages in Germany. Some time, during the night, it seemed as if the spirit of song was haunting the chamber and mixing itself with my dreams; and finally the music, soft yet strong, grew so powerful that I started from my sleep. The next act was to spring from my bed and to throw up a window opening upon the street. There was a spectacle below quite in unison with such dreams. The moon was about half an hour from setting, and cast a dim light on objects around. Along the middle of the street was a procession of pilgrims, in double file; they seemed, to my glance, to be all in white; and their rapid gait, in the dull moonlight, appeared more like the flitting of ghosts than the tread of earthly forms. As they passed, they were singing a hymn to some tune that harmonized with the scene and the occasion. They soon grew indistinct, and their hymn floated on the night air as if spirits were singing; and then we had again only the deserted street and the splashing of water in the fountain below.

At sunrise I was again aroused by singing from many voices in the street; and found, on looking out, that it came from another company of pilgrims winding up from the river and entering the church. After concluding their worship, they proceeded on their way. Other processions succeeded; and during the whole day, pilgrims were passing on towards Maria Zell. I found, on inquiry, that they were from the rural districts of Styria; that it was customary to make appointments each year, for particular districts, and that this was the year for pilgrims from that region.

I began my journey early on the following day: and as the road, since leaving Gratz, had been most of the time ascending, and was now fairly among the German Alps, the scenery on every side was marked with grand and striking features. I knew that there were pilgrims not far ahead, and by rapid walking soon joined a company of thirty-five, seated on the grass, at their morning meal. They appeared to be a family party; and there was a venerable-looking man at the head of it, by whose word they were governed, as they presently arose and formed a procession in double file. They were all provided for the journey with huge loaves of bread, which the women carried on their heads. Not long after setting out, the leader uncovered his head, and all the other men doing the same, the whole party engaged in solemn prayer; still, however, continuing their walk. This over, the hats were replaced and they all commenced singing a hymn. The effect was very fine. Their voices were good; the tune was a pleasant one; the grandest and most sublime forms of nature were all around us; a stream was dashing by our side, mingling its sounds not inharmoniously with the singing; and the gentle moving of the forest trees, as we passed along, seemed by the graceful motions and the soft murmurings, to intimate that nature herself was joining in the worship offered to nature's God. I looked in the faces of my companions, and read there clear signs of the sincerity of their devotions. Thus we travelled on, the whole party engaged in singing and praying alternately, for more than an hour; at the end of which time we arrived at a little chapel by the roadside, which they entered in order to commence more formal devotions.

Here I left them; and passing on, I soon joined a party of about 150 resting in the little town of Oflands; and this company, being more miscellaneous, was organized more carefully than the other. They occupied much of the time, as we proceeded, in singing and prayer: a slight rain, lasting two or three hours, did not interrupt either the journey or their devotions.

They also stopped in the afternoon; and I proceeded and

joined a party of about 250, a little further on the road. Their singing, as we travelled on, had the finest effect imaginable: for the rain had now ceased; we were quite up, among the highest parts of the Alps; the softening influences of evening were beginning to be felt upon the scenery, and upon our feelings; and, if to this, we add that the voices were good, and the airs musical and sweet, some idea may be formed of the evening walk, as our procession passed, winding among the mountain tops.

About sunset, we came to a small village, and stopped to rest. I walked a little to one side, so as to have a view, at leisure, of the mountain scenery: for the spot commanded a most extensive prospect; and every Alpine height was now steeped in its own peculiar hue, running through the richest shades of blue, purple, green and yellow; while over some, floated canopies of vapor with ever-changing colors, which no human art could imitate. I soon, however, thought it best to return to my company:—but they were gone, nor could I find them anywhere! The road in each direction was in sight, for some distance; but they were not there. I looked around, perplexed and troubled: till, at last, happening to raise my eyes, I espied them scattered thickly over an adjoining hill-side so steep that I had previously not thought of looking for them there. It is called the "Seherberg;" and is so steep, that, in climbing it, I often had to dig holes in the turf with my feet before trusting myself to the next step. On the way up, I passed four pilgrims at prayer, on a more level part of the ascent. When I joined the company again, which was on the summit, I found them all on their knees, in an open area among the trees. Their faces were toward their homes; and their leader was repeating something which seemed to be half-vow, half-prayer. Suddenly they all rose, and faced in the contrary direction; when, kneeling again, they repeated their devotions: and then, all rising, they broke, with full, strong voices, into a

7

hymn, the cadences of which were well adapted to the scene and the time. In double file, as before, and still singing, they descended the hill by a slope more gentle than on the opposite side; and, at the bottom, we passed a large stone, which many of the company stepped to, and kissed. We came, soon after this, to a large tavern, which the pilgrims immediately filled, as their resting-place for the night. I went on to another, four miles distant; but which I found, on arriving there, to be already filled, like the other; I however succeeded there in getting a bed.

On the morrow I joined this latter party, and went with them towards the shrine. At the expiration of a couple of hours, a bright object, like a gilded sun on top of a steeple, shone among the trees; and now, by a little way-side chapel, the whole company stopped for formal prayer. Soon afterwards we reached the precincts of the village, Maria Zell; but before entering it my companions stepped aside to make their toilet at a stream crossing the road. At the church I found many others advancing on their knees through the court-yard toward the shrine.

We may, from these scenes, have probably some idea of the circumstances attending the going up to the festivals at Jerusalem, in those ancient times. The chief difficulty with the German pilgrims was in finding accommodations for the night: but in those southern countries, people, when at home, often sleep from choice in the open air. The *simlah*, wrapped around the Jewish travellers, with the girdle folded and laid on a stone for a pillow, was all that was needed in that climate. Such was doubtless the night-rest of their Patriarch Jacob, when, travelling in this same country, he saw, in his dream, the angels ascending and descending; and so, in the morning he called his open-air *hostelrie*, where the bright stars had shone down upon him, and heaven's vault was the dome,—a fit place for dreaming of angels—Bethel, or *the house of God.*

The object of the Jewish festivals was " to perpetuate the memory of great events; to keep them firm in their religion by ceremonies and the majesty of divine service ; to procure them certain pleasures, and allowable times of rest; and to renew the acquaintances, correspondence and friendship of their tribes and families, which, coming from distant towns in the country, met three times a year in the holy city."[1] The periods for the festivals were : for the Passover, just when the harvest was ripening, but the gathering had not yet begun ; for Pentecost, fifty days after this, when the harvesting had been finished ; for the feast of Tabernacles, just before seeding time had commenced :—periods, consequently, when time among agriculturists could very well be spared : and the Jews were generally cultivators of the soil. Then, as regards weather, the feast of Tabernacles was about our 15th of October, before the rainy season had set in : Pentecost was at a time when not a cloud is ever seen in Palestine, but yet prior to the hot season : the Passover was on the 14th Nisan, which month corresponded to the latter part of our March and beginning of April; and at the 14th Nisan we may consider the weather of that country to have recovered from the wintry storms, and to have become settled and clear; for, from the middle of April to the middle of September, rains and thunders are there little known.

The weather, therefore, for these journeys we may believe to have been clear, but not warm, and favorable for travelling : the time could easily be spared, and the periods came when the heart was open for rejoicing and thankfulness. We may easily imagine the members of families, male and female, including the children fit for travel (for all seem to have gone, although it was compulsory only on the adult males) starting together, joining other families from their

---

[1] Calmet.

neighborhood, or on the road ;—cheerful, happy parties, and all the happier for the "pic-nic" kind of living on the way; making the journey easy, since there was no occasion for hurrying, and they were subject to little expense on the road. The morning and evening and other occasional devotions added a sacredness to the day ; and the cheerfulness in other incidents of the journey had only a better zest from this devotion.   Their grand and noble hymns—(and time, even to our day, has furnished no grander or more sublime hymn-ology)—were chanted ; and, often and often, the full tones, in that rich Hebrew language, rose in sublime anthems in the clear air, amid the very regions of which those anthems spoke ; the mountains and plains, all witnesses of God's miraculous powers, seeming now to take a voice and to join the singers in the great anthems of praise.   The cattle in-tended for the coming sacrifices helped to carry the offerings of the first fruits or other burdens of the travellers : the horns of the oxen were sometimes gilded ;—trumpets were blown before the processions, to herald joyfully their ad-vances towards the holy city, the temple, and the altars. The children had with them their pet lamb or kid, also decked and sporting along, unconscious of the death so closely awaiting it ; and resting at night with the head of the child nestled against it—the animal itself still, as always before, a part of the family group.   It was to be the coming sacrifice,—was thus a part of their religion itself—was to go before God accepted by him, from and for them ; and was to open their way towards paradise, and so was a sacred object even in its sportiveness : and then again, the children while hanging around their pet, with many a secret grief at the near final parting, were told of Abraham, leading even his favorite son for sacrifice at the same Mount Moriah to which they were travelling, and of his faith which they could now all the better appreciate from the trial required of themselves.   Thus were infused into their young hearts the lessons of their religion by practical teachings so well understood and never to be forgotten.

But, on the whole journey, apart from the beauty of the scenery amid which the roads were laid, there were to all minds and hearts, historic lessons of strangest character and highest interest. If we suppose the festival journey to be from the northern part of Galilee, we see the travellers soon on the great plain of Esdraelon, vast in extent, and rich in beauty, on which rose the dome-shaped Tabor, with a town perched on its fortified heights. But the interest in natural beauty was sure to be mixed with grander thoughts; for there, on Tabor, had their countryman, Barak, ranged his host of 10,000 men, while Sisera, with his immense army, and his 900 chariots of iron, waited to engage the Israelites on the plain below. There had the fearless prophetess, Deborah, without whom Barak had said that he would not go down, cried out to him, "Up, for this is the day: is not the Lord gone out before thee?" And so they had rushed down; and the whole plain was soon covered with the flying enemy, slaughtered till not a man was left, except Sisera, who was spared to be slain by a woman's hand, because Barak had doubted God. How heartily, as the travellers passed on, did they now chant Deborah's song of victory, "Praise ye the Lord for the avenging of Israel"—ending with "So let all thine enemies perish, O Lord."[1] Far to the west of them now rose gradually on the edge of the plain and in full view, Carmel, with its history of Ahab's heathen priests, gathered there by order of Elijah;—the altars prepared there; the priests cutting their own flesh in frenzy, and calling on their gods in vain; and the heavenly fire, at Elijah's prayer, descending and consuming his sacrifice, and licking up the water in the trenches around. Soon the way laid by Jezreel, with its story of Elijah's hurried arrival there with

---

[1] Judges iv. and v.

the king, after the prophets of Baal had been slain in Kishon, on the western side of Esdraelon; and of the windows
of heaven then opened in rain; and also of Jezebel's fearful end under the walls of Jezreel.[1]   On their left, also, lay
Endor, telling of Saul's night journey thither from the
neighboring mountain of Gilboa, where his army lay encamped: and of the summons to the spirit of Samuel, and
of the king's heart-rending cry to the dead prophet, "God
is departed from me and heareth me no more."[2]   Further to
the east they could see the isolated hill of Scythopolis (Bethshean) with precipitous sides, and a castle on its summit,
against the walls of which the decapitated body of Saul had
been nailed by his triumphant foes.[3]   What lessons of most
powerful interest there were in all this journey to their festivals!   Soon now, toward the southern side of Esdraelon,
they passed the isolated range of Gilboa, 1,300 feet high,
where Saul was defeated and slain: and here, with their
chanting, mingled saddest notes, as filled with the memory
of the great slaughter of their countrymen, they sang the
lament of David, "The beauty of Israel is slain upon thy
high places: how are the mighty fallen!   Tell it not in
Gath, publish it not in the streets of Askalon; lest the
daughters of the Philistines rejoice, lest the daughters of the
uncircumcised triumph.   Ye mountains of Gilboa, let there
be no dew, neither let there be rain upon you, nor fields of
offerings;[4] for there the shield of the mighty is vilely cast
away, the shield of Saul, as though he had not been anointed
with oil.   How are the mighty fallen in the midst of the
battle!"[5]

Their journey might lead also by Sychem and Jacob's
well; and they could picture the patriarch returned once

---

[1] 1 Kings xviii.; 2 Kings ix.   [2] 1 Sam. xxviii.   [3] 1 Samuel xxxi.

[4] Gilboa is to this day remarkable for its barrenness,

[5] 2 Samuel i.

more to his native land, and finding here for a while, his home; and here, too, looking upon the two mountains, Ebal and Gerizim, they were reminded of the strange scene of blessing and cursing in the ancient times, to each item of which all Israel gathered there said, *Amen.*

Shiloh also was on their way, **with its** mementos **of** the ark resting there for 328 years: **and of Samuel brought up** there: and of the sudden death of Eli, when it was **announced** to him that his countrymen were routed in battle, and his children slain. Then **they** passed Bethel, **where** Jacob had his dream of the angels;—their whole **journey** from home to Jerusalem being indeed, through **regions** where history took to them a living and speaking form.

Thus in prayer, and in singing their grand old hymns, and in pleasant intercourse they passed on; until at last, having reached the heights of Scopus, they paused in mute admiration and joyfulness: and then they broke out in **shouts** of loudest praise: for, from this elevation, they looked down over a **wide** scene of beauty, in the **midst of** which lay "the joy of the whole earth," their **own blest,** sacred city,—Jerusalem.

On the road the crowds had **thickened, new companies all** the while uniting;—not as for one of our modern gatherings, **but for a deeply sacred and yet a glad purpose:** devotion and **joy mingled harmoniously and beamed on every** face; old associates **were** there with cordial greetings; · friends met from all parts of Palestine to strengthen the heart-bonds already formed.

Of the feasts of Tabernacles and Passover we shall have notices in a future **part** of this work. The ceremonies at Pentecost were brief, **and we give them here as a suitable** conclusion to this part of our subject. The word Pentecost signifies the 50th; and was used because this feast was on the 50th day, that is, the expiration of seven weeks from the second **day of the** Passover feast. **The object of it was** to bring the Jews to acknowledge in the sanctuary at this, the ending of their harvest, the dominion of God over the fruits of the earth; and also to thank him for the law given on Mount Sinai, on the fiftieth day after their coming out from Egypt. Assembled at Jerusalem, they formed into companies of twenty-four persons each, to carry their first-fruits in a ceremonious manner. Each company was preceded by an ox appointed to be sacrificed, his head crowned with garlands of olive branches, his horns sometimes gilded, a player on a flute preceding him. The offering of first-fruits consisted of two loaves of wheat bread, barley, grapes, figs, olives and dates. Each man carried his basket, and the king himself was not exempt from this act. They walked in pomp to the temple, singing hymns: and having arrived there before the priests, the Levites sang the 30th Psalm. The bearers then brought their baskets before the priest, and said:

"A Syrian ready to perish was my father; and he went down into Egypt, and sojourned there with a few, and became there a nation, great, mighty and populous," &c. "And now, O Lord, I have brought the first-fruits of the land, which thou, O Lord, hast given me."[1]

They placed the baskets beside the altar, and after prostrating themselves, were free then for the social enjoyments of the occasion.

Such was the nature of the Jewish institutions, and such their legitimate actions;—a pleasing spectacle where religion and social joy were combined, and each helped to give a zest to the other; and where all life was made grand by its intimate relationship to God.

---

[1] Deut. xxvi. 4–10: see also Numbers xxviii. 26–31.

CHAPTER VIII.

THE UNWRITTEN WORD—THE TALMUDS, &c.

BUT, over this fair spectacle of ordinances and worship, and over the Jewish heart, a cloud had been gradually drawn; and it was every day darkening more and more. It came from the substitution of forms for the essence of religion; from assumptions and pride in their leaders, and the hypocrisy which these engender; from innovations by the Pharisees; and especially from *The Unwritten Word,* (*oral traditions*) of which the Pharisees were the authors; an instrument which it will be readily seen must, from its mysterious and undefined nature, have been capable of giving immense power to its possessors. The Jewish history of this very singular claimant of divine authority is thus condensed by Isaac Nordheimer D. P., Professor of oriental languages in the University of New York, drawn by him from the writings of R. Moses Ben Maimon, commonly called Maimonides,[1] the highest authority among the Jews:

"All the laws given to Moses on Mount Sinai were accompanied by their interpretation; as it is written, 'I will give thee tables of stone and the law and the commandments' (Ex. xxiv. 12). 'The law' means written law, and 'the commandments' its interpretation, the oral law. Although this oral law was not preserved in writing, Moses taught it all to the Seventy elders composing his Beth-din or tribunal. Eleazer the priest, Phineas his son, and Joshua, were likewise instructed by Moses, especially the latter, who was his

---

[1] He died A. D. 1205.

own immediate disciple. From Joshua, who spent his whole
life in teaching it, the oral law was transmitted to many of
the elders of the people; and from them and Phineas it
was received by Eli. It then passed successively, through
the hands of Samuel and his tribunal, David and his
tribunal, Abijah the Shilonite and his tribunal, Elijah,
Elisha, Jehoiada the priest, Zechariah, Hosea, &c., &c., [the
whole list is given by the Jews] to Hillel. R. Gamaliel,
his son, imparted it to his son Simon, from whom it was
received by his son Gamaliel, [Saul's teacher], who was
followed by his son, Simon the 3d. After him came his son
R. Judah, generally called 'our holy Rabbi.' This R.
Judah compiled the *Mishna*. From the death of Moses to
his own age, no book had been composed for public instruction containing the oral law; but, in every generation the
chief of the tribunal, or the prophet who lived at the time,
made memoranda of what he had heard from his predeces-
sors and instructors, and communicated it orally to the
people. In like manner, each individual committed to
writing for his own use, and according to the degree of his
ability, the oral laws and information he had received
respecting the interpretation of the Bible, with the various
decisions which had been pronounced in every age and
sanctioned by the authority of the grand tribunal."

R. Judah had become fearful that these traditions might
fall into oblivion, and thus, A. D. 160, wrote them out,
forming the *Mishna or Second Law*, as above described. An
edition of this book published in Amsterdam 1698–1703,
is in six volumes, folio; and the vastness of the work shows
us not only how difficult (if indeed possible) it was for any
memory to retain it, but also what immense means it afforded
the Rabbis, by its very vastness, for imposing on the Jewish
people, coming to them as these traditions did, as *the word
of God.* Indeed, the oral law, at a very early time, began
to claim more power than the Written Word of the Penta-

tcuch. Before we proceed to give authority for this assertion, we must speak also of a consequent work, the *Gemara*, (i. e. *completion*), called so because in this book the oral law is supposed to be completed, or fully explained. The Gemaras contain an exposition of the contents of the Mishna, and discussions on disputed points of doctrine, also historical and biographical notices, legends, disputations on astronomy and sympathetic medicine, aphorisms, apologues, parables, short and pithy sermons, and rules of ethics and of practical wisdom in general. There are two Gemaras, one called the Jerusalem Gemara, compiled at the city of Tiberias, about seventy years after the writing out of the Mishna, (or A. D. 230). The other, the Babylonian Gemara, was prepared a few years later: this latter, as published in Berlin in 1715, fills 12 folio volumes. The Mishna and Gemara form, together, what is called the *Talmud*, or, referring to the two Gemaras, "the Talmuds," from the Hebrew *Lamad, to learn*. The Mishna is divided into six portions: 1, on seeds and agriculture; 2, festivals; 3, women; 4, laws of civil life; 5, things holy; and 6, purifications. Being written out so soon after our Saviour's time, it may be considered a fair exhibition of the excrescences which had at his time grown upon the Jewish religion, and which Christ so often and so severely denounced. The Talmud, as respects its claims to authority, says: "The written law is narrow; but the traditional is longer than the earth and broader than the sea." "The words of the scribes are lovely above the words of the law; for the words of the law are weighty and light, but the words of the scribe are all weighty." "The Bible is like water; the Mishna like wine: he that hath learned the Scripture, and not the Mishna, is a blockhead."

A great English scholar, Dr. Lightfoot, believing that an examination of these books might afford important information respecting those earliest times, and help us thus in understanding the New Testament, gave nearly all his life to this subject; and Christian students must ever feel grateful to him for an undertaking so full of difficulties and attended with so much that was utterly wearisome and disgusting. He says in his own quaint language respecting the Talmuds: "The almost unconquerable difficulty of the style, the frightful roughness of the language, and the amazing emptiness and sophistry of the matters handled, do torture, vex and tire him that reads them. They do everywhere abound in trifles, in that manner as though they had no mind to be read; with obscurities and difficulties, as though they had no mind to be understood: so that the reader hath need of patience all along to enable him to bear both trifling in sense and roughness in expression."

Speaking again of the representation of the Supreme Being in the Talmud, he says: "With regard to this fundamental doctrine of all religions, we must forbear to quote what would be offensive to the pious in perusal. Suffice it to say, that it speaks of God as the author of sin; as needing atonement; as contracting pollution; as inferior to the Rabbis in knowledge: this, and more horrible blasphemies, are of common occurrence."

Surely there was great need for a Divine Teacher, and for a Deliverer to appear! Quotations from these books will be given in another part of this work.

In searching for the origin of the abuses just detailed, we have no occasion to go very far; for the Scribes and Pharisees, "hypocrites," as the Saviour often declared them to be,[1] "making the word of God of no effect through your traditions, which ye have believed,"[2] readily furnish us with the clue to them all.

"*Scribe* denotes generally any man learned, and is opposed to the word rude or clownish. More particularly the word *Scribe* denotes such as being learned, of a scholastic educa-

---

[1] Matt. xii. 13–33; xv. 7.　　　[2] Mark vii. 13.

tion, addicted themselves especially to handling the pen and writing. Such were the public notaries in the Sanhedrim; registrars in the synagogues; amanuenses, who employed themselves in transcribing the law, phylacteries, short sentences to be fixed upon door-posts, wills of contract, divorces, &c. But, above all, the fathers of the traditions were called *Scribes,* (who were, indeed, elders of the Sanhedrim), which is clear enough in such like expressions, 'The words of the Scribes are more lovely than the words of the law;' i. e., *traditions are better than* **the written law.** 'Scribes of the people' were those elders of the Sanhedrim who were not sprung from the sacerdotal or Levitical stock, but from the other tribes: the elders of the Sanhedrim, sprung from the blood of the priests, were the scribes of the clergy; the rest were scribes of the people." [1]

The Pharisees, called so from the Hebrew word *Pharash,* signifying *to separate,* have been noticed in a previous chapter; and it is necessary to mention them here only as coming before us in history about the time when we have the first distinct notices of the traditional law. They and the Scribes were its conservators, and doubtless also its originators. That all the Pharisees were wicked men is not to be supposed; for we have record of individuals of probity belonging to this sect; but these were the few exceptions, and the character of the rest is emblazoned in our Saviour's public denunciations of them, the truth of which they did not dare to deny. It is not wonderful that such men, vainglorious and haughty, ambitious, overbearing and hypocritical, should persistently oppose the Saviour, and that he should so constantly warn the people against them and their works.

There was another sect among the Jews called the Essenes, a quiet people, living by themselves, and almost entirely cultivators of the soil. Josephus speaks of them as only 4000

---

[1] Lightfoot

in number, and says, "They are Jews by birth, and seem to have a greater affection one for another than the other sects have. These Essenes reject pleasures as an evil, but esteem continence and the conquest over our passions to be virtue. They reject wedlock, but choose out other persons' children while they are pliable and fit for learning, and esteem them to be of their kindred, and form them according to their own manners."[1]   In another part of his book, however, he intimates that some of them married, and that they were more numerous than as above described: but they do not seem to have exercised, or cared to exercise, any great influence in national affairs.

Another Jewish sect, the Herodians, were, however ambitious of such power, and stood boldly forward not only as the advocates of the Roman government, but also of principles corrupting their countrymen.   They took their name apparently from Herod the Great, and seem to have drawn their sentiments from him, namely: 1st, That the dominion of the Romans over the Jews was just, and that it was their duty to submit; and 2d, That in the present circumstances, they might with a good conscience follow many of the heathen modes and usages.[2]   Twice the Pharisees combined with them in attempts to entrap and destroy the Messiah; and no further proof can be needed of the bitter hostility toward him by the former sect than their union thus with men whose avowed principles in national affairs were so utterly hostile to their own.

We have now, through these preliminary remarks a view of the surface of Jewish society, and of some of its internal workings; but after all there was a deep under-current of feeling and belief which we have not reached, and cannot reach.   The power of the insolent Pharisee over the masses was tremendous, backed as it was by the traditional law

---

[1] De bel. ii. 8, § 2.   Prideaux—see Calmet.

claiming to be that of God, and which they might change into any form which seemed expedient: yet the **people were** ever ready to break from them, and the rulers were **ever** fearful of such revolt by their followers. **We may** know from this, that **in the** Jewish heart was a broad substratum of right feeling, which no Pharisaic cunning could **destroy.** While the Pharisees and **the Sadducees and Scribes and** Doctors, **looked coldly on Christ, or sneered, or tried to de-stroy him, the people heard him gladly, followed him with** admiration, **wanted to make him a king; and more than** once **set their old doctrinal masters at defiance in their love** to Christ, and their joy **as they followed in his train.** Where the general heart was so moved by him, there **must have been** much good and right feeling in it, notwithstanding the cor-rupting influences which their leaders had long and hypo-critically exercised over the land.

The Jews had never been a popular people among other nations, and they could not **be.** Exclusive, antagonistic to all other religions; repelling **all** intercourse as adapted **to** bring heathenism among them; believing **themselves to be a nation chosen of God** from all the inhabitants of the **earth, and** favored of **Him, they shut their hearts** against all other people in **that** *adversus omnes alios hostile odium, hatred amounting to hostility against* **all** *others,* **described by** Tacitus (Hist. **Lib. v. 5), and were regarded by** other nations in return **with hatred mixed with contempt.** "Credat Judeus" —*let a Jew believe it,* expresses Horace's contemptuous opin-ion of their credulity. Their literature, even their poetry, was scarcely known beyond themselves; yet their poetry was **the** most sublime extant, and even to our day it has not been **excelled.** Their **prophetical writing rises to a grandeur** of **sentiment and language without a parallel; and the father** of Grecian critics **on style, Longinus, quotes the opening of** the first chapter of **Genesis as the highest known specimen of** the sublime. While Pharisaism and the heavy curse of the *traditional* religion were like a crushing weight upon the land, there **must have** been a mighty power **in the** original Jewish faith to **keep** religion alive at all **under** such a malign influence.   **Alive it was;** and now springing **up** once more with **vigor at** that cry from the Jordan, "the kingdom of heaven **is** at hand," with **the** subsequent declaration, "Behold the Lamb of God, which **taketh** away the sin of the world."

CHAPTER IX.

PRESENT JEWISH VIEW OF THAT PERIOD.

THESE preliminaries in the last three chapters will enable us to take a comprehensive view of the circumstances attending the public ministry **of** Christ: but the reader would probably **be gratified by seeing** what **are the** present Jewish views of those times **and circumstances. We** therefore make extracts from a **recent** work, "A general history of the Jews," by one **of** their own people, Jost; **considered** by them **as** the most profound historian of the **age. It was** written in German, and portions have been **translated by** Rev. James Murdaugh, **D. D.;** from which we **make our quotation. Its deeply** interesting character will **render unnecessary any apology for its length, or** for inserting it here in the text instead of in a note.

Jost says:

"Herod the Great tore in pieces all the framework of society, and gave it a **new construction.** Under him the people so visibly lost their **national** peculiarities, that they **seemed** ready to **become extinct.** Trodden down and oppressed by a tyrannical government, they turned their eyes towards the Holy Scriptures and their law, for comfort and consolation. They acknowledged themselves justly punished for their backsliding; and although the sanctuary and the sacrifices continued, yet every one could see that a priesthood which the king conferred on whom he pleased, and of whose incumbents he had deposed four and slain **two, and a sanctuary which** the king **beautified merely as a permanent temple, the** sanctity of which **he was no way concerned to** maintain, could by no means satisfy the **requisitions of God's** government, and of the Judaism resulting from it. **Besides,** the national tribunals were disregarded, **and the king alone** enacted laws and appointed tribunals **on every occasion,** according to his pleasure. The people had no protection, **and** they were harassed with acts of individual violence; some were carried away by ambition, others by self-interest; some acted from compulsion, others from bigotry and hypocrisy. What would be the result of such a state of things, **was a** question which interested **every friend of the** public weal; **and it was answered variously. One** party adhered to the doctrine **of Judaism, and looked for deliverance by a** regent of the house of David; **another party were for waging war with everything of a foreign character; and a third party declared the kingdom of God to be at hand,** in the way **of a general repentance and reformation.**

"**1. The first party** connected themselves with the doctors of the law, and adhered to their schools. At the head of these schools, during the whole reign of Herod, stood two men entirely disconnected with political life, who devoted their time to the study and exposition of the doctrines of the law; namely, **Hillel of Babylonia,** renowned for the mildness of his disposition, his kindness and calmness, **and** Shammai, **a man bold, vehement and decisive.** Both were distinguished **for learning, and both** framed systems **of** Judaism, though they frequently clashed in regard to their

8 *

legal conclusions on particular points. And hence their schools were afterwards opposed to each other, and were characterized, that of Hillel for adhering more to the sense and import of Scripture, and that of Shammai for a rigid adherence to the letter. Both of these men mingled so little in the transactions of their times, that they became mythical personages. Only some particular sayings, characteristic of each, have come down to us. Thus Hillel inculcated as the fundamental principle of Judaism this maxim: *Love thy neighbor as thyself.* On the necessity of an early prosecution of knowledge, with his accustomed brevity, he said: *Unless I for myself, who will? If I only for myself what do I become? If not now, then when?* On the nothingness of the world, compared with spiritual life, he said: *The more flesh, the more worms; the more wealth, the more care; the more wives, the more poisoning; the more maid-servants, the more unchastity; the more men-servants, the more thieving,—but the more knowledge, the more life; the more reflection, the more intelligence; the more benevolence, the more union. Gaining a good name is a good thing; but a knowledge of the law procures immortality.* Respecting union he said: *Separate not yourselves from the many. Do not account yourself safe until your dying day: and judge not your neighbor until you stand in his place.* From Shammai we have only a few sayings. *Make the study of the law the business of your life. Say little and do much. Be beforehand with every one.* Yet the virtues of the man are particularly eulogized. By the influence of these two men, Rabbinism, or the authoritativeness of the teachers of the law, became predominant; Sadduceeism was nearly extinguished, and the interest of students in the application of the doctrines and precepts of the law to human conduct was amazingly shackled. By the Rabbis of after ages, Hillel was honored as being next to Ezra, the restorer of the law. (Succa 1, end). To him in particular, has been ascribed the distribution of the whole law into six parts: 1, of seeds; **2,** of women; 3, of festivals; **4, of** possessions and property; 5, of sacred things; 6, of things clean and unclean; a distribution which has been permanently maintained. Under these six titles are arranged **all that Judaism teaches** respecting the law; **and** the whole, collectively, **has** since been **called MISHNA, (Deuterosis) or the second** rescension of the law. **Yet all instruction was,** at that time, given orally. Hence, **though many persons understood the** law, yet there **were few who had talents for** teaching. Possibly **the** *Semicha,* **or the consecration of** public teachers by the imposition of **hands, which their** principal doctors practiced, originated in **this period. For** not long afterwards the learned were always called *Rabbis;* which word became a title, and was an object of ambition. The introduction of such a mode of investiture greatly increased the power of the Rabbis, or rather established it on a firm basis. Rabbinism directed its aims against paganism, and the dominion of the senses in common people. To all who intrenched themselves **in this bulwark, the civil** government became a matter of indifference, **because it did** not secure the proper object. From that **period, the adherents to Rabbinism have** had a world of their own in **which they** lived and for which they died. We **may also remark that the Rabbis** for a **number of** centuries **continued their labors to** bring Judaism to **perfection. The men who took** the lead in **the work set out with a** very good **idea,** namely, to give to Judaism an enduring shell or covering that should defend it against all the storms to which it might be exposed. But many of their followers embraced only the shell, and sought for salvation in outward observances, in much prayer **and fasting, in strenuously** combating **the slightest deviation from very trivial prescriptions; and thus, either they were** altogether in error **respecting the kernel of doctrine, or they** put on an apparent **sanctity as a cloak to conceal** their moral conduct. The majority were enthusiasts in the proper sense of the term, and lived only in an ideal world.

"2. On the other hand, there was at that time a *large party* who contemplated a full restoration of the Jewish commonwealth, and who overrated their own power.

*   *   *   *   *   *   *   *
*   *   *   *   *   *   *   *

"3. A third party was actuated by totally different views. In the interpretation put upon the law by the first party, they could see only a tissue of external sanctity; and in the zeal of the second party, only a useless effort that must draw after it the loss of what little union remained in Judea. Far from both, many, especially among the more plain common people who had no thirst for distinction, and no solicitude to maintain the fallen commonwealth, hoped for deliverance from the fluctuating state of things, and particularly from the evils of immorality, in accordance with the generally proclaimed oracles of the prophets. There can be no doubt that this expectation of a kingdom of God which should arise out of Judaism, and be a very different thing from what others anticipated, was very prevalent, especially among the later Essenes. They preferred a still and quiet life of devotion, and served the public chiefly as peaceful counsellors, and revered wise men. The spirit alone, the divine, the all-subduing spirit, could put an end to their calamities; burst the fetters of the law on the one hand, and of worldly-mindedness on the other, and by his truth, bring not only the Jews, but all the Gentile world, to an internal tranquillity; which their religions, in combination with worldly power or oppression, could not secure. These views more or less matured, pervaded and animated a very considerable number of Jews, who waited only for the manifestation of God, in order to see the work of redemption in successful operation. Their aspirations for it increased as the calamities multiplied.

*   *   *   *   *   *   *   *

"Recognizing the sinfulness of men by nature as a fundamental principle, the Jews anxiously desired to find an atonement for sin. This was symbolized by sacrifices and by baptism. *John*, surnamed the Baptist, born a little prior to Jesus, and also destined to a high calling, travelled up and down the wilderness like the ancient prophets, proclaiming, 'The kingdom of heaven draws near.' Kindly greeting all who resorted to him, he baptized many in the Jordan, and preached repentance as a preparation for the coming of Christ; whom moreover, he recognized in the person of *Jesus of Nazareth*. Jesus, also honoring the national custom, received consecration from him. Exciting high expectations in his childhood, and astonishing people by his wisdom in discourse with the doctors of the law when twelve years old, he at the age of about thirty, entered on his course as a public teacher. In Galilee his discourses had an overpowering influence; and soon his triumphant superiority in reasoning with the Pharisees and Sadducees in their own way, procured him general esteem and veneration. The mentally diseased often from mere internal conflicts exposed to exquisite pain, found relief by him; and other sufferings he was able to alleviate by his healing word. After various miracles which were beheld with amazement, but which did not so penetrate the soul as did his instructions, Jesus announced his vocation as the *Christ*, the Anointed One, the Saviour of the world, the Son of God, and in general as the person foretold by the prophets under various attributes; and of course also as a *king*, yet not over an earthly realm, but over the spiritual world which was to be new created. His friends who were in some uncertainty respecting his mysterious character, were at length brought gradually to the conviction that he was the Deity himself, manifested in a human form. The Pharisees who were advocates of the enlarged oral law, and especially of the expected glorious appearing at some time of a restorer of the commonwealth, saw in his denial of the holiness and atoning efficacy of certain precepts of the law, and in the announcement of his grand position, that redemption is to be sought for in a renovation of the soul, an entire prostration of their own system of doctrine.   Although no one of the renowned doctors of Judaism encountered him in debate, yet he had to answer a great many captious questions, and often to hear his doctrine branded as heresy.   This occurred especially at Jerusalem, where his adversaries took occasion from certain expressions, to accuse him of treason which the civil relations of the country easily offered the means of doing.   A Sanhedrim assembled under the Romish governor Pontius Pilate, found him guilty; and Pilate, contrary to his own convictions, yielding to the urgency of the excited people, ordered him to be crucified.   But the execution of the Sanhedrim's sentence had an effect very different from that contemplated.   The headlong procedure in disregard of the usual forms of justice, strengthened and united his followers. They saw in the transaction not merely the execution of an innocent person, but a conspiracy against the Deity with which he was filled, and by whose spirit actuated, he for the salvation of all, gave up his body to torture and contumely. From the period of Christ's crucifixion, his followers ceased to be Jews, and of course pass out of the province of our history into that of the church of Christ.   The Jews themselves did not at the time view this transaction so important as they must afterwards have found it to be."

CHAPTER X.

AT THE JORDAN—DISCIPLES CALLED.

WAS this the Christ? The multitudes around John in their scrutinizing, earnest, anxious mood, might well be astonished while looking at him, just proclaimed to be The Son of God; who was to baptize with the Holy Ghost; whose shoe's latchet the Baptist had declared himself not worthy to unloose. The admiration of the throngs toward John had increased to the highest degree as the strange ascetic had stood before them, day after day, so earnest in manner and so bold in his denunciations; a revivification, apparently, of their long dead, best beloved prophet; his appearance itself captivating their fancy and awakening enthusiasm, while the rite he was administering was, alone, a proclamation of wonderful revolutions to come. But was this the Christ? For he to whom John pointed was a simple personage, in ordinary costume: one like themselves, except that grandeur of expression in face, and that dignity combined with simplicity and unassumingness of manner, which always belong to true greatness even in men. Here they produced a *Presence* which was indeed felt. But yet, with their expectations of worldly glory and honor and pomp in the Messiah, the crowds shrank from believing. "Was this he," they thought, "who was to rescue them from the Roman dominion, and to build up a mightier earthly kingdom than any one ever yet known; to flash over all the world his own glory and that of the Jewish name?"

Greatly agitated they gazed, wondered, argued, doubted. Many a person has done the same ever since respecting this Christ. The human mind is dazzled by displays of outward glory, and desires **them as the immediate** foundation for its reverence.   Men **require a** mixture of awe for their devotion. **Had** Christ **come in pomp and majesty,** with the retinues of **the great men of earth, there is many a** heart **at** present **doubting or repellant that would gladly** open to receive **him.** **But** surely, **so received, the heart could** never *feel* him as it **does now.   He was to be** *the Teacher and the Example* as well as *the Redeemer*, **and where, if such earthly** pomp and circumstance **had been** around him, where could **ever have** been the force of such a sermon as that on the Mount, **or of his** parables, or of his injunctions respecting humility in soul **and** action, **or indeed** of all his great teachings felt now to **be the life of** the world? **where** the power of his example, **before which every human heart now** bows down in rever- **ence,** though it **may not** imitate? where that blessedness of **fellowship recognized in him by the lowly in** life? how could **any of this have been, if he had come** amid exaltations **and had** so dwelt on the earth?

He knew all this, and so he came, not only as man, but as man **in** humility and in commonness among men : **but yet,** with the consciousness which **he carried** within him, what an impressiveness **of** internal power and grandeur there was to be recognized, on observation, as he appeared there among the astounded **crowds about** John ;—astounded by the seeming contradictions, **such** lowliness **yet** such greatness claimed **for him by the Baptist** and through John by heaven itself. **They were amazed and confounded ; they** reasoned, **doubted ; yielded willingly to doubts, for they clung to** the old expec- **tation of coming Jewish earthly grandeur,** unwilling to let it go.

On the following day, while two of John's disciples were standing near by, Jesus **came** in sight, **and** the Baptist's face again took the glow of inspiration, **as he** cried :

"Behold the Lamb of God !"

The two disciples, how they were thrilled by the words !

What a flashing of brightest thought in their minds! What a glory of hope! Could it be? John had said it. They left their former master to follow the new. Christ turned to them :—

" What seek ye?"

" Rabbi, where dwellest thou?" they said, apparently confounded by their having no ready answer to his sudden question.

" Come and see," was his reply; and they went to see how humble indeed was his place, and how unpromising as to earthly comforts was to be any discipleship to him.

They were the first followers of Jesus. One was Andrew, the other is unnamed, but was doubtless John, a man blest with a true and affectionate nature; one who could, most of all the men with whom Christ came in contact, appreciate the greatness of the love of Jesus for our race, and who was the most beloved in return. The record of this incident is from him, and in his modesty he has refrained from naming himself as of the first to join his Lord. The two remained with the Messiah through the day.

On the morrow Andrew, stimulated by the power of his new convictions, restless under them and deeply earnest, searched for a brother then at Bethabara, a man quick, ardent, sympathetic and impulsive, often uncertain yet always with a readiness to drop error when seen and catch at truth, and to acknowledge and grieve for error; in short, one of that class whose firmness of fidelity we cannot always trust, yet who always win on us and whom we admire and like in spite of their weaknesses and faults. It was Peter; and Andrew on finding him cried with joy:

" We have found the *Messiah!*"

The brother came promptly, for the cry met with quick sympathies in his sensitive nature—came, gazed, took in the force of the wonderful Presence there was in Christ, and was addressed by him:

9

"Thou art Simon the son of Jona: thou shalt be called **Cephas**,"[1] (*Kephas*); the Messiah, as he said this, probably pointing to an adjoining cliff or high rock as an intimation of the future prominence of this disciple in the church.

Another night was passed at Bethabara, such a night as people have who in the dim light spend their time in surmisings and agitations about subjects of great national and individual welfare; for there were many reasonings and doubts and fears and hopes among this emotional people, about John's declarations, and about John, and especially about him upon whom the Baptist had now concentrated the attention of all.

On the morrow Christ thought it best to leave this region for Galilee; but before going he called another individual to be his disciple, Philip of Bethsaida, a town just beyond the northern end of the lake of Galilee, and the residence also of Andrew and Peter. To Philip he simply addressed the words,

"Follow me;" and the injunction was promptly obeyed.

There was authority in the voice, mixed with all tender-

---

[1] The Aramaic כיפא, (*Kepha*), the language used on this occasion, is from the Hebrew *Keph*, כף, and the use of the latter may help us to the true significance of the name given to Peter.   The author, after careful and thorough examination, can find this word used but twice in the Old Testament, both times in its plural form, כפים, (*Kephim*), Job xxx. 6, literally, "To inhabit the caves of the earth *and the rocks;*" Jer. iv. 19, literally, "They shall go into thickets *and into rocks;*" each instance evidently indicating a cliff or prominent rock: the Greek, πετρα, (Matt. xvi. 18), also means rock.   Commentators suppose that "stability" and "firmness" are here indicated as the qualities of Peter, to be his characteristics after the descent of the Holy Ghost on the day of Pentecost: but we know, (Gal. ii. 12–14), that he was not stable subsequently to that event.   As Christ was accustomed to seize upon objects in nature for his elucidations, if we will suppose him on this occasion to have pointed to a cliff or high rock of which there was abundance at the Jordan valley, and to have intimated by this word that Peter should have a similar prominence among the Apostles, the expression becomes very significant and adapted to the occasion, as well as strikingly prophetic.

ness and kindness; and Philip felt it: nor could he have been a stranger to what had previously occurred. A new joy filled him as he opened his heart to the power of his convictions, and to the glory of being the follower of such a master, privileged to be near to Christ, to see him and hear him, and to be distinguished by him: but the joy of Philip was quickly subject to a check.

There was among the throngs at the Jordan a man, Nathaniel by name, belonging to Cana in Galilee, a town about eight miles north of Nazareth. He was an individual of great singleness of life and character, pure in heart and an ardent lover of the truth; discriminating also and cautious against error, but readily open to conviction. To such a man the rumors and the excitement at Bethabara could not be otherwise than known; and inasmuch as he was looking earnestly and longingly for the fulfillment of Israel's great hope, he had probably this very morning been in retirement for prayer respecting this present engrossing topic. He had doubts peculiar to himself; for the proximity of his home to Nazareth, whence Christ had come, made him acquainted with the character of that place, which he believed to be bad. He was now met by Philip full of ardor and zeal, who exclaimed to him,

"We have found him of whom Moses in the law, and the prophets, did write, Jesus of Nazareth, the son of Joseph!"

"Can there any good thing come out of Nazareth?"

"Come and see."

He followed Philip towards Christ, who when he saw him said to those around:—

"Behold an Israelite indeed, in whom is no guile!"

The words doubtless had reference to the entire singleness of the man's purpose in his present seeking for light; and the earnest seeker spoke out in wonder,

"Whence knowest thou me?"

To which the response was given:

"Before that Philip called thee, when thou wast under the fig-tree, I saw thee."

"Rabbi, thou art the Son of God; thou art the king of Israel."

"Because I said unto thee, I saw thee under the fig-tree, believest thou? thou shalt see greater things than these. Verily, verily, I say unto you, Hereafter ye shall see heaven open, and the angels of God ascending and descending upon the Son of man."

Still greater was the amazement in all who heard.

CHAPTER XI.

AT CANA IN GALILEE.

THE events in the former chapters, it will be remembered occurred in Judea; but we are now to follow the Messiah into Galilee. John's baptizings had been about twenty miles from Jerusalem, probably a little to the north of east from it; and this capital city or its neighborhood might possibly appear to be the best spot for the first general teachings and miracles of Christ.

But they were not. Judea was intensely and inveterately Jewish, in the worst meaning of the word. In the great proud capital were the schools of their Doctors; and every one was not allowed to appear there as a public teacher;[1] for although the form of authorization may not have been fully established then, as the Talmuds state to have been afterwards the case, when to be qualified, an individual must have been for some years as *Collega* of a Rabbi, and then

---

[1] See Matt. xxi. 20: also Tholuck on this passage.

promoted to the work of instruction to others; yet, under Shammai and Hillel, in the time of Herod the Great, the school had in all respects taken this shape. Christ's authority to teach would be questioned there at the very outset, and difficulties be thrown in his way, and people's ears closed by authoritative injunctions. There too was the high seat of all scholastic iniquity in **the Unwritten Traditional Law,** with which he was to come into violent antagonism; and in which, unbounded invention and authority could be united so as greatly to embarrass his **work.** There Pharisaic pride, Sadducaic vanity and **insolence, and Herodian** freethinking would **if** necessary lay **aside** their distinctive tenets, and at once combine against **him**; and his followers, **men of** humblest rank and uninstructed, would there **be** thoroughly scorned, for they belonged to a class against whom the Pharisee's code shut up the kingdom of heaven.

Why did **he** choose **such men for disciples?** the reader asks. The answer will manifest itself **to any one who** will notice how education, as conducted **in that country,** dwarfed and perverted the intellect, and helped **to make it impervious** to **the truth.** It **was important** in **these new** doctrines to have as much as possible a *tabula rasa,* a **clear page,** on which to write the truths which **Christ came to** communicate to the **world.** Even **these chosen** men, **John,** Nathaniel, Andrew, **Philip,** etc., **were always mistaking the** doctrines of their master, especially **such** as referred to the fact that his kingdom was not of **this** earth.

Galilee was a region very different from **Judea.** Although **densely** populated, it had no very large cities, but was an **agricultural country with numerous villages;** its inhabitants **mostly a people of simple habits, frank, genial in** feeling, open to instruction **and ready to respond to any** benevolent acts. Their **bravery of** disposition **was shown soon** after this **in the fact that** Josephus, **when collecting forces for**

9 *

the defence of his country, was able in this small district, to raise an army of 100,000 men. He says of this region,

"Those two Galilees, [upper and lower, but essentially one] of so great largeness, and encompassed with so many nations of foreigners, have always been able to make a strong resistance on all occasions of war; for the Galileans are inured to war from their infancy, and have been always very numerous, nor hath the country been ever destitute of men of courage, or wanted a numerous set of them; for their soil is universally rich and fruitful, and full of the plantations of trees of all sorts, insomuch that it invites the most slothful to take pains in its cultivation, by its fruitfulness; accordingly it is cultivated by its inhabitants, and no part of it lies idle. Moreover, the cities lie very thick, and the very many villages which are here are everywhere so full of people, by the richness of their soil, that the very least of them contain above 15,000 inhabitants. In short, if any one will suppose that Galilee is inferior to Perea in magnitude, he will be obliged to prefer it before it in its strength; for this is all capable of cultivation and is everywhere fruitful."[1]

After calling the five disciples at Bethabara, as mentioned above, Christ proceeded to Galilee; and just after his arrival, went to a marriage feast at Cana, to which he, his mother and disciples were invited.

We will accompany him there, and notice carefully all the singular facts of this feast; for some of them have been nervously shrunk from, especially in modern times, as things difficult to be explained.

We observe first the company and the occasion.

The latter was one of the holiest, as well as of the most joyful, events in human life; so holy that a large part of the

---

[1] De Bello, III. 3, § 2.

Christian church has considered it a *sacrament*, or a solemn religious ceremony establishing new covenants between God and his people; nor can its joyousness ever detract from its religious aspects; for religion is itself always a new joy in the heart. We look therefore at the presence of Jesus on this occasion, as only giving new sanctions to a holy and blessed rite, the gladness in which is but an additional beauty to what is so beautiful in itself. That there could be no rudeness and no coarseness in the mirth there, and no excesses in any enjoyment sanctioned by such a presence, we have the assurance in all else that we know of his pure and holy life, and of his teachings, which descend with a searching power into the very thoughts of the soul of man. We see Christ then, in this scene, as in perfect harmony with the occasion; and combined with his grandeur of aspect and with his gentleness and kindness to all, we mark his sympathy also with the happiness of the time and circumstance; and we love him more from seeing how he entered into the gladness, as well as into the sorrows of human life.

Among the company present there was a very singular sensation. Watchings, whisperings, uneasy earnest movements, unusual at such a time were noticed during all the feast. The five disciples, who were there, could not help but give information of the occurrences at Bethabara; and from this sprang up a scrutiny and a wondering, which spread quickly throughout the assembly. The impression was as it might have been if their outward vision had caught glimpses of a dim, undeveloped form of an angel floating in the atmosphere of their room,—now partly revealed, now hidden in obscurity; and as if they were expecting to hear the angel speak. There could be no tendency to unseemly merriment in that house; but there was an impressiveness as of a strange presence: and yet no one could look into those features of Christ so full of love to all men, without knowing that this impressiveness was not painful, but only added to the general holy and genial affections of the time and place.

There also was the mother of Christ, among the guests. She knew, and had entire faith in him in all respects: and while as attentive as others, she was trying to still her heart in the full strength of her faith. But a mother's heart would not be stilled, and her nervous anxiety followed him everywhere. With what entireness of affection she loved that son! How glorious he was to her! What reverence was mingled with her love! How perfect her faith! And yet, the future? she could not divine it: and in the present, she was anxious and nervous through the great power of her love.

The Jewish wedding feasts usually continued through seven or eight days; and on this occasion, at the last of it, the supply of wine was exhausted. The mother of Jesus came to him to tell him that this was the fact. It is difficult at any time, to enter into a mother's feelings, and the difficulty here is enhanced by the peculiarities of the case. Did she, overhearing the whisperings and surmisings, and probably the objections, and possibly scornful rejoinders by some, wish too eagerly for a miracle by one whom she knew to be so wonderfully endowed, in order that he might silence objectors and scorners? Was she anxious to hurry demonstrations of the Divine power, which she believed would be eventually made? to interpose her maternal anxiety in a place where she ought to have had faith in the Divine? The answer given her would seem to indicate this: but still not relinquishing her hopes, she directed the servants,

"Whatsoever he saith unto you, do it."

There were several water-jars present which he directed to be filled with water which was done: then he said, "Draw out now and bear unto the governor of the feast." The latter, ignorant of what had been done, tasted the fluid.

It had become wine! The ruler called for the bridegroom, and said :

"Every man at the beginning doth set forth good wine ; and when men have well drunk, then that which is worse : but thou hast kept the good wine until now."

The only additional remark in the Gospel concerning this circumstance is, "This beginning of miracles did Jesus in Cana of Galilee, and manifested forth his glory ; and his disciples believed on him."[1]

This is all in St. John's Gospel ; but the world has ever since remarked freely, especially in these later days, and sometimes with equivocal innuendo, sometimes with inferences honestly yet injuriously drawn ; and the subject has become one that seems to require further comment in this place.

The writer of this work was once about to sit down to a dinner party in Washington, the whole company consisting of clergymen except the lady of the house. In the conversation, before dinner was announced, questions were put to him about the Navy and its usages, etc., and he mentioned how he had been led to entire abstinence even in the use of wines by the importance of adding all possible power to his injunctions respecting the evils of intemperance in ships. The clergymen objected that "this was seeming to try to make one's self better than Christ ;" that "He drank wine and sanctioned the use of it in his first miracle ;" and that "what he had sanctioned no man ought to gainsay. For themselves they would not dare to put their example against His." In conclusion, we sat down to dinner with decanters of Madeira before us, a present from Ex-President John Quincy Adams to our host, and the present writer was the only person of entire abstinence on the occasion. Now these were, undoubtedly, conscientious men, honest in their belief ; and

---

[1] John ii. 2.

it is because honest conscientious men have such a view of the matter (while many others less scrupulous take courage by their example) that some comments on the subject are here introduced.

Among religious people there is often a shrinking from allusion even to the wine-making at Cana, and sometimes in these later days a strange effort by friends of total abstinence at arguments which will not bear examination, and which perhaps cause a revulsion of feeling, a result quite opposed to that which the arguments were intended to effect. It is best to deal openly with the subject. Our Saviour's conduct needs no attempt at apology from man, and no hiding over or shrinking from; indeed this very subject of Christ's first miracle comes before us as *a singular test to ourselves* of what is our disposition, or wish, or our heart's deep inclination respecting both him and ourselves. What do we wish to believe? How do we desire to come to conclusions? What are we *willing* to choose as our own action?

We will take a broad view of the subject of wines, making our remarks however as succinct as the case will admit. We notice:

1. *New wines,* not yet fermented, the *must* of ancient and modern times. Until fermentation (in which the alcoholic principle is formed) takes place, all wines are a perfectly harmless as well as pleasant drink. The vintage season in Palestine is in August[1] and September; the wine then made if left undisturbed by transportation will continue in its original condition for several months, the author is informed till spring, and this feast at Cana was at some time before the Passover, which occurred in March or April.

---

[1] The author purchased at Jaffa, in August, a bunch of grapes two feet long, and heard of others still longer, all of length inconvenient to be carried in the hand and making necessary such an act as we read of in Numbers xiii. 23. The grapes which are white, small and sweet are disposed scatteringly in the cluster, which is remarkable chiefly for its length.

2. *Wines in which fermentation is quite prevented.* This may be done by boiling and other processes, but most easily by the former, which was often done. The wine was somewhat thickened, but the purpose of prevention was entirely answered, and the drink remained harmless and sweet: it could be diluted with water when used, and was then an agreeable as well as harmless beverage. Columella, a Roman writer on agriculture, says, "Some people boil away a fourth and others a third of the *must.*"

3. *Wines drugged in order to prevent or check fermentation.* A vast variety of recipes for this are given in the ancient Roman and Greek writers. The Greek wine of the present day is unpalatable to foreigners on account of its turpentine-taste received from this cause. In Roman wines alcohol was so unusual that according to Pliny the Falernian was the only one that could be made to burn with a flame. *Solo vinorum flamma accenditur.*[1]

4. *Wines such as we see now in common use as a beverage in France and Italy.* Rev. Dr. Duff, in his journey through France, says of their wine: "In this its native, original state, it is a plain, simple and wholesome liquid, which at every repast becomes to the husbandman what milk is to the shepherd, not a luxury but a necessary; not an intoxicating but a nutritive beverage." The author of this book, in more than six years of cruising along the shores of the Mediterranean, never as far as he can recollect, saw a drunken man among the natives, although wines were used by them almost as freely as water is with us.

5. *Sweet wines.* A recent traveller in Palestine, W. C. Prime, who appears to have given the subject of wines there, as well as in other countries, a thorough consideration, says, that the good wines of that country are all *sweet*, he having seen sour wine only twice in Palestine, and "this was

---

[1] Lib. 14; cap. 13.

vile stuff." At Tiberias, by the Lake of Galilee, when desirous of replenishing his stores, he was taken to a wine cellar where were six different kinds of Galilean wine. "Some," he says, "was **new and raw**, unripe and unpleasant, the bitter **taste of grape seeds** predominant; other was better, more like a **Baune Burgundy** sweetened. One jar was not a little like **dead champagne, and that** which she [the owner] thought best of all was heavier than port, thick, **oily and sweet, strong and sharp** in the throat, but cloying to the taste. I have never seen anything like this wine elsewhere, except in Jerusalem, in the house of one Mordecai, where I tasted the same. The Jews esteem it above all other wines. **They take** but little of it at a time, using it **as we do a preserved fruit or jelly.**" He considered this cellar at Tiberias "a fair representation of the same repository" in ancient times; and we now remark on this subject of *sweet* wines that the alcoholic principle in them is but slightly formed by fermentation; for their sweetness "is due to undecomposed grape sugar, the ferment being exhausted before all the sugar is changed. This excess of sugar preserves the wine from further decomposition. Where the sugar is wholly decomposed the **wines** are called 'dry,' as claret, Burgundy, port, sherry, &c."[1] There being little fermentation, consequently in them but little alcohol can be formed.

6. Finally, we notice that these last wines just enumerated have in them the **following per centage** of Alcohol: *Port* from 21 to 26: *Sherry*, 13 to 18: *Claret*, 14 or 15: *Madeira*, 19 to 26:—this, even when they are genuine, which we know to be in our country very rarely the case; the wines in use here being manufactured **in a** great degree from vile and noxious drugs. Alcohol as a distinct principle, was not known until A. D. **1313**, and consequently

---

[1] Youman's Chemistry.

could never have been infused into the ancient beverages, as it is constantly done with those of modern times, even **into** the best of the genuine ones now in the market.

The whole subject is now before the reader, and he is left to draw conclusions for himself, as he doubtless will do: but any person **ought** to question **very** closely **his own** feelings before he can allow himself amid such a variety of innocent beverages as is above exhibited, to conclude that Christ performed an act that can in any wise encourage our modern usages in intoxicating drinks. The whole course of his pure and holy life was utterly **set against any such encouragement**; and we do violence to all his teachings and all his example, when we try to deduce any aid to ourselves in countenancing the strongly alcoholic wines of our day. Saint Paul's rule is clearly defined and commends itself to every man's convictions of right. "Take heed lest by any means this liberty of yours become a stumbling-block to them that are weak."[1] "It is good neither to eat flesh, nor to drink wine, nor anything whereby thy brother stumbleth, or is offended, or is made weak."[2] Paul had drawn this principle **of action** from **the** true spirit **of all Christ's** teaching and example; and men are assuredly contravening both when they quote this act at Cana in support of a contrary course.

In reference to any loss of enjoyment by following **the** strict temperance rules, the author will take the liberty here to mention a reply which he recently made to a friend who with a bottle of champagne before him was taunting him jocosely on the loss of such enjoyment. "No, I am not a loser but a gainer by abstinence in such a cause, for I am *all the while* drinking champagne in my heart." The answer did not make a convert then, and probably it will not now; but still **it tells the truth.**

---

[1] 1 Cor. viii. 9.   [2] Romans xiv. 21.

10

CHAPTER XII.

THE TEMPLE.

AFTER these events at Cana, Jesus with his mother and disciples proceeded to Capernaum, by the lake of Galilee; but they remained there only a few days, for the Passover was approaching, and it was according to the requirements of their law that he should go up to Jerusalem for the observance of the festival.

Certain occurrences on this occasion require for the better understanding of them, that we should have a knowledge of the temple and its precincts; and we enter upon a description of it the more readily, because it was in itself a very grand object, as well as being a most important part of the Jewish system. The Messiah will come before us frequently in connection with this edifice and its surroundings, and we must endeavor to have it all clearly before our minds.

This spot was the central object of the Jews' affections both at home and wherever they were scattered over the world. The very stones were precious in their eyes. In distant lands the theme to their wondering children was the former glory that rested abidingly on Mount Moriah; the presence of God as seen and felt there, the Urim and Thummim, the Ark, the bright cloud upon the mercy-seat, the spirit of prophecy;—all connected with the first temple which Solomon had built and had dedicated with sacrifices of sheep and oxen "that could not be told nor numbered for multitude," and with prayers; while in "the holy place" within, "the priest could not stand to minister," "for the glory of the Lord had filled the house of the Lord." That temple had long since been destroyed by the enemy's hand; but its splendor and its honor from heaven were yet a living remembrance in the hearts of all the Jews.

Then had come the second temple built by Nehemiah, far inferior to the other,—the foundations laid while the old men among them who had seen the glory of the first, " wept with a loud voice," as they remembered it; and the younger were shouting with joy at the prospect of restoring the former worship; "so that the people could not discern the noise of the shout of joy from the noise of the weeping of the people: for the people shouted with a loud shout, and the noise was heard afar off."[1]

Such were some of the grand and the tender associations connected with this sacred spot: but it had others also deeply interesting; for Moriah was supposed to be the place where Abraham erected the altar for offering his son; and it was certainly there that David interceded for his people, and built an altar at the time when the destroying angel was scattering pestilence over Israel,[2] because the monarch had numbered his subjects, trusting in them rather than in God.

This second temple being unsuited to the grandeur of the purposes for which it had been erected, and having also become ruinous from age, Herod the Great determined to pull it down and to erect a larger one; and finally he succeeded in placing before the Jewish people that great " Mountain of the House," as they termed it, vaster in size and more magnificent in its architectural claims, than was the case even with Solomon's temple itself.

Mount Moriah is a short rocky ridge 318 yards wide, running north and south; having on the east the deep valley of Jehoshaphat, separating it from the Mount of Olives, and on the west a shallower valley called the Tyropeon, (also valley of the Cheesemongers), 117 yards across,[3] immediately beyond which rose the heights of Zion lined with

---

[1] Ezra iii. 12, 13.   [2] 2 Sam. xxiv. 25.   [3] Robinson.

its battlemented walls. Solomon had by means of a wall built on the eastern side, and perhaps also across the southern part of this ridge, and by filling it up, formed a platform for his temple; but Herod faced each side of Moriah with a wall forming a rectangular substructure suited to the temple with which its heights were to be crowned. The foundation of this wall can still be traced nearly in its whole extent; while at the south-eastern angle it has an elevation of twenty-five feet in its original condition. This and similar remains afford us an opportunity of studying some of the peculiar characteristics of Jewish architecture in those ancient times, among which may be mentioned what travellers to that region have generally called *bevelled* stones, a wrong term which conveys an incorrect idea of this style of embellishment. The word *rebated* is the proper one, and the wood-cuts here appended will show what it means. The appearance is that of a raised panel on the face of the stone, the edges of the panels being about two inches from the joints which are carefully and nicely made. The blocks are of good white limestone, and some of them have measured from twenty-four to thirty feet in length.

Front view of a rebated wall, characteristic of the ancient Jewish Architecture.

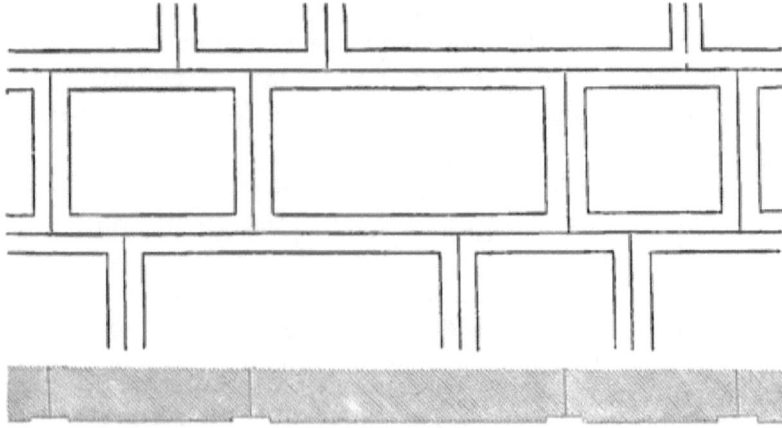

Profile Section of the same.

These walls having been carried to an elevation which though doubtless less than that given by Josephus—400 or 500 feet—was still considerable, the inclosed space was filled up with arched ways and earth; and thus at a proper height a platform was made for their sacred purposes. Let the reader now imagine these outside walls to be carried still higher so as to enclose this platform as in a court, and to be battlemented. This court according to Josephus was 625 feet square,[1] and was paved with marble of various colors; and against the wall all around was a cloister or covered space the roof of which was of carved and ornamented wood-work, the columns supporting it of marble, each column a single stone. In southern countries where people live much in the open air, covered places for general resort are a great convenience, and the pillared spaces around the Grecian temples were for such a purpose as well as for ornament. The Greeks however, finding these insufficient, soon began to erect what were called Stoæ—inclosed courts with paved corridors, and had many of them. The Stoic sect of philosophers received that

---

[1] He says a furlong square, and doubtless meant the Roman furlong, equal to 625 feet of our measure; but this must be too little even according to his own showing; for it would not allow room for the measurements which he gives of the Sanctuary (or more holy place), within. The Talmuds give 750 feet for each side; and these are the dimensions adopted in the accompanying plan in this book. The ground is now occupied by the Turks as their sacred enclosure, the *Haram es-Sheriff*, with the Mosque of Omar, a forbidden place to any but Mohammedans; but the foundations of the old wall of substructure have been carefully measured. They are according to Dr. Barclay on the East 1523½ feet; North 1038; West 1600; South 916; agreeing nearly with those of Robinson and of Catherwood. This doubtless embraces the Castle of Antonia, which adjoined the temple on the North, with an extent of ground according to Josephus, equal to that of the temple courts. (De bel. v. 5, § 2). If we take the southern half of these measurements, and allow for the necessary inward slant of so high a wall and an offset above, we come very nearly to the dimensions in the Talmuds, thus settling a much-discussed and difficult subject.

10 *

name because **Zeno** their teacher delivered his lectures in one of these resorts, the **Stoa Poecile.** The Romans had also numerous stoæ, sometimes private ones connected with their city palaces or their villas.

These cloisters at the temple were thus in accordance with the habits of those countries and times ; but here they were also not only very beautiful in themselves but were a magnificent frame-work for the more holy places inclosed. On the north and east and west, they were formed by triple rows of columns (including half-columns against the wall) the pillars five feet in diameter and twenty-seven in height, with Corinthian capitals and a double spiral at the basis.[1] The rows of columns were thirty feet apart, the whole height of the cloister fifty feet, and above it, at the outer edge, were the battlements of the wall. The southern cloister was on a still larger scale ; for here were four rows of columns, the outer and inner rows being as on the other sides, but the two middle ranges had twice the height of the others, with a width between them of forty-five instead of thirty feet. The western end of this central colonnade opened upon a stone bridge 350 feet long leading across the Tyropeon valley and connecting the temple with **Mount Zion.** Portions of the first or eastern arch of this bridge remain in their original condition and show the width of the bridge to have been fifty-one feet. It was doubtless the main thoroughfare for conducting the beasts to the temple for sacrificial purposes.

In addition to this outlet by the Tyropeon bridge, there were seven of a different kind; one into Antonia, and the others either by long flights of outside steps or by subterranean passages, of the latter of which some remains may yet be seen. In the present southern wall crossing Moriah is a double gateway, within which is a vestibule represented in

---

[1] Josephus.

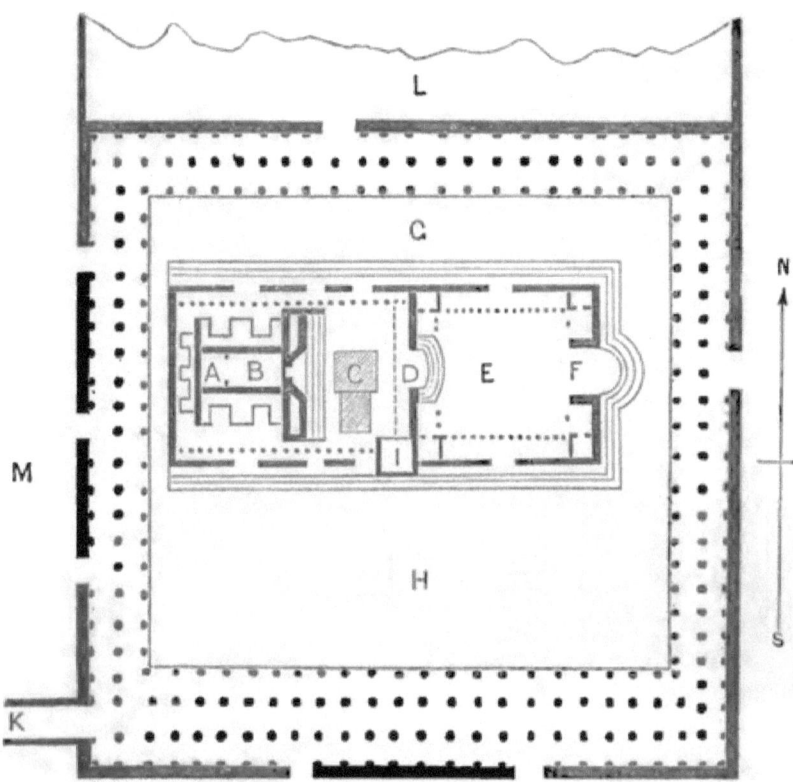

Plan of Herod's Temple, formed after Josephus, the Talmuds and Lightfoot.
On a Scale of 250 feet to an inch.

A. Holy of Holies.

B. Holy Place.

C. The Great Altar, with inclined plane to its summit.

D. The Court of Israel, entered from E by the Gate Nicanor.

E. Court of the Women; rooms in its corners for various purposes. Like that of Israel, it had cloisters at its sides.

F. "The Beautiful Gate of the Temple." (See Acts iii. 2.)

G and H. Court of the Gentiles. Of the cloisters surrounding this, the one on the east is Solomon's Porch; that on the south is the Royal Porch.

I. Sanhedrim Room.

K. Bridge leading over the Tyropeon.

L. Part of the Castle of Antonia.

M. Probable place of the Xystus.

The waved lines at the sides and rear of the Temple represent chambers; three stories of these at the sides and two at the rear.

The gates of the cloisters are marked according to authority; but except at the castle of Antonia and the bridge and perhaps one other on the west, they probably mean the commencement of subterranean descents.

There were numerous other chambers of less size about the cloisters and courts, but they could not be marked on such a plan as this.

115

Remains of the bridge connecting the temple court with Mount Zion.

the second cut on this page. It is the commencement of a double vaulted archway of pure Jewish architecture, which by a passage 258 feet in length conducts to an opening into the Haram area above, as doubtless it formerly did to the temple courts.

Vestibule to underground passage leading upward to the ancient temple courts.

We return to contemplate once more the various objects at the summit of this "Mountain of the House," where the pillared cloisters, rich as they were in architectural effect, engaged the attention only for a moment or two. The great court which they inclosed was called the court of the Gentiles, and was open to all the world; but the more sacred spot "The Sanctuary" could be visited by Jews only. This latter was a little to the North[1] of the centre of the court, and was on more elevated ground; it was 170 cubits from North to South, and 335 from East to West: its front toward the East. It was ascended to, on all sides by fourteen steps, on the uppermost of which was a balustrade of open stone-work three cubits high and elegantly wrought: In this balustrade, at short intervals, were pillars with inscriptions in Greek and Roman letters, declaring that "no foreigner should go within that sanctuary." Within the balustrade was a level space ten cubits wide, called "the Chel," and vacant, except that, toward its western end, the council room of the Sanhedrim, built partly on the more sacred ground of the temple court, was there extended so as to embrace also the Chel. Not only were foreigners excluded from these boundaries, but the sight of all within them was prevented by a wall forty cubits high, running all around the sanctuary along the inner border of the Chel. The Gentile in the court without might hear the voices of the chanters, and see the smoke of sacrifices ascending from the great altar, but even his vision might not profane the holy places, except so far as it could be indulged through the large gateways, of which there were nine in this wall, four on each side, and one at the east. These gateways were large, and were covered over with silver and gold: but the one at the east, called "The Beautiful Gate,"[2] was the most magnificent of all. It was of Corinthian brass,

---

[1] On authority of the Talmuds.   [2] See Acts iii. 2.

and fifty cubits in height: its doors were forty cubits high, and were "adorned after a most costly manner, as having much richer and thicker plates of silver and gold upon them than the others. These nine gates had that silver and gold poured upon them by Alexander, father of Tiberius."[1] Additional steps led up from the Chel to this magnificent gateway; and passing through it, the visitor would find himself then in what was called "The women's court," an area 135 cubits square, and surrounded by cloisters, formed by columns as in the larger court without. Private passage-ways at the entrance gave the women access to their separate place, probably above the cloisters; for, although this was called the "Court of the women," it was frequented by the other sex as much as by them. It was the place for that most extraordinary scene of dancing, which we shall notice, by-and-by, in describing the Feast of Tabernacles.

The "Court of the Women" had four gates, one on each side: the Beautiful gate on the east, and opposite to it on the west a large and very rich one, called Nicanor. This last was reached by an ascent of fifteen steps from the women's court, and gave admittance to the higher platform and court, called "The Court of Israel," sometimes termed simply "The Court." This was 135 cubits from north to south and 187 from east to west, with columns and cloisters as in the other courts. But the reader must not suppose this area to be all plain, as in the women's court, for here was the great altar and beyond it the temple itself. Standing at its eastern gate of entrance, Nicanor, (it had three others on each side), the visitor would see before him, at eleven cubits distance, a low wall running across the court and separating him from the "Court of the Priests;" beyond that, at eleven cubits, the great altar, thirty-two cubits square and ten in height,

---

[1] Jos. De Bel. v. 5, § 3.

with an inclined plane of ascent on its southern side. Then, beyond the altar, was the Temple.

This last stood on a platform the highest of them all. Its porch or entrance, 100 cubits wide and of the same height, was reached in front and at its two ends by twelve steps commencing not far from the altar and formed in pairs, three cubits between each pair. Josephus says : " The outward face of the temple in its front wanted nothing that was likely to surprise either men's minds or their eyes, for it was covered all over with plates of gold of great weight, and at the first rising of the sun reflected back a very fiery splendor, and made those who forced themselves to look upon it to turn their eyes away just as they would have done at the sun's own rays. But the temple appeared to strangers, when they were at a distance, like a mountain covered with snow, for as to those parts of it that were not gilt they were exceeding white. On its top it had spikes with sharp points to prevent any pollution of it by birds sitting upon it. Of its stones some of them were forty-five cubits [sixty-seven feet] in length, five in height and six in breadth."[1]   It was of such as these that the disciples said to Christ, " Master see what manner of stones and buildings are here ;" as if such solidity might set at defiance all common human events. Indeed, every part of the Mountain of the House combined great massiveness with richness of decoration and often with elegance. The front of the temple was pierced by an immense open entrance seventy cubits high and twenty-five cubits broad, of which Josephus says, " This gate had no doors, for it represented the universal visibility of heaven, and that cannot be excluded from any place." It seems to have been an arched way sixteen feet in depth (the thickness of the front) with sides highly enriched with architectural devices, and in this open-

----

[1] Bel. v. 5, § 6.

ing was trained the celebrated vine of beaten gold, the clusters to which were five or six feet in length.[1] Of this vine the Talmud says: "For men would be offering some gold to make a leaf, some a grape, some a bunch, and these were hung upon it, and so it was increasing continually."[2] **Tacitus** calls the building *immensæ opulentiæ templum*.[3]

This was only the porch of the temple which narrower than the porch extended **back at** right angles to it, so that the whole structure was in a **form like this** ⊥. **Back** of this lofty arched way was another fifty-five cubits high and sixteen wide, and then were folding **doors** twenty cubits **high** and **each** five cubits wide, giving admittance towards **the** body of the temple; next to **these a** veil, in the rear of **this,** folding doors similar to the last. The outer pair were commonly called by the Jews "the great door of the temple," because it had "a great front;" and of this we have the record, "the morning sacrifice was never killed till this door was opened," and that "he that was to slay the sacrifice killed him not till he heard the noise of the great gate opening."

None but the priests could **pass these doors, and entering** they would **find** themselves **now** in "the Holy Place," a room forty cubits long, **twenty wide, and sixty** in height; "the floor planked with fir-boards and **then gilt with gold;"** the walls and ceiling of cedar both gilt likewise; the walls carved into branches and **open flowers** to the height of fifty cubits, above **which were** windows admitting light. In this room were the seven-branched golden candlestick four-and-a-half feet high; the table of show-bread, two cubits long by

---

[1] Josephus De Bel. v. 5, § 4. Tacitus says, "But because their [Jewish] priests when they play on the pipe and timbrels wear ivy around their head and a golden vine has been found in their temple, some have thought that they worshipped our father Bacchus, the conqueror of the east, whereas the ceremonies of the Jews do not at all agree with those of Bacchus."

[2] Lightfoot.   [3] De Jud. lib. v. cap. 8.

one in breadth, and the altar of incense a cubit square and two cubits in height.

Beyond these at the end of this room hung a veil, and a cubit further on, a second veil, this second the one spoken of by Josephus and others as "the veil of the temple." This latter was the one rent at the time of our Saviour's death. No one might lift these veils and pass beyond except the High Priest alone.

The room to which this gave admittance, "The Holy of Holies," was twenty cubits square and as many in height, and was gilt throughout, the floor as well as the walls and ceiling; the walls also enriched with precious stones. "In this there was nothing at all. It was inaccessible and inviolable, and not to be seen by any, and was called the Holy of Holies."

Attached to each side of this main building were three stories of small chambers for temple purposes;[1] a similar set two stories in height being also at the western end. The central or main building rose considerably above all these. The walls in these edifices were of great thickness (five or six cubits) and solidity, as was requisite in a country subject to earthquakes. The porch extended fifteen cubits on each side beyond the main building and its attached chambers; the steps leading up to it have been described as in pairs, three cubits between each pair, and on these successive platforms, or "degrees of steps," the priests stood when they sounded the trumpets, and also when accompanied by other instrumental music they chanted the psalms.

Women were admitted beyond their own court, only when they brought sacrifices; the Jewish men might come into the court of Israel; they and the women also were allowed to pass the low boundary inclosing the court of priests when they came to touch the sacrifices they were about to offer on the great altar within that court.

---

[1] They are supposed to have given rise to the words: "In my Father's house are many mansions," &c.   John xiv. 2.

What a contrast to those temple scenes in the ancient times;—the old worship, the innumerable sacrifices, the rejoicing crowds at the festivals, the priest, the rabbi, the lordly Pharisee;—to all this, what a contrast now in the scenes among the Jews at Jerusalem, to which city they yet come, often from far distant lands, to pray and mourn and die! At retired spots, by the remains of this ancient wall of the "Mountain of the House," they may be very frequently seen with their lips at the joints between the stones, praying so that their breath in supplication may pass towards

Jews' praying-place at the foot of the ancient Temple Walls.

the sacred ground. No one but a Mohammedan is allowed to enter on the paved court above, once the temple precincts; but the hearts of the Israelites still warm with affection towards their holy place, and when they die their bodies are

carried across the Kedron and buried on the lowest slopes
of the Mount of Olives, so that the shadows of Moriah may
be cast across their graves as the sun declines. They believe also that in this valley of Jehoshaphat will be the final
scene of the judgment-day, and that those who rise there
will have peculiar advantages.

Extensive vaults of masonry have been for some years known
to exist under the southern end of the site of the Temple courts
and Temple, but quite recent explorations have brought to
our knowledge many still more interesting facts respecting
excavations below those grounds; among them a reservoir,
736 feet in circumference and forty-two in depth, estimated to
have a capacity of two millions of gallons, supplied in ancient times by the aqueducts from Solomon's pools seven
miles distant towards the south. The discoveries "tend to

Underground reservoirs recently discovered beneath the site of the Temple at Jerusalem.

show that by a series of subterranean tunnels and valves its
abundant waters could be used at will for flushing the cess-
pools and sewers connected with the temple, and carrying
off all the blood and filth, as the Talmud informs us down
to the bottom of the Kedron."

In the great Mosque of Omar, in the Haram, is a rock of

ruddy limestone projecting above its floor, and regarded with great veneration by the Turks. It is irregular in form, nearly sixty feet in its greatest diameter, and rises five feet above the marble floor.

It is supposed by some to be the spot of Abraham's altar, and to have been under the great altar of the ancient temple. At its south-east corner is a door leading down to an excavated chamber about fifteen feet square and eight in height. The rock overhead is pierced with a hole three feet in diameter, and directly beneath this in the floor of the chamber is another hole with a pit beneath, called by the Turks the Well of Spirits, of unknown depth.

A channel runs northward to this sacred rock from the great cistern above described, enters the Well of Spirits, then passes on northward 120 feet to a large double cistern hewn in the rock. From thence a tunnel descends eastward, is joined by an aqueduct from the great tank at the northern side of the Haram area, and appears to descend toward the Kedron. The Mishna says, "Beneath the altar was a cave whereby blood and filth were conveyed down into the Kedron valley, and the gardeners there paid as much as purchased a trespass-offering for the right to use it for fertilizing their gardens."

These explorations have been made chiefly by M. Pierotti, formerly engineer in the Sardinian service, but more recently employed by the Pacha of Jerusalem. They are imperfect, and doubtless much yet remains to be discovered.

Vast subterranean chambers recently discovered under the part of Jerusalem called Acra, will be noticed in another part of this work.[1]

---

[1] The cubit referred to in this chapter is most probably *Roman* (equal to 18 inches of our measure) as Josephus, from whom the measurements are taken, was writing for the Romans. The Jewish cubit was equal to 21.8 inches.

11 *

CHAPTER XIII.

THE TEMPLE CLEANSED—NICODEMUS.

FROM Capernaum the Messiah had proceeded to Jerusalem to be present at the Passover, and having arrived there he went up into the temple. It was to the Jews the greatest of all their celebrations in the reminiscences it awakened, and was in parts of it a very solemn and in other parts of it a very joyful festival. The Jews came to it from even the most distant regions, and the numbers congregated at Jerusalem were calculated on one occasion for a statistical report to be sent to the Roman emperor, and were estimated at two millions seven hundred thousand.[1]

The reader who has perused the foregoing chapter and has in his mind the grandeur of this Mountain of the House, the courts, the altar and temple, would now imagine a scene suited to the place and the solemnities. But there was one far different,—a scene of desecration of the sacred spot, of filth, of barter and sale, and of the unholy passions which the love of money begets. In order to understand it fully we must follow Lightfoot in some of his details.

"There were thirteen treasure-chests at the temple which by the Jews were called *Shoperoth*, which signifies properly trumpets, because trumpet-like they were wide at the bottom and narrow at the top, that money put in might not easily be got out. Two were for the half-shekel that every Israelite had to pay for the redemption of his soul or life, for which the law is given, Exodus xxi. 30: one chest for the payment of the last year, if he had missed to pay it at

---

[1] See Josephus, De Bel. vi. 9, § 3.

the due time; and the other for the present. On the first day of Adar [the month preceding Passover month] which answers to our February, there was a general notice given throughout the country that they should provide to pay the half-shekel; and on the 15th of that month the collectors sat in every city to gather it; and they had two chests before them, as were at the temple; and they demanded the payment calmly and used no roughness or compulsion.—On the 25th day of the month the collectors began to sit in the temple, and then they forced men to pay; and if any one had not wherewith to pay they took his pawn, and sometimes would take his raiment perforce. They had a table before them to count and change the money upon.

"A man that brought a shekel to change and must have half a shekel again, the collector was to have some profit upon the change, and that addition was called *Colbon.* * * The Talmud and other authors discourse largely about this colbon, and who was to pay it, and who to be quit from it, and how much to be paid and to like purposes; but the general conclusion is still for some profit, which exaction was that which caused our Saviour to overthrow the tables of the Colbonists (John ii. 15; Matt. xxi. 12); for these receivers began to sit in the temple for that purpose but eighteen or twenty days before the Passover, and continued for that time when the concourse of people was greatest, and after it was over and done.

"And so the market that was in the temple, the sheep and oxen, it is like, were not constantly there, but for such times of concourse, when the multitude of people and sacrifices were so exceedingly great; though indeed there was merchandizing of other things there all the year in the taberne or shops that we have spoken of [in the Court of the Gentiles just inside the eastern gate]. The place where the marketing of the sheep and oxen was, was the great space of the Mountain of the House [Court of Gentiles] that lay on the south side of the courts; for on the west and north the rock was too straight for such matter; and on the east was the most common entrance of the people, and these cattle would have stopped up the way.

"These collectors of the pole-tax (half-shekel) probably sat about the east gate Shushan, as being the chiefest entrance."[1]

There were besides those enumerated, money-chests for eleven other distinct kinds of collections, all in the temple courts; and these last remained throughout the year.

What a scene there was therefore,—not for a day, but continuously through their feasts,—in that large court belonging to the temple! In addition to the lambs for the Passover supper, there were many thousands of sheep and oxen slain at this festival. They were brought up here for sale; and while from the great altar within the sacred enclosure rose up the smoke of the sacrifices; from this adjoining outer court came strange discordant noises jarring terribly on the feelings of all who were there for devotional purposes. With the sounds of the sacred instrumental music or the chantings in front of the temple,—the great Hallels of the occasion,—were mingled the tramp and lowing of cattle, the sharp angry words of buying and selling among this demonstrative people, the loud and stern demands of the Colbonists or collectors requiring the half-shekel often from the poverty-stricken or reluctant, from whom their garments were taken by force when the money was not paid. The worst feelings of the human heart were cultivated there, and Devotion, even at this their most sacred time, was driven away or fled disgusted from the place. The whole scene was an outrage upon the time and occasion, and upon decency itself; and must often have been felt to be so by every right-thinking man. Therefore now when Christ

---

[1] Lightfoot—Temple service.

reached that temple-court, and glancing around yielded to the sentiment which these outrages occasioned, there were many other persons doubtless ready and most willing to give their aid.

He cleared the temple-court of its abominations.

His disciples as they saw his face lighted up by his emotions beheld a verification of the Psalmist's words, "The zeal of thine house hath eaten me up."[1] Before the glance of his eye the conscience-struck traffickers fled: the cords from the loosed animals supplied him with a scourge, which indeed was scarcely needed; for his words, "Make not my Father's house a house of merchandize," stirred up that which had been latent in every heart, and brought a tide of conviction which carried everything before it, the buyers and sellers retreating as best they could. The Colbonists fared no better amid their exactions; for the poor found a friend, the money-chests were overturned and the tables cleared away.

Strange scene indeed it was where people everywhere fled or were palsied in their convictions of the righteous dealing by a seemingly weak individual; but when it was all over, the temple was in a new condition, cleansed now and restored to its legitimate use.

But who was this,—people asked—who was this, the principal in this act? They turned to gaze at him; and the rulers also came immediately with the pertinent inquiry, "What sign showest thou unto us, seeing that thou doest these things?"

It was indeed a bold invasion of their rights which they had for so long a time abused, in giving what might be called their sanction to these abominations: and they came to him indignant, and also filled with astonishment at what he had effected with such slight means—a strange power

---

[1] See John ii. 17.

that seemed to be in him and of which they might well be
jealous, conscious as they were of their own iniquity.
Troubled, wondering, angry, resentful, their hearts were
now in singular contrast to the strange, new quiet in those
courts, and to the peace that had succeeded the turmoil. A
new sacredness hung over the spot, where the smoke of sacrifice seemed to go up purer than before, and where the
chanting of the Hallels had more the breath of heaven;
but heaven was not in the hearts of these men, whose
character the Baptist had already pointed out and held up
before their eyes.

To their inquiries now, Christ gave an answer in the
figurative language of the country; and for the present,
their curiosity as to his authority for such acts was not
gratified.

CHAPTER XIV.

NICODEMUS—JOHN'S IMPRISONMENT.

THE Messiah appears, during this visit to Jerusalem, to
have performed some miracles of which we have no
record; but which occasioned a visit to him by a Ruler, upon
whom recent circumstances had taken a strong hold.

This Ruler—Nicodemus by name—came by night.

Why by night? It may be that he thought his visit
would have fewer interruptions at that hour; but the course
of the conversation seems to point to a less commendable
reason, in which moral timidity may have been involved.
The admiration which he felt now, he afterwards continued
to cherish, but still in secret; until finally, amid the heart-

rending scenes of the crucifixion, all other feelings gave way before his reverence and love. Nicodemus rose up then, in manly, Christian strength.

Now he sought the Messiah in the darkness, and was introduced: and they sat there in the dim light. How striking the difference between the two! Nicodemus reverent, yet wanting boldness openly to acknowledge his reverence; irresolute, yet drawn to Christ by a strong power of affection; inquisitive, yet probably fearful of being convinced. On the other hand, Christ so gentle to his visitor, yet so determined, not wishing to repel, yet so earnest in inculcating **that truth** on Nicodemus which the Ruler needed most.

Nicodemus began the conversation.

"Rabbi, we know that thou art a teacher come from God: for no man can do these miracles that thou doest, except God be with him."

The answer seems to have plunged, at once, into Nicodemus's case, when Christ replied with emphasis:

"Verily, verily, I say unto thee, Except **a man be born** again, he cannot see the kingdom of God." **You must have** the new birth, which will make of you another being; **will** change your very soul, and make you decided for the truth, whithersoever your convictions may lead you, whether before the Sanhedrim or **before kings, for my sake.**

The word "new birth" **was not a strange one** to Jewish ears. "**If any man** become a proselyte, he is a child new-born;" "The Gentile that is made a proselyte, and a servant that is made free, behold, he is like a man new-born,"[1] **are** words from their ancient Rabbis; **but** it was a new doctrine to be urged upon one already a Jew; and Nicodemus received it **with expressions of surprise.**

An entire change of soul wrought by the Holy Spirit was inculcated **upon Nicodemus: and then** Christ, in showing

[1] See Lightfoot *in loco.*

that the heroism which is to be a consequent of it and which was needed by the visitor, was not required of others while he was shrinking from it himself, spoke of his own future,—"And as Moses lifted up the serpent in the wilderness, even so must the Son of man be lifted up: that whosoever believeth in him should not perish, but have eternal life." But the teachings on this most interesting occasion went much further; and tell us that "God so loved the world, that he gave his only begotten Son, that whosoever believeth in him should not perish, but have everlasting life;" a sentiment which, if Jesus had never uttered any thing else, would be sufficient to be the life of the world. Many a perishing sinner has found it so to be. It contains in itself what, to use common language, may be termed "a whole body of divinity."

The Messiah, after this, remained a short time in Judea, during which his disciples were administering the new ordinance of baptism to the multitudes offering themselves. Reports were quickly carried to the Pharisees that the number even exceeded those who were resorting to John;[1] and the disciples of the latter hearing a similar rumor, hurried to their Master with a complaint to similar effect. John stopped complaints quickly by declaring that the Messiah "must increase, but he must decrease. He that cometh from above is above all: he that is of the earth is earthly, and speaketh of the earth: he that cometh from heaven is above all. * * He that believeth on the Son hath everlasting life: and he that believeth not the Son shall not see life; but the wrath of God abideth on him."[2]

But the career of the Baptist was approaching towards its close. After remaining for a while at Bethabara, he had removed to "Enon near to Salim," a spot apparently about six miles north-east from Jerusalem, where, in a valley

---

[1] John iv. 1, 2.   [2] John iii. 26–36.

sometimes narrowing till it becomes a rock-lined ravine, half-a-dozen springs of the purest water burst from rocky crevices at various intervals, and form a stream "rivalling the atmosphere itself in transparency, of depths varying from a few inches to a fathom and more, shaded on one or both sides by umbrageous fig-trees, and sometimes contained in naturally-excavated basins of red mottled marble—an occasional variegation of the common limestone of the country;" the quantity of water "sufficient to drive several mills."[1] John had been preaching and administering the new ordinance for about a year and a half, when he was seized by the soldiers of Herod Antipas, and was hurried off to the castle of Macherus, situated towards the southern end of Perea, and not far from the north-eastern borders of the Dead Sea. His voice, which had rung out so boldly against all wicked men, while it was also gentle to the penitent, had now given unpardonable offence in the royal household itself, and the implacable, deadly hate of a woman had been aroused.

Herod in one of his journeys had become enamored of Herodias, wife of his brother Philip, and although she was his niece he persuaded her to leave her husband and form a new connection with himself. John fearlessly denounced the libertine act, and so brought upon himself the wrath of the king and the vengeance of the still more vindictive paramour. Herod doubtless gave out the report such as we have seen in a former chapter as stated by Josephus, but the result to John a year and a half after this fully verifies the Scripture account.

We accompany the bold, brave man to his place of con-

---

[1] These extracts are from Dr. Barclay's "City of the Great King;" and biblical geographers must feel greatly indebted to our countryman for establishing so undoubtedly the site of "Enon near to Salim" which had previously been a matter of uncertainty, but was generally supposed to be in Galilee, near Scythopolis (Bethshean), although it was difficult to harmonize the place with Scriptural accounts.

finement; we see him whose life had always been so free and untrammeled, shut up, and wearing away his energies in the prison-house; we watch him day after day wondering whether relief would not come, whether the tyrant would not relent, whether the Divine power would not interpose, and we find him still a prisoner there, till his heart was weary and sick amid his blighted hopes.

CHAPTER XV.

IN SAMARIA AND GALILEE.

CHRIST was immeasurably in advance of the Jewish nation in all his doctrines, and this advanced position added greatly to the difficulty in successful teaching; for, not only were the minds of his hearers slow in comprehending him, but moreover the truth when comprehended was frequently quite out of harmony with all that they had ever before conceived. The idea of man's universal brotherhood, so familiar to our minds through Christianity, was an entire novelty to the Jews, and was utterly repulsive as well as new. Even after the descent of the Holy Ghost at Pentecost a miracle was necessary in order to bring Peter to enter for the sake of religious instruction into the house of a devout Gentile, and he was reproved by his brethren for doing so: "Thou wentest in to men uncircumcised, and didst eat with them."

We must bear in memory all this cramped and fettered condition of the national mind as we follow the Messiah and his disciples in their journeyings, and in his glorious teachings to them or to the assembled multitudes.

He did not remain long in **Judea, but** returned to Galilee, passing through Samaria which **was the** most direct way.

About twenty-five miles from **Jerusalem the** road descends into **a plain extending** northwardly about twelve miles, and about half **way** along this plain brings the traveller to where a narrow valley between two mountains opens suddenly at his left. **This spot** is exceeded in interest only **by Jerusalem** itself; for, of those two **mountains, that** on the south is Gerizim, the northern is Ebal; **and the traveller is here** also by a well unmistakably dug **by the patriarch** Jacob, while a small edifice a **short way off** shows undoubtedly **the** burial-place of the **remains of Joseph brought** from Egypt [1] in that long journey **of forty years.** It is **gratifying** to be able so fully **to identify all** these places after **such** a lapse of **time.** The **mountains** are about 800 feet in height, rugged, and in places precipitous, and with only a few olive trees **to relieve their** desolate appearance. **The** valley between **them is 400 yards wide, and ascends** gently **westward** till at a distance **of a mile and a half we come to** the city of **Nablûs, the Shechem of ancient times lying on its** southern side. From **this onward toward the west it widens,** is abundantly **supplied with springs, and is a region of extreme fertility; six miles' travel in that direction brings us** to **the city of Samaria. Gerizim has on its summit exten-** sive **remains** of **its ancient** temple; **near its foot, on the** great plain, is Jacob's well; Joseph's tomb is a little **to the** north of the well, just where the middle of the narrow **val-** ley opens to the plain.

It is easy standing there to imagine the scene, when, in Joshua's time, all Israel were gathered there, according **to** the former command of Moses, one-half on each mountain; those **on** Gerizim **to utter the blessings, and** those on Ebal the curses previously **detailed, to each of which as uttered**

---

[1] Ex. xiii. 19; Josh. xxiv. 32.

| Gerizim. | Jacob's well. | Joseph's tomb. | Ebal. |

Viewed from the East.

the whole congregation were to respond *Amen*—a wonderful and most solemn scene. It is easy also to imagine the Samaritans in generations afterward, when half-heathenish from the admixture of foreign nations they had been refused fellowship by the Jews, and had erected a rival temple in Gerizim, ascending to it with a grim hatred and jealousy of their neighbors, who boasted of their superior claims to Divine favor.[1] So too we may conceive the undisguised contempt for them by the Jews, felt and sometimes manifested as the latter had to traverse their country in passing directly between Judea and Galilee. Notwithstanding that " what a Samaritan ate as food became from that fact as swine's flesh in the eyes of a Jew ;" that " no Samaritan might be made a proselyte," and " no one of them would

---

[1] One beneficial result of this jealousy has been to bring down to us, through a period of 2800 years, two distinct copies of the Pentateuch, without fear of there ever having been collusion between the copyists. Both copies are alike. The Samaritans still exist at Nablûs as a distinct people ; few however are left, and the nation seems to be near extinction.

by any possibility in Jewish estimation attain to everlasting life;" still there were probably some Jews residing there for trade, as they did also among the Gentile nations.

With such feelings as the ancient history of this most interesting region was adapted to produce, Christ and his disciples had travelled along this plain leading by the two mountains, and reached the celebrated well about the middle of the day. Wearied he sat down there to rest, while his followers went into the city to purchase food; and as he sat, there came to the spot to procure water a woman from whom he asked a drink. There is still, not far from the well, a village called Aschar which may be the same place as Sychar, from which she came, but more probably she was from Shechem, the present Nablûs, and came this distance for water on account of a superstitious belief in the efficacy of Jacob's well; for her life was one that might readily lead her to any extraneous help in an endeavor to quiet her conscience. In reply to the request for drink she questioned the Messiah, "How is it that thou, being a Jew, askest drink of me, which am a woman of Samaria?" and a conversation ensued in which he said to her, "But whosoever drinketh of the water that I shall give him shall never thirst; but the water that I shall give him shall be in him a well of water springing up into everlasting life." Other words there were from him, some of which were astonishing indeed, coming from one of his nationality; for he said, "Woman, believe me, the hour cometh, when ye shall neither in this mountain, nor yet at Jerusalem, worship the Father;" and soon afterward he declared to her his Messiahship—authority sufficient for breaking down all the old distinctions of time and place, and making a fraternity of all the nations of the earth. "The hour cometh," he said, "when the true worshippers shall worship the Father in spirit and in truth: for the Father seeketh such to worship him."

The disciples now arriving from their mission were sur-

12 *

prised to find him in social conversation with a woman of Samaria, but they kept their wonder in silence, not daring to question him.   But if astonished at this, how much greater was their astonishment when not long afterward they saw him proceed to Shechem to be there *a guest of the Samaritans.* The woman had gone up to the city and had spread such reports of him that the citizens came out and "besought him that he would tarry with them," which he did for two days.

His disciples might indeed well be filled with wonder; for it was an entire breaking down of the old wall of separation: it was an entire giving up of all old feelings of pride, contempt and hatred: it was a substitution of affection and kindness: it was an opening of the Jewish heart to take the hated Samaritans in.   They were not prepared for this; and shrinkingly they followed their Master with many a protest in the lowest depths of their nature; many a recoil which their feelings for Christ, full of love and reverence as they were and full of confidence, could yet not prevent them from having, and probably at times also manifesting.   Peter's impulses were ever ready to break out, and often got the mastery over him in secret if not in public. Even John, full of love as he was, came with reluctance into this strange fraternizing with men so long despised and slighted, if not hated.   Indeed there must have been a great tumult in the souls of all these disciples, as during those two days they not only had to witness but to become sharers in this new condition of fellowship with Samaritans; as recoiling all the while, they were yet held to their fidelity by the wonderful force of that love and goodness which they saw to be in Christ?

What a power there is in thus teaching by example! Long afterward when their Master had ascended to heaven and had left them to their own guidance under the help of the Holy Spirit; when Peter was sent to Samaria to preach and to establish a church among the dwellers there; and when John far off at Ephesus and Smyrna, had to seek for companionship and brotherhood chiefly among Gentiles; then they remembered these scenes at Jacob's well and at Shechem, and they blessed God for such a teacher, by example as well as by precept.

The Samaritans were powerfully affected by both, and when he left their city they declared,

"We know that this is indeed the Christ, the Saviour of the world."

In Galilee to which he now proceeded, reports concerning him were spreading rapidly; for people from all that region had been to the Passover: and they were telling everywhere what they had seen and heard at Jerusalem. Among that simple agricultural people, accustomed to regard with reverence everything belonging to their religious metropolis, the news was astounding:—and deepest interest, wonder, hopes, doubts, agitations of all kinds, met Christ and his disciples here, and were depicted on people's countenances wherever he went. An added rumor now gave intensity to this interest; for it was asserted that in Samaria, he had declared himself to be the *Messiah, the Christ.*[1] Astonishing as this claim was to every one, it gathered force as people gazed and listened; for he began immediately to preach in their synagogues, and it was evident to their apprehensions that there was something most extraordinary in his words and looks. He "had returned in the power of the Spirit:" and if in after times the face of Stephen was "as it had been the face of an angel," as filled with the Holy Ghost he spoke before the council of Jerusalem, what must have been the sight here as Christ preached in these synagogues, his countenance lighted up with the Divine expression, his eyes gleaming in the supernatural afflatus, his doctrines sublime

---

[1] See John iv. 26.

though clear, his manner having the stamp of authority, while at the same time it was winning and gentle! The result might well be as we are told in the Scripture that it was, "He was glorified of all."[1]

Proceeding thus onward he came again to Cana, the scene of the marriage feast. There a man hurried into his presence. What a look there was in that man's eyes of entreaty, hope, anxiety: all that would be in a father's face when a son was sick, near to death, and here might be relief! He was a nobleman of Capernaum which was about fifteen miles distant: he had heard that Christ had returned from Judea to Galilee, and had hastened to him, and his beseeching cry was "to come down and heal his son." His entreaty seemed to be warded off:

"Except ye see signs and wonders ye will not believe."—

—He broke in with the exclamation,

"Sir, come down ere my child die."

"Go thy way; thy son liveth."

—The man must have sprung to his feet with joy; for he believed. He hurried homeward; and was met on the road by his servants coming to inform him that his son was alive, and that the fever had left him. On inquiry it was known that the relief came when the healing words were pronounced at Cana: and the father "believed, and his whole house."[2]

---

[1] Luke iv. 14–15.   [2] See John iv. 46–53.

CHAPTER XVI.

AT NAZARETH.

IT was putting the claims of Jesus to be the Messiah, the Christ, to a very severe ordeal for him now to visit Nazareth, where he had been brought up, where he had worked at the trade of his reputed father, a carpenter, and where all feelings of jealousy if not of indignant wrath at such claims would certainly be aroused, and might result in violence itself.

Yet he went. And although the inhabitants appear to have been exceptional among the frank and genial Galileans, as we conclude from Nathaniel's remark about the place; yet here at the very outset of his ministry, he proclaimed himself as fulfilling the prophecy respecting the Messiah. Could these people have ever found in his long residence among them—his youth and manhood—aught else than a perfect life, they would on this occasion have overwhelmed him with vituperation : but in their crowded synagogue there was but one voice raised—there could be but one, and that was only against the astounding nature of his claim. "He the Christ ! !" We will soon enter into the synagogue with him, and witness that scene.

First, of the place itself and its surroundings, amid which Jesus had been brought up.

No portions of Palestine are so grand in general features, or so interesting in detail as those immediately surrounding Nazareth and in view from the adjoining heights. The town lies imbedded in a range of hills running east and west, forming the northern boundary of the plain of Esdraelon, which spreads out immense in extent, yet with scenery varied in every part. The eastern edge of this plain may be said to rest on the Jordan, along which it extends north and south about twenty-four miles. Carmel running north-west and south-east, forms its other boundary. Only the western end about seventeen miles across can be called level, its eastern portion being rolling like our prairies; while also in that part rise Mount Gilboa, 1,300 feet high, Little Hermon, 1,862 feet, and Tabor, 1,800 feet, the last connected with a spur running out from the Nazareth range. The foot of Tabor is about six miles east from Nazareth.

Nazareth as it is now, viewed from the South-East.

This town is reached by a short valley running up from the plain, and rests on the western side of a recess a mile in length by half a mile in width. It contains now about 3000 inhabitants, probably about the same number as in the Saviour's time. Thompson says, " The valley is certainly small, but then the different swellings of the surrounding hills give the idea of repose and protection."[1] Among the hills are precipitous rocky bluffs adjoining the town.

Robinson who was by no means given to enthusiasm in

---

[1] "The Land and the Book."

his descriptions, thus speaks of the prospect from the hill immediately back of Nazareth, the summit of which is 1,100 feet above the sea;—a spot to which doubtless the Saviour had often withdrawn for enjoyment and reflection, while his earthly life was growing up in that grandeur which harmonized so well with this scene. That traveller says: "I walked out alone to the top of the hill over Nazareth, where stands the neglected Wely of Neby Isma'il. Here quite unexpectedly, a glorious prospect opened on the view. The air was perfectly clear and serene; and I shall never forget the impression I received, as the enchanting panorama burst suddenly upon me. There lay the magnificent plain of Esdraelon, or at least all its western part; on the left was seen the round top of Tabor over the intervening hills, with portions of the Little Hermon and Gilboa, and the opposite mountains of Samaria, from Jenin westward to the lower hills extending towards Carmel. Then came the long line of Carmel itself with the convent of Elias on its northern end, and Haifa on the shore at its foot. In the west lay the Mediterranean gleaming in the morning sun; seen first far off in the south on the left of Carmel; then intercepted by that mountain, and again appearing on its right, so as to include the whole bay of 'Akka, and the coast stretching far north to a point N. 10° W. 'Akka itself (Ptolemais, now St. Jean d'Acre) was not visible, being hidden by intervening hills. Below, on the north was spread out another of the beautiful plains of northern Palestine called el-Buttauf; it runs from east to west, and its waters are drained off westward through a narrow valley to the Kishon, (el-Mukatta) at the base of Carmel. On the southern border of the plain the eye rested on a large village near the foot of an isolated hill, with a ruined castle on the top; this was Sefuriah, the ancient Sepphoris or Dio Cæsarea. Beyond the plain of el-Buttauf, long ridges running from east to west rise one higher than another until the mountains of Safed overtop them all, on which that place is seen—'a city set upon a hill.' Further towards the right is a sea of hills and mountains, backed by the higher ones beyond the Lake of Tiberias, and in the north-east by the majestic Hermon, with its icy crown. * * I remained for some hours upon this spot, lost in contemplation of the wide prospect, and of the events connected with the scenes around. In the village below, the Saviour of the world had passed his childhood; and although we have few particulars of his life, yet there are certain features of nature which meet our eyes now just as they once met his."[1]

Among such scenes Jesus had lived, doubtless in far more hearty communion with them than with his townsmen of Nazareth. He might now look for a more favorable reception of his teachings in any other part of Galilee than in this place; for, even if its people had been of a better description of character than they were, still the jealousies felt towards one who had grown up among them with no advantages of education or position, and who yet had suddenly become distinguished by fame, and was asserting such remarkable claims, would predispose them to regard him with suspicion if not with hostility. The rumors that must have been brought to them were startling;—the proclamation of John, the scenes at Jerusalem, the miracles, his teachings in the synagogues; there was in all this something to shake their prejudices and to puzzle and perplex them; but they argued, "Are not his parents here with us; his brothers and sisters?" Prejudice still had rule; and the very greatness of his claims made the barriers to their belief in him the stronger. When the citizens of Nazareth heard, therefore, that he had come among them, and was about to proclaim his doctrines in their synagogues, there was a great agitation in the community;—anger, disdain, envy, and probably old dislikes, against one who had in life and char-

---

[1] "Biblical Researches."

acter always been so different from themselves;—all this mingling with the intense curiosity, which was in every one's heart. One thing, **they** reasoned, might possibly satisfy them, namely, a miracle; and they might feel that they had **a** higher claim to miracles than Cana, or even Jerusalem itself. Report had told them of wonders performed in both these places; perhaps they would **witness similar, or even** greater **things,** in Nazareth. **So they hoped.** Candor and fair judgment could not be expected among **such a people**; and a teacher given to expediencies **would have avoided, in** this preaching **in** their synagogue, **anything** that would be offensive to them; that is, any prominence to the high claims of being the Messiah, and any allusion to their desire for a miracle to gratify curiosity. But Christ was not given to consult expediencies rather than the truth.

People had hurried to the synagogue. He was there also; his face had long been a familiar one in that place. The congregation looked upon it variously; some trying whether they could discover in it traces of that mysterious power with which he was said to be endowed; some resistingly, **yet** still, **in their** unwillingness, **half-impressed by a strange** Presence that there was in him; some scouting **it all; some** stupidly curious; all **watchful, and with few exceptions,** predisposed to be skeptical, whatever **might occur.** The service began. The whisperings and **surmises and** cavillings had now ceased. All felt the power of the solemn worship stealing over their disturbed hearts; and they perhaps felt that there was an additional impressiveness, as if some supernatural power was breathing over them and through all the room.

The doxology was sung; then came the reading from the **Mosaic law; then the second** doxology was chanted:—still there **had been no unusual** demonstration,—only the sentiment that **a supernatural** power might possibly **be in their** midst, and a consequent impressiveness **which people could**

13

read in each other's eyes, with a half-subdued, a half-angry manner, as if the heart was resenting what it could not help but feel.

Now came in order the reading of the prophets. It was customary for the ruler of the synagogue to invite readers and speakers, unless some one voluntarily offered himself; and Jesus presented himself for that purpose now. He opened at the prophecy of Isaiah, and read :—

"The Spirit of the Lord is upon me, because he hath anointed me to preach the Gospel to the poor; he hath sent me to heal the broken-hearted, to preach deliverance to the captives, and recovering of sight to the blind, to set at liberty them that are bruised, to preach the acceptable year of the Lord."

It was a well-known prophecy referring to the Messiah; and often, through the long years since Isaiah's time, had the Jews fed themselves with glorious hopes from these words and those immediately following. He closed the book and handed it back to the minister, and sat down,—the posture of speakers.—What a breathless silence there was in that assembly! He broke it by saying:

"This day is this Scripture fulfilled in your ears."

It was a re-assertion of that which they understood he had claimed, now made directly before them; but hostility was for the present repressed; for there was something in his look and manner that made astonishment keep other feelings in check; that strange Presence giving authority to his words.

By Presence is meant that something undefinable which has impressiveness in any company where a person of great distinction and worth is felt to be;—in this case greatly heightened by "the power of the Spirit" which had previously been noticed as "returning with him into Galilee."[1]

---

[1] Luke iv. 14.

The people of Nazareth whispered to each other, "Is not this Joseph's son?" and the question would express not only astonishment, but, among many, rage also at his claims. There was a mixed feeling; and it would soon show itself among these demonstrative people. He saw their feelings, and gave them a warning; for he now began to speak again, and as he did so silence fell on the assembly.

"Ye will surely say unto me this proverb, Physician heal thyself! whatsoever we have heard done in Capernaum do also here in thy country."

Their hopes were high, their curiosity now most intense. Was he going to perform a miracle there? But he always reprobated idle curiosity, and especially that which would desecrate the miracle-working power for its gratification. So now he gave the reproof. They were wound up to the highest expectancy, and he spoke, "Verily I say unto you no prophet is accepted in his own country. But I tell you of a truth many widows were in Israel in the days of Elias, when the heaven was shut up three years and six months, when great famine was throughout all the land; but unto none of them was Elias sent, save unto Sarepta, a city of Sidon, [a heathen place], and unto a woman that was a widow. And many lepers were in Israel in the time of Eliseus the prophet, and none of them were cleansed save Naaman, the Syrian [a heathen]."

There was a storm of rage. Every angry feeling in them was roused at this intimation that the heathen might be preferred before them. They rushed upon the speaker, and forgetting all else than what they considered so gross an insult to their nation and themselves, they hurried him out of their town to an adjoining precipice, bent on hurling him over. But their rage was futile. The super-human power was now exerted; "he passed through the midst of them and went his way," leaving them to subdue as best they might their impotent wrath.

He came thence to Capernaum, and now he made that city his home,—such a home at least as his frequent journeys and labors would admit; for his time on earth was not to be one of quiet enjoyment, but of self-denial and of labor wherever the good of others should require.

CHAPTER XVII.

THE LAKE OF GALILEE—CAPERNAUM.

HOW gem-like amid its beautiful environments, even in our day, is the Lake of Galilee! but how much more beautiful in those ancient times! Its immediate surroundings are sufficiently marked with what is grand in nature to give it something of that character, but it is chiefly remarkable for a gentle, quiet, lasting beauty which never tires; for this beauty has every variety of form, and changes at every hour of the day. Every one who reads the Gospels appreciatingly feels that he must love this lake on account of its associations, but it is a place very lovely in itself and in the natural surroundings with which it is enriched.

The approach to it is thus described by Dr. Olin, one of the most graphic writers of travels in the Holy Land. He had been journeying all the day over the plain of Esdraelon, which, after leaving Mount Tabor, may be said to continue (though with a more undulating surface) in a northeasterly direction quite to the lake. Toward evening he came to a level spot of great fertility and under cultivation, the thick grass on its waste places sprinkled over with flowers, and he says, "My attention had been so fully occupied with this scene of loveliness and these unusual tokens of industry and cultivation, always the more striking from being rare, as not

to have heeded our progress until we reached the eastern
border of the plain. We were now upon the brow of what
must appear to the spectator at its base a lofty mountain
which bounds the deep basin of the sea of Galilee, and forms

LAKE OF GALILEE AND THENCE TO NAZARETH AND NAIN.

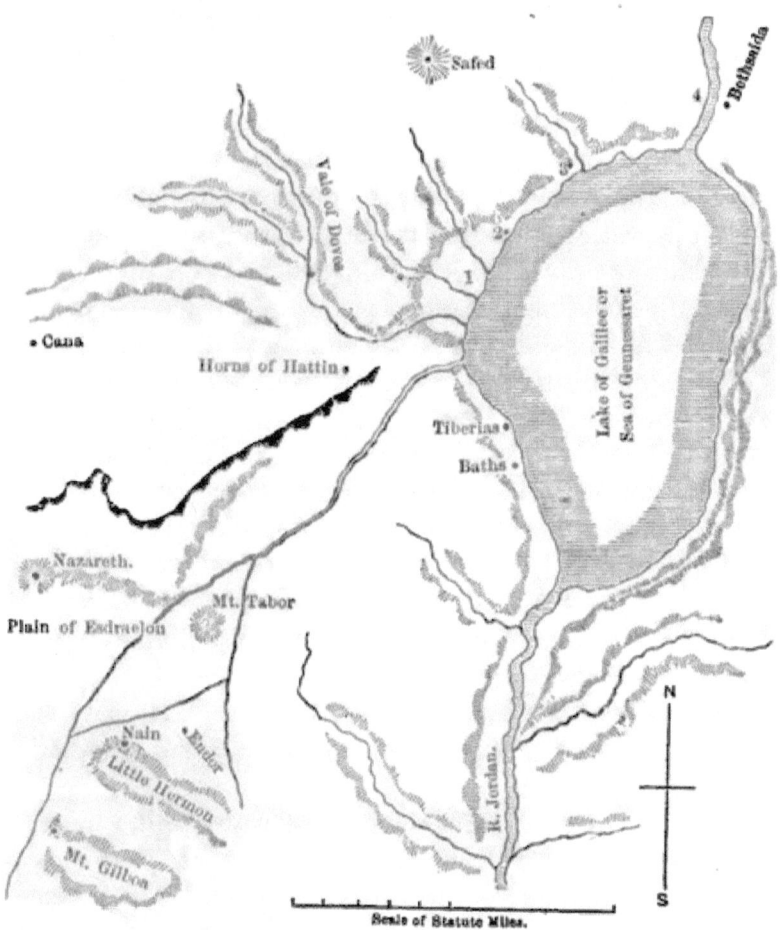

1. Plain of Gennesaret.
2. Khan Minyeh—supposed site of Capernaum.
3. Tell Hûm—supposed site of Capernaum.
4. Probably an extension of Bethsaida into Galilee.

the last step in the descent from the very elevated plain over which we had been journeying during the long day. The sun had just set behind us in a blaze of red light which filled the western sky for many degrees above the horizon, and was slightly reflected from the smooth glassy surface of the beautiful lake whose opposite shore was visible many miles on the right and left, rising abruptly out of the water into an immense and continuous bulwark several hundred feet in height, grand and massive but softened by graceful undulations and covered with a carpet of luxuriant vegetation from the summit quite down to the water's edge. Beyond the lake stretched out a vast, and to our eye a boundless region filled up with a countless number of beautiful rounded hills, all clad in verdure, which at this moment was invested with a peculiar richness of coloring. In the remote distance, though full in our view, the snowy top of Mount Hermon was still glittering and basking in the beams of the sun, while a chaste, cool drapery of white fleecy clouds, hung around its base. The green graceful form of Mount Tabor was behind us, while on the broad and well-cultivated plain the numerous fields of wheat, now of a dark luxuriant green, contrasted very strongly and strangely with intervening tracts of ploughed ground. Independently of sacred associations this was altogether a scene of rare and unique beauty, nay, of splendid magnificence."[1]

Dr. Clarke, the English traveller, says, "It may be described as longer and finer than any of the Cumberland lakes."

It is in shape an irregular oval, fourteen miles in length by seven at its widest part, the waters of great transparency and 165 feet in their greatest depth. On its eastern side the mountains rise abruptly, but with green, sloping sides, and great billows of such hills pass to the east as far

---

[1] Olin's Travels.

Safed.

Tiberias.

Mount Hermon.

Hills east of the lake.

THE LAKE OF GALILEE, or SEA OF TIBERIAS. (Viewed from the south.)

as the eye reaches, green but uninhabited; as seems to have been chiefly the case also in the ancient times. On the southwest the mountain sides are in successive off-sets like huge terraces a thousand feet high in the aggregate; and there, four miles from the southern end of the lake, is Tiberias, once a place of some eminence for its hot baths and schools, now decayed and almost in ruins from earthquakes of recent date. Passing northwardly from Tiberias along the western border of the lake we come at the distance of three miles, to Mejdel, the ancient Magdala, and soon afterwards to a spot where the mountains sweep backward for a short space and leave room for the rich plain of Gennesaret. This plain, for reasons which will presently appear, must receive our particular attention, which indeed apart from historical associations, if only for its extreme richness it might well deserve. It lies opposite the widest part of the lake, a little more than midway along toward the north, and is nearly triangular in shape, about three miles in length by a mile and a-half in its greatest width; is perfectly level and only a few feet above the water. It is a place of surpassing fertility. In those eastern countries wherever water can be procured for irrigation, the vegetation is most exuberant, and even the sandy shore at Jaffa, seemingly pure silex, is changed by artificial watering into richly-productive gardens; but at Gennesaret the soil, a dark loam, is of itself of the greatest natural richness, while four very large fountains afford water that in ancient times was carried by artificial channels all over the plain. On its south-west side is what is now called the "Round Fountain," inclosed by a low, circular wall, 100 feet in diameter, the water about two feet deep, and beautifully limpid and sweet, bubbling up and flowing out rapidly in a large stream to water the plain below. Ten minutes' travel northwardly from this, conducts to another very copious stream coming down through a break in the mountain; and at the northern end of the plain we have another large fountain gushing out from beneath the rocks, while around this, near the celebrated *Khan Minyeh,* other smaller fountains are clustered. Close by this last spot the mountain comes back again to the lake, and sends a short promontory out into its waters; but a fountain a mile further north, still larger than any of the former, and strong enough to turn several mills as it bursts from the rocks, had its waters formerly conveyed by artificial channels to the plain of Gennesaret, about which they were distributed by similar means. The abundant supply of water, the natural fertility of the soil, the depth of the plain, 622 feet below the level of the Mediterranean, and with a hotter climate consequently than the table-land above, together with the adjoining lake, make this spot a very choice one in Galilee, and it had a wide reputation in ancient times. Josephus says of it: "The country also that lies over against this lake hath the same name of Gennesaret; its nature is wonderful as well as its beauty. Its soil is so fruitful that all sorts of trees can grow upon it, and the inhabitants accordingly plant all sorts of trees there; for the temper of the air is so well mixed that it agrees very well with those several sorts, particularly walnuts, which require the coldest air, flourish there in vast plenty; there are palm-trees also which grow best in hot air; fig-trees also and olives grow near them which yet require an air that is more temperate. One may call this place the ambition of nature, where it forces those plants that are naturally enemies to one another to agree together; it is a happy contention of the seasons, as if every one of them laid claim to this country, for it not only nourishes different sorts of autumnal fruits beyond men's expectations, but preserves them a great while. It supplies men with the principal fruits—with grapes and figs continually—during ten months in the year, and the rest of the fruits as they become ripe together through the whole year; for besides the good temperature of the air it is also watered from a most fertile fountain."[1] Khan Minyeh at the northern end of this plain is distinguished as the place selected by many travellers for the site of Capernaum. There is a mound there with some ruins, and if sentiment only were to be consulted we should readily choose this spot by the cluster of fountains, where the adjoining **upward** slopes of ground allowed the view to extend **fully** over the garden-like plain, as well as over the beautiful lake. Arculfus, a French bishop at the close of the seventh century, mentions **Capernaum** as existing in his time and seen by him from the opposite side of the lake, and the description he gives corresponds only to this site at the fountains **by Khan Minyeh.** Robinson says that taking into consideration all the circumstances of historical allusions and descriptions, he is disposed to rest in the conclusion that this is the place.

But there is another spot three miles to the north of this which puts in claims considered by many travellers to be of a more valid kind. The **road** on leaving Khan Minyeh, crosses a projection of land, and then keeps along the lake by the large fountain Tabiga already noticed, so copious as to turn several mills; and then two miles further it reaches a projecting point or rather **curve of the** shore slightly elevated **above the water, half a mile long by a quarter in** breadth, covered with ruins of buildings, among which are many columns and remains **of an edifice 105** by 80 feet in extent. The name of **the place Tell Hûm,** is thought by Thompson to be from *Kefr-na-Hâm,* the word Kefr or *village,* having given way to Tell or *mound,* from the heap of rubbish there. That writer is fully in favor of the claims of this spot: and the English exploring party recently sent out **by an** Association in London, assert that they have **not only established the identity of this with Capernaum, but** that they have laid open the foundation of the syna-

---

[1] De Bel. cxi. 10, § 8.

gogue of our Saviour's time. **They** probably refer to the large building noticed by Robinson and Thompson, the beautifully colored marbles of which were from a mountain not far from the place. The remains of the dwelling-houses are of the black, compact basalt of the country, and may be said to extend to the fountain of Tabiga; probably in the whole extent of shore to the plain of Gennesaret was a continuation of dwellings, the great water-power of this fountain being adapted to draw a large population to its neighborhood. This town at Tell Hûm was certainly one of some consequence.[1]   Josephus speaks of having been taken to *Capharnuome* or *Capernaum*, after a fall from his horse in which he was hurt near the northern end of this lake.[2]

In either case, whether Capernaum was at Khan Minyeh or Tell Hûm, it was in a beautiful as well as most populous region. The whole of the plain of Gennesaret was doubtless like a garden with many valleys interspersed or bordering on it; and all the country above on the west, was full of habitations and in the highest state of culture. Indeed the whole region from the sea of Galilee westward, quite across the plain of Esdraelon to the Mediterranean, was probably by far the most fertile and populous part of Palestine.

---

[1] The distance from Tell Hûm to Nain might be an objection to this site, if we suppose that Christ made the journey from Capernaum to Nain (in this case twenty-five miles) in one day. See Luke vii. 11.

[2] *Life*, § 72.

CHAPTER XVIII.

AT CAPERNAUM AND THROUGH GALILEE.

ON the Sabbath after his arrival in the city the Messiah went into the synagogue and taught. People were astonished. It was not the jargon of the Scribes full of obscurities, and often of absurdities, such as have come down to us through the literary remains of their Rabbis, but was clear, within the comprehension of his hearers, practical, and had an authority in the manner of delivery corresponding to the words. No hesitancy or appearance of doubt in him who spake; but it was the language of one who knew; whose eye swept through all parts of his subject, the heavenly as well as the earthly, the Divine as well as the human, and who felt that he had power and authority thus to speak.[1] "They were astonished at his doctrine," says the history, "for his word was with power."[2] In the synagogue was a demoniac, whom he healed by his word; and afterward in the house of Peter, he restored to health also by his word, the mother-in-law of that disciple sick of a fever.

Thus the early part of the Sabbath was passed in Capernaum; a time full of wonder and of strange surmisings among the people. Twice had this teacher declared himself to be the Messiah; once in Samaria, and again in Nazareth: but he was so different from the Messiah whom the nation had expected: for here was no earthly pomp or glory, and no manifestation of a desire for kingly power; but on the other hand humility, indifference to rank, and abnegation of all human glory. Yet there was a strange mightiness in

---

[1] Mark i. 22.   [2] Luke iv. 32.

14

him. The spirits obeyed him. Disease left the wan and haggard frame at his command, and health flashed over the system: his very presence had a power in it; his manner so gentle and winning, still inspired respect; his face through which the inner being spoke out, seemed to be stamped with Divinity itself.

Such was this teacher, as he had appeared that day, in divine instructions in the synagogue, and afterward among the people, filling them with many contradictory and perplexing thoughts. His healing powers, however, they could understand, and these stirred them immediately into action; and there was a hurrying to and fro not only in the city but in all the country round about. For the warmest and most active, as well as the most blessed sympathies of human nature were reached in this case; and people were carrying to the bedsides of the afflicted the cheering news that a healer was among them whose power both for mental and for bodily distress, was equal to every disease. If we would appreciate the gladness of such tidings, we must remember the condition of medical science even among the most learned practitioners at that time. There was a medical school at Antioch in Syria, and one at Alexandria; but the facts on which the true principles of that science are built, are of subsequent discovery; and in Palestine at the period spoken of, physicians were rare and were little to be relied on when they could be procured. The sick were left to perish unaided, or were administered to blindly and with doubtful result. A modern traveller speaking of a Missionary Christian physician with whom he was journeying in this same region of country, says of him, after they had stopped one evening, subsequently to a day's explorations,— "Dr. Kelley is still busy with his patients who are all Druses and Mohammedans. How eagerly they listened to him,—he has so won their hearts by his benevolent aid! It is truly touching to see how the poor and miserable come to

him for help for the body, and how they go away from him
with the first tidings [of Christ] that ever met their ears."[1]

Evening came on in Capernaum after this preaching in
the synagogue; and the shadows of the Galilean hills were
cast over the beautiful lake, and went ascending the green
sides of the opposite mountains,—a fair, quiet, Sabbath-
evening scene without; but within the city all was fermentation and bustle. "All the city was gathered together at
the door" of the house where the Messiah was staying. The
whole region was stirred up, for the fame of Christ as a person wonderful in healing as well as in teaching had been
rapidly spread abroad. As people heard of this certainty
of cure, they hurried joyfully to communicate the intelligence to the sick. What intelligence it was! The wan
from suffering grew flushed with hope: the wasted found
sudden energy, and came panting on toward the Great
Healer, or cried to friends for transportation: the despairing had new words of comfort whispered in their ears, and
took courage for one further effort: volunteer aid was ready
for those who needed it: and speedily among the crowds of
the curious blocking up the street, were intermingled all
forms and stages of disease trying to force their way. The
dying,—could his power reach them? So the anxious
friends queried as they bore their precious burdens slowly
and tenderly along. The chronic cases of many years,—
could they be healed? The plaintive voice so long sharp-
ened by pain, and almost unused to any other than outbursts of
anguish,—could this ever be changed into joy and praise? O
make way! Let them see that Jesus: let them reach this
Deliverer: let them come before him that he may see the
distorted or wasted form and be moved to pity! And on
they struggled; sometimes shrieking in agony as the crowd
unwittingly jostled the couch; sometimes so death-like that

[1] Van de Velde.

consciousness was gone,—hope however attending, and shown in the tender looks bent over the sufferer. And as the sick were borne along, the healed met them with shouts of joy and praises to God; while the wondering crowds could scarcely believe their own senses as they saw them return as if brought alive from the dead. All who came were healed,—the diseased both in body and mind.

Thus the night settled down over Capernaum an agitated city, full of wonder, full also of joy.

The Messiah, however, did not continue there long; for much work remained to be done in other parts of Galilee. Rising in the morning, long before day, he went to a retired place for communion with Heaven; but the disciples came to him there with the annunciation that "all men were seeking him."[1] The multitudes followed immediately after, with the entreaty that he would stay with them; but he replied, "I must preach the kingdom of God to other cities also; for thereto am I sent."[2]

Peter and Andrew, and also James and John, had before this returned temporarily to their former occupation as fishermen; but having here received a more formal call to discipleship, they were with him again; and henceforward continued to be his followers until the end of his ministry.

He proceeded now to traverse Galilee once more, preaching and healing as he went. The multitude joining and following him had become very great; for his fame had extended throughout Syria, and to the great cities of Decapolis east of the Jordan; and people from all those regions, and from Jerusalem, and Judea generally, as well as from all parts of Galilee were hurrying to him: and the sick were brought,—"all sick people that were taken with divers diseases and torments, and those which were possessed with

---

[1] Mark i. 37.   [2] Luke iv. 43.

devils, and those which were lunatic, and those that had the palsy; and he healed them."[1]

What strange sensations there must have been among all these multitudes in Galilee, so intent and scrutinizing, watching the sick coming up, and beholding them immediately depart well and sound; joining, if only from sympathy, in the words of the healed men glorifying God; amazed at all they saw, amazed at what they heard; and yet, with all this, doubting. They could not doubt respecting the miracles; for these were obvious to their senses, and were public and repeated, till there could be no question about this astonishing power in the Messiah, and respecting the endorsement thus given from Heaven, of his teachings and his claims. Yet they were not satisfied. They walked in a maze of thoughts. The Jewish mind had been concentrated on itself for so long a time, so dwarfed amid narrow prejudices, that it was difficult to give it enlargement of thought, and especially such enlargement as Christ was now endeavoring to produce —a belief in the brotherhood of mankind.

Our wonder at the Jewish obtuseness and their unwillingness to believe, except in their own way, may however be lessened, if we observe how, even at present, Christian churches adhere persistently, each to their own forms or creeds, and are unable, perhaps unwilling, to see truth in others; and how a desire of personal self-glorification often unsuspected by ourselves, may enter into our zeal for church-establishments when we should be zealous only for Christ.

The Jewish people were obtuse to the truths now preached. There was wonderful power as well as beauty in these truths which their hearts acknowledged: there was a strange Presence in him around whom they were crowding, a seeming glow from heaven itself shining out through his coun-

---

tenance; and his miracles had the stamp of divinity upon them; but when he spoke to them of a kingdom in men's hearts and souls, embracing *equally* Jew, and Roman, and Greek; making a brotherhood of all men, making it a duty to love even their enemies, whose iron heel was pressing their necks, their feelings revolted, and the glorious truths of the new kingdom fell idly on their ear. Their very belief in the coming of a Messiah was of just such a nature as to increase their selfishness and pride and arrogance, and to cause them to be earthly in their most cherished hopes; for was he not to make them the supreme rulers on the globe? This they believed, and their hearts rioted in the thoughts of their coming worldly triumph. Thus the multitude, as they followed Christ, and saw and heard, did it in much darkness of mind—a cherished darkness which most of them did not wish to have turned into light. But still they had glimmerings of truth: some sought for more; some believed.

So they proceeded, closely attending the Messiah in his progress through Galilee, watchful, often admiring, always full of wonder, and full of excitement.

—But one day they all recoiled in horror and dismay from the presence of Christ; for there was suddenly before him and at his feet a form that scarcely seemed to be human, so disfigured was it with leprosy, the foulest and worst disease known in their land, considered also to be contagious when in its advanced forms, such as were clearly exhibited in the present case. The Jews regarded it as a visitation of Providence, and called it ."the finger of God;" emphatically, "the stroke." Persons afflicted with it were excluded, by their law, from society, and were compelled to prevent any accidental approach to them by giving a distant warning cry of "Unclean, unclean!" How this man, if man he might now be called, had come to break through this law, it is impossible to say. Probably, a sudden hope had made him desperate in boldness; the crowd had given way before him in horror and alarm: and there he was now at the feet of Christ, with a plaintive and broken cry.

"Lord, if thou wilt, thou canst make me clean."

A competent writer says of this disease: "A recent leprosy may be healed, but an inveterate one is incurable. * * The common marks by which, as physicians tell us, an inveterate leprosy may be discerned, are these: the voice becomes **hoarse**, like that of **a dog** which has **been long** barking, and comes through the nose, rather than through the mouth; the pulse is small and heavy, slow and disordered; the blood abounds with white corpuscules, * *; the eyes are red and inflamed, and project out of the head, but cannot be moved either to the right or left; the ears are swelled and red, corroded with ulcers about the roots of them, and encompassed with small kernels; the nose sinks, because the cartilage rots; the nostrils are open, and the passage stopped with ulcers at the bottom; the tongue is dry, black, swelled, ulcerated, shortened, divided into ridges, and beset with little white pimples; the skin is uneven, hard, and insensible; even if a hole be made in it, or it be cut, a putrefied sanies issues from it instead of **blood**."[1]

An American author, who, **during a residence of more** than thirty **years** in Palestine, **has seen the disease in all its** forms, thus describes its **progress as presented** to his eyes: "The hair falls from **the head and eyebrows**; the nails loosen, decay and **drop off**; joint after joint of the fingers and toes shrink up and fall away. The gums are absorbed and the teeth disappear. The nose, the eyes, the tongue and palate are slowly consumed, and finally the wretched victim sinks into the earth and disappears, while medicine has no power to stay the ravages of **this fell disease or even to** mitigate sensibly its tortures."[2]

Such was the nature of the disease of this man, who,

---

[1] Robinson's Calmet.   [2] Thompson's "Land and the Book."

"*full of it*,"[1] had now prostrated himself at the Messiah's feet, with the cry, "Lord, if thou wilt, thou canst make me clean." Abject he was in all but his faith. Loathsome, but glorious in faith. The body a horror, the soul resplendent through his faith. His tongue scarcely uttering intelligible sounds; but pronouncing the words of faith that brought salvation. How the crowds, crushing against each other, in their horror and desire to avoid contact with him, gazed and watched for the result! It came immediately.

"I will, be thou clean;" and Christ touched him.

At the word, a transformation took place. The hideous disease was gone; all the foul signs were swept away from his person, and he rose to his feet clean and sound,[2] a well man. With a thrill of joy—such as no thought in our mind can reach—he looked down upon himself; found that he could use all of his limbs; felt the soundness all through his system; saw the people no longer shrinking from him in abhorrence, but gazing in admiration and kindness, and approaching him—lately so shunned,—to satisfy themselves of this amazing change. His plaintive cry, "Unclean, unclean," was exchanged for thanksgivings and loud rejoicings amid the congratulations which soon poured upon him from the multitudes around. The man's burst of joy over, the Messiah charged him not to publish this abroad: for, in the strange city where they now were, the running of crowds, and the confusion and uproar, might give offence to the authorities, as well as interrupt his work of teaching; but the man's wild joy could not be restrained, and he published and "blazed it abroad." The Messiah, in consequence, could no longer openly enter the city, but kept outside, away from its thoroughfares: the people, however, came to him there, crowding from every quarter, far and near, in order to be healed.[3]

---

[1] Luke v. 12.　　[2] Mark i. 42.　　[3] Luke v. 12–15: Mark i. 40–45.

But we must return to that miracle, to observe the central person in the wonderful scene: for, above all other interests, above the wonder of the cure itself, come before us the majesty of Christ himself, and the calm dignity of his words, I WILL, uttered in that quietude of conscious power which could **have been witnessed** only in one to whom infinite power had been forever familiar and who **felt its** existence in himself. We see this also in all **his other** miracles; and it is even more remarkable than the miracles themselves;—*a quietude in the perfect consciousness of power; a simplicity of omnipotence*, which reminds us of the command recorded in the Bible, " *Let there be light:* and **there** was light."

CHAPTER XIX.

THE PARALYTIC HEALED.

THERE was, soon afterwards, another scene where the Divinity within **Christ** asserted its rights and its powers, in a yet more **striking degree. After** healing the leper, he **had** spent **some** days in **still further** teachings and miraculous cures, through the country; and then had returned to Capernaum; where, the rumor of his presence having been quickly spread, multitudes began to gather about him as before. They came in such crowds "that there was no room to receive them, **not so** much **as** about **the** door: and he preached the word unto them."[1]

The houses in those countries are built about a court-yard, and the annexed cut will give us an idea of the general

---

[1] Mark ii. 2.

plan of construction of those of the better kind. It is that of the dwelling of an American merchant in Damascus, in which the author was lodged, during a visit to that city in 1834: and as habits are unchangeable in the East, it may be considered as an example of the houses in use in the times of which we are writing.

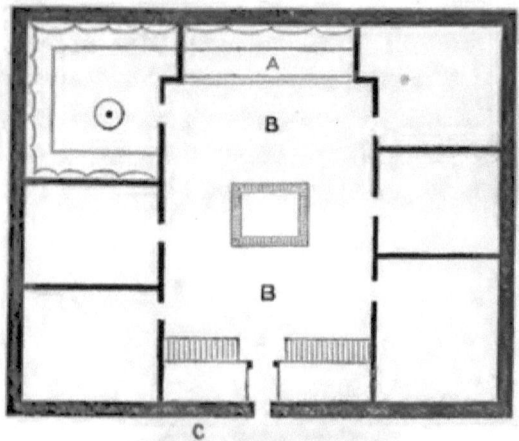

Plan of a Damascus house.

This house was entered by a narrow door from the street C. where the exterior was such that the building looked as if it was ready to fall and crush us rather than to give us shelter. Then there was a narrow, and dark arched way, and at the further end of this another door, passing which we were in a scene of a far different kind. This was an open court, B. B. about fifty feet by forty, paved with differently colored marbles, with a fountain in the centre lined with vases of flowers; and at the further end a lofty arched way forming a recess ten feet in depth and extending nearly across the court. This recess A. was elevated above the court, and had at the rear, a *divan* with cushions of richly colored silks. This lofty recess with its luxurious couch had a most inviting appearance; but just before reaching it, a rival attraction was presented on our left by a room

intended for the hot hours of the day;—a chamber with
dim light, a fountain near the door with a delicate jet of
water just gurgling enough to soothe and lull to sleep, a
raised pavement richly carpeted, and along the walls cushions as in the outer *lewan*. The walls of the court and
chambers were enriched with gay colors in tasteful patterns,
or with poetical inscriptions; and the wood was colored so
as to represent japanned work of various designs.

The reader may perhaps suppose this to be one of the
palaces of the city, but it was a dwelling scarcely above the
ordinary kind. We were taken, the day after our arrival to
visit the palace of Abdallah Bey, which had three or four
distinct courts, and where we counted eight fountains: also
that of Ali Aga, and next to that of Abdi El Belzah Aga,
all of large proportions and exhibiting a great display of
wealth and of rich architectural adornment.

Capernaum had undoubtedly far inferior architectural
pretensions to the dwellings in Damascus: but the plan
above given shows the taste of those eastern countries; and
the court-yard and the arched open recess were considered a
necessity in every house, if within the means of the owner.

It was probably in such a recess raised above the court
that the Messiah was teaching on the occasion now before
us; while the "Pharisees and doctors of the law sitting by"[1]
occupied the divan, in his rear, and the densely packed
crowds filled the court in front.

The court may be shaded by an awning drawn across: or,
as the author has often seen, by vines trained overhead, or
sometimes in part by loosely fastened boards.

Thus we may have the scene before us in this case:—the
speaker with his face lighted up in his glorious teachings;
the Pharisees and doctors of the law watching with keen
scrutiny and sifting every word uttered; the multitudes full

---

[1] Luke v. 17.

of wonder and admiration and full of awe: for "the power of the Lord," we are told, "was present to heal them."

What a scene it was! How grand was that Presence where the Divinity was making itself clearly impressed, glowing in the expressive features and giving tone to the intonations of voice;—*superhuman love speaking and teaching and manifesting itself in every word.*

·—Suddenly there was an interruption, and it was from a very singular cause.

Out in the street four men had come bearing on a couch a paralytic who was unable to help himself. A new hope had seized him and them when they heard that Christ had returned to Capernaum, and with the quick tenderness of friendship they had been hurrying the sick man toward the Messiah, when presently they were brought to a stand by the crowd filling every spot about the door. It was found impossible to proceed; for the archway was packed closely by human beings trying to catch the words of the Great Teacher within, and the people either could not or would not give way. A fear came over the sick man, such a fear as can be known only to one long diseased and helpless, but who is suddenly roused by a great hope, and now that hope made seemingly vain. He turned his feeble gaze on the multitude full of entreaty, but they did not move; exhortations from friends were of no avail; probably every one believed that an effort to get through such a crowd must be in vain. But the friends were not to be baffled by difficulties; they persevered, and they succeeded.

The house-tops in those cities are flat and are a common resort for the natives by day, and often their sleeping-places at night. It is easy also, as the author has often found, to pass from house to house over the low parapets, and although in this case the doorway from the street was crowded and the stairs of this court-yard could not be reached, yet in other courts access to the roof could be gained, and thus the

spot right over the head of Christ as he stood in the recess
teaching could be reached. The loose boards or awning being then moved aside[1] the couch could be let down directly
in front of the Saviour and by his feet.

The crowds below **as they saw the couch descending let**
down with such tenderness and **care, and** saw the anxious,
earnest faces of the friends **above, were deeply moved; a**
common sympathy swept all **other, feeling before it, as all**
bent toward the helpless, **sad object before them in intensity**
of gaze at him and at Christ. **None could doubt the result**
after **such** healings as they had witnessed, and especially
when they saw the gush of sympathy in the face of the Messiah, but amongst the hearers there was a start of wonder—
in some of **horror** at the words they heard from him:

"Man thy sins are forgiven thee."

"Who is this which speaketh *blasphemies?* Who can
forgive sins but God alone?" were the swift thoughts filling
with repulsion the hearts of those immediately about Christ.
But although **he** knew these thoughts **there was no** disclaimer by him but a full sanction to **their conclusions.**

"What reason ye in your **hearts? Whether is easier to**
say, **Thy** sins be forgiven **thee, or to say, Rise up and walk?**
But that ye **may know that the Son of man hath power upon**
earth **to forgive sins** (he said to the sick of the palsy), I say
unto thee, **Arise and take up thy couch and go unto thine**
house."

The man rose well **and sound. It was** wonderful not
only to see the fullness of strength flushing through all

---

[1] Mark says, "uncovered the roof where he was;" Luke, "they let him
down through the tiling with his couch," διὰ τῶν κεράμων, which here
in our Bible is translated *through* the tiling. In Acts ix. 25, however,
διὰ is translated *by*, not *through*, διὰ τυ τείχους, by the wall. Also in 2 Cor.
xi. 33, διὰ *by* the wall. The Greek word κεραμοι, originally meant tiles;
afterward it was used for any kind of roof or covering. The passage
here undoubtedly means *by* the roof or edge of the roof.

that body just before this so worn and utterly helpless, but to witness the sanction from God himself in this miracle to the claims of Godhead from Christ!

Jehovah had in their writings always declared himself to be "a jealous God;" and well might such a declaration be impressed upon them surrounded as they were with heathen temples and with false claims for deities adapted to lead their hearts astray; but here was one charged with claiming the rights of Divinity, and in not a word abnegating these claims but endorsing them, yet sustained by Jehovah in this wonderful miracle before their eyes.

The lately paralytic was there sound and strong, and what a rejoicing in his new power there was in him. Among the spectators there was a tumult of sensations, amazement, awe, fear, sealing for a few moments their tongues. Then came a rush of joy over all other feeling, and of glorifying God; and as they went to their homes they repeated to each other, as well indeed they might, "We never saw it in this fashion; we have seen strange things to-day." [1]

Among them was one even more exuberant with joy—he who was carrying his bed homeward, shouting out along the streets of Capernaum his gloryings to God.

But discussions respecting the events of the day were continued with deep earnestness long afterward at their homes. The Pharisees and Scribes especially were thoroughly perplexed. There was such a strange power in that teaching; there was such a greatness in the speaker uttering his doctrines with authority, and these doctrines so clear and practical, and carrying to the heart conviction of their truth. His position had all the marks of humility in life; yet real greatness can afford to be voluntarily humble, and there was even a grandeur in this retiracy and unpretendingness of Christ, mingled as they were, with a latent power to which

---

[1] Mark xi. 1–12; Luke v. 18–26.

there seemed to be no bounds. With this humiliation in his appearance he was claiming the attributes of God! It was blasphemy in man; was he man? Their own eyes satisfied them as to his human **form,** but yet in his words, his doctrines, his face, there shone out what might well be Divinity enthroned for a while on earth. What a Divinity, too, in his manner of address to **the sick man;** his word simply to be healed, and he was healed, **as in the old manner** when God spake and it **was done.**

And yet if he were the Christ, **the Messiah, God** with men, **so** unpretending and unambitious, so humble in all **his** surroundings and contented with them, what was to **become** of their nation's hope of dominion and glory? Judea was still to remain trampled under foot; its expected triumphs a dream. **Why** should he appear also as he did? Why in the form their eyes beheld? Why not, at least, in some pomp and circumstance of honor?

Thus in doubts and queryings, and in feeding the heart with worldly passions, these Pharisees and Scribes wandered off from the truth. How many other men have **since that** time done the same!

CHAPTER XX.

AT JERUSALEM—ALSO AT CAPERNAUM.

THE Messiah had given recently another proof of his preference **of what** was right above what was popular, by calling Matthew, **a** publican, from the very receipt **of customs** to be **a** disciple. Accompanied by him and by **others** selected **to** this office, he went now **again to the Passover at**

Jerusalem disregardful of what the Rabbis and Doctors would say of his retinue taken from a class despised by their learned men, and called by them "earth" and "worms" fit only to be trod upon.

Indeed the whole party from Galilee were sufficiently humble in their dress, and were unpretentious in manner; yet one of them was Lord, not of Judea only, but of the earth; and two of his followers have left writings the value of which it will require the fullness of eternity to show. Souls in this world and in the next, will not cease to bless the records of Matthew and John.

There was a pool at Jerusalem called Bethesda, having five porches or colonnades attached to it, under the shelter of which were a great number of men, "blind and halt, and withered," waiting for the "moving of the water" in the pool. "For an angel went down at a certain season into the pool and troubled the water: whosoever then, first after the troubling of the water, stepped in was made whole." A very singular fountain with a similar periodicity of flow, which the writer of this book has himself seen, still exists at Jerusalem. A few days after the author's arrival in that city, he was one day going alone on the outskirts during the sickness of his friend and guide; and on the side of the valley of Jehoshaphat, not far below the old temple walls, he noticed an opening in the hill-side with steps leading down. He descended some distance—twenty-seven steps cut in the rock;—and at last in the dim light, was just about stepping into a pool of water, when a timely discovery saved him from the partial bath. The fountain was about eighteen inches deep, and a few feet across, the water perfectly clear, but with a slightly foreign taste. Returning there a few days after this, he was astonished to find instead of the clear fountain, only a muddy puddle, with but a quart or two of water left. Others have noticed the same periodicity in this fountain[1]—called the Fountain of the Virgin. A subterranean channel leading from it has since that time been explored and found to conduct to the pool of Siloam: and this "Fountain of the Virgin" is itself doubtless supplied by artificial conduits, from sources under the temple site, or perhaps from Acra. Its periodicity, though of course natural, has never been fully **explained.**

The Messiah on this occasion **of his visiting the pool of** Bethesda, stopped near **a man—a** cripple for thirty-eight years,—lying there with longings to feel **the power of the** water; often tantalized with a sudden hope; then springing up with painful effort as the water was troubled, but only to be disappointed by seeing others more active than himself step in and be healed.

"Wilt thou be made whole?"—the words were addressed to him.

"Sir, I have no man when the water is troubled to put me into the pool: **but** while I am coming another steppeth down before me."

"Rise, take up thy bed and walk."

There was power as well as authority **in that voice. A** movement! strength! **the man was on his feet, whole and** sound and strong! He **did not know the Healer, who, in-** asmuch as many were assembling **had withdrawn: but he** did **as directed, took** his bit of mat or couch and started for his home.

But it was the Sabbath: and the Jewish leaders meeting him, reproved him for the breach of its sanctity by carrying a burden on that day. He told them of the directions given him; and afterwards having met the Messiah, and discovered who it was that had **healed him, he** informed them that it **"was Jesus who had made him whole."**

---

[1] See Robinson's Bib. Researches, and also Thompson's "Land and the Book."

15 *

Christ was now in a city where whatever was fierce in bigotry, lofty in religious assumption, or deadly in malice when such prejudices were wounded, had their climax; and the part of a teacher is not only to exhibit truths, but to expose their opposites for condemnation. In Jerusalem he must therefore soon come into collision with the rulers, from whom when once their ire had been aroused, only the fiercest measures of revenge might be expected, so far as the Roman power would permit. Of the Messiah's opinion of these men, "hypocrites," "serpents," "generation of vipers," we have a record further on in history; and from the first, he knew them thoroughly in all the baseness of their nature and of their designs. Nor did he among them ever cease to place the full power, both of his teachings and his example, on the side of truth. We are too apt in our considerations of the gentleness, the mildness, the benevolence and the unconquerable love of Christ in this his ministry, to lose sight of the *moral force* there was in him, and which it was that led to the plots against his life; and as far as these rulers were concerned, brought him finally to suffer on the cross. This force made no parade of itself, and was seldom a prominent object in his character, often seemingly latent, but it was ceaseless in operation and ever felt: and where there was a necessity, then it came out fully, and openly, and decidedly, as we see in his cleansing the temple, and in the woes hurled there afterward on the Pharisees, and indeed through all his ministry on earth. His religion was indeed to be forever aggressive against all wickedness; and he was himself aggressive; but we recognize even in this, such a greatness of love that it often hides all else from our eyes; and so to many persons in our day, Christ appears to have been tame and passive, when the fact is that the actually aggressive force in him is veiled from us by his more striking traits of benevolence and love. Even in the scene which comes immediately after this in Galilee, his *anger*[1] was deeply blended with grief at man's hardness of heart.

When the healed man from the pool of Bethesda informed the rulers who it was that had directed him to carry his bed on the Sabbath, they immediately came to the Messiah with a murderous purpose in their hearts. He had before been obnoxious: they now began their plots for his life. His very first words to them were an assertion of the right through the Godhead in him, to act as he had done.

" My Father worketh hitherto, and I work."

They understand him perfectly, and they " sought the more to kill him, because he not only had broken the Sabbath, but said also that God was his Father, making himself equal with God."[2]

But there was no retraction on his part; only re-assertion in a more positive form. * * " For as the Father raiseth up the dead, and quickeneth them ; even so the Son quickeneth whom he will. For the Father judgeth no man, but hath committed all judgment unto the Son: that all men should honor the Son, even as they honor the Father." The address was continued in the same clear and decided language, with declarations of the power in heaven belonging to him, and of his supremacy in the judgment to come.[3]

While returning from Jerusalem to Galilee, as he was passing through a field of grain, his disciples being hungry plucked some of the ears, rubbed them in their hands and ate ; a practice still always considered allowable in that country: but this was on the Sabbath, and some watchful Pharisees in the company taking offence at what they considered a breach of the holy day, drew his attention to the act. He replied to them, closing with the remark, " The Son of man is Lord even of the Sabbath day."[4]

---

[1] Mark iii. 5. [2] John v. 18.
[3] See John v. 19–47. [4] Matt. xii. 8.

They had begun now to watch him, in order to find occasions for accusation, and he met their scrutiny readily ; for it would give him only the better opportunity for impressing his doctrines.   An occasion for this offered itself soon after his return to Galilee.

He had gone to the synagogue on the Sabbath and had taught as usual, after which he noticed in the congregation a man having a withered hand.   Scribes and Pharisees were attentively observing both him and this individual, to see whether they might not find there another charge against him of violating the Sabbath.   He knew it.

" Rise and stand forth in the midst," he said to the man ; and he did so.   Turning to the Scribes and Pharisees who were then plotting for his life, he said : " I will ask you one thing ; Is it lawful on the Sabbath days to do good, or to do evil ? to save life, or to destroy it ?"

They did not answer ; and he " looked round about on them with anger, being grieved at the hardness of their hearts ; then towards the man,—

" Stretch forth thy hand."   He did so : it was whole as the other.

Those men who were plotting murder there in their hearts on the Sabbath, and yet would not sanction an act of mercy on that day, lest its sacredness should be violated, now went out ; and immediately, for their fell purposes, formed a combination of a very singular kind with another Jewish sect. These were the Herodians, a set of men who it will be remembered had become the advocates, first of Herod the Great, and were such now of his sons, Herod Antipas, king of Galilee and Perea, and of Philip of Gaulonitis ; maintaining that the Roman government was just, and that it was the duty of the Jews to submit ; also that in the present circumstances they might follow with a good conscience, many of the heathen practices and modes.   Nothing could be more at variance with the Pharisaic doctrines of a strict adherence to their law, and of their proclaimed maxim, that God only was their king, and that it was wrong to submit to any other: yet these Pharisees now went forth from the synagogue, "and straightway took counsel with the Herodians against Jesus, how they might destroy him."[1] The Herodians might easily be persuaded that the Messiah was setting up a kingdom in opposition to that of their Master, Herod Antipas; or, at all events, that dangerous tumults against the government might arise among a people at this moment so excited about a promised mighty King. The two sects, Pharisee and Herodian joined here in compact, their antagonistic principles made to act in concert, through their greater enmity toward Christ.

With what feelings then of rage and jealousy must they have looked on the events which immediately ensued at Capernaum;—throngs brought by his fame from all parts of Palestine, and from beyond its limits;—people crowding around him; the sick, in the multitude of applications, endeavoring if only to touch him in order to be healed; and demoniacs falling down before him, crying out, "Thou art the Son of God." We are puzzled here again, as we often are in reading the Gospels, by the notice of what is unknown in our own time, and seems to have been peculiar to the period of which we are writing, that is, men possessed of spirits of various kinds. In our entire ignorance as to the extreme thinness of the veil which separates the visible from the invisible world, and how easily it may be pierced by supernatural force when occasion requires, while to us it is so impervious, we can only content ourselves with the query suggested in a former part of this work, that if the powers of heaven are to be shaken when the Son of man comes to the judgment, how much more must they have been shaken during that wonderful period when he laid aside his glory

---

[1] Mark iii 6.

which he had with the Father, and was a sojourner on our earth?   But these are facts about which we are little capable of reasoning, as indeed we must be, whenever we try to peer into the supernatural, and to query about the mighty unknown wonders it contains.

The scene at Capernaum had become an exciting one. People had come from Tyre and Sidon on the north, and even from Idumea and its capital Petra on the south; from the east of the Jordan, and from Jerusalem, and all parts of Judea;[1] and a vast multitude were congregated, brought together by the fame of the Messiah's teachings and his deeds.   Through these crowds the friends of the sick men were still hurrying them; and people's sympathies were every moment excited by such sights;—by the wan and feeble, and the distorted by disease; by eyes raised imploringly from couches; or by faint voices entreating them to give way, that the Great Healer might be reached in time; by the halt and lame, trying to force an approach; and by the blind, asking to be directed amid the dense masses; while here and there over the various noises, rose the acknowledging cry of the demoniacs: "Thou art the Son of God."   The scene indeed, might easily become tumultuous, especially through the instigation of enemies; and the Messiah at last withdrew to the lake, where near the shore, a boat had been placed for his use.   From this, his teachings could be more readily heard than among the dense throngs which had been pressing on every side.[2]

---

[1] Mark iii. 8.   [2] See Mark iii. 7-12; Matt. xii. 15-21.

CHAPTER XXI.

SERMON ON THE MOUNT.

AFTER the scenes in our last chapter, Jesus sought in the evening somewhere back of Capernaum, a retired spot for prayer; and there he remained all the night in communion with Heaven. He needed rest after such a day as we have just been describing; but he felt still more the need of the refreshment which such communion only could afford.

Earth must have been to him lonely. Even his friends had few ideas in common with himself; and with all his teachings, quite to the last of his ministry, his immediate followers themselves did not understand the nature of the kingdom which he was endeavoring to establish. Where, indeed, could he find any one to join with him in that vastness of love which was for all mankind, or to comprehend its nature? His views of things were infinitely wider than those of the men around him, or of any man; his knowledge embraced both worlds, the seen and the unseen; he was infinitely above all others, and thus to him there must have been a solitude on the earth into which no one could come bringing that companionship which even the highest natures long for, that full communion which makes the greatest happiness of our being. He had such fellowship with others as could be found in relieving their distress, in elevating them toward heaven by his teachings, and in ever doing them good by the mightiness of power at his command; but companionship there was none, and there could be none upon the earth.

His full communion could be only with heaven; and in

such a night as this, when retiring from all human beings, he put himself away from earthly things, then was his solitude broken, for the companionship of heaven came fully to him again.

Thus he spent the night, and until the morning waked up the world to activity once more, and his work of teaching and healing was to be resumed. That day's teaching is among the most memorable things of earth, for it gave us the SERMON ON THE MOUNT.

The narrow thoroughfares at Capernaum were ill adapted to be a place for extended and formal teaching, and no house could contain the multitudes thronging about him; and recently he had been compelled to take a boat from which as it lay by the shore he could address them; now he led the way back of the city to the heights of the table-land, which, as already mentioned, here overlooks the lake. Seen from below, the shore there has a mountainous aspect, rising to the height of 600 or 700 feet, although when examined from above, the ground shows itself to be only the termination of the great Esdraelon. These heights are not uniform, however, but are broken into irregularities of elevation and depression, and one of these highest parts, called "The Horns of Hattin," is pointed out by tradition as the scene of the interesting gathering on this day. This is, however, seven miles from the nearest admitted site of Capernaum, and seems to be too distant for the record as given in the Gospels; the actual place was more probably on one of the more elevated heights back of the city itself. Wherever it was, our minds can easily bring before them the more strking objects in this region, some of which doubtless are alluded to in the address.

From the plain of Gennesaret a deep valley or ravine extends westwardly and then curves round toward the north, its rocky and often precipitous sides rising to the height of 1000 feet, and giving shelter to vast flocks of pigeons, from which the place takes its present name, *Wady Hamam* or *Vale of Doves.* "Behold the fowls of the air:" (we may suppose them then floating along overhead); "for they sow not, neither do they reap, nor gather into barns; yet your heavenly Father feedeth them. Are ye not much better than they?"

Palestine in the spring is remarkable for the abundance and brilliancy of its wild flowers, and the delivery of this sermon was just after the Passover, and therefore some time in April. Dr. Olin, when near this spot, was struck with "the great profusion of flowering plants." "The tall grass," he adds, "waved with every breeze, and we seemed to be in the midst of a sea of vegetation." "Consider the lilies of the field," said Christ, "how they grow; they toil not, neither do they spin; and yet I say unto you, that even Solomon in all his glory was not arrayed like one of these. Wherefore, if God so clothe the grass of the field, which to-day is, and to-morrow is cast into the oven,[1] shall he not much more clothe you, O ye of little faith?"

Within sight to the northward was a sharp peak rising to a height of 2650 feet above the Mediterranean, and now crowned by the city of Safed, among the houses of which are numerous *rebated* stones, which prove that the place was one of importance in those ancient times. This peak rising high and distinct above all other objects, with its city, gave striking force to the admonition: "Ye are the light of the world. A city that is set on a hill cannot be hid. Neither do men light a candle, and put it under a bushel, but on a candlestick; and it giveth light unto all that are in the house. Let your light so shine before men, that they may see your good works, and glorify your Father which is in heaven."

The place was indeed fitted well to be the scene of that

---

[1] Wild grass and weeds when dried were used for heating ovens. See "The Land and the Book."

16

sermon; the open vault of sky above, the lofty elevation
where the morning air was wafting the incense of flowers
toward heaven, the wide prospect—nature all around in its
purity and grandeur seeming ready to say *Amen* to the pure
and great word of **Nature's God** uttered there to men for
man's imperishable soul. We cannot but contrast the scene
of that morning with the one at Sinai—its barren crags with
the thunder and lightning making people stand afar off in
fear, and remark how characteristic the two scenes were of
the two dispensations to which they belonged.

Another remark forces itself here on our notice, and that
is the contrast between Christ mingling with the people, and
Shammai and Hillel, the celebrated Rabbis and founders
of schools in Herod the Great's time; those two men
described by Jost as mingling "so little in the transactions
of their times that they became mythical personages;" and
we contrast also their celebrated sayings with the clear,
direct, practical doctrines in this sermon on the Mount.

The disciples of Christ had become numerous, and he had
now out of them selected twelve whom he named *Apostles*,[1]
that is, "persons to be sent forth," who were to be more
especial attendants on his acts and teachings and witnesses
for him before the world.

They accompanied him in this ascent of the mountain
back of Capernaum, as did also many persons from the city
and regions adjoining.[2] When on reaching the summit
he sat down—the position for teaching—the multitudes
gathered closely around, and their curiosity was intensified.
The circumstances seemed to show that the teaching would
be of a more important character than usual. What would
it be? We can see them closing together, so as not to lose
a word of what might be uttered; their eager faces, their
silence of attention and their listening attitudes giving evi-

---

[1] Luke vi. 13.   [2] Inferred from Matt. vii. 28.

dence of the deep interest which they felt. Were angels also listening? We believe they were, and generations since that of the tempted and tried and weary and sad and of the longing on earth for heaven, and for light in darkness, and for a sure foundation for faith and peace, have gone to those words and have found them just what their souls needed most. **Yet there is no eloquence of words in** them, no overwhelming grandeur of thought or sentiment; on the contrary, the language is very plain and the thoughts **and sentiments are marked with** great simplicity; but we feel, while reading, that **the soul's God** and Maker is speaking to the soul, speaking to it in kindness **and love. The** scene was a great one, where those words ever since that time so productive of blessings to men were uttered. In our thoughts we glance over those intensely interested multitudes, to fix our eyes where theirs were fixed, on the central object of that assembly, on those features of God-like expression, those eyes lighted up by unutterable love; on the lineaments where the Divinity enthroned was taking form to the human eye. **In all that grand scene of nature he** shows himself worthy to be highest over nature and in **heaven, and** we hear him speaking worthily even for him; for **they are the words of eternal life.**

When the occasion **was over, and the people were return-ing** down the mountain **towards their homes, they went** thoughtfully, not yet recovered from the astonishment which had settled upon them, while observing his doctrines and his manner: for they all felt as they acknowledged among themselves, that he had "taught them as one having authority, and not as the Scribes."[1]

We can see the better how well they might be surprised when we come to read of the usual instructions in their synagogues, and to notice the frivolous subjects of the teach-

---

[1] Matt. vii. 29.

ings there. In order that the reader may himself form some idea of these, we here give quotations from Rabbinical writings adduced by Lightfoot: for "although the words which he quotes were committed to paper subsequently to the birth of Christ, yet they are generally considered as correct representations of the moral and religious opinions which the Rabbis inculcated and which the Jewish people imbibed and observed in the days of our Saviour's ministry."[1]

We present some extracts made by that scholar, classified under different heads.

"*Absurd legends and stories.*—'R. Judah sat looking in the law before the Babylonish synagogue in Zippor: there was a bullock passed by him to the slaughter, and it lowed. Because he did not deliver that bullock from the slaughter, he was struck with the tooth-ache for the space of thirteen years.' Adam, when first formed, reached from earth to heaven, and had a tail like an orang-outang. Og, of Basan, walked during the deluge by the side of the ark, and some-times rode astride on it; from one of his teeth Abram made a bedstead. The wings of the bird Bar Juchne, when extended, cause an eclipse of the sun: one of her eggs, which fell from her nest, broke down 300 cedars and inun-dated sixty villages, &c., &c.[2]

"*Opinions relative to the Sabbath.*—'It is not only permit-ted to lead a beast out to watering on the Sabbath day: but they might draw water for him and pour it into the troughs, provided only they do not carry the water and set it before the beast to drink, but the beast comes and drinks it of his own accord.' 'Women may not look into a looking-glass on the Sabbath day, if it be fixed to a wall.' 'He that hath tooth-ache, let him not swallow vinegar to spit it out again: but he may swallow it, so he swallow it down. He that

---

[1] Preface to Lightfoot's works, by J. R. Pitman, A. M.
[2] These legends are fully equaled among Arabs of our time.

hath a sore throat, let him not gargle it with oil; but he may swallow down the oil, whence if he receive a cure, it is well. Let no man chew mastich or rub his teeth with spice for a cure: but if he do this to make his mouth sweet, it is allowed.'

"*Superstition with* **regard to** *amulets, charms,* **magic,** *&c.*— The senior who is chosen into the council ought to be skilled in the arts of astrologers, jugglers, diviners, sorcerers, &c., that he may be able to judge of those who **are** guilty of the **same.'** 'The chamber Happarva, in the temple itself, was built by a certain magician, whose name was Parvah, by **art** magic.' 'Four and twenty of the school Rabbi, intercalating the year at Lydda, were killed by the evil-eye,' i. e., sorceries. The Talmud, after cautioning its votaries against drinking water by night, lest it should cause dizziness and blindness, instructs them, if they so drink, to guard against these maladies by repeating *Shivriri, Vriri, Riri, Iri, Ri.* 'When a child laughs in its sleep in the night of a Sabbath, or a new moon, the demon Lilith **is toying** with it: then let the parents thrice exclaim, **Begone cursed Lilith, and at each** exclamation pat the nose of the child.'

"*Hypocrisy in prayer.*—'R. Joachin **said,** I saw R. Jannai standing and praying in the streets of Zippor; and **going** four cubits, and then praying the additional prayer.'

"*Puerile and ridiculous descriptions.*—They detail the number of angels and demons, their mode of birth, precise names, magnitude and stature, residences and peculiar offices. Equally childish are **the** reveries of the Rabbis, relative to the chorography of Paradise, its various divisions and names thereof. With the same accuracy they mark out the different compartments of Hell or Gehinnon; the extent and inmates of each section, the various intensities of penal fire and the processes of purgation.

"*Drunkenness as a matter of religion.*—'Rabba saith, A man is bound to make himself so mellow on the feast of

16 *

Purim that he shall not be able to distinguish between cursed be Haman and blessed be Mordecai.'

"*Absurd calculations.*—'The ladder of Jacob is the ascent of the altar and the altar itself. The angels are princes or monarchs. The king of Babylon ascended seventy steps: the king of the Medes, fifty-two; the king of Greece, 180: the king of Edom—it is uncertain how many.' They reckon the breadth of the ladder to have been about 8,000 parasangs, i. e., about 32,000 miles, and the bulk of each angel was about 8,000 English miles in compass.

"*Punctilious washing of hands.*—The Rabbins delivered, 'The washing of hands for common things (or common food) was unto the joining of the arm.' 'The second waters cleanse whatsoever parts of the hands the first waters had washed. But if the first waters had gone above the juncture of the arm, the second waters do not cleanse, because they do not cleanse above the juncture. If, therefore, the waters which went not above the juncture return upon the hands again, they are unclean.' There are a great many injunctions on this subject.

"*National vanity.*—'If one sees one of the Gentiles fall into the sea, he shall not fetch him up; for it is said, Thou shalt not stand up against the blood of thy neighbor. But such an one is not thy neighbor.' 'The nations of the world are likened to dogs.' 'An Israelite that slayeth a stranger sojourning among them is not to be put to death by the Sanhedrim for it; because it is said, If a man come presumptuously upon his neighbor.' 'If any one's ox shall gore his neighbor's ox; his neighbor's not a heathen's; when he saith *neighbor's*, he excludes heathen's.' 'The dust of Syria defiles, as well as the dust of other heathen countries.' 'Wicked heathen's little ones, all men confess they shall not come into the world to come.' 'Whosoever lives within the land of Israel is absolved from all iniquities. And whosoever is buried within the land of Israel is as if he were buried under the altar.' 'The men of Israel are wise, for the very climate makes wise.'

"*Subtle distinctions.*—Any spittle found in the city was clean, except that which was found in the upper streets. The hinges of the gates of the temple were heard as far as a Sabbath-day's journey eight times numbered. The hinges indeed not farther, but the gates themselves were heard to Jericho. There is a dispute upon that precept, Levit. xvii. 3: If any one kill a bird upon a holy-day, the Shammean school saith, 'Let him dig with an instrument and cover the blood.' The school of Hillel saith, 'Let him not kill at all, if he have not dust ready by him to cover the blood.'

"*Intricate questions.*—Whether a man may bless God for the sweet smell of incense which he smells offered to idols? Whether a man at his devotions, if a serpent come and bite him in the heel, may turn and stoop and shake it off or not?

"*Logical deductions.*—The Jews do gather 613 precepts, negative and affirmative, to be in the whole law, according to the 613 letters in the two tables, and so many veins and members in a man's body. 'While he asketh necessaries for himself, let him not use any language but the Syriac, because the angels do not understand the Syriac language.'"

More in the same style might be adduced, but this is sufficient to show the truth of Lightfoot's account of the Talmuds, that "the amazing emptiness and sophistry of the matters handled do torture and tire him that reads them."

Immediately on returning from the mountain to Capernaum the Messiah was called upon again to exercise his power of miraculous healing; the request was brought this time by the elders of the city. Jewish elders were the princes of tribes and heads of family associations. It was seldom that the Jewish rulers showed him any honors, for there seems to have been small affinity between him and them; but they now came by entreaty of a Roman centurion who instead of bearing himself haughtily among them, they said, "loved their nation, and had built them a synagogue." **His servant was** sick of palsy, apparently in those frightful spasms when paralysis is verging on apoplexy, and was "grievously tormented." The centurion fearing, perhaps, that his being a foreigner might **stay** the benevolent hand of Christ, asked the elders to **solicit him to** come and heal, but modesty overwhelmed him even in this solicitude; for while the Messiah accompanied by the rulers **was on the** way to his house, friends of the officer were sent to say that their master did not deem himself worthy to receive such a visitor: "But speak only the word, and my servant shall be **healed.** For I am a man under authority, having soldiers **under me; and I say to** this man, Go, and he goeth; and **to another, Come, and he** cometh; and to my servant, Do **this, and he doeth it."** The Messiah **turned** to the elders with an expression of admiration at the man's strong faith, **and added,** that many such of other nations should enter the kingdom of heaven, while unbelieving Jews should be cast into outer darkness, where "there shall be weeping and gnashing of teeth." They went no further, and the centurion's friends returning immediately found the servant well.[1]

CHAPTER XXII.

NAIN. .

THE writer of this, while looking out one day from an upper window of his lodgings in Pera, a suburb of Constantinople on the opposite side of "The Golden Horn,"

---

[1] Matthew viii. 5–13; Luke vii. 1–10. Matthew speaks of the centurion as having come himself; on the law-maxim *qui facit per alium facit per se;* *any one who performs an act by another performs it himself.*

NAIN.　　RIVER KISHON.　PLAIN OF ESDRAELON.　MOUNT TABOR.
(Viewed from the east.)

saw just below him a procession advancing rapidly up the
street. It was headed by persons carrying on their shoulders a species of bier or couch, on which was the dead body
of a young girl—one who might have been sixteen or seventeen years of age. There was no coffin, simply the open
couch, and the deceased lay there dressed in white garments,
such as she had worn while living, the face uncovered,
flowers scattered about the head and the dress and bier; all
reminding one but little of death, for the features were like
those of a person in a quiet sleep.

But still there was unmistakably there the majesty of death,
that majesty which every one recognizes, and before which
we are always filled with awe.

We come now to speak of a scene in Galilee connected
with death.

The reader will remember that parallel to Carmel, the
southwestern boundary of Esdraelon and near to it, is the
short range of Mount Gilboa, and then also parallel but a
little farther to the north another similar range, called Little
Hermon. From the northern side of this last a short spur
of table land projects, on which in those days was a small
city, called Nain, overlooking the plain below, with Endor
not far off, and Mount Tabor about five miles to the north.
The time of this scene was near the close of the day. Scarcely
a finer spot could have been chosen for seeing the quiet of
evening fall over the great landscape of Esdraelon than was
this plateau of Nain, from which objects below were all distinct—the numerous villages, the orchards, the signs of busy
husbandry, and the fields of waving grain; for the time we
speak of was at the harvest season over that immense plain.
But as, in our history, we may consider ourselves outside of
Nain, looking down over the interesting scene, we hear the
quiet of the evening suddenly broken by loud wailings from
a procession issuing from one of the city gates, and direct-
ing its course toward an adjoining burial-place. It was a

funeral procession conducted with all the demonstrations belonging to such an occasion in the East.

"The grief of the orientals formerly on the occasion of death, was as it is at this day in the East, very extreme. As soon as a person died, the females in the family with a loud voice set up a sorrowful cry. They continued it as long as they could without taking breath, and the first shriek of wailing died away in a low sob. After a time they repeated the same cry and continued it for eight days.

"A box or coffin was not used except in Babylon and Egypt. The corpse was wrapped in folds of linen and placed upon a bier, and was carried by four or six persons to the tomb. * * The mourners who followed the bier, poured forth the anguish of the heart in lamentable wails; and what rendered the ceremony still more affecting, there were eulogists and musicians who deepened the sympathetic feelings of the occasion by a rehearsal of the virtues of the departed, and by accompaniment of melancholy sounds."[1]

The greatness of the concourse[2] attending this funeral at Nain, showed the respect entertained for the afflicted family, and how wide was the sympathy felt in this particular case. The deceased had been an only son: his mother was a widow; and the mourning here had the depth that can come only from such utter desolation as was hers. The Jewish dead were always buried outside their towns: and the procession had now left the city gate,—a long line of mourners filling the evening air with their lamentations and cries. The corpse was borne on a couch, with the face uncovered, as was the custom in that country:—those calm placid features, and that depth of appalling repose in the corpse, contrasting strongly with the agitations of the mourners and

---

[1] Jahn's Archæology. See also Matt. **ix. 23**, and **xi. 17**.

[2] Luke vii. 12.

the loud cries and lamentations as the procession moved rapidly on.

Another large company had just been ascending the hill; and now it came upon the mourning **train,** which it stopped; and that voice which we **have** listened **to so often,**—those gentle tones, so full also **of the power of command,** said to the mother,

" Weep not."

The Messiah accompanied **by his disciples had** again left Capernaum, **in his unremitting labors of teaching and heal-**ing; and **on** his way to **this** place **had been joined by a** large concourse, all wrought upon by the feelings which such a time must have inspired, curiosity, reverence, wonder, **and** in many of them love: for, if only by his healings, the best affections of their nature had been roused. It had been an agitated throng: until as they had ascended the hill at Nain, the noises of all agitation had grown hushed under the influ-ences of the sounds of grief from the mourning procession. But the cries of grief also suddenly ceased: and **then there** was a quick gathering of both companies around **the bier,** expectation **in its intensest form manifesting itself in every** face, with awe such as the **presence of death always begets;** and hope **also perhaps,** although **they might think them-selves** hoping against **hope.**

For **here on that bier was manifest** the power **that over-**comes all powers. **It was death.** Could he reverse **that** decree ?

So they crowded in a dense mass around the corpse, silent though deeply agitated, and gazing with awe on the calm stony face of the dead man, the quiet of which seemed to be almost **a mockery** of their **throbbing hearts,** their parted quivering lips, their strained **eyes.**

In the deep silence **of the scene, all heard the words ad-**dressed to the mother, " Weep not:" and **they noticed the** tones of unwonted compassion observable even in him who

17

was always so compassionate. He touched the bier and spake,

"Young man, I say unto thee, arise."

—It was death no more. The chest heaved, the features relaxed, the eyes opened; the marble paleness and rigidity passed away. Life was there; the true breathing, active, perceptive life. The eyes of the restored man had a bewildered, wondering expression, as if asking what all this meant; but the ear immediately recognized his mother's tones of joy :—

"My son, my son!"

He sat up and began to speak; and the crowd freed from the spell of deathlike stillness, sent up loud praises to God. They cried out joyfully and confidently, "A great prophet is risen up among us:" "God hath visited his people."

Amid this scene of their rejoicing there was a more subdued yet touching spectacle, where the Messiah was delivering to the mother the young man freed from the wrappings for the grave; and where her joy and gratitude were trying to find vent in broken words; and where she clasped her recovered son tightly to her heart, as if to feel of a certainty that it was all real, and that she might thus secure herself from losing him again.[1]

CHAPTER XXIII.

CASTLE OF MACHERUS—JOHN'S DEATH.

FAR over all Galilee, and through all Judea, and even into the remote southern borders of Perea, went the report of this greatest of all possible miracles, stirring up

---

[1] Luke vii. 11–15.

wherever it spread, a belief that God had visited his nation. But yet even amid that flush of joy at Nain, and the **cries of** Glory to God by that empty bier from which Christ **had** just raised the dead, the shout was about a *prophet* **come,** not about the Messiah. **God, they** believed **had not forgot-**ten his people, and had **sent them a great prophet ; but they** kept their minds obstinately blinded **against any Messiahship,** except according **to the old opinion, of their glory and do-minion to be extended over all the world.**

The rumor of this scene, and the rejoicings and hopes it gave rise to, reached away down to the castle of Macherus, John's place of strict confinement, where the vengeance of the tyrant ruler and of his wicked wife had never once relaxed. John had disciples still, who were allowed to visit him ; and they came now and told him of what had occurred at Nain.[1] He had at this time been about a year in prison, and the long confinement had worn on the spirit of the bold and ardent man. It must have been to him indeed, a very wearisome time ; and often and often he had thought during **his** confinement, of the sensual tyrant revelling **in power** and luxury, and enjoying freedom, while **he the man of God** was left seemingly **deserted of all aid human or divine.** Doubts of God's **goodness mix up with such thoughts as these, and have to be repelled by a powerful and active** faith ; **but often in spite of faith, they will yet return. If** Jesus was the Messiah,—so the Baptist might have queried, —why was he John, left deserted, to pine away in solitude and confinement ? There was in Christ the power of won-derful miracles ; why was it not exercised for him, the mes-senger sent to prepare the way ? Jesus had even raised the dead ; **why** was there no word to set him the living, free ? There **was no feeling of rivalry or envy in** John, **nor had there ever been ; but his was a condition where the soul pines**

---

[1] Luke viii. 18.

and loses force under long restraints, and where its own thoughts and its chafed feelings sometimes become its worst tormentors. The various reports about Christ; the questions started by the Rabbis; the objections from the poverty of appearance and simplicity of life in Jesus; the general disposition through the land to receive him only as a great prophet;—all this must have reached John,—perhaps in distorted rumors; moreover the gloom of confinement is always fruitful in doubt. So, calling two of his disciples, he sent them to Jesus, with the simple but pertinent question—

"Art thou he that should come, or look we for another?"

The Messiah made no immediate reply, when the message was delivered; and the messengers wondering at his silence stood aside to look on the spectacle now presenting itself. It seems to have been at Capernaum;[1] but wherever it was, the sick and afflicted were now coming around him, and he was healing all who came. Among them were numerous blind men,[2] groping, stumbling, pushing their way among the crowd, with the energy of the great hope that was in them, and with their plaintive cry to Christ for help. It was, indeed, an exciting scene;—the crowds of applicants; the anxiety and sympathy of friends; the pathetic earnestness of all; the gladness and rejoicings of the relieved; the wonder of the blind, as sight was given; their exclamations at what they saw; their earnest gazings on that face, all radiant with the divine benevolence; their thanks and praises, shouted out in return for this blessing, as the strange scenes of life were all developed to their eyes; as, turning their sight everywhere, upon earth, and sky, and lake, and upon the loved face of friends, and upon the gazing crowds around, and then back again upon the Messiah, they drank in the joys of their new and wonderful life.

The disciples of John looked on and saw it all; and they

---

[1] Inference from Matt. xi. 23   [2] Luke vii. 21.

heard, from the crowds, of similar miraculous cures of other afflictions: and now, the Messiah calling them, **charged them to** go and report to their master what they had witnessed and heard; **and,** also, that **"to the poor** the **gospel is** preached." **No** word **of censure on John for** his doubts; but only this declaration, **"Blessed is he whosoever** shall not be offended **in me."**[1]

—Was this all?—So these messengers **might have said,** as **they went on their long** journey **back to John's gloomy prison-house at Macherus.** What they had seen **and heard was** decisive as to the Messiahship; **but could there be no** token of deliverance for John himself? **no hope to be car-** ried back to the prisoner, so wearied, so worn, and **so sad?** not one word from this great, loving soul of Christ, so **full of** benevolence to all around him, so ready to help the abject? no cheering hope to their master of earthly help from Him? There was none. And thus it ever is in the mysteries of God: often he seems to leave us deserted, even **when** we look **most for** his help: but, *"Blessed are they whosoever shall not be offended in him."*

John's life **was, however, now** about **to have a tragic end.** The deadly **hate of the wife of Herod** had **never lost sight of him: and she feared also the influence he might have on** the **Tetrarch, who in his heart respected and honored the** Baptist,[2] **both as a man and** prophet. **At the first of his** confinement she had tried to instigate the **tyrant to have** him executed;[3] but a fear of John, and of the influence he had over the people, restrained the ruler: but now an oppor- tunity suddenly offered, of which she immediately availed herself. Herod, on his birth-day, gave a great supper to **his lords and captains,** and **chief estates** of Galilee; and **when all were inflamed with wine, the** daughter **of** this **woman came in and danced for the amusement of** the com-

---

[1] Luke vii. 23.   [2] Mark vi. 20.   [3] Ib. 19.

pany. The dancing in the east, unlike what it is with us, is mostly a slow and graceful posturizing, with a gentle movement of the arms and body: and it is often, also, lascivious. It is seldom that any woman of rank or dignity takes part in it; and among the Jews, it was highly indecorous for a woman even to appear at any time before strangers without being veiled: but, in this case, all seems to have been forgotten in the madness of the hour; and, in that madness the Tetrarch, in return for the exhibition of herself swore to give her what she might ask, even if it should be the half of his kingdom. The oath was before all the lordly company: and the girl, with high gratification, withdrew immediately to consult with her mother as to what she should demand. The fiendish woman sprang at the opportunity; and told her to require the head of John the Baptist in a charger. The demand was made; and a feeling of horror passed through the company. The king would have canceled his promise; but it was made so publicly, and in the presence of such high officers, that pride and the fear of incurring ridicule, forbade it; and the order for execution, as she had required, was given. The head of John was delivered in a salver to the girl, and from her to her mother.

The disciples of John came and received the body and buried it; and then passed on to Galilee to communicate the circumstance to the Messiah.

How many of such mysteries of human life remain to be cleared up when the great day of reckoning shall come, and Christ shall sit for the eternal judgment! In the meantime, we walk by faith, and not by sight; and, amid seeming incongruities in providences, we have the words still repeated down from the old times, "*Blessed is he whosoever shall not be offended in me.*"

CHAPTER XXIV.

THE TWO DINNERS.—HEALINGS.—NAZARETH, &C.

THE query how, with all these miracles before them, could the Jewish rulers fail to be convinced? has sometimes been asked with a secret sentiment perhaps at the bottom of it that the miracles were not what they claim to have been. Demonstrations such as these profess to have been, if perfectly clear and satisfactory, must have been fully convincing, such querists say. People were not convinced, therefore these demonstrations themselves were doubtful. We have not room here to discuss the subject of miracles, except so far as it refers to the Jews: in its wider aspects, it will be found fully and satisfactorily argued in other books.

As to the Jewish rulers, they were clearly unwilling to believe; and with such unwillingness, they soon found means for parrying the evidence. Quickly their unwillingness grew into a set hostility: and we need not go back to those times in order to see how enmity will darken the reason, and warp the judgment, and grow ingenious in finding arguments for abundant nourishment to itself.

To yield their belief that Christ, inculcating humility both by doctrine and example and saying that his kingdom was not of this world, was the promised " Messiah, the Prince," would be to give up all their dearest earthly hopes, their expectations to see the hated Roman power humbled, and themselves triumphant over the world. Fidelity to their old prophets, who they believed had predicted this earthly glory; fidelity to their nation, to their families, to everything hopeful for the future, seemed from the first to forbid their receiving Christ. Soon the feeling grew into hatred, for he was denouncing the *Traditions*, their greatest source of power; he was drawing the people after him and away from them. The Jewish hate had seemingly a rancor belonging only to itself, and **Christ and every one** connected with him might look for it in its most subtle and deadly forms.

Therefore **as** respects these miracles **which were so open and so** decided **in** character (as well **as** numerous) **that the facts** could not be controverted, the Pharisees and Scribes met these facts in their own peculiar way, as the following incident will show:

The Messiah **was again** passing through all Galilee, "**preaching and showing the glad tidings of the** kingdom **of God,**"[1] **and there was brought before him "one** possessed **with a devil, blind and dumb," whom he healed, so** that the **man both spake and saw. There was a cry of** admiration from the spectators:

"**Is not this the son of David?**"   **The** Pharisees rejoined,

"**This** fellow doth not cast **out devils but by Beelzebub the** prince of the devils."

He cut short their logic:

"Every **kingdom divided** against itself **is** brought to desolation, and every city or house divided against itself shall not stand. And **if Satan cast** out **Satan, he is** divided against himself: how shall then his kingdom stand?" **and** then, **after some other remarks, he gave a** terrible warning respecting the sin of which they had just been guilty:

"**All manner of sin and blasphemy shall be** forgiven **unto men: but the blasphemy against the** Holy Ghost shall **not be forgiven unto men.** And whosoever speaketh a word against the Son of man, **it** shall **be forgiven him;** but whosoever speaketh against **the Holy Ghost, it shall** not be forgiven him, neither **in this world, neither in** the world to

---

[1] Luke viii. 1.

come. * * O generation (brood) of vipers, how can ye, being evil, speak good things? for out of the abundance of the heart the mouth speaketh."[1]

Soon after this he was invited by a Pharisee to dine in his house, and he went, but he found himself there in the midst of an assembly—Pharisees and Scribes and Lawyers—from whose presence nothing but hostility could be expected. In those countries, for a man to invite another to break bread with him is to place the latter at once under the protection of the host, who is bound then to defend him if necessary even with his life; and in all nations persons who invite a stranger to dinner are expected by the rules of hospitality to have the company at least not hostile to the guest. The Messiah, on looking around in this room, could see faces in which enmity if concealed for the present was ready at any moment to break forth, for they were the class of men who had already leagued with the Herodians for his destruction.

At the outset the captious spirit of his host was displayed, because the guest had not conformed to a Jewish practice proper to some extent, but which the Pharisees had inwrought into their system of traditional law, so as to give it prominence among those things making religion consist in external observances of their own prescription and not in the heart. "For the Pharisees and all the Jews, except they wash their hands oft, eat not, holding the tradition of the elders. And when they come from the market, except they wash,[2] they eat not. And many other things there be, which they have received to hold, as the washing of cups and pots and brazen vessels and tables." On another occasion than the present, when Christ was upbraided with the practice of his disciples on this subject, he replied, "Well

---

[1] Matt. xii. 22–34.

[2] For their silly rules in this washing, see page 186 of this book.

hath **Esaias prophesied of you** hypocrites, as it is written, This **people honoreth me with** their **lips,** but their heart is far from me. **Howbeit, in vain do they** worship me, teaching for **doctrines the commandments of men.** For laying aside the **commandment of God, ye hold the tradition of men,** as the **washing of pots and cups:** and **many other such like things ye do.** And he said unto them, Full **well ye reject** the **commandment of** God, that ye may keep your **own tra-**dition. For Moses said, Honor thy father and thy mother; **and, Whoso** curseth father or mother, let him die the **death; but ye say, If a man** shall say to his father or mo-**ther, It is Corban** [devoted to God], that is to say, a gift by **whatsoever thou mightest be** profited **by me,** he shall be free. **And ye** suffer **him no more to do aught for his** father or his **mother: making the word of God of none effect** through **your tradition which ye have delivered: and many such** like **things do ye."** [1]

Such was the system **upheld** by **the** individuals whom Christ beheld around him now at this dinner, and by one of whom, his host, he was immediately cavilled at for not conforming to one of those traditionary rules. His reply was direct and pointed: "Now do ye Pharisees make clean the outside of the cup and the platter; but your inward part is full **of** ravening and wickedness. * * * Woe unto you, Scribes and Pharisees, hypocrites! for **ye are as** graves which **appear not, and the men that walk over them** are not aware **of them."**

"**Master, thus saying thou reproachest us also.**"

The speakers now were the lawyers **present,** men whose **business in life it** was to expound the unwritten law. He turned to them:

"Woe unto you also, ye lawyers! for ye lade men with bur-dens grievous to be borne, **and** ye yourselves touch not the bur-

---

[1] See Mark vii. **6-13.**

dens with one of your fingers. * * Woe unto you, lawyers! for ye have taken away the key of knowledge; ye entered not in yourselves, and them that were entering in ye hindered."

The scene presently became a tumultuous one, for the Scribes and Pharisees "began to urge him vehemently and to provoke him to speak of many things; laying wait for him, and seeking to catch something out of his mouth that they might accuse him."[1]

On his return to the Lake of Galilee, the multitudes still pressing about him in great numbers,[2] he sought refuge as on a former occasion, in a vessel by the shore, and taught them thence, conveying his teachings as was very often the case, in parables.[3] A parable is "an allegorical representation of something in real life or nature from which a moral is drawn for instruction," and was a mode of teaching common among a people so fond of figurative language.

In the evening he directed the vessel to be launched out, so as to proceed to the other side; and quite wearied, he sank into profound sleep at the stern. One of those sudden squalls to which the lake is subject came rushing down from the mountains, the waves rose and surged into the boat till it was near foundering, when the disciples awoke him: "Master, Master, we perish." He rebuked the wind and water, and there was a calm. They said to each other, "What manner of man is this that even the winds and the sea obey him?"

On the eastern shore he healed two demoniacs who had been "exceeding fierce, so that no man might pass by that way."

When he had returned to the western side of the lake a great feast was made for him by Levi, (Matthew), one far different from that at the Pharisee's house; for his fellow-guests here were the despised and outcast members of so-

---

[1] Luke xi. 37–54. [2] Matt. xiii. 1, 2.
[3] Luke xii. 1–59; xiii. 1–9; Mark xiii. 1–53.

ciety—publicans and sinners, "for they were many and they followed him." They were invited in to the feast, and Matthew, it will be remembered, had been himself a publican. The prying eyes of the Scribes and Pharisees followed him here, and these men came now to his disciples with indignation, complaining, "How is it that he eateth and drinketh with publicans and sinners?" Christ had been looking on the guests with tenderness of regard, for they were men whose ears were open to truth, and their very outcast position in society made them draw near to him who was ever the friend of the lowly. He answered, "They that are whole have no need of the physician, but they that are sick; I came not to call the righteous, but sinners to repentance."

A very beautiful spectacle indeed it was—the crowds of the lowly in life, often the despised, gathering about him as one of whose sympathy and kindness they were sure; while he, though so truly great, was never among them in a *condescension* of goodness, but with a truth of love whose superiority could be felt only in its trying to elevate all and draw them up to itself; his purity never soiled, and the Divinity within him never lowered by this mingling with the abject of earth.

Once more, after this feast with Levi, came an urgent appeal for help; this one from a Jewish ruler, a father, who hurried to Christ and worshipped him.

"My daughter is even now dead, but come and lay thy hand upon her and she shall live."

The Messiah went, and on the way a woman long diseased, who touched but the hem of his garment, was healed. In the ruler's house he restored the daughter to life.

He had passed out again, and was on his way along the street, when there was raised after him a loud and most plaintive cry—

"Thou Son of David, have mercy on us!"

These words seem to be almost ringing in our ears, so true

they are to nature, like the language of simple earnestness in entreaty, and so sad from suffering. They were from two blind men, who had been informed that Jesus was passing, and who fearing to lose a moment raised the cry.

He made no immediate response, but they continued calling after him with plaintive appeal, "Thou Son of David, have mercy on us!" and they followed him into the house. He said to them :

"Believe ye that I am able to do this?"

"Yea, Lord."

"According to your faith be it unto you ;" and he touched their eyes. Light flashed in ; they saw; their ecstasy was loud.

"See that no man know it," he said to them ; but they knew not how to be silent, and went proclaiming their joy and the deed all abroad.

Yet, with all this fame of miracles wrought throughout Galilee, where men had glorified God everywhere for his having come, the Messiah was at this period rejected again at Nazareth, even although this town was but a short distance (eight miles) from Nain, where he had recently given life to the dead.

He was now making a third circuit through Galilee, visiting all the cities and villages, teaching in their synagogues preaching "the gospel of the kingdom, healing every sickness and every disease among the people."[1] He came to Nazareth in his journey, and again as usual went to their synagogue on the Sabbath-day to preach. The citizens crowded there as before, full of curiosity, and were puzzled and greatly perplexed. They looked and listened with astonishment, as words of power fell from his lips, and as they witnessed the greatness of the being before them in that depth of wisdom and that extent of knowledge of

---

[1] Matt. ix. 35.

18

Divine things which was shown in his discourse; his preaching also upheld by such miraculous powers as rumor had brought to their ears, and which many of them may have witnessed themselves.   Yet, with a pertinacity which only a determined and set jealousy could produce, they clung to the old ideas and said, "Is not this the carpenter, the son of Mary, the brother of James and Joses, and of Juda, and of Simon?   And are not his sisters here with us?"   Swayed back and forth during this discourse; one way by the power of his words, by his quiet majesty of manner, and by that strange, singular Presence which forced the acknowledgment from enemies, that "Never *man* spake like this man;" and then carried again into the opposite by the humble circumstances of his bringing-up, they settled at last into offence at his claims, and he left them; nor does it seem probable that he ever again returned to Nazareth.

"A prophet," he said, "is not without honor but in his own country, and among his own kin, and in his own house." He laid his hands there on a few sick persons and healed them.

But the work of teaching was more than one individual could perform, unless his presence was miraculously multiplied, so large was the field of labor, and the necessity for teaching so great; for ideas had to be again and again repeated in the ears of people so long misled by false teachings, and made obtuse by the Pharisaic absurdities.   Therefore the Messiah now paused in his course to prepare his twelve apostles and to send them out to teach, with power also to heal.   They were not to excite the prejudices of the Jewish people at present by teaching beyond their own nation, the time for a far wider mission being not yet come. They were to go out, two together, and in simple manner, trusting in God for what in respect to food and shelter might be needed on the way, and with a still higher trust in him, if they should be brought before governors and kings for their Master's sake. The Spirit of God was to be in them, and to help them in all such trials. What was to be their reward? Honors and applauses? **No;** but, on the contrary, they were to be hated of **all men for his name's sake.** They were to *endure.* That was to be their lot, *endurance;* and this to the end ; **and after life was over, then was to be** their reward. People had accused him of being leagued with Beelzebub, "the prince of devils," thus associating him with one believed by the Jews to be the author of all pollutions and abominations in heathen worship; and "how," he said, "could they, his disciples, hope **to escape?**" But in all this they were to be strengthened and supported from on high, and finally their reward would come. They were to go in the loftiest heroism, both physical and moral, and must not dare to shrink from duty. "He that findeth his life shall lose it; and he that loseth his life for my sake shall find it."

Such were the instructions and the admonitions and warnings given : **thus** he sent them forth,—the **first ministers** of his word.

CHAPTER XXV.

"LET US MAKE HIM A KING."

THE rumors of what Christ was doing had reached the royal palace, and were creating great perplexity among its inmates. The base tyrant, now probably at his Galilean capital, was far from feeling at ease after the death of John; for the murder had left behind it, in the royal actors in that scene, a guilty conscience and its attendant alarms.

The sensation was increased by a rumor that John was risen from the dead; for that was the belief of some in the palace when they heard of these wonderful scenes in Galilee; their guilty fears at once suggesting that he had come back perhaps to be an avenger in their midst; others said that it was Elijah restored from the dead; and some of them more indefinitely, that "one of the old prophets was risen again."

Herod said, "John have I beheaded; but who is this of whom I hear such things?" and he desired to have a sight of the individual causing such a sensation throughout the land.[1]   He was not gratified however at this time.

The twelve now returned to the Messiah at Capernaum, giving an account of what during their recent mission, they had done and taught.

They found such multitudes about him, that he had not opportunity for even the needed refreshment of food. Crowds were coming and going continually, and making constant demands upon his time and energies; and nature became now quite exhausted, and could endure it no longer. He could refuse no one coming thus with earnest appeals to his sympathy and kindness; but rest was absolutely needed for his human frame; and therefore, having directed his disciples to have a boat prepared privately, he sought the requisite retirement by crossing the lake toward its north-eastern shore.

But the crowds followed.   Some of the company had recognized him in the boat when leaving the city; and the multitudes passing round the head of the lake, were soon gathered about him once more, on the other side.   His sympathies were deeply stirred by their earnestness, and his compassion moved by their moral destitution; "for they were as sheep not having a shepherd."   Having had some

---

[1] Luke ix. 7–9.

rest in the boat, he recommenced there both his teaching and healing. For the sick had also continued to reach this place, having helped themselves along, or been carried by their friends.

The mountains east of the lake have already been described as rising in green rapid slopes; and these appear to have been more a pastoral region than the western side. But on this occasion, the slopes were quickly covered by a crowd amounting to 5,000 men, besides women and children,[1] all actuated by the deepest earnestness, which they had shown by having followed him so far. To persons with such a feeling, the Messiah's kindness and tenderness were ever open; and he continued his instructions and his healing till a late hour in the afternoon. His disciples then came to him and said:

"This is a desert place, and now the time is far passed: send them away, that they may go into the country round about, and into the villages, and buy themselves bread: for they have nothing to eat." He answered:

"They need not depart; give ye them to eat." The disciples were astonished at the order.

"We have here but five loaves and two fishes," they said.

"Bring them hither to me."

They were brought; and he directed the disciples to make the people sit down in companies on the grass. He took the bread and fishes; and looking up to heaven, he blessed and brake the loaves, and gave the food to his disciples;— the disciples then distributing it about among the hungry people. They ate abundantly, the food seemingly exhaustless; for it never failed in that unstinted meal: and afterward, when all were satisfied, what remained was gathered up by his orders, making twelve baskets of fragments.[2]

---

[1] Matt. xiv. 21.   [2] Mark vi. 31–44.

18 *

Astonishment took possession of all the multitude, for they knew how scant had been the first supply, and by what a miraculous power it had been increased : and, as they had sat there on the grass, their eyes ranging over the thousands so fully satisfied, their feelings took words, and by-and-by these words began to have a singular purpose. The scene brought to their minds what they had read concerning the bountiful supply afforded by Jehovah himself to their fore-fathers on the deserts of Arabia. Here was a similar miraculous provision of food ; what was left after feeding so many thousand being even more abundant than the origi-nal quantity. The visible power of God seemed to have come down into their nation once more. Why not recog-nize it ? they thought and said. They had been listening that afternoon to teachings such as had never been heard from any one on earth before, so pure, so godlike : they had gazed with affection mingled with awe, on those features where a divine love seemed to be enthroned : they had seen this person receiving the diseased with such readiness and gentleness : and had seen them after they had been healed, dismissed with such words of kindness, that their hearts were all in harmony with their mental convictions, as they said to each other, "This is of a truth, the Prophet that should come into the world."

But they went further. Enthusiasm is contagious ; and it is apt to be progressive. Daniel had spoken of the Mes-siah as THE PRINCE, and their whole nation, and even foreign nations, had been expecting a mighty king. Here was the Messiah now among them. "Let us make him a king !"

He had been so humble in his mode of life, and so retir-ing and unambitious, that they must act for him,—so they thought,—and put him into the high place which the prophet had designated for him, and for which he was so well quali-fied. With Jesus for king, what might not their nation

become? Such wisdom, such majesty, such power over the
laws of nature, even creative power in his hands, all seemingly only waiting to be raised to that position of honor
which was their right! There might be resistance from
Herod; but that Tetrarch was already trembling with imaginary fears in his palace. There would doubtless be hostility from the Roman government; but what government,
or what array of arms, could withstand such power as was
ever resting quietly in their Messiah, waiting for exercise?
There would be acquiescence on the part of their Scribes
and Pharisees, when they once saw that the glory of their
nation and wide dominion were to be the result. So the
multitude could readily argue: and thus the excitement on
that mountain-side increased, till whispers turned into outspoken words, and words into open demonstration; and
presently there was evidence that they were coming to take
the Messiah " by force, to make him a king."[1]

But his kingdom was to be of a far different nature from
that;—one in the hearts of redeemed men, and to be eternal:
and knowing the intentions of the multitude, he quieted
and dismissed them before they could commit themselves in
the eyes of the authorities; and then "departed again into
a mountain himself alone,"[2] for communion with heaven.

He had previously sent his disciples back to the boat with
directions to proceed to Bethsaida,[3] on the other side of the
lake; for there was a town of that name in Galilee, to the
north of Capernaum, or more probably the Bethsaida of
Gaulonitis extended also across to the west of the Jordan.
This lake lying so far below the level of the Mediterranean,
as if it might be in a deep basin scooped out in the earth;
is subject to sudden and violent storms which come rushing
down from the vast high plateaus lying to the east and

---

[1] John vi. 15.
[2] See Mark vi. 33–44; John vi. 1–16.   [3] Mark vi. 45.

north-east of this, and also from the snowy Hermon, from which regions they are drawn down as into a funnel by the gorges and ravines worn by the water-courses converging about its north-eastern side. A traveller who had encamped one evening in one of the valleys leading down to it on the east, says, "The sun had scarcely set when the wind began to rush down towards the lake, and it continued all night long with constantly increasing violence, so that when we reached the shore next morning, the face of the lake was like a huge boiling caldron. * * We subsequently pitched our tents at the shore, and remained for three days and nights exposed to this tremendous wind. We had to double-pin all the tent ropes, and frequently were obliged to hang with our whole weight upon them to keep the quivering tabernacle from being carried up bodily into the air."[1]

A storm somewhat similar, appears to have caught this boat with the disciples, when out upon the lake. Coming from the northward it would be contrary, and any effort to make headway against such a fury of the wind would be in vain: nor would it be safe to run before the gale, for that would put their vessel in danger of being immediately "swamped."[2] Their only safety was in keeping "head to wind," by a ceaseless and most vigorous use of their oars,

---

[1] "The Land and the Book."

[2] These storms in their suddenness and violence and want of premonition, appear to resemble the "Northerners" which sometimes sweep the Gulf of Mexico, from the Mississippi to Vera Cruz. An officer of high rank in our navy, informs me that he was once lying at the anchorage near the latter, at the island of Sacrificios, in company with the British frigate Madagascar, when a northerner sprang up so suddenly that the ship had not time to secure all her boats. One broke adrift and floated off, on which the gunner called for volunteers to help save it, "for the honor of the ship." A crew offered, and they and he started for the purpose, running of course before the wind. Such was the fury of the gale that soon afterwards, the stern of their boat lifted on one of the short seas, was carried up, and the boat turned over "end for end." Every one on board perished.

amid those short, chopping seas, where any relaxation of their struggle would cause their boat to be filled and to **sink.** The meal on the hill-side had been late in the evening. Midnight came now and passed over **this boat and** its inmates out on the water, **contending with** the storm, and drifting into the middle **of the lake.** Their strength and hearts might well **be giving way in this struggle, and in the** seeming abandonment of **them by their Master; and thus** also the **fourth watch (three** o'clock)[1] **arrived, the boat still** tossed **and in danger** of foundering. Suddenly **they saw** what seemed to be some one walking on the water, **and approaching them.** Fright seized them, and they thought **it** an apparition; for it might well seem that only a spirit could walk on those curling foam-covered waves; but they were quickly reassured by the well-known voice of the Messiah.

"Be of good cheer; it is I; be not afraid."

One of them—the impulsive Peter—cried out:

"Lord, if it be thou, bid me come unto thee on the water;" and he was bidden. He **was on the** sea immediately: **and** just as Christ **has often been to others, so he was to Peter,** treating him **according to his faith.**

Soon **the heavy waves beginning to dash high against the disciple, who had been so far walking safely on the water,** he forgot that the power which could make him **walk at all,** could sustain him in the heaviest seas: his faith gave way, and losing it, he lost **the** Saviour's help, and began to sink. We need not censure this disciple; for we ourselves in our trials, often forget that God's arm is **just as** strong for **us in rough** weather as in mild, and **then** we **also** find **the water** beginning to **close over us.** He cried **for assistance, and the**

---

[1] **The** Jews had now adopted the **Roman mode of reckoning, and the** fourth watch commenced **at three o'clock.**

outstretched arm of Christ held him up, while the Master, in gentle reproof, said:

"O thou of little faith, wherefore didst thou doubt?" The storm ceased when they reached the vessel, and the disciples falling in worship before the Messiah exclaimed:

"Of a truth thou art the Son of God."[1]

They landed at Gennesaret, and as soon as it was known that he was there, news was spread through all the country adjacent; and quickly the diseased were carried in beds and laid in the street that as he went by they might but touch the hem of his garment. All who touched were healed.[2] So, also, wherever he went through the villages or cities or country, the sick too numerous to have special cases attended to were brought by willing friends and placed in a similar manner, and as he passed by them and they touched his garment they found their health restored.[3]

It must seem strange that people should run into the extreme one day of wishing to force the Messiah to be king through admiration of him, and that the next day, in consequence of his teaching, even many of his regular followers should desert him—the desertion so general indeed that he said to the twelve, "Will ye also go away?" Peter spoke up quickly in reply, "Lord, to whom shall we go? thou hast the words of eternal life. And we believe and are sure that thou art that Christ, the Son of the living God." The discourse that gave such umbrage was delivered in the synagogue at Capernaum,[4] and contains passages in which profound spiritual matters are figuratively introduced—subjects at which captious persons might take offence. Perhaps the audience were captious in consequence of their disappointment the day previous, and disposed to avenge themselves for their high-wrought but unsuccessful enthusiasm on

---

[1] Matt. xiv. 22–33; Mark vi. 45–51; John vi. 15–21.
[2] Matt. xiv. 34–36.   [3] Mark vi. 56.   [4] John vi. 22–71.

that occasion. It is a part of our nature to run into extremes.

Passing now beyond the boundary of Palestine on the north he healed there the daughter of a Syrophœnician woman, but soon afterward returning he went to the region south-east of the Lake of Tiberias, and in the brief narrative of the Gospels we again perceive him on one of the usually solitary mountains of this district; but it was not solitary now. Not far off were most of the cities of Decapolis, and the fame of the Messiah had been spread over all the country, and soon great multitudes had come to him, "having with them those that were lame, blind, dumb, and maimed, and many others, and cast them down at Jesus' feet; and he healed them."[1]

There comes up before us a scene of uncommon beauty and interest as we read of those healings on that mountain. There the blind restored to sight saw him whom their eyes immediately sought sitting fitly vaulted over by the dome of heaven, and in his grandeur of Presence suited to be the centre of those wide surroundings of nature—the great temple of nature not made with hands, where in the exercise of Divine power through love to men he showed himself to be the fitting Deity. What gladness there was around him as the lately maimed and halt found that they were so no longer; as the lately dumb broke forth in joyful exclamations carrying with them the sympathies of all; as the lately blind glanced at the varied sights of grandeur and beauty on every side, but ever turned their eyes quickly to rest them in reverence and love on him whose face seemed to be reflecting heaven over our earth!

But the multitudes lingered, "and they glorified the God of Israel,"[2] until at last, as in a former case, there was danger

---

[1] Matt. xv. 30.   [2] Matt. xv. 31.

of suffering from hunger. The Messiah calling his disciples, **expressed his compassion,** adding:

"**I** will **not** send them away fasting, lest they faint in the way."

"**Whence should we have so much bread** in the wilderness, as to fill so great a multitude?" **they** asked, for the number was four thousand men, besides women and children.

"How many loaves have ye?" and they answered:

"Seven, and a few little fishes."

He directed the people to be seated as on the former occasion, and having given thanks he broke the bread and gave the food to his disciples for distribution to the hungry multitude. **When all were satisfied** seven baskets of fragments yet remained.[1]

CHAPTER XXVI.

THE TRANSFIGURATION.

IN the extreme north of Palestine, and among the broken ridges which surround the base of the snow-crowned Hermon, **the waters of a** large fountain, called Banias, burst from **a cave, and form at once a stream of** considerable size. **This is one of the three sources of the Jordan.** At an early **period the cave, the large fountain, and the** picturesque country around, overtopped by Mount Hermon, made this spot a much frequented resort. **Near to** Banias on an elevated table land, which is bounded by ravines and precipitous descents, stood a city of ancient date, but much enlarged and embellished by Philip, son of Herod the Great, Tetrarch

---

[1] Matt. xv. 29–48; Mark viii. 1–9.

of Batanea, Trachonitis and Auranitis,[1] to whom in the division of Herod's kingdom this district had fallen. He had thought the enlarged city worthy of the name of his patron, Tiberius Cæsar; and Philippi, **from his own name, was** added to distinguish it from the other Cæsarea on the Mediterranean and present political capital of Judea. So **this** was called Cæsarea Philippi.

The Messiah, **after having dismissed the multitudes con-gregated on the** mountain in **Decapolis, returned to the western side of the lake from which he passed northwardly** toward the region above described. There lacked now **only** about nine months of the time of his crucifixion, and **during** this journey he appears to have wished the twelve for their own sakes and for future purposes to make demonstrations before each other of their opinions respecting himself. They had been thrown everywhere into the society of doubting and captious men, and had heard the Pharisees and Doctors make objections and quote authorities, and had witnessed their rancorous hostility increasing every day. He wished the twelve to make it manifest to each other whether **they** were infected or not, and **he put the question to them—**

"Whom do men say **that I the Son of man am?"** they answered :

"Some say **that thou art John the Baptist; some, Elias,** and others, Jeremias, or one of the prophets?"

"But whom say ye that I am?" Peter answered :

"Thou art the Christ, the Son of the living God."

"Blessed art thou, Simon Barjona, [Son of Jona]: for flesh and blood hath not revealed it unto thee, but my Father which is in heaven," said the Messiah : and he then proceeded to give to that disciple a prominence of position in his future church.[2] The frank, prompt, generous nature of Peter had much in **it that was** attractive, notwithstand-

---

[1] Luke iii. 1.   [2] Matt. xvi. 13–20.

ing the vacillation and timidity which he sometimes displayed.

The physical and moral courage of the twelve, was indeed after a while to pass through terrible ordeals; and Christ had warned them at the very outset of their apostleship, that they should be delivered up to the councils, and be scourged in their synagogues, and be brought before kings and governors for his sake; adding also, what was the hardest of all to bear, "Ye shall be hated of all men for my name's sake."

The remainder of that discourse is startling on account of its positiveness, and its exacting nature; and it presents to us Christ—not tame, as people often imagine him to have been, but decided; and not only firm in present purpose, but drawing a terrible impressiveness from future scenes. He had said, "He that loveth father or mother more than me, is not worthy of me: and he that loveth son or daughter more than me, is not worthy of me. And he that taketh not his cross, and followeth after me, is not worthy of me."

On this present occasion he said, "If any man will come after me, let him deny himself, and take up his cross, and follow me. For whosoever will save his life, shall lose it; and whosoever will lose his life for my sake, shall find it. For what is a man profited, if he shall gain the whole world, and lose his own soul? or what shall a man give in exchange for his soul? For the Son of man shall come in the glory of his Father with his angels; and then he shall reward every man according to his works. Verily I say unto you, there be some standing here, which shall not taste of death, till they shall see the Son of man coming in his kingdom."

Was he exacting? Principle is always exacting. Patriotism is exacting. Love to one's country exacts the offer of life, requires the mother and father to give their son, the daughter to give her brother and the wife her husband, to the battlefield and to death, if this be necessary. Why should religion be less decided in its demands than principle or country? The Messiah had just been telling his disciples "how that he must go unto Jerusalem, and suffer many things of the elders and chief priests and scribes, and be killed, and be raised again the third day;" and he was not only himself filled, but he was trying to fill them also, with the greatness of the work he came to perform, and which it was to be their duty to advance. Religion, such as this, is full of the grandest of all thoughts and all emotions, has them for its groundwork, and they make an essential part of itself.

The grandeur and glory of heaven is, in such thoughts and feelings given to the earth: and while listening to such words from Christ, we are readily prepared for what came, soon afterwards—the scene of the transfiguration.

Six days subsequently to the discourse related above, he took Peter, and James, and John, and conducted them "into a high mountain apart." The scene which followed there is one which painters have very often tried to depict, but always without success; for how can any one represent the glory of heaven impressing itself on aught of earth: least of all can they do it, as here shining out through Christ. We are told that when Moses came down from receiving the law on Sinai, his face shone so that Aaron, and all the children of Israel shrunk away in amazement, and "they were afraid to come nigh him." He was himself not aware of the wonderful glory in his face, till he saw their fright as if something supernatural were before them; and afterwards, "he put a veil on his face,"[1] and repeated this, after every subsequent descent from the presence of God. When Stephen was before the council at Jerusalem; all that sat there "looking steadfastly on him, saw his face as it had

---

been the face of an angel :"[1] and both this event and that at Sinai, may aid us in our endeavor to comprehend the

---

[1] Acts vi. 15. The reader has **perhaps heard** of death-bed scenes, where the face of the departing **one has been** suddenly lighted up, and has taken expressions, as if the spirit about to be released was reflecting the heavenly glory already so near at hand.

The author of this book lately witnessed **a very wonderful scene** of this description, which he will here briefly sketch.

There was a husband feeble as an infant, in a **sudden illness, and** thought to be near to death : in another chamber in the same **house,** was his wife also ill, and about to die. She had, just before this, when **at a** distance, been informed of his condition, and had hastened on to **nurse** him ; but in **consequence** of the fatigue of the journey operating **on an already feeble frame, was herself** immediately stricken down with a rapid disease. **She was a person who,** through life, had always seemed **to belong rather to heaven than to earth ; so pure,** so true, so lovely she **was, so great in all excellence. It was** the Sabbath, at night, a few days **after** her illness had commenced. **She** recognized in herself the approach **of** death, and asked to be **carried to** her husband's room. The **request** was met with remonstrance, but she persisted :—" You would not prevent a dying wife from going to take a last farewell of her husband?" She was put into a large easy chair, and thus carried and placed by his bedside. Many messages had passed between them during the day ; but they now met ; and it was in this brief meeting that the wonderful scene referred to occurred. *Her face and all its expressions became angelic*—just like a reflection of heaven itself;—there was a transfiguration,—an effulgence over all the features amazing to behold. Six other individuals were present, all of mature years, and this remarkable change was noticed by every one of them. Both of the sick persons were incapable of saying **much, but she uttered a** few words of blessing and of farewell. **She sat there, a heavenly brightness and joy on her face, looking like a seraph ready to take the upward flight. This lasted about twelve minutes, at the end of which time her weakness compelled** them **to remove her to her** own apartment. **When** placed **again on her** bed, she made an **audible** prayer, the breathings of which seemed not to belong to earth. Then the forecloudings of the approaching last scene overshadowed the mind ; and so continued for about twenty-four hours, when death came ; and, without a struggle, her spirit passed as if angels had gently carried it away.

The death-bed of Senator Foote (U. S. Senator from Vermont), also presents an example of the manner in which **the** thin veil between the heavenly **world and ourselves is** sometimes penetrated **by** mortal vision.

scene of the transfiguration now witnessed in the region of Cæsarea Philippi. But they can lead us only to a partial appreciation of it: for what mortal can fully understand the event or the glory of an occasion when Heaven came down and enveloped the mountain top, and *the Divinity in Christ glowed forth through his mortal frame*, while Moses and Elias stood there beside him; the veil between the two worlds withdrawn from before the apostles' vision, so that the supernatural became revealed. There "His face did shine as the sun, and his raiment was white as the light. And behold, there appeared unto them Moses and Elias talking with him." The apostles were filled with mingled awe, and fear, and delight; and the impulsive Peter, in his tumult of thought, cried out with a request, as if he could hope to make it all permanent. But such scenes belong permanently only to a world not stained with sin. A bright cloud overshadowed them; and from it proceeded a voice, "This is my beloved Son, in whom I am well pleased: hear ye him." The disciples fell prostrate, their faces to the earth, before Jehovah himself who was felt to be present in this amazing scene; fear now filling their hearts. From this overwhelming agitation, they were restored by the touch and voice of him who stands now between the terrors of the Unknown

---

The scene is thus described by a member of Congress, who was with him on the occasion.

"At seven o'clock, the dying senator expressed a desire to see once more the light of the sun in the heavens, and the capitol on which it shone and where he had so long served the people of his state and country, and where his associates were soon to assemble. They lifted him up. His eyes were already dim; and he sank back on his pillow. The words of the 23d Psalm were read and a solemn prayer delivered by one who was dearest to him of earth. He called her to his side, and folded her in his arms, asking, "Can this be death? Has it come already? Then looking with eyes of celestial radiance, and lifting up his hands, he said: 'I see it! I see it! I see the gates wide open! Beautiful! Beautiful!' And then, without a pang, he immediately expired.'"

19 *

and us, and who says still to us when prostrate, as he did to them, " Arise, and be not afraid." When they arose, and " had lifted up their eyes, they saw no man, save Jesus only." He charged them not to make these circumstances known until after his rising from the dead.[1]

CHAPTER XXVII.

DISPUTES AMONG THE APOSTLES.

ON their return to the place where the other apostles had been left these were found undergoing an examination by the Scribes, a great multitude of people also being around, who as soon as Christ was seen, hurried to him with glad salutations. Immediately a father was on his knees before him crying for compassion on his only child, a lunatic, whom he had brought to the disciples and presented in vain to be healed. But now there was hope, for the Messiah himself was there, and his power was equal to the cure. With a reproof to his hearers for their want of faith he directed the child to be brought before him, and he turned to the beseeching parent:

" If thou canst believe, all things are possible to him that believeth."

" Lord, I believe; help thou my unbelief," cried the father, with tears.

The helpless boy fell to the earth in a fit, but the Messiah took him by the hand and lifted him up, and the happy father had him quickly in his arms entirely restored.[2]

---

[1] Matt. xvii. 1–9.   [2] Mark ix. 2–9.

They left that region for Galilee, and as they travelled onward the Messiah's mind was looking forward to the painful end of the journey at Jerusalem, for he who could work miracles for the relief of all others must in that approaching frightful endurance on the cross work none for himself; and the human nature in him so mysteriously united to the Divine, had the full force of the anticipations of what was now soon to occur. Nevertheless he went steadfastly on. He tried again to prepare his disciples for what was coming, and repeated to them that he should be betrayed to his enemies and be put to death and should rise again, but they did not understand him,[1] and the only effect was a deep sorrow, in which they felt too much awed to seek relief in questioning him on the subject, though it filled their hearts.

But even in this time of sadness a most unseemly question was started among them—who should be greatest in the approaching kingdom of their Master? and here we are again reminded how little in common there was between him and them, his chosen followers, and how solitary he was in the world. Man was formed for companionship, and the kind and loving nature of Christ was peculiarly fitted for its enjoyments, but there could be little companionship for him anywhere among the Jews even among his followers themselves. In this respect he could emphatically say, "The foxes have holes, the birds of the air have nests, but the Son of man hath not where to lay his head."

On their arriving at Capernaum he called the apostles, and to his inquiry about their disputes they made no reply, but stood silent and abashed. He then took a little child, and setting him in the midst of them, he said:

"Verily I say unto you, Except ye be converted, and become as little children, ye shall not enter into the kingdom of heaven. Whosoever, therefore, shall humble himself as

---

[1] Mark ix. 30–32.

this little child, is greatest in the kingdom of heaven. * * * He that is least among you all, the same shall be greatest."

The Messiah was now about to take his final leave of Galilee, but previous to his departure he sent out from Capernaum seventy disciples to go before him "into every city and place whither he himself should come." As he returned no more to this region their mission was chiefly, it would seem, into the country east of the Jordan (Perea), where and in Jerusalem his time after this period was chiefly spent. The seventy had nearly the same directions and the same authority as the twelve on the former occasion when sent through Galilee.

He was himself now going up to Jerusalem for the Feast of Tabernacles, and was about to pass permanently from the simplicity and frankness and generous nature of the people in these rural districts to the capital and to a region of country over which its influence held sway, and was to encounter at almost every step the superciliousness and pride and captiousness of the Pharisees and Doctors and Scribes.

The Messiah chose for this journey to Jerusalem the way through Samaria; and in that country immediately occurred one of those incidents which showed the bitter hostility between its inhabitants and the Jews. He had sent messengers before him to one of their villages to make ready for his coming; but the citizens of that place when they found that he was going to Jerusalem would not receive even him, all regard and curiosity giving way before their jealousy of the rival city and people. John, the most gentle of the disciples, was enraged at this treatment, and he and James united in a request that the Messiah would allow them to call down fire from heaven to consume the place. The reply was, "Ye know not what manner of spirit ye are of. For the Son of man is not come to destroy men's lives, but to save them."

How soon were these disciples to witness far greater

indignities offered to him in that city which boasted that God had especially chosen it for himself!

They proceeded on their journey, and were entering another Samaritan town, when was heard that loud, plaintive appeal for help, now become familiar to the ears of his followers. The cry came from ten men, who stood far off; since they did not dare to approach him, the laws of that country prohibiting it; for they were lepers. But from that distance the cry rang distinctly in the ear, it was such an earnest, beseeching one:

"Jesus, Master, have mercy on us!"

That disease, so loathsome and horrible in itself, had the further horror of cutting off those afflicted with it from all relatives and from home; and it could never have the alleviations which in other cases sometimes almost make sickness feel like a luxury, so tenderly is it ministered to by friends. The leprous man could have companionship only with other horrible objects like himself; and so these ten men stood together that day, isolated from all others, and raising their piteous cry. The Jewish laws, (Levit. xiii. 43–46), said, "If the rising of the sore be white reddish, in his bald head or in his bald forehead, as the leprosy approacheth in the skin of the flesh; he is a leprous man, he is unclean: the priest shall pronounce him utterly unclean: his plague is in his head. And the leper in whom the plague is, his clothes shall be rent and his head bare, and he shall put a covering upon his upper lip, and shall cry, 'Unclean, unclean.' All the days wherein the plague shall be in him, he shall be defiled; he is unclean; and he shall dwell alone, without the court shall his habitation be."

A recent traveller in Palestine, says, "In my walks about Zion to-day, I was taken to see the village or quarter assigned to the lepers lying along the wall directly east of Zion Gate. I was unprepared for the visit, and was made positively sick by the loathsome spectacle." Meeting them also outside the city, he says, "they held up towards me their handless arms, unearthly sounds gurgled through their throats without palates—in a word, I was horrified."[1]

So, as Christ was entering this Samaritan village, how intensified was the cry of those ten men, as if all existence were centred in that moment of hope. It came from them broken, gurgling, distant, but was heard.

"Jesus, Master, have mercy on us."

The company around all turned with earnestness toward him. His disciples were Jews, and had the jealousy of Jews toward the people of this country. Would he perform his miraculous healing here, especially as they had just been rejected from one of the towns because they were of the race hated by this people and were going to Jerusalem? The disciples, not yet recovered from their indignation, felt that here would be a good opportunity, by refusing these people help, to impress upon them a lesson of hospitality to strangers travelling through their country. The villagers also were gathering, and watching to see how it would end; and there was agitation and excitement on every side; while, in the confusion incident to such curiosity, the sad cry from the lepers standing afar off was distinctly heard.

What was the result? It was to be according to the faith of the applicants: and of this faith there was to be first, an open demonstration.

"Go show yourselves unto the priests," he said to them.

They went; and in going felt themselves healed. The terrible disease had disappeared from their system; their eyes saw the newly restored flesh, each on the other and on himself; they felt the new health coursing through their veins. We might imagine them now, all aglow with gratitude, hurrying back to thank their Divine Restorer; but history gives a different account. Only one returned for

---

[1] "The Land and the Book."

this purpose: he was a Samaritan. He came, glorifying God, and fell down on his face at the Messiah's feet with expressions of thanks. The Saviour said, "Were there not ten? But where are the nine? There are not found that returned to give glory to God, save this stranger. Arise, go thy way: thy faith hath made thee whole."[1]

CHAPTER XXVIII.

JERUSALEM—FEAST OF TABERNACLES.

DURING the last of those scenes recorded in the preceding chapter, the Jews from all Palestine, and regions adjoining, and even from remote parts of the world, had been flocking towards Jerusalem. The Feast of the Tabernacles, to which they were hastening, was their most cheerful festival, the שמחה, *festivity* or *mirth*, called so by way of pre-eminence: a time of great rejoicing; all conducted in a manner and at a season to give a peculiar zest to their joy. The Passover was a season of more impressive solemnity: this feast of Tabernacles was a time more given up to mirth. Plutarch calls it a *bacchanalian season;* but there was certainly neither drunkenness nor rioting in it, though it must be confessed that there were scenes in this festival that, to a person imperfectly informed, might easily appear like the drunken orgies of Bacchus in heathen countries.

The Rabbins were accustomed to say of this feast, "The man who has not seen these festivals, does not know what a jubilee is;" and the Talmud, "Whoever hath not seen the

---

[1] Luke xvii. 11–19.

rejoicing that was upon the drawing of this water, hath never seen any rejoicing at all."[1]

It was a double festival; 1st, to commemorate the living in tents during the journeying of their forefathers from Egypt;[2] and 2d, it was a thanksgiving for the fruits of the year,[3] answering thus to *our own Thanksgiving Day.* The time corresponded to our October: the fruits and harvests had then been gathered in: a time of rest for the husbandman had come: the garners were full: hearts were ready for rejoicing: and so, at this season, Jews from all directions moved towards their great city and their far greater temple, to have a week of festivity and worship, mingling religious devotion with the outpourings of the general joy. The people all lived, during that week, in booths made of branches of trees, erected on the flat house-tops of Jerusalem, or in the country adjacent; great taste was exhibited in the construction of these booths: rains never troubled the country at this period: the habits of the people were simple, and there was no inconvenience to them in such an out-door life: it was a gathering, not of distinct families, but of the one great family of the nation; and everybody came prepared to be happy, and to give outward demonstrations of joy.

We may imagine, from our own yearly Thanksgiving-Day and the family gatherings on that occasion, what were the feelings of the Jews when the whole people old and young came up to their great national Thanksgiving, of divine institution, in which it was a duty to be joyful before God for the blessings of the year. For seven days, no one, was allowed to eat or drink or sleep outside of the booths, which on the morning of the eighth day were all removed, although still the eighth day was the chief one of the festival, for it was the last, and they believed that upon the manner in which it

---

[1] Lightfoot.   [2] Leviticus xxiii. 42–43.   [3] Ex. xxiii. 16.

was observed depended the rains and crops for the ensuing year. During the seven days supplications and sacrifices were offered for the whole world, but the solemnities of the eighth day were wholly on their own behalf.

There was a place a little below Jerusalem, probably in the valley of the Kedron, where willows were cultivated for use in this festival; for each individual was obliged to provide himself with what they called *the lulabb*, a bundle of two twigs of willows, three of myrtle, and a leaf of palm, tied together with a gold or silver or silken band, also a willow branch to lay before the altar. When they went up to the daily ceremonies in the temple they carried the *lulabb* in their right hand, and a pomecitron branch with fruit on it in the left. The children from early age were taught to sway the *lulabb*, and to join in the singing, and in their innocence and half serious gaiety they formed an interesting part of the great scenes of this festival on the temple heights. The Talmud said: " A little child as soon as he knows how to wave a bundle is bound to carry a bundle." Prepared with these the people came to the usual morning sacrifice which was at the earliest dawn, and this morning sacrifice itself had also a distinguishing feature belonging only to this feast. Wine was always a part of the daily offering; but now a priest went to the pool of Siloam at the outlet of the Tyropeon valley, and with pomp and ceremony brought water from it in a golden vessel, the trumpets sounding as he reached the great court of the temple. He proceeded up the inclined plane of the altar to where two basins were standing, one with wine; into the other he poured the water, and both fluids being then ceremoniously mixed they were poured over the morning sacrifice, the trumpets and cymbals sounding while was sung, " With joy shall ye draw water out of the wells of salvation," (Isaiah xii. 3). This part of the solemnities did not profess to be of divine institution, but had been established of old, they said, in memory of the

20

water so bountifully bestowed on their ancestors in the desert, and as the Rabbis testify was meant to be a symbol of the benefits to be some time poured out and dispensed by the Holy Spirit.[1]

The Pool of Siloam as it is now; viewed from the south-east.[2]

When the libation was finished, and the smoke of the sacrifice began to ascend, the music recommenced, and their great hymn, the Hallel, rose on the morning air from the voices of that immense throng in these greatly elevated courts of the temple. The great Hallel consisted of the cxiii. cxiv. cxv. cxvi. cxvii. and cxviii. Psalms, and when they came to the beginning of Psalm cxviii., " O give thanks," &c., the whole company waved their branches toward the four

---

[1] Bloomfield.

[2] It occupies undoubtedly the site of the ancient pool of this name, but is probably smaller. Its dimensions are fifty feet in length by from fourteen and a-half to seventeen in breadth, with a depth of eighteen and a-half feet. The water has now only a depth of three or four feet, being let off at that height by channels which conduct it to the garden below. It is supplied from sources beneath the site of the ancient temple, where seems to be a syphon which makes its flow periodical; thence it is conducted to the Fountain of the Virgin noticed in chapter xx. of this book, and thence under Ophel to this place. Its outlet is properly at the arched way in this picture, but owing to some defect in the masonry it escapes otherwise into the pool below.

quarters of the world, as they did also when they came to the "Hosanna," (or "Save now, I beseech thee, O Lord"), and again at the latter clause of the same verse, "O Lord, I beseech thee send now prosperity." The same shaking of the branch was repeated when they came to the last verse of that Psalm, "O give thanks unto the Lord, for he is good; for his mercy endureth forever," and which was the finishing of the Hallel.

When this daily sacrifice was completed then commenced the additional sacrifices peculiar to this occasion; *i. e.,* on each day fourteen lambs and a goat; on the first day also thirteen bullocks; on the second, twelve; on the third, eleven, and so diminishing till on the seventh day seven bullocks were offered. At this sacrifice hymns peculiar to it were also sung; on the first day the cv. Psalm; on the second, the xxix.; third day, the l., beginning at v. 16; fourth day, xciv., at v. 16; fifth day, xciv., at v. 8; sixth day, Ps. lxxxi., at v. 6; the seventh day, Ps. lxxxii., at v. 5; and we may very easily imagine the effect of the sound of so many thousands of voices on those temple heights, while the smoke of the sacrifices was curling upward toward the open sky. Sometimes the voices ceased, and the trumpets and cymbals were substituted, and then again the Hosannas burst forth like the voice of a great ocean during a storm.[1] Every individual was required to go round the altar with his *lulabb* each day; on the seventh day seven times.

Thus it was during the day, but in the evening a very strange scene commenced, and for this we will quote from Lightfoot, whose quaint language is so well suited to such descriptions.

"At the time when the water was brought from the pool of Siloam and poured on the altar they had not the liberty for their jollity, because of the seriousness and solemnity of the

---

[1] Lightfoot: *Temple Service.*

service then in hand; but when all the services of the day were over and night had now come, they fall to their rejoicing for that matter, which rejoicing is equally strange both for the manner and the cause. The manner was thus:

"They went in the court of the women, and there the women placed themselves upon balconies round about the court, and the men stood on the ground. There were four candlesticks or beacons of exceeding bigness and mounted on exceeding great heights overtopping the walls of the court of the 'Mountain of the House' at a great elevation. The pipe of the temple began to play, and many Levites with their instruments in great abundance, standing on the fifteen steps that went down out of the court of Israel into the court of women, and whosoever of them and of the priests were musical, either with instrument or voice, joined his music. In the meanwhile the greatest grandees of the people, as the members of the Sanhedrim, the rulers of the synagogues, doctors of schools, and those that were of the highest rank and repute for place and religion, fell a dancing, leaping, singing and capering, with torches in their hands, with all their skill and might, whilst the women and common people looked on; thus they spent the most part of the night. And the more they abased themselves (like David before the ark) in this activity, the more they thought they did commendably, and deserved praise.

"At last, far in the night, two priests standing at the gate Nicanor, do sound their trumpets; and then come down to the tenth step and sound there again; they come down into the court of the women and there sound for the third time; and so go sounding all along the court, till they come to the east of it; and there they turn themselves and look back up toward the temple and say thus, 'Our fathers who were in this place turned their backs upon the temple of the Lord, and their faces towards the east, towards the sun, but as for us we are towards him and our eyes towards him.'

" As the grandees danced, some of them would say thus, ' Blessed be thou, O my youth, which hast not shamed my old age;' and these were called ' Men of performance;' and others would say, ' Blessed be thou, O my old age,' which hast gained my youth ; these were ' Men of repentance;' and both of them would say, ' Blessed is he that hath not sinned, and he that hath sinned, and his sin is **pardoned.**'

" At length, weariness and sleepiness and satiety with their mirth, concludes the jollity, till another night. * * * This was the celebration of the feast of Tabernacles day after day, only there was this difference among the days: that on the night before the Sabbath that fell within the feast, and on the night before the eighth day, which was a holy-day, they used not their dancing, singing and rejoicing. On the eighth day they had the same solemnities with the days before, ate the pome-citrons, which they might not do before, and at night had the great rejoicing in the court of the women, and thus they concluded the feast: and therefore, this by the Evangelist is called not only the last day, but also the *great* day of the feast, because it was a holy-day, and because it was the conclusion."[1]

A very strange scene surely ; and if we now suppose ourselves on the Mount of Olives, which looked directly down upon the temple area and the whole city; upon the lighted-up booths on the tops of the houses and over the whole country around; upon the immense columns at each angle of the women's court, with the blazing fires on their summit ; and on the torches of the dancers waving to and fro, and circling about in intricate lines ; and then listen to the murmur from more than two millions of wakeful people at the festival, mingled with the sounds of musicians and singers on the temple steps, we shall have a tolerably fair idea of what this great festival of Tabernacles must have been.

"Temple Service."

The distinguished Jewish authority, Maimonides, says of this dancing: " Because it was the rejoicing for keeping the law, to which no joy can be comparable ;" and therefore, he adds, " the common people and **every** one that would were not actors in this rejoicing; **for they** neither sang nor danced," but were only spectators: **but the** actors were the **great** men of wisdom and religion.[1]

A remarkable passage occurs in the Talmud **respecting** this festival. " Rabbi Levi saith, ' Why is the name of **it** called drawing of water? Because of the drawing or pouring out of the Holy Ghost; according as it is said, With joy shall ye **draw water out of the** wells of salvation.' "

Such were the scenes at the feast **of** Tabernacles repeated day after day, **for seven days, with** the slight exceptions above noticed; **and it was evidently a** time of great hilarity, mixed with so much of a religious **character** as to give in their minds a sanction to great enjoyment. They felt it a duty to enjoy **the** present with thankfulness for the past; while also, from the solemnities of the eighth day, they might look for blessings on the coming year.

CHAPTER XXIX.

THE MESSIAH AT THE FEAST OF TABERNACLES.

" WHERE is he?"

The number of people estimated by Josephus, to be usually present at a Passover feast was, as already stated, two millions, seven hundred thousand ;[2] and we may suppose that it could not be much less on such an occasion as

---

[1] See Lightfoot—*Temple Service.*   [2] Bel. vi. 9, § 3.

this. The temple ceremonies occupied but a small portion
of their time; and great sociability must have prevailed
amid so large an assembly. We may easily suppose what
was the universal theme; and the great variety of forms in
which it was discussed.

The Messiah had not yet made his appearance there; for
such scenes as those described in our last chapter could have
had little attraction for him; and he had resisted the solici-
tations of his kinsmen in Galilee to go up early to the feast.
These last "did not believe in him;"[1] for "a prophet is not
without honor, save in his own country;" and the claims of
the Messiah must have been startling to his own connections,
as we know they were to the people generally in Nazareth.
We of our time, who know what has been the operation of
his doctrines through eighteen centuries, and who can com-
pare them with those of all other teachers, and see how pure,
how perfect, and how God-like they are; and can trace also,
the greatness of his life down to the wonderful self-sacrifice
in its close; and who also are free from the Jewish prejudices of that day, and their extravagant expectations respecting the Messiah, may wonder at the obstinate resistance to
Christ, and especially to the force of all those miracles
wrought before their eyes. But we know how the Pharisees
parried off this last; and we must remember how cramped
was the Jewish mind, how narrow their intellectual horizon,
and how enslaved by fear the largest portion of them were
to men ruling by the power of that mysterious undefinable
unwritten law; those rulers denounced by Christ as "hypocrites;" "for," he said, "ye compass sea and land to make
one proselyte; and when he is made, ye make him twofold
more the child of hell than yourselves."

At this feast were two sets of men putting the question,
"Where is he?"—the rulers, who did so openly; and the

---

[1] John vii. 5.

multitudes, who through fear of them,[1] "murmured[2] concerning Christ," giving in suppressed tones, their opinions: some saying, "He is a good man; others, 'Nay; but he deceiveth the people.'" There was among both classes an anxiety concerning him; in the rulers it was mingled with fear as to what his influence on this vast excitable multitude might become; among the people was an intense desire to decide respecting him, by what their own eyes might see. The people from Galilee brought astonishing rumors of the miracles performed in their country, very great in number, and wonderful in character, which were here detailed in low tones; the very caution used lest the rulers should hear them, only sharpening the curiosity of the hearers. Men from Decapolis, and from the region north of Galilee, also described what they had seen; and the inhabitants of Jerusalem itself could tell of the miracle at the pool of Bethesda, made more famous by the consequences which immediately ensued.

It was known that there had been a breach between Christ and their rulers, and that issue had been fully made; they seeking his life and even uniting with the hostile element in the Herodians to effect their purpose; and he denouncing them as hypocrites, "transgressors of the word of God by their traditions," and "blind leaders of the blind."[3] It seemed as if it might be extremely perilous for him to appear at the festival. Amid the hopes and fears on both sides the question was often repeated,

"Where is he?"

Suddenly, in the middle of the feast, it was reported that he was in the city, and even in the temple, teaching there. Such public places, and especially covered porticos, as in the

---

[1] John vii. 13.

[2] The word Γογγυσμός, translated murmuring, means literally a *buzzing*, very significant of their low tones in this conversation.

[3] Matt. xv. 3, 14.

case of the *stoœ* in Greece and Rome, were the favorite resort of teachers in those days; and the Messiah appears to
have immediately proceeded to the cloisters of the temple,
a place very well adapted to his purpose.

The Jewish rulers were confounded. Pharisees and
Scribes from Galilee had brought them accounts of his teachings in that region, and of the effects produced on the people there;—how these admired and followed him, and
approved his doctrines; and here he was now in their very
temple-courts, apparently about to produce there similar effects. It was a bold act,—this invasion of their own
precincts, and this placing of himself publicly before them,
both rulers and people in Jerusalem, as a teacher. And how
attentively the multitudes were listening to him! The
rulers looked out from the Sanhedrim room, and observed
among the thickly-packed masses the form of the Teacher,
his earnest impressiveness of manner, the wonderful characteristic of that Presence which seemed to belong to him; a
glow in the face, that seemed to come partly from his earnest words and the nature of his teachings, and partly from
his inner being. They saw, and were filled with both wonder and alarm. It was evident that their combinations
against his life had not frightened him into silence; and
here now he was producing effects on those vast crowds
which might render any further efforts against him dangerous to themselves. What authority had he to teach? was
a question which it seemed to be too late now to put, although this appears to have been his first teaching in Jerusalem; for the fixed attention of the multitudes, and their
lighted-up and earnest faces, appeared to be fully endorsing
his teachings, although the proceedings now were altogether
out of regular order. He had received no authorization
from their great schools, and indeed could never have received there such doctrines as he was now promulgating,—
especially when the denunciations of the Traditional Law

came from his lips. There was an originality, with a freshness and a clearness and convincing power in what he said, which were different from the mumblings and jargon of their schools; but it was all unauthorized. Surprised and confounded, the rulers could not prevent admiration from mingling with their wrath; and yet their words, as they reached his ears, implied half a sneer:—

"How knoweth this man letters, having never learned?" He answered:

"My doctrine is not mine but his that sent me:" and then he proceeded to the declaration of a truth springing from the deepest philosophy of our nature.

"If any man WILL DO the will of my Father, he *shall know* of the doctrine:" a sound philosophy, yet very little regarded by men. Our emotional nature governs us more than does our intellect. What, from the influence of our feelings, we wish to believe, we generally end with believing. Our reason is a single element: the emotions are multifarious, often unsuspected by us, and when wrong making readily-admitted apologies: they crowd around the reason, and overshadow and blind it. Therefore, when we wish to seek truth, our first effort should be to look at our hearts, and to be certain that we desire it: and most of all, ought we to be certain that we are willing to take with it also its consequences, making it *practical* as fast as it is gained. Then shall we know truth. "If any man *will do* his will, he shall know of the doctrine."

The Divine Teacher then referred to the annulling of Moses's law, notwithstanding their hypocritical professions of respect for it: for, basing their acts on such professions, they formerly (after the cure at Bethesda) "sought to slay him."

"Why do ye go about to kill me?"—The people living in Jerusalem were aware of that purpose in their rulers: but it was a new idea to strangers: and the audience in the temple cried out in astonishment, "Thou art mad: who goeth about to kill thee?" He reasoned with them then about his former healing, and about the vindictiveness shown on that occasion, adding, "Judge not according to appearance, but judge righteous judgment." It had now become a scene of excitement among those people so given to strong, outward demonstrations and to quick emotions. Some of the people of Jerusalem said: "Is not this he whom they seek to kill? But lo, he speaketh openly, and they say nothing unto him. Do the rulers know that this is the very Christ?" which remark was met immediately by objections; "We know this man whence he is: but when Christ cometh, no man knoweth whence he is."

Their objection is another example of the difficulty which truth had to encounter in Judea; for a belief was current that there was to be a two-fold manifestation of the Messiah; the first at Bethlehem, after which he would straightway

Bethlehem as it is now: viewed from the North.

disappear and be hid. Then again, he would show himself; but from what place or at what time that would be, no one knew. They believed that at his first appearance at Bethlehem, he would do nothing remarkable: in his second coming rested the hope and expectation of the nation.[1]

The Messiah met their objection, "when Christ cometh, no man knoweth whence he is," by referring to his divine origin; and now his enemies—all the while watching an opportunity—made an effort to seize on him. But in this they did not succeed, "because his hour had not yet come."

There was, however, after a while a more formal and official effort to put an end to these proceedings, and to seize upon his person. The Pharisees were informed that numbers of the people were believing on him, and saying among themselves, "When Christ cometh, will he do more miracles than these which this man doeth?" which was a logic so clear to the understanding of the multitudes, and so conclusive, that it soon became alarming in its results. The reports from the Galileans here at the feast, had spread widely among the multitudes, who were mostly country people like themselves, who did not stop to argue much, but came by a quick way to conclusions; and the effect was becoming epidemic. In a little while the public sentiment in Christ's favor might break through all those restraints of the leaders, which had kept the people in check.

This danger must be met at once: and for this purpose the power of the Sanhedrim was invoked.[2] The chief priests were also called upon for help; for here, even in the temple, and near the altar and amid the festival celebrations, had this exhibition been made of the popular feeling in his favor.

"There were several ranks of priests; all connected with

---

[1] The large building on the left in the wood-cut is the church over the reputed place of the nativity. The town is undoubtedly on the site of the ancient Bethlehem.

[2] This is clearly the inference from John vii. 45–52.

the temple. 1st. The *plebeian priests*, namely, such as were not of the common people, but wanted school education, and were not reckoned among the learned nor such as were devoted to religion. For seeing that the whole seed of Aaron was sacerdotal, and priests were not so much made as born, no wonder if some ignorant and poor were among them. Hence is that caution given, 'that an oblation be not given to a plebeian priest,' and the reason is added, ' Because whosoever giveth oblation to a plebeian priest doth all one as if he should give it to a lion, of which it may be doubted whether he will tread it under feet, or eat it or not. [These men performed offices at the altar, being instructed for such duty at the time].—2d. There were others who were called *Idiot and private priests*, who, although they were both learned and performed the public offices at the altar, yet were called *private*, because they were priests of a lower and not written order.—3d. The *written degree of priests* was four-fold, besides the degree of the high priest: 1, Heads of ephemeries or courses, which were twenty-four in number: 2, Heads of families in every course: 3, Presidents of various offices in the temple: 4, Any priests or Levites indeed, (although not in these orders), that were chosen into the chief Sanhedrim. Chief priests, therefore, here and elsewhere, where the discourse is of the Sanhedrim, were they, who, being of the priestly or Levitical stock, were chosen into that chief Senate."[1]

The chief priests and Pharisees sent officers, probably from those connected with the Sanhedrim or temple, with directions to watch for a proper opportunity to seize upon him : and from that time he was closely followed and observed ; his words were weighed by the spies ; keen eyes were constantly upon him scrutinizing his actions ; and official authority was waiting, till there should be some

---

[1] Lightfoot.

occasion when the seizure might be made without raising a tumult among the people. Matters semed to be coming to a crisis. All this time an under-current of admiration and of hearty affection among the multitudes was growing stronger every hour. He said to the people, "Yet a little while am I with you, and then I go unto him that sent me. Ye shall seek me and shall not find me, and where I am thither ye cannot come." These words perplexed both enemies and friends.

The feast lasted, strictly speaking, only seven days;[1] yet in the law there is also mention made of eight days;[2] and the eighth came gradually to be considered the greatest of all. In Josephus, (Ant. iii. 10, § 4), the eighth day, together with the first, is designated as the time of especial rest. The singing and dancing the night previous had been intermitted, as that was the beginning of this, a holy day, —the Jewish day always commencing at sunset. The booths were on this day taken down; the *lulabb* was laid aside; and the pome-citron was eaten, which could not be done on any other day. The libation of water with wine had now a more important meaning than on any other day; for on the eighth day, according to the Talmud, "Judgment is made of the waters, and God determined what rains shall be for the following year." The Talmud says, also, "Why doth the law command, saying, 'offer ye water on the feast of the Tabernacles?' The Holy, blessed God saith, 'offer ye waters before me on your feast of Tabernacles that the rains of the year may be blessed to you." "In the feast of Tabernacles it was determined concerning the waters." "Why do they call it the house of drawing? Because thence they draw the Holy Spirit."[3]

---

[1] Lev. xxiii. 34: Deut. xvi. 13.
[2] Lev. xxiii. 36: Numbers xxix. 35: see also Nehemiah viii. 18.
[3] Lightfoot.

Rains in Palestine are far more uncertain than with us, and therefore on this last great day of their feast their religious exercises took an unusually interesting form. With the deepest earnestness they raised their voices in the Hallel; with the most hearty devotion they joined in the exercises of the sacrificial offering, and particularly the one peculiar to this feast, the water-libation.

This eighth day of the feast arrived. On the morrow the crowds were to disperse, and to return to their distant homes. It had been such a festival as they had never witnessed before, one of strong excitements, of discussions among themselves respecting this Wonderful Being possessing such miraculous powers, and so interesting in his teachings. They had seen him with their own eyes, and had heard him—that face so striking from the Divinity glowing in all its lineaments, and so winning, and that voice so gentle in its modulations, mingled however so strangely with authority. They did not wish to go away only half-satisfied, and now on this last day they watched for him, and when he came listened for his words with peculiar attention and a greatly increased interest. Their feelings yearned toward him, for he had spoken to their hearts, and his words had reached those eternal longings which the soul has for an inner life, calling for it with an earnest, unceasing cry.

The first words from him this eighth morning startled all who heard him; they were such an answer to all those longings:—

"If any man thirst, let him come unto me and drink. He that believeth on me, as the Scripture hath said, out of his belly shall flow rivers of living waters."[1]

That very water of Siloam, carried now by them in a tankard and received at the altar with loud sounds of the trumpets and cymbals and peculiar rejoicings, and when poured

---

[1] John vii. 37, 33.

on with the wine in libations, accompanied by the loud Hallels of the immense multitudes, was believed by them to be significant of the pouring out of the Holy Spirit, indicative of some mighty, direct, supernatural influences; and here now that Wonderful Being, wonderful beyond all that they had ever seen or heard of called to them :

"If any man thirst let him come unto me and drink ;" and said, moreover, that those who thus came to him should be the means of allaying the thirst of others. Did not their souls thirst with a ceaseless cry to have the feeling assuaged? Every man there knew and felt this to be the case.

Many said when they heard him :

"Of a truth this is the prophet;" others, their hearts fully responding to his words,

"*This is the Christ.*" Some replied :

"Shall Christ come out of Galilee?" And in their ignorance of his birth-place they quoted against him the Scriptures which said that he ought to come from Bethlehem. Thus a disputing arose among the crowd, and there was an agitation in those temple precincts; the sacrifices at the altar continuing in the meanwhile. Some would have seized him, but the Roman garrison in Jerusalem was on these occasions particularly careful to repress tumults, and there was a lofty watch-tower at the south-east corner of Antonia from which every part of the temple courts was overlooked.[1] There was consequently no violence to him at this time.

The officers sent by the Sanhedrim to watch him and to seize him if a safe opportunity for doing so should offer,

---

[1] Jos. De Bel. v. 5, § 8. "And as the entire structure (of Antonia) resembled that of a tower, it contained also four other distinct towers at its four corners, whereof the others were but fifty cubits high, whereas that which lay upon the south-east corner was seventy cubits high, that from thence the whole temple might be viewed." For this tower see the view in chapter xxxviii. of this book.

now came and presented themselves before their superiors in session in the council chamber.

"Why have ye not brought him?" was the angry demand. They answered:

"Never man spake like this man."

With eyes flashing scorn and anger the Pharisees spoke out:—

"Are ye also deceived? Have any of the rulers or of the Pharisees believed on him? But this people who know not the law are cursed."

One voice in the Sanhedrim was raised for the purpose of checking such proceedings, rather however in expostulation with the rulers than in defence of Christ. It was that of Nicodemus, not yet bold as he afterwards became, but still not willing by silence to seemingly endorse their action.

"Doth our law judge any man before it hear him, and know what he doeth?" he asked; and the remark brought a storm of wrath upon him.

"Art thou also of Galilee? Search and look, for out of Galilee ariseth no prophet."

Their hatred led them to malign even their own best prophets and to falsify history, for Elijah was from Galilee, as was also Jonah and perhaps Nahum and Hosea.[1]

This council seems to have broken up in tumult of passion: "And every man went unto his own house."[2]

Another scene of dancing and similar festivities during that evening formed the closing event of the Feast of Tabernacles.

---

[1] Alford. [2] John vii. 11-53.

21 *

CHAPTER XXX.

BETHANY AND ROAD TO JERICHO—A PARABLE.

AWAY from the turbulence of the city.   It is very pleasant to accompany the Messiah as we may now do to
a quiet retreat in the country, and to a family of friends
whose feelings were all in harmony with his own.

Across the Kedron and directly opposite the city on the
east is the Mount of Olives, a range about two miles in
length and having three rounded summits, the central one
appearing to the eye the highest as seen from the city.   This
is 114 feet above the average height of Mount Zion and
227 above the Haram area.   This mountain with its grace-
fully curving outline is a beautiful feature in the landscape,
and the olive trees scattered over its sides are still numerous enough to justify its ancient name.   It has now scarcely
a dwelling on it, but in those former days it was perhaps
studded all over with houses and gardens, and must have
presented as looked on from the city a very charming scene.
The writer of this work has still a glow at his heart as he
remembers how, after having entered Jerusalem by night, he
early on the following morning on reaching the house-top and
looking out had directly before him this mountain, over the
middle summit of which the sun was showing its first beams
in a cloudless sky.   Nor was the view enjoyed afterward from
the summit of the mountain less exhilarating, taking in as
it did an immense extent of country, the "chatoyant tints"
of the high mountain of Moab and Ammon and Pisgah's
top, the Dead Sea, the plain of Jericho, and the verdure
marking the course of the Jordan, while the utter desolation of "the wilderness of Judea," just to the east of the

spectator, gave force by contrast to the variegated habitable country in all other directions, and especially to the valleys just on the west and to the city picturesque in itself and rich as is no other on earth in thrilling associations.

Two shorter roads cross the mountain going directly up by zigzag, while a third, the caravan road of former times as it is still, ascends slantingly along the south-eastern part, and toward its summit crosses through an opening among the rocks. This last road and this opening where a person coming from the east first gets sight of the city, are all places very dear to the Christian; for along this way the Messiah doubtless came when making his public entry into Jerusalem, and at this highest point where the view of the city opened upon him he wept over the devoted place. If we are proceeding eastward from Jerusalem by this road, then after following it around the southern end of the Mount of Olives, we descend along some spurs on the eastern side, and at about two miles from the city come to a village of about twenty houses in a dilapidated condition, but pleasantly situated, for a fountain with sparkling water gushes from the side of the hill, and olive trees abound, which Robinson describes as musical with the songs of nightingales..

The name of this place sends a gush of tender and pleasant feelings into the Christian heart; for this is Bethany, undoubtedly on the site of the town of that name in our Saviour's time. It lies in a nook on the south-east side of one of the spurs of Olivet, and a writer says of it, "the broken ground and glens [just below on the south] and 'braes' with the glimpses of the deep descent which leads to Jericho, save it from being common-place, and give to it a certain wild, sequestered, Highland character of its own. When it was well cultivated and well wooded it must have been of all the places near Jerusalem the most peaceful as well as the most picturesque."

Here was a family consisting of two sisters, Mary and

Martha, and a brother, Lazarus, hospitable, genial and kind, among whom the Messiah could find a most welcome fellow-ship in his feelings, and also companionship as far as he could have companionship on earth.   To this place he re-

Bethany as it is now; viewed from the south.[1]

tired after the harassing scenes of that last day of the festi-val; and soothing indeed must have been the quiet of the retired spot as well as the warm sympathy of this family. But such indulgence was not to be protracted, and in the morning he returned to the temple for further teaching, and "all the people came unto him." The Scribes and Phari-sees came also, bringing a case before him, which they hoped would place him in a dangerous position with regard to the Roman government, or to the people. The Mosaic law required the individual brought into his presence to be put to death: and they demanded of him a decision. If he should decide according to the ancient law, it would be as-suming a right reserved by the Roman power exclusively to

[1] This is from a stereoscopic picture, the full accuracy of which may therefore be relied on.

itself; if against the law, then the rulers would charge him before the people with trying to abrogate the Mosaic ordinances. He relieved himself from the dilemma in a manner which put the rulers themselves to confusion and shame.[1] The teachings in the temple then proceeded; but they were continually interrupted by cavils and efforts of the rulers to bring him into odium among the multitudes; and **finally** with a charge,

"**Thou art a** Samaritan and hast a devil;" **and again :—**

"We know that thou hast a devil," which charges he met fearlessly; in his reply, claiming covenant rights as inherent in himself and not received through **Abraham. He ended** with the declaration,

"Before Abraham was, I am;" on which their fury broke all bounds; and from the repairs going on in the temple area, they took up stones to stone him. He however escaped from their hands.[2]

In reading these teachings and **discussions, we must re-member the** *sententious* **nature of the language in these coun-**tries, not only in that time **but also in our day; a mode of** speaking often **very** different from **our own.**

From an occasion probably **occurring at this period, we** have one **of the most beautiful of his parables: and as his** words **were** often suggested **by the scenery about him, we** may suppose the parable **to have been delivered at** Bethany, or **near to** it; this town being just on the edge of the dreary "wilderness," which extended the whole way thence to Jericho and the Dead Sea. We remark here also that Jericho was one of the cities appropriated to Priests and Levites, and that at the times of which we are writing, 12,000 of **them** resided in **that** city. The road towards it from Bethany is thus described by an **American traveller."**

"The road beyond Bethany [eastward] continues to de-

---

[1] John viii. 2–11.   [2] John viii.

scend, though a number of ridges extend across from the
north, terminating at a valley on our right, into which our
road pretty soon declined. We followed this valley for
three hours or more in a direction nearly south-east. The
whole region is formed of limestone rock, commonly broken
and precipitous, and shooting out spurs into and athwart the
straitened way, so as to make our progress slow and laborious. We were perpetually clambering over rocks and going
down broken, precipitous declivities, which though really
productive of no other evil than delay and fatigue, often
threatened more serious dangers. A little grass [April 20],
and a few stunted trees appeared in the valley and on the
hill-sides, upon the first part of the route, just enough to
relieve this dreary region of the aspect of absolute steri-
lity which characterizes the deserts of Arabia. [He then
arrives at a fountain and the remains of a Khan, midway
between Jerusalem and Jericho. The bottom of the valley
beyond the Khan is sparingly supplied with verdure; the
mountains on either side are bare, and 'exceedingly dreary].'
At the end of perhaps an hour-and-a-half from the Khan,
we left the valley to the right hand and entered upon a region far more rugged than that through which we had previously passed. The verdure gradually diminished, till at
length not a shrub or blade of grass was visible. Still there
was less bare rock than before, nor was it of so dark a hue.
The surface of the stone was more loose and shelving, and
in many places reduced to debris. The road runs along the
edge of steep precipices and yawning gulfs, and in a few
places is overhung with the crags of the mountain. The
aspect of the whole region is peculiarly savage and dreary,
vieing in these respects, though not in overpowering grandeur, with the wilds of Sinai. The mountains seem to be
loosened from their foundations and rent to pieces by some
terrible convulsion, and then left to be scathed by the rays
of the sun, which scorches this naked land with consuming

heat.'"[1] The place is still infested with robbers, as of old.

A lawyer,—one of those persons whose business it was to explain the Mosaic ordinances, but more especially the Traditionary Law, asked the Messiah,

"Master, what shall I do to inherit eternal life?" and this dialogue followed,

"What is written in the law? how readest thou?"

"Thou shalt love the Lord thy God, with all thy heart, and with all thy soul, and with all thy strength, and with all thy might, and thy neighbor as thyself."

"Thou hast answered right: this do, and thou shalt live."

"And who is my neighbor?" said the lawyer. Jesus answered,—

"A certain man went down from Jerusalem to Jericho, and fell among thieves, which stripped him of his raiment, and wounded him, and departed, leaving him half dead. And by chance there came down a certain priest that way; and when he saw him, he passed by on the other side. And likewise a Levite, when he was at the place, came and looked on him, and passed by on the other side. But a certain Samaritan as he journeyed, came where he was; and when he saw him he had compassion on him, and went to him, and bound up his wounds, pouring in oil and wine, and set him on his own beast, and brought him to an inn, and took care of him. And on the morrow, when he departed, he took out two-pence and gave them to the host, and said unto him, 'Take care of him; and whatsoever thou spendest more, when I come again, I will repay thee.' Which now of these three, thinkest thou, was neighbor unto him that fell among the thieves?

"He that showed mercy on him."

---

[1] Dr. Olin. See also Josephus. Bel. iv. 8, § 2.

"Go and do thou likewise."[1]

The lawyer completely thwarted in his purpose, and made to condemn himself, must have winced under the application. He, an official expounder of the oral law was directed, in a manner which he could not refute, to take a Samaritan as an example, when this oral law said, "If one sees one of the Gentiles fall into the sea, he shall not fetch him up; for it is said, Thou shalt not stand up against the blow of thy neighbor. But such an one is not thy neighbor."[2]

The Messiah himself remembered the ten lepers recently cured in Samaria, of whom only one returned to show his gratitude, and that one a Samaritan.

CHAPTER XXXI.

THE MAN BORN BLIND.

IT is always an interesting spectacle when bold, simple, plain truth comes into antagonism with the cunning chicanery of men. Truth is almost sure to gain the victory, even to human apprehension; and its opposite writhes all the more under defeat, because the means producing this have been so simple.

A case of such a nature in Jerusalem, comes before us now in this history; the opponents being on one side, a street beggar; on the other, the Jewish Sanhedrim; the former single and alone, even his parents being afraid to

----

[1] Luke x. 25–37.   [2] Lightfoot.

sustain him, though conscious that he was right; the latter armed with power, and using as an instrument of terror, a new decree,—that "if any man did confess that Jesus was the Christ, he should be put out of the synagogue." There were three degrees of excommunication among the Jews: the first or slightest of which was separation from the synagogue, and a suspension of intercourse with all Jews whatsoever. It lasted thirty days; and, if the individual did not repent, the time might be doubled or tripled. The second kind of putting out of the synagogue was called the *curse.* It was pronounced with imprecations in the presence of ten men; and it so thoroughly excluded the individual from all communion whatever with his countrymen, that they were not allowed to sell him even the necessaries of life. The third degree was solemn and absolute exclusion from all intercourse and communion with any other individuals of the nation; and the criminal was left in the hands of God.[1]

The Messiah had returned from Bethany to Jerusalem, and was passing along one of its thoroughfares with his disciples when they came upon an object that might well excite commiseration—a man blind from his birth. In the disciples, however, the case gave rise to a psychological query, and they turned to the Messiah with a question which appears singular to us, but which arose out of notions more or less current at that time: "Master, who did sin, this man or his parents, that he was born blind?" The belief in metempsichosis, or previous existence of souls, was universal among the Pharisees; but as, in their opinion, the souls only of good men could be removed into other bodies, while those of bad men were subject to eternal punishment,[2] such a belief could not have given rise to this question. Lightfoot says: "It appears from this dispute that the ancient opinion of the Jews was that the infant from its first quick-

---

[1] Jahn's Archæology.   [2] Jos. Bel. ii. 8, § 14; Antiq. **xviii.** 1, § 3.

ening had some stain upon it.   And the great doctor, Judah, (compiler of the Mishna) was originally of that opinion himself."   The sweeping remark of the Pharisees in verse 24 of this chapter[1] intimates that both the man and his parents were originally guilty of sins with which they themselves could not be charged.

The Messiah replied to the disciples that the cause of his being so born was in God's own purposes for good, always wider than any individuality ; to which he added some other remarks, and then he spat on the ground and made clay with the spittle, and having anointed the eyes of the blind man he bade him go and wash in the pool of Siloam, which was at the outlet of the Tyropeon valley, and probably not far from where this incident occurred.

What did the man himself think of this?   The blind are quick-witted, and also sharp in hearing ; and his obeying so promptly the direction shows that he fully understood who was addressing him and what were his powers, and the poor man must have been trembling with the excess of hopes. He stopped not, however, for inquiry or further remarks, but stumbling in his haste, earnest, almost wild with expectation, he hurried on, reached the fountain, washed, SAW.

Could he believe it himself?   And yet there before him were objects all revealed—houses, earth, trees, sky, men— a world open all at once upon him full of its strange, moving scenes and its beautiful sights.   How often had he wondered how things looked! now he saw.   How often had he tried to imagine what color was! there were colors everywhere now, though he knew not their names.   There was the water gurgling at the fountain, with its old familiar sound ; he *saw* it now ; yonder was a mountain—Olivet, was it?   Yonder—yes, that he knew must be the temple ; yonder the bridge high in the air spanning the valley of the

---

[1] John ix.

Tyropeon. That hill and city on the left of the bridge he knew must be Zion and Jerusalem. Great, glorious, grand, all was to him beautiful, wonderful! But where was Jesus, he who had given all this blessedness to him? The man turned back again up the Tyropeon valley, and went toward the city, stumbling now even worse than before. Distant objects seemed to be close by, and he put out his hand to touch them, for his eyes had not yet learned to measure distances. He raised his foot at inequalities yards off, and brought it down, almost falling as he did so on level space. He was more uncertain and puzzled in his movements than he had ever previously been, and he went on hesitating and almost falling on the even road, yet amused at his mis-steps, and delighted at everything he saw.

But his ears, so sharp always, were listening with painful earnestness for that voice which he was sure he would recognize; he wanted to see *him.* Other voices he soon heard, and they were in loud dispute:

"Is not this he that sat and begged?" some asked.

"It is he," some remarked.

"He is like him," said others. The man said:

"I am he."

"How were thine eyes opened?"

"A man who is called Jesus made clay and anointed mine eyes, and said unto me, Go to the pool of Siloam and wash, and I went and washed and I received sight."

"Where is he?"

"I know not."

He would have been rejoiced to know, but he had at present no further opportunities for searching, for the Jewish rulers had their watchful agents about the city, and before the man could do further mischief to their cause by satisfying the curiosity of the people he was seized and led before the Sanhedrim itself.

It was the Sabbath-day when all this occurred.

The Sanhedrim were excited by what they saw and heard. The man was before them with eye-sight as good as theirs; everybody said he had been born blind. If so, it was a miracle of the clearest and most decided character, and could not be contradicted. What should they do? He had been a street beggar, and every person knew him, and knew what the extent of his affliction had been. He could not be silenced, for the fame of this event was already spreading everywhere about; they could, however, perhaps confound him by questions, and make him contradict himself, or through fear swerve off from any acknowledgment of the healer. They would try.

They asked him how he had received his sight: and he answered, as he had before done to the people in the streets.

"This man," they said, "is not of God because he keepeth not the Sabbath day:" for, some of the Rabbins expressly forbade applying saliva at all to the eyelids on the Sabbath: others allowed it in case of inflammation of the eyes.[1]

" How can a man that is a sinner do such miracles ?" said other members of their council.

Their own Sanhedrim was becoming divided. They tried him again :

" What sayest thou of him, that he hath opened thine eyes ?"

" He is a prophet," replied the bold man, bluntly and decidedly.

But there might be hopes from his parents: they might be induced, through fear of excommunication, to give the subject another character, perhaps to prevaricate, or at least be led to contradict their son. They were sent for, and made their appearance before the council. The latter asked:

---

[1] Lightfoot, *in loco.*

"Is this your son, who was born blind? how, then, doth he now see?"

"We know that this is our son, and that he was born blind: but by what means he now seeth, we know not: or who hath opened his eyes we know not: he is of age; ask him: he shall speak for himself."

The poor man looked at them. They were his parents: and, O how often, in childhood and manhood, he had desired, with most intense longing, to see their faces, to know what were their features, how they looked. He saw them now, his own father and mother, standing there; and the longings of those many years were being satisfied. He was not able, yet, to read emotion in features; but his quick ear knew, long ago, all the intonations of their voices: and he knew, at this time, only too well, what these intonations in their reply meant; and that they were basely abandoning their son to the Sanhedrim, through fear, in the very hour and joy of his recovery; leaving him to run the risk, alone, among those cunning men.

The rulers addressed him again. He was bolder now, even than before; bold in his indignation at the meanness of these rulers, who, he saw, were hoping to browbeat his parents into a contradiction of their son's words, and a denial of the greatness of his blessing; and bold, also, through determination to adhere to his true Friend of that morning, who had given him the blessing.

"Give God the praise," they said, "we know that this man is a sinner."

"Whether he be a sinner or no," he answered, "I know not. One thing I know, that whereas I was blind, now I see."

"What did he to thee? how opened he thine eyes?" They hoped ·for some stumbling or contradiction in his words. The brave, quick-witted man seems now to have been in a quiet, secret enjoyment of their dilemma. Indig-

22 *

nant that this insolent and crafty tribunal should tempt him to a falsehood, and to deny his benefactor, and to assist in the downfall—and perhaps violent death of one who had raised him to a joyous life, his contempt broke through all bounds, and threw a cutting sarcasm into his answer.

"I have told you already, and ye did not hear: wherefore would ye hear it again? will ye also be his disciples?"

"A stormy scene ensued. They saw now that he knew of Christ as one making many disciples:—how could he, the shrewd beggar, help knowing it, when the passers by at his thoroughfare had, for days, been full of talk about the Messiah? They saw that he had been playing with their ill-disguised hate and revengeful purposes towards Christ; and, losing their dignity, they broke upon him with revilings:

"Thou art his disciple; but we are Moses' disciples. We know that God spake unto Moses: as for this fellow we know not from whence he is."

He answered, as before, in assumed simplicity, but severe sarcasm:

"Why, herein is a marvellous thing that ye know not from whence he is, and yet he hath opened mine eyes. Now we know that God heareth not sinners; but if any man be a worshipper of God, and doeth his will, him he heareth. Since the world began was it not heard that any man opened the eyes of one that was born blind. If this man were not of God he could do nothing." Their reply to his logic was only a fierce invective loaded with Pharisaic assumption and scorn,

"Thou wast altogether born in sins, and dost thou teach us?" And so they drove him out of the Sanhedrim's presence.

There is a very beautiful appendage to all this; and it is in the gentleness and childlike simplicity of the brave man, when, not long afterwards, he met the Messiah himself.

His observations on the human face had not given very satisfactory results; for they had shown him angry and malignant passions at work; the cowed, timid looks of his parents; the workings of disputatious curiosity; the angry scenes of the Sanhedrim; the violence of gesture and manner, when they **drove him out.** He knew that the benevolent being, **who** had given him **the great blessing, was not** to be sought among such **men as these; but where and** when should **he see** him, and hear those well remembered tones **of** kindness again? He heard them suddenly. The Messiah had knowledge of this violence in the council chamber, and had perhaps come to look for him; and the man's eyes were, at last, fixed on the features so different from those in the Sanhedrim; and he heard the same tones that had thrilled him before. He was asked:

"Dost thou believe on the Son of God?"

"Who is he, Lord, that I may believe on him?"

"Thou hast seen him, and it is he that talketh with thee."

"Lord I believe." **And he worshipped him.**[1]

CHAPTER XXXII.

THE FEAST OF DEDICATION.

IT will be remembered that under Antiochus Epiphanes "the Illustrious," or "the Madman," (B. C. 167), the second temple at Jerusalem, built by Zerubbabel, was defiled; **the exercise of the Jewish rites of religion was forbidden; a** statue of the Olympic Jupiter was **placed on the** great

---

[1] John ix. 1–38.

altar, and sacrifices to that god were there offered by the Grecian priests. When the nationality was restored by the Maccabees, and the city was in part recovered (B. C. 165) by the brave Judas, of that race, he found shrubs and weeds growing in the courts of the temple, and a scene of complete desolation over the desecrated grounds of Moriah. With loud lamentations, and with the sounds of martial music, the Jewish people went up to the temple; and while a portion of them, with arms in their hands, kept watch on the Syrian garrison still holding the adjacent citadel, others purified the grounds, constructed a new altar, provided vessels for the temple services, and instituted, on the 25th of December,[1] the Feast of Dedication, to be continued seven days, which was ever afterwards held sacred in the Jewish calendar. The other three great feasts could be celebrated only at Jerusalem, but this might be observed at their homes. It was a time of great rejoicing; and as lights were kept burning in every house throughout the night, this festival had also the name of Phōta, or Lights.

The anniversary of this feast occurred not long after the events named in the last chapter, and one day during its continuance, as the Messiah was walking in the east cloister of the temple—Solomon's Porch—he was surrounded by the rulers coming evidently with no friendly intent. They addressed him :—

"How long dost thou worry our minds;[2] tell us plainly if thou be the Christ?"

The elements were wintry around that lofty colonnade, but no sky could be more dark and lowering than were the purposes of those men; for the city was deeply affected by the miracles of Christ, and the Pharisees were every day finding themselves more powerless among the people, while their thirst for vengeance was daily increasing. Every effort had

---

[1] Alford.   [2] Ἕως πότε τὴν ψυχὴν ἡμῶν αἴρεις.

shown how futile their anger was becoming, and worse than that how easily they might be foiled by the very singleness and simplicity of the means used for their defeat. They had tried repeatedly to entrap the Messiah, either by efforts to lead him into the intricacies of their law, or by questions intended to involve him with the government, or by placing him in situations where whatever might be his action, troubles they hoped would ensue.

" How long dost thou trouble our souls?" they said now, as with faces marked indeed with trouble they encircled him in that portico, ready for any violence that opportunity might suggest, yet feeling the strong necessity for caution; for the tower seventy-five feet high at the south-west corner of Antonia looked directly into this portico, and Roman soldiers were as in all other festival times, especially on the watch.[1]

The Messiah said in answer to their question:

" I told you, and ye believed not; the works that I do in my Father's name, they bear witness of me;" and we can imagine him looking calmly and placidly upon them as they scowled and winced at this simple and powerful logic. For the multitudes around listening to this dialogue would all remember the miracle of the man born blind and restored to sight. He added:

" But ye believe not because ye are not of my sheep, as I said unto you. My sheep hear my voice, and I know them, and they follow me; and I give unto them eternal life; and they shall never perish, neither shall any pluck them out of my hand." Then, finally, he gave the climax to their rage by declaring:

" I AND MY FATHER ARE ONE."

There were stones lying near; they seized them and threatened to stone him.

---

[1] Jos. Bel. ii. 12, § 1.

"Many good works have I showed you from my Father; for which of those works do ye stone me?" he said.

"For a good work we stone thee not, but for blasphemy, and because that thou, being a man, makest thyself God."

He made no disclaimer to this charge in his reply, but they listened, forbearing violence till he added:

"If I do not the works of my Father believe me not. But if I do, though ye believe not me, believe the works; that ye may know and believe that the Father is in me, and I in him."

Again their wrath became furious, and there was a rush in order to commit violence, but he passed safely from among them—"his time had not yet come."[1]

He crossed over the Jordan into Perea, and it is a relief, as we read his history, to find him once more away from that city of turbulence and violence and of corrupt men false in doctrine and hypocritical in life.

He was now breathing the pure country air among a people of more simple habits and more open to the truth. It will be remembered that he had some time before this, while yet at Capernaum, sent out seventy of his disciples with directions to go "to every city and place whither he himself would come." They had recently returned to him at Jerusalem, making report of their mission with joy;[2] and in his thanksgiving on that occasion we have words referring to his selection of such men:

"I thank thee, O Father, Lord of heaven and earth, that thou hast hid these things from the wise and prudent and hast revealed them unto babes; even so, Father, for so it seemed good in thy sight."[3]

Indeed, the scenes which we have just been witnessing in Jerusalem show clearly the wisdom in the Messiah's choice which excluded such men as the schools produced.

---

[1] John x. 22–39.   [2] Luke x. 1.   [3] Ibid. verse 21.

The people resorted to him in Perea, and believed on him there. They said, "John did no miracle: but all things that John spake of this man were true."[1]

CHAPTER XXXIII.

RAISING OF LAZARUS.

"I AM the resurrection and the life: he that believeth in me, though he were dead, yet shall he live: and whosoever liveth and believeth in me shall never die."

What a power there is in words!

Those words of Christ have been like symphonies over the world, ever since they were uttered; reaching the dull ear of the dying; floating about the solitary home of the mourner grieving for friends laid in the grave; meeting us, inscribed on the church-yard gate, as if heaven itself had been writing on its portals; and through all life, giving us the courage to meet calmly the fearfulness of its end.

"I am the resurrection and the life: * * * whosoever liveth and believeth in me shall never die." The history connected with those words is a very remarkable one.

The Messiah, as just narrated, had gone to Perea to deepen the instructions given there by the seventy, and for other labors in that large, and in some portions of it populous, region. He was yet, however, somewhere in the neighborhood of the Jordan, when a message from the family at Bethany reached him, with a very touching, though modest appeal :

"Lord, behold he whom thou lovest is sick."

The message did not ask him to come back ; but the sim-

---

[1] John x. 41.

ple fact of its being sent had evidently in it some kind of expectancy, either that he would come, or that he would send a healing communication, or at once speak relief. He who could open the eyes of the blind, and had cured so many in Galilee by a word,—among them the distant son of the nobleman at Capernaum,—could heal now his sick friend by a similar mandate, even if he should not come to him: he who was so ready to relieve strangers, and had stopped before the beggar at the wayside to speak words of pity and help, would not surely fail now, in the instance of those to whom he was so much attached. The message came from the sisters of Lazarus, stating the case respecting their brother in simple but affecting language:

"Lord, behold he whom thou lovest is sick."

But he sent no healing word back again: nor did he appear disposed himself to go: for he continued still two days in the same place. Such seeming abandonment in their distress, of those who had showed him hospitality so often, might very well excite wonder in the minds of the disciples. This family were among the few of his open and avowed friends, defying the edict of the Sanhedrim: but he seemed now to forsake them in their hour of pressing need. His remark, when the message from Bethany reached him, might appear to his twelve followers to have even a tinge of selfishness in it: "This sickness is not unto death, but for the glory of God, that the Son of God might be glorified thereby." They watched him anxiously; for no one could know that family at Bethany, as they did, without loving them; but still there was no message thither; no word of relief. Finally, he said:

"Our friend Lazarus is dead."

The disciples were shocked and distressed. Just so had he treated John. Was this treatment of nearest friends a sample of what they themselves might expect? They had rejoiced in his supernatural powers, and had felt that, whatever afflictions might come upon them, they had a friend in their Leader, who through the greatness of his power was equal to every extremity. But was this case, and was John's an example of his relief? He had told them that they should be persecuted for his **sake**; and had **drawn** many a dark picture of the sufferings **they** were to endure; and had called upon them **to brace themselves up** for **endurance**: what then? **To be deserted in the end? They had always** comprehended **his meaning** imperfectly. **His words had a** mystical sense **to them**, containing promises **of final victory and** rewards; but all these promises had **come** to them darkly and were but half understood. His *present* kindness, goodness, and power had been their trust; but here was a manifestation that startled them, a desertion **to** their apprehension of a beloved friend **and** a kind family: Lazarus was dead!

In the meanwhile, those sisters at Bethany had watched by the bedside of the dying man; mingling **with** their afflictions, as they saw life ebbing **away,** many a discomforting thought of him **who** might **so** easily have helped, **and** did not help. They had to keep this grief to themselves; **for** they could **not**, before their visitors and **sympathizers at** the bedside, speak **words that might seem to be disparaging** to Christ, or containing reproach: and these thoughts were all the more corroding and heavy because they had to be kept **hidden** within their **hearts. They** had listened, with painful nervousness, for quick footsteps bringing news of his coming: none came. Hope rose at every unusual sound out by the door, and died away, and rose again; and still kept flickering on, as the life, too, was flickering there, **on** that bed of pain.

All in vain :—in vain!

The blow came at last. **They had** been cherishing **a double hope, both of Christ's quick presence, and his word** of healing: all was lost. They had **now a double grief, the**

23

crushing weight from their brother's death, and also from that apparent neglect by one whom their brother and they had so much loved and trusted, and by whom he might have been, but was not, saved.

They buried the corpse in the usual manner; their friends from the village and from Jerusalem condoling with them, and giving the usual loud tokens of grief. These friends sometimes—and the sister could not help overhearing them, if indeed, the words were not spoken for their hearing—sometimes wondered why Jesus had not come or sent help; occasionally intermingling words of doubt about his power or affection, or censures for his neglect; but the sisters had to keep their own thoughts and feelings crushed down within themselves,—a very heavy weight on their already overburdened hearts.

When he had announced the death of Lazarus to the disciples he had added: "And I am glad for your sakes that I was not there, to the intent that ye may believe; nevertheless let us go unto him."

Thomas, referring doubtless to the late attempt at Jerusalem to stone him, and to his own predictions about his approaching death, said to the other disciples, "Let us also go that we may die with him." They now proceeded toward Bethany; by slow stages, however, for they were four days getting to that town, although the distance was not very great.

Their journey was in the winter time,[1] and lay across that desolate region of the Wilderness of Judea, always gloomy, but doubly so at this season of the year. As the apostles followed the Messiah over the bleak, cold waste they had time for many reflections, and their reflections might well be of a sombre kind, corresponding to the scenes around. They had left home, occupations, domestic comforts, in order to follow this new Master, proclaimed by John to be the Son

---

[1] Just after the Feast of Dedication.

of God. Bright visions of earthly glory and power had been flashing before them, but not one of these had ever yet been realized. On the contrary, they had been scoffed at by the rulers at **Jerusalem,** and their Master himself was near being stoned **in** the very temple by the agents of the Sanhedrim. **He** had miraculous powers undoubtedly, but **he** never exercised them **for** any aggrandizement of himself and followers, as may have **been their chief expectations in** leaving all to follow him. He had just been telling them what they might expect **in future. Honors, power, glory,** rank? No, but stripes, persecutions, hatred, and death by violence. He had promised them comfort from on high, and had given assurance of his help; but here was Lazarus, the beloved friend, neglected in his need and now dead. What, as respected themselves in the dreary prospect of the future?—more dreary far than this utter desolation of nature around them, the crumbling, chalky cliffs, the shelterless wastes, the sharp, biting winds, the wintry skies, frowning down on the wide, bleak scene below.

They drew their garments around them, their hearts more gloomy than the skies or the wastes of the wilderness; and so they travelled over those **long miles, till at last they came in sight of Bethany, no cheerful greeting however awaiting** them **now as in the former times.**

The **Messiah did not enter the town at** once, but remained on its outskirts; intelligence, however, was immediately carried to Martha, one of the sisters, that he had come. She hurried out, and that deep additional grief as of a felt neglect broke out before him:

"Lord, if thou hadst been here my brother had not died." She added, "But I know, that even now, whatsoever thou wilt ask of God, God **will give it** thee." He said:

"**Thy** brother shall rise again;" and she replied:

"I know that he shall rise again in the resurrection at the last day."

"*I am the resurrection and the life;* he that believeth in me, though he were dead, yet shall he live; and whosoever liveth and believeth in me shall never die. Believest thou this?"

"Yea, Lord; I believe that thou art the Christ, the Son of God, which should come into the world."

Leaving him there she hurried back to her sister Mary with the news:

"The Master is come and calleth for thee."

The lamentation on such occasions lasted eight days, and there were many mourners and sympathizers in the house, who seeing Mary rise hastily and go out followed her, saying:—

"She goeth unto the grave to weep there."

Hurrying on, the whole company of visitors came immediately in front of the Messiah, and found Mary at his feet, where she also had let out her bitter grief in the same cry as that of Martha.

"Lord, if thou hadst been here my brother had not died."

The company around joined their weeping with hers. The Messiah was convulsed with strong emotions in his deep sympathies with human griefs, for this scene was but a sample of what is ever occurring in our world. He asked:

"Where have ye laid him?"

"Lord, come and see."

"Jesus wept."

"Behold," said the company, "how he loved him." Some of them asked:

"Could not this man, which opened the eyes of the blind, have caused that even this man should not have died?"

Again as they were advancing toward the tomb came over him that convulsion of grief. There could be no longer a doubt in the mind of any one, of his affection for Lazarus, and of his deep sympathies in the distress before him; and the feelings of the sisters, if any doubts had crept into them,

were fully satisfied. In silence they reached presently the
place where the body had been interred—a cave with a stone
in front closing the entrance. The mourners were thinking
of the gloom and desolation within, the horror of that abandonment **by the** world to corruption and the worm, when
the silence was broken by Christ's ordering the stone to be
taken **away.** Martha interposed **a remonstrance that by this**
time the body must be offensive, **for it had now been there**
four days; but he replied:

"Said I not unto thee, that if **thou wouldest believe, thou**
shouldest see the glory of God?"

The scene changed immediately, for now every one supposed that there was some strange demonstration at hand.
The solemnity of mourning and the wailing cries ceased,
crowds pressed forward, a low murmur of voices went among
them: "What was meant? Corruption had advanced in
the body, death's work had been fully sealed by decay, all
power now seemed to be in vain. What would he attempt?"
The mourners at Bethany, from Jerusalem, seemed to have
been from the higher classes,[1] and strange feelings were
at work in their hearts, some of **these not** friendly to Christ.
But curiosity **was uppermost.**

By this time the stone had been rolled away. **They could**
see within where the dim light half revealed the scene in
which **death held his fearful rule;** the silence and gloom all
made more impressive by **the deeply** earnest life-scene at the
mouth of the cave. For solemnity had given place to intense curiosity, and the agitated faces of the crowd showed the
fulness of their emotions; every lineament drawn into the
utmost tension of expectancy. The company tried to read
in the face of the Messiah his intentions, or they peered into
the entrance of the tomb, all so quiet and death-like there.

---

[1] See John xi. 31, 33, 36 and 45, in connection with John's distinction
between "the Jews" and "the people," in vii. 12, 13.

23 *

Christ's features still showed the marks of his recent strong emotions, but his face, though sad in its deep sympathies, had yet on it the grandeur of power and command.

The first commotion from this expectancy ceased, and was succeeded by a painful silence among the crowd. They gazed on Christ; and when his lips now opened, their hearts throbbed as if about to burst in their emotion. But it was not as they expected. It was in prayer.

"Father, I thank thee that thou hast heard me. And I know that thou hearest me always: but because of the people which stand by I said it, that they may believe that thou hast sent me."

Turning then to the grave, he said in a loud voice,—

" Lazarus, come forth !"

There was a sound in the cave, where all had just been in that stillness of death ; a rustling, as of a movement there ; a further noise of motion ; and Lazarus presently stood before the gazing, excited, frightened, shrinking throng; his body still swathed, as customary with the dead, and a napkin bound over his face. This was removed ; and the features, though shrunken and emaciated by the disease, *were full of life. The sisters had their loved brother again !*

The feelings of the crowd had been worked up to such a pitch of tension that it seemed as if their nature could scarcely have stood the trial of that scene much longer ; but now they breathed freely again, and their full hearts found vent, some in tones of joy, some in praises and thanksgivings, and in congratulations to the family and to Lazarus himself. Some of them turned wondering, glad, and believing eyes on the Messiah himself, and received full faith in him into their own hearts, with a reverence and affection that filled them with new and thrilling joys. Some went straight to the Pharisees to tell them what had been done.

In Jerusalem there was a commotion in consequence. The news of the miracle, the most wonderful that could be performed, spread rapidly over the city; and the members of the Sanhedrim were called together, much puzzled, and now greatly alarmed.

"What do we?" or, "What shall we do?" they said; "for this man doeth many miracles. If we let him thus alone, all men will believe on him; and the Romans will come and take away both our place and nation."

But Caiaphas, then high priest, relieved them from their dilemma by declaring authoritatively:

"Ye know nothing at all, nor consider that it is expedient that one man should die for the people, and that the whole nation perish not."

They took him at his word, prophetic and not fully understood even by himself; and from that day forth "they took council together for to put him to death."[1] They believed that Christ or themselves must perish: and the manner in which his fame was spreading, and the astounding nature of his miracles gave them, now, but a little time for choice.

CHAPTER XXXIV.

IN EPHRAIM AND PEREA.

THE site of Ephraim, the city to which the Messiah retired with his disciples after raising Lazarus, and the determination of the Sanhedrim in consequence,[2] is not fully known at present, but is supposed to have been where el-Taiyibeh is now situated. This is a town twenty miles

---

[1] John xi. 1–53.   [2] John xi. 54.

N. N. East of Jerusalem, and on such a lofty eminence as to overlook portions of the wilderness of Judea, adjacent to it on the east, and also the valley of the Jordan, with part of Perea beyond the river. From this he made visits to the neighboring country, and also extensive journeys through Perea; but there is some obscurity attending this part of our Saviour's life. Doubtless it was active; and critics place, during these few months, the healing of the infirm woman in a synagogue, exciting the indignation of the rulers of that place of worship, because it was done on their Sabbath-day.[1] On another occasion he was dining with a Pharisee on the Sabbath, when a similar case occurred. The hospitalities of the house were no safeguard against the machinations of his enemies, and "they watched him."[2] A man afflicted with dropsy was brought there, perhaps in order to produce results on which the Pharisees and lawyers who were also guests, might bring against him a charge of violating the Sabbath. He knew their thoughts, and said, "Is it lawful to heal on the Sabbath day?" They considered it best to be silent; and taking the man, he healed him, and sent him away; saying to the company, in the same strain with which he had recently silenced the rulers in the synagogue: "Which of you shall have an ass or an ox fallen into a pit and will not straightway pull him out on the Sabbath-day?"[3] The people rejoiced at "the glorious things done by him."

The Messiah observed the jealous eagerness of the guests to have the places of highest honor at the feast; and he gave them on this occasion some admonitions on the subject, ending with the declaration, "For whosoever exalteth himself shall be abased; and he that humbleth himself shall be exalted." Then, turning to his host, he added, in a similar strain:

"When thou makest a dinner or a supper, call not thy

---

[1] Luke xiii. 10–17.   [2] Luke xiv. 1.   [3] Luke xiv. 5.

friends, nor thy brethren, neither thy kinsmen, nor thy rich neighbors; lest they also bid thee again and a recompense be made thee. But when thou makest a feast, call the poor, the maimed, the lame, and the blind; and thou shalt be blessed; for they cannot recompense thee; for thou shalt be recompensed at the resurrection of the just."

We have next, in these journeyings, a scene altogether characteristic; and with it some parables, which have ever since been food to the souls of men wherever they have been heard.

We are told, "Then drew near unto him all the publicans and sinners for to hear him. And the Pharisees and Scribes murmured, saying, This man receiveth sinners and eateth with them." The Jewish Rabbis stalked with a lordly step among those of inferior degree; they felt it necessary to sustain their reputed sanctity by a distance of manner, and by the exclusiveness of caste: but it was not so with Christ.

Therefore we may readily imagine with what feelings of attachment, as well as of wonder, the multitudes followed him; gazed upon those features so divine in their expression; felt attracted by that Presence which seemed not to be of earth, not awed into a fear of approaching; and listened to his words, so different in their meaning, and in the tone in which they were uttered, from anything else which they had ever before heard.

We also who have followed him through so many scenes where angry passions were raging tumultuously about him, may find it a relief to sit down now and listen quietly to his blessed words.

"What man of you," he said, "having an hundred sheep, if he lose one of them, doth not leave the ninety and nine in the wilderness, and go after that which is lost, until he find it? And when he hath found it, he layeth it on his shoulders, rejoicing. And when he cometh home, he calleth together his friends and neighbors, saying unto them, Re-

joice with me; for I have found my sheep which was lost.
I say unto you, that likewise joy shall be in heaven over
one sinner that repenteth, more than over ninety and nine
just persons, which need no repentance.

"Either what woman having ten pieces of silver, if she
lose one piece, doth not light a candle, and sweep the house,
and seek diligently till she find it? And when she hath
found it, she calleth her friends and her neighbors together,
saying, Rejoice with me; for I have found the piece which I
had lost. Likewise, I say unto you, there is joy in the presence of the angels of God over one sinner that repenteth.

"And he said, A certain man had two sons; and the
younger of them said to his father, Father, give me the
portion of goods that falleth to me. And he divided unto
them his living. And not many days after, the younger son
gathered all together, and took his journey into a far country,
and there wasted his substance with riotous living. And
when he had spent all, there arose a mighty famine in that
land; and he began to be in want. And he went and joined
himself to a citizen of that country; and he sent him into
his fields to feed swine. And he would fain have filled his
belly with the husks[1] that the swine did eat; and no man
gave unto him. And when he came to himself, he said,
How many hired servants of my father's have bread enough
and to spare, and I perish with hunger! I will arise and
go to my father, and will say unto him, Father, I have

---

[1] It is much to be regretted that in our English version of the Scriptures, this word (κεράτιων) is thus translated. It should have been *pods*,
and refers to the fruit of the *carob*, a tree frequently to be seen in those
countries. In Cyprus there are large orchards of them, and the fruit is
there fed largely to the swine. It grows in pods from six to ten inches
in length, resembling those of our honey-locust, lined inside with a ge-
latinous substance. The tree (*ceratonia siliqua* of Linnæus) is an ever-
green, and resembles our apple-trees, though more bushy and thick-set
and with longer leaves, of darker green: in Cyprus it produces very
abundantly, but through Palestine in smaller quantities.

sinned against heaven, and before thee, and am no more worthy to be called thy son : make me as one of thy hired servants. And he arose, and came to his father. But when he was yet a great way off, his father saw him, and had compassion, and ran, and fell on his neck, and kissed him. And the son said unto him, Father, I have sinned against heaven, and in thy sight, and am no more worthy to be called thy son. But the father said to his servants, Bring forth the best robe, and put it on him ; and put a ring on his hand, and shoes on his feet : and bring hither the fatted calf, and kill it ; and let us eat, and be merry : for this my son was dead, and is alive again ; he was lost, and is found. And they began to be merry. Now his elder son was in the field : and as he came and drew nigh to the house, he heard music and dancing. And he called one of the servants, and asked what these things meant. And he said unto him, Thy brother is come ; and thy father hath killed the fatted calf, because he hath received him safe and sound. And he was angry, and would not go in : therefore came his father out, and entreated him. And he answering said to his father, Lo, these many years do I serve thee, neither transgressed I at any time thy commandment : and yet thou never gavest me a kid, that I might make merry with my friends : but as soon as this thy son was come, which hath devoured thy living with harlots, thou hast killed for him the fatted calf. And he said unto him, Son, thou art ever with me, and all that I have is thine. It was meet that we should make merry, and be glad ; for this thy brother was dead, and is alive again ; and was lost, and is found." The whole of this beautiful parable has individual, personal application; but probably, at the close of it, we are to understand the Jewish feeling at the incoming of the Gentiles.

This period during the Messiah's last retirement from Jerusalem—spent probably chiefly in Perea, in order to deepen the instructions by the seventy—abounds in parables and practical admonitions; among the former, that of the Rich Man and Lazarus, and also one showing to every person who feels himself to be a lost sinner, how he must approach to God.

"Two men went up into the temple to pray: the one a Pharisee, the other a publican. The Pharisee stood and prayed thus within himself, God, I thank thee that I am not as other men are, extortioners, unjust, or even as this publican. I fast twice in a week, I give tithes of all I possess. And the publican, standing afar off, would not lift up so much as his eyes unto heaven, but smote upon his breast, saying, God be merciful to me a sinner. I tell you, this man went down to his house justified rather than the other; for every one that exalteth himself shall be abased: and he that humbleth himself shall be exalted."

A scene occurred during this visit to Perea, which painters have often endeavored to exhibit on canvass, but which is far beyond the powers of art to reach. It is easy to portray man in the coarser passions, and grosser exhibitions of his nature: but the more any individual rises into the true heaven-like nobility of soul; and the grand thoughts and great emotions of such nobility show through the eyes and take expression on the face, the more the act of copying verges upon the impossible. Who then can paint the Messiah, in any scene, but especially in that to which we now refer?

It was that of his receiving the little children brought to him in order that "he might put his hands on them and pray." His disciples rebuked those who brought them, but he checked them:

"Suffer the little children to come unto me and forbid them not; for of such is the kingdom of God. Verily I say unto you, whosoever shall not receive the kingdom of God as a little child, he shall not enter therein."

He took them up in his arms and put his hands on them and blessed them.[1]

His kindly, genial feeling toward children, and the manner in which he attracted them toward himself, form one of the most pleasing characteristics of his ministry on earth. Often we are lost in wonder, and often we are awed by the incidents of this ministry, but there is a charm to all our finer feelings of admiration and love as we observe the children clustering about his knees, and see from all those scenes how strong must have been the sympathy in them toward him and in him toward them. He speaks of their likeness to the kingdom of heaven; he tells us that unless we become humble like a child, have its full, unquestioning love and confidence, but in our case toward God, the humble yielding up of ourselves to Him, as children give themselves into their parents' arms, we cannot see the kingdom of God. The oldest of us are indeed scarcely more than infants in the wide stretch of our existence.

The greatest men are more frequently than otherwise noted for a childlike simplicity of manners, and Coleridge says, "Men of true genius give themselves up to the first simple impressions of common things. They are content to wonder and smile and admire, just as they did when they were children; it is the opening of the heart to all sweet influences."

One of the most beautiful things in the world is a person mature in years, but still keeping the heart fresh as in early life. Individuals may sometimes be seen even of advanced age, but with feelings all genial and kind and responsive, in their heart-life never growing old. But such persons are rare. The writer of this work has had the happiness to number among his intimate friends one of this class, a person (lately deceased) of the highest scientific reputation

---

[1] Matt. xix. 13–15; Mark x. 13–16.

24

abroad as well as at home, but more remarkable still for carrying the bloom and freshness of life even beyond his eightieth year. He loved children, and they always loved him.

CHAPTER XXXV.

JERICHO.

A STRANGER travelling in the times of our Saviour, eastwardly from Bethany along the high-road already described, would, after five or six hours spent in crossing that dreary Wilderness of Judea, be then startled by a view as if some sudden enchantment had operated upon his sight. Standing on a hill-top, all around him as bare as barrenness itself can be, he would now look directly down on one of the most verdant and most perfectly beautiful spots on the face of the globe, a mass of deepest and thickest verdure, a garden-like place twelve miles or more in length by seven in width, all in the highest cultivation; palms, the most beautiful and graceful of trees ever seen in any country, waving their feathery tops as in groups or singly all over the landscape they rose high above other trees of great variety and beauty; a large city also with signs of wealth about it, palaces, a castle for defence, a hippodrome, an amphitheatre, villages and scattered dwellings amid the unbroken garden, fountains and rivulets gleaming in the sunshine, a river meandering along the farther edge of this vast plain, beyond the river a narrow plain backed with a range of lofty mountains, and on the right a lake or sea stretching on till hid by some mountain spurs.

The plain was that of Jericho; the city was one called by the same name; the river, the Jordan; the wide expanse of water, the Dead Sea; the mountains on the east, the range of Nebo, Moses' place of mysterious burial by unseen hands.

Even now, although almost entirely forsaken and lying waste, this plain of Jericho still breaks most agreeably on the traveller's eyes, so long blinded by the glare from the white hills of the Wilderness. What then must it have been in those days we are speaking of when Jericho was among Jewish cities exceeded in size only by Jerusalem, and when the plain was the pride and boast of all the nation for its fertility, its extraordinary productions, and its climate (called "Egyptian") seeming in temperature as if some choice spot of an intertropical country with its heat had been taken up and set down here in a region entirely different! This tropical nature of the climate made the place a favorite retreat in winter for those who might wish to escape from the bleakness of the "Hill Country" of Judea, and of the capital itself.

The conformation of the ground here is singular. It looks as if an immense region had been scooped out of the general natural elevation in that country, making room for a great plain, for a sea, and for a river, all sunk down to an unnatural depth. The Dead Sea, to which the southern end of this plain extends, has its surface 1312 feet below that of the Mediterranean,[1] and therefore a traveller coming from the "Hill Country" of Jerusalem, and the equally elevated grounds of the "Wilderness," seems here to descend into a chasm in the earth, which indeed is really the case. Yet in this chasm flows the Jordan to discharge itself here into that sluggish lake; and the plain of Jericho which at its southern end borders on the Dead Sea, has but a small elevation above the stream. Travelling on this plain toward the river we

---

[1] Stanley's Sinai and Palestine.

come, on approaching it, to a descent of fifty or sixty feet; then there is again a level for a short space, and then about six feet below is the Jordan fringed with willows and rushes, its width here from eighty to a hundred feet, its depth ten or twelve, and its current very strong.[1]

The great depth of this plain with the reflection of the sun upon it from the bare surrounding hills, will account for its tropical growth of plants and trees. The palm grew here in such luxuriance that in the days of Moses (Deut. xxxiv. 3), Jericho was already designated as the "city of palm trees." Josephus speaks of the palms in his day, as being "of many sorts different from each other in taste and name;" and adds: "The better sort of them yield an excellent kind of honey, not much inferior in sweetness to other honey. This country will produce honey from bees: it also bears the balsam, which is the most precious of all the fruits in that place; cypress trees also, and those that bear the myro-balsam; so that he who should pronounce this place to be divine, would not be mistaken, wherein is such plenty of trees produced as are very rare and of the most excellent sort. And indeed, if we speak of those other fruits, it will not be easy to light on any climate on the habitable earth, that can well be compared to it,—what is here sown comes up in such clusters: the cause of which seems to me to be the warmth of the air, and the fertility of the waters; the warmth calling forth the sprouts and making them spread, and the moisture making every one of them take root firmly, and supply that virtue which it stands in need of in summer time."[2] He adds: "The ambient air is here, also, of so good a temperature, that the people of the country are clothed in linen only, even when snow covers the rest of Judea."

Herod the Great had built there a palace for himself,

---

[1] Robinson.　　　　[2] Bel. iv. 8, § 3.

which was afterwards repaired and ornamented with great splendor by Archelaus: also an amphitheatre and a hippodrome, and on a spur of mountain overlooking the city, a citadel, and in it a very fine and strong building dedicated to his mother, and called Cypros.[1]

This hippodrome came by-and-by, to have a strange history connected with it, one of the most singular in all the records of purposed crime. For Herod, when that dreadful disease which ended his life was growing upon him, and he found that he must die, determined that there should be, by compulsion, a general mourning throughout Judea at his death. He ordered the principal men of the Jewish nation to assemble at Jericho: and when they had come, had them shut up in the hippodrome. He now sent for his sister and her husband, and laid before them his plan, which was that, at his decease, his soldiers should be let loose upon these men, and all of them should be put to death, in order that "the whole nation should mourn from their very soul, which otherwise would be done in sport and mockery only. So" continues Josephus, "he deplored his condition with tears in his eyes, and obtested them by the kindness owed from them as his kindred, and by the faith they owed to God, and begged of them that they would not hinder him of this honorable mourning at his funeral. So they promised him not to transgress his commands."[2] His orders, however, through the mercy of the intended executioners, were not carried into effect, which Josephus says, was considered as a great "benefit" by the nation.

It is difficult to determine the northern limits of the plain of Jericho; but it is about twelve miles from north to south, and seven in width.

The soil is described by Robinson as of extreme fertility, which was in those ancient times assisted widely by large

---

[1] Bel. i. 2, § 9.   [2] Antq. xvii. 6, § 5.

24 *

and copious fountains, most of which still remain. About
four miles from the Jordan, is the fountain called now *Ain
Hagila,* three-and-a-half feet deep and of purest water,
sending forth a stream which waters the whole plain below.[1]
To the northwest of this, and also in the plain, is *Ain es
Sultan,* bursting forth from the foot of a group of mounds
which probably designate the site of the Jericho of Joshua's
time, which seems after its destruction at that period never
to have been rebuilt. This gives a supply of sweet water
"which runs off through the plain in a stream twenty feet
wide, and from eighteen inches to two feet deep, and afterwards divides into many little rivulets,"[2] used for irrigation :
and three miles northwest from this, is the still larger fountain of *Duk,* with a stream sufficient in volume to have formerly turned mills, ruins of which are now on its banks.[3]
In addition to this, there have been lately discovered portions of an immense reservoir, formed by damming up the
waters of a valley (*Wady Kelt*) having its outlet into the
plain on its western side, near the opening of which valley
is supposed to have stood the Jericho of our Saviour's time.[4]
Of the numerous artificial channels, elaborately constructed
for the distribution of all these waters, there are still extensive remains.

Bordering northwardly on the Wady Kelt, and just over
this supposed site of the ancient city, is the Mount Quarantana, standing out quite distinct from all the other bare
hills, which, by their semi-circular sweep towards the west
make room for this plain.

To a person standing on the plain in the morning, and
looking southwardly, a heavy fog in that direction usually
shuts out all objects from the sight ; but, as the sun gets
higher in the sky, the mists roll heavily away, and that

---

[1] Robinson.   [2] Durbin's Observations in the East.
[3] Robinson.   [4] Ibid.

strange phenomenon, the Dead Sea, lies all exposed. The Jordan pours its waters into this sea, and there they are lost; there is no outlet to it, no life in it: every living thing that enters it dies; the wind sometimes ruffles the water, but the sullen, lead-like waves fall without any glad murmur upon the shore, and the surface soon subsides again to its dull appearance as of some immovable molten substance. When earthquakes shake the country around, there come up, from the depths of this sea, huge masses of asphaltum which float towards the shore, as if they might be dark messages of woe from the cities sunk beneath. A fruit growing by this sea, though fair to the eye, is found when bitten into, to be composed of a film for the exterior, inside of which are only dry filaments and dust. An adventurous traveller some years ago, launched a boat upon this sea, determined on explorations: he was found a few days afterwards, on its banks, gasping and exhausted; was taken to Jerusalem, but scarcely lived to reach the city; the memory of what he saw perishing also with him. A party of our own countrymen afterwards made the attempt, and lived through it: but one, the bravest and the best, came from it drooping and ill, and died immediately afterwards at Beyrut, in a vain attempt to reach his home. Near the southern end of the sea, the awe-struck visitors to its shores will find a hill entirely of salt; and will think of the strange circumstance attending Lot's family in the destruction which once came over this place.

The climate of the plain of Jericho is, in summer, insufferably hot, made more trying by a sight of the snow-clad summit of Hermon looming up in the clear atmosphere, and distinctly visible, although 100 miles to the north. East of the Jordan, at this spot, is a plain about three miles wide, immediately beyond which rises the vast range of Mount Nebo; and both that mountain, and the plain between it and the river, had associations of absorbing interest in the Jewish mind. For, over this range, the immense hosts of their forefathers had poured down, and there on that plain they had rested, after their journey from the place of bondage; their wanderings of forty years, concluded now: and on that high, sky-line of Nebo, Moses had stood, forbidden by the Almighty to go further; and there he had taken his view of the Promised Land.   How attentively had he gazed over the whole region; his vision extending to the Mediterranean whose gleaming waters were fully in sight; to the sands of Arabia spread out far to the south; to the snowy Hermon on the north :—between them a fair, pleasant country,—but which he was not to enter.

This great leader and lawgiver—one of those men mentally and morally of colossal proportions, whom earth but rarely produces, who had spoken with God on Sinai, was forbidden to lead them further; and for an incident which must have risen up in the Jewish memory, at this time of the ministry of Christ, with peculiar force.   One rash word spoken in anger had caused this exclusion of Moses from the promised possession; and this great range of Nebo, the barrier which he might not pass, was forever to the Jewish mind a remembrancer of God's determination that no human being should ever dare to invade any divine right.

On one occasion during that long journey through the wilderness of Arabia, the people had been murmuring for water; and Moses and Aaron were told by Jehovah to strike with their rod a certain rock, whence water would then flow.   They proceeded to the act, but gave not God the glory.   "Hear now, ye rebels; must we fetch you water out of this rock?   *   *   And the Lord said unto Moses and Aaron, Because ye believed me not, to sanctify me in the eyes of the children of Israel, therefore ye shall not bring this congregation into the land which I have promised

them."[1] Aaron was buried, during the long journey, on
Mount Hor; and here, on Nebo, the steps of Moses were
stayed; and there he died and was buried; and that lofty
mountain range before Jericho,—so strangely like an even
wall or barrier built far up into the sky—told, and to the
last will tell, of God's isolation in his Divine majesty and
power. No man dare ever say WE before him in that
greatness of his glory, or in the exercise of aught even of
his communicated power.

Yet here was one. He had just said, "I and my Father
are one." He had repeatedly asserted prerogatives belonging only to God: the power to forgive sins; the supreme
seat in the great judgment to come, when all the world
would be gathered before him, and he be seated in the glory,
and power, and dominion belonging to Jehovah: when
charged with making himself equal with God, he had
not denied it; and he was at this time at the Jordan, on his
way to Jerusalem, where his entry into the city would be a
triumphal one, and where the immense crowd attending and
meeting him on the way would shout to him "Hosanna,"
that is, "Save, Lord, we beseech thee;" "Hosanna in the
highest;" an invocation given only to God, but which was
there to be addressed to Jesus, without reproof or check
from him.

And even here in Jericho, with Nebo looking down upon
him, would be performed by him one of the greatest of
those miraculous acts, to which he was always appealing as
confirmation of the justness of his claims.

God only can perform a miracle. That is, only He who
has established nature's laws as irrevocable, can reverse them;
and here now, by that spot which Moses could not pass,
because he had on one occasion not sanctified God, here

---

[1] Numbers xx. 10–12.

Jehovah was going to establish, by his own act, the claims of one always asserting equality with God.

CHAPTER XXXVI.

THE MESSIAH AT JERICHO: BLIND MEN HEALED.

THE Messiah was now on his way once more toward Jerusalem. His disciples, on a former occasion, when he was about to go to Bethany in order to restore Lazarus, and had declared to them his intention of going into Judea, had said, in alarm, "Master, the Jews of late sought to stone thee, and goest thou thither again?"[1] That subsequent miracle at Bethany had produced in the rulers a more deliberate and determined purpose to put him to death;[2] and now, when he indicated his intention of proceeding to Jerusalem, his followers showed both amazement and fear.[3] Their apprehensions as they followed him in Perea, on the road toward Jerusalem, took a more gloomy cast from his own words on the way; for he began here to repeat what he had before intimated of the closing scenes of his ministry, only more definitely and more clearly, and with a declaration that these were near at hand. "Behold, we go up to Jerusalem; and the Son of man shall be delivered unto the chief priests, and unto the Scribes; and they shall condemn him to death, and shall deliver him to the Gentiles; and they shall mock him, and scourge him, and spit upon him, and shall kill him; and the third day he shall rise again."

The journey, therefore, along the roads of Perea, was a

---

[1] John xi. 8.   [2] Ib. verse 53.   [3] Mark x. 32.

sad one. Dim as were the apprehensions of his disciples respecting the nature of his kingdom, they still understood language so unmistakable as this; and saw that they were about to lose him, who had so long been their leader, and teacher, and their constant friend. Much there had been about him which they had tried in vain to comprehend; but his kindness to them, even among the strange enigmas of his ministry that had so often puzzled them, had been uniform; and even when he had observed occasion to reprove them, it had been done with such gentleness as to strengthen their attachment and love. One exception there was in this feeling of affection toward him, but that was confined to a single individual and was not yet made clearly manifest. In following him, they had often been thrown into the society of opposers; and sometimes they had been made to feel the secret force of hostility when people were backward in manifesting it towards himself. Questions innumerable concerning him had been propounded to them, often such as they were unable to answer, frequently on subjects greatly puzzling to their own minds. They were Jews still, only half enlightened by all his teachings; for the Jewish mind seemed to need a miracle to break through the old incrustations which enveloped it: but their feelings were truer than their intellects; and in their hearts, they had appreciated that grandeur in the character of Christ,—that true greatness, which could afford to be humble; the wonderful power, not in his teachings only, and his miracles, but in his gentleness and love to all, and especially to themselves.

Respecting his kingdom, promised by the Baptist, sometimes alluded to by himself, they had heard many disputations among his friends and enemies, and in these they had often shared. Their interest in this subject was strong and personal. Ambition had its power over their hearts; and even during this sad journeying towards what their Master had declared would to him end presently in sufferings and shame and an ignominious death, James and John, aided by their mother, preferred a request, that they might have the preference (sit next to him) in his glory, respecting which, however, their ideas must have been very indistinct.

"Are ye able," he asked, "to drink of the cup that I shall drink of, and to be baptized with the baptism that I am baptized with?"

"We are able."

"Ye shall drink indeed of my cup, and be baptized with the baptism that I am baptized with: but to sit on my right hand and on my left, is not mine to give, but it shall be given to them for whom it is prepared of my Father."

The ten heard of the request, and were indignant, and he took the occasion to enjoin humility and mutual kindness on all :—

"Whosoever will be chief among you, let him be your servant: even as the Son of man came not to be ministered unto, but to minister, and to give his life a ransom for many."

No wonder that, amid all their darkness of intellect and selfishness of nature, their Divine Master was greatly admired and loved!

They crossed the Jordan now for the last time with him; and entered upon the garden-like plain of Jericho, which presented at every step scenes of busy life. If anything could win an individual off from sad and disturbing thoughts, it might have been found in the sights now around them; where the rivulets, led carefully from so many fountains, gurgled pleasantly by the road-side; or, crossing the path, were lost amid the profuse vegetation which they aided in this most prolific soil; where fruits and flowers constantly greeted the eye; and where birds were filling the air with their melody. The labor of the husbandman was here abundantly rewarded; and a profitable trade existed between this favored region of gums and palms, and other parts of the country: the balsams of Jericho were sought also by foreign nations and valued at their courts.

The business of a tax-gatherer was here an unusually profitable one; but here, as elsewhere, odious to the Jews. A man in that office might be thoroughly honest, and even far more than usually benevolent; but he would still be looked upon with suspicion and dislike. He wore the Roman badge of servitude, and was connected with a class disreputable for extortions and overreaching; and any increase in wealth would make suspicions attached to him only the stronger. Zaccheus, the chief of these tax-gatherers at Jericho, was a man of the widest and largest charity; and of strictest probity also; for while the Jewish law required restitution two-fold in case of wrong-dealing, he gave back four-fold to any one whom he might unwittingly have injured. Yet he was "a sinner" in the estimation of the people here, and was so branded: his occupation alone was a sufficient cause for condemnation in their eyes.

He had heard of Christ: and there was very much in these reports, not only to awaken his curiosity, but to enlist his feelings of affection;—for they spoke of the Messiah's wide benevolence, his kindness, his gentleness to all, mixed yet with power. He had never spurned any one seeking help: he had shown himself the friend of the humble and the slighted by the world; publicans themselves had gathered around him, and had not been repelled. When charged with eating with such, and with sinners, he had said that he came not to call the righteous, but sinners, to repentance. The heart of this man had warmed toward Christ:—and now this great and wonderful being was there in Jericho. But the tax-gatherer, repelled by the citizens, and taunted with sharp epithets, dared not thrust himself forward among that throng, which now, as the Messiah advanced along the highway, was continually growing more and more dense; and Zaccheus being a small man, there seemed to be no

25

probability of his even getting a sight of him whom his heart was already prepared to reverence.   But there is a tree in that country with branches near to the ground; and, one of these being just in advance of the company he hastened to it, and drew himself up till he could see over the heads of the advancing throngs.

The Syrian sycamore.[1]

They came on: and, now, opposite to him, was that face he had so longed to see; that great being, of whose power and benevolence and divine wisdom he had heard so much. . But what was his astonishment when he found the eyes of

---

[1] This tree is entirely different from our sycamore.   Its branches grow out near the ground, and its large widely spread roots extend upward like buttresses to the trunk.   These roots take such a strong hold on the ground as to give the greatest force to the passage in Luke xvii. 6, " Be thou plucked up by the root," &c.   It bears fruit like figs, growing directly from the large branches.

the Messiah turned directly and attentively upon him; and to hear himself addressed—

"Zaccheus, make haste and come down, for to-day I must abide at thy house."

If the tax-gatherer was astonished, equally so were the multitudes; and while the former hurried down and joyfully accompanied the Messiah, a displeased murmur ran among the people, "that he had gone to be guest with a man that is a sinner." They could not understand it, and self-invited too! "Was he ignorant of the man's occupation?"—thus the murmurs ran among the crowd—" or was this done purposely to give an open defiance to all their prejudices and feelings of caste? or was it done in contempt of themselves?" Some turned away in disgust, others followed to the door, curiosity still strongest in their minds: all were displeased.

In the meantime the two, followed by the disciples, had entered the tax-gatherer's house. A stir and commotion within the dwelling at such an unexpected Presence, wondering looks fixed intently on that face of benignity and kindness, peering eyes outside trying to have cognizance of what was going on; such was the scene as Zaccheus standing before the Messiah said, in a sort of a defence of himself from what he knew was the general impression respecting his business and life—

"Behold, Lord, the half of my goods I give to the poor, and if I have taken anything from any man wrongfully I restore him fourfold."

"This day is salvation come unto this house," was the answer, "forasmuch as he also is a son of Abraham. For the Son of man has come to seek and to save that which was lost."

But through all this scene in the receiver-general's house, and doubtless throughout the city also, there were rumors and whisperings foreign to the scene itself, greatly exciting the people wherever they were heard. These were, "That the *kingdom of God should immediately appear.*" [1]   The origin of the rumor was, doubtless, in a distorted report of the Messiah's recent declaration respecting his going up to Jerusalem.   He was known to be on his way to that city.   Something decisive it was believed from his own words was then to ensue.   He had spoken of his death as to occur there, but also of his rising again.   What could this last mean, they supposed, but the assumption of that earthly power and glory so long awaiting the Messiah, prophesied of him for so long a time?   We shall see in a few days how strong was the under-current in his favor among all the multitudes, and how quickly it could bear them into open demonstrations in his favor.   His fame had spread throughout the nation. People *felt* him to be great.   This feeling of his greatness was that which led the Pharisees after he had denounced them, to be so inveterate and so deadly in their hostility.   A common man they could have disregarded.   All felt that Christ was very far above that.   His very humility of appearance gave to the mightiness of power evident in him a stronger relief; his very gentleness and kindness made more striking the grandeur of character that sat so majestically, and withal so naturally on him in all that he did and said.   The Pharisees hated him, because he had this force, this grandeur, this wonderful Presence, which no humility in appearance or in life could annul or conceal, which his humility only made more prominent and more striking; he was himself the truest exemplification of his doctrine, "The first shall be last, the last shall be first."

So the Pharisees hated and feared him.   He had denounced their hypocrisy and their abrogation of God's law by their traditions.   He was carrying the hearts of the people away from them, and they felt that their power was on the wane. The multitudes, although often murmuring at Christ's words

---

[1] Luke xix. 2.

or actions, as in this recent one of going to be a guest with Zaccheus, still returned to him with new fealty and affection; for their hearts responded to his greatness without assumption, his force without harshness, his gentleness and kindness to every one.

He spent the Sabbath at Jericho. **At his leaving the city vast multitudes attended him, for in addition to the usual** curiosity this new **rumor** of the mighty revolution soon to be—the new kingdom—was filling men's minds and occupying their tongues. Advancing onward they had reached the edge of the city, the great crowd causing a bustle as they pressed around him, when above all their noises rose suddenly a very distinct and most earnest cry—

" Jesus, thou Son of David, have mercy on me !"

It ceased for a moment or two, and over in the direction from which it had come were now heard angry objurgations and efforts to stifle the cry, but immediately the voice rose louder than before, " Jesus, thou Son of David, have mercy on me !"

It was from **a** beggar, Bartimeus by name, a blind man sitting by the road-side, that the cry **had come. The sounds** of an unusual crowd had **fallen on his ear, as he sat there in** darkness, the light of **broad day quenched to his sightless** balls. The multitude **increased and were excitedly talking** as of something unusual **on the road. He stopped his own** petitions for alms to inquire **what** it meant, and was told that " Jesus of Nazareth passeth by." What a thrill shot through the blind man ! Jesus there ! He raised the cry.

It was offensive, however, to many of the crowd, for Son of David was one of the titles which in all Jewish belief **was to be applied to** the Messiah, **and** unbelievers quickly **threw in their angry commands to him to be silent;** enraged **men crowded about him, indignant, sharp tones and harsh** words **rung in his** ear, but with **a blind** man's quick instincts he understood at once both them and his only hope,

25 *

and he cried out only the louder in that cry of his earnest faith.

Presently the angry men about him were pushed aside, and a friendly voice said,

"Be of good comfort; rise: he calleth for thee."

Jesus had stopped when the cry reached his ear, and had directed that he should be brought to him. The blind man dropping his outer garment in his haste, was led—how he hurried those leading him! they seemed to be so slow!—and now he felt that he stood before the Messiah. The colloquy was too earnest to be other than brief.

"What wilt thou that I should do unto thee?"

"Lord, that I might receive my sight!"

"Go thy way; thy faith hath made thee whole."

LIGHT! yes, there was light poured into those balls: a world of faces flashed upon him, all of them with such intensified and startled looks;—all but one, and on that, calmness and benevolence ruled; that gentle face of Him blessing, even in his very look, those who had faith for the blessing. Him he saw, and a loud cry of gratitude, and praise, and of glorifying God burst out; not from the healed man only, but from all the company around. They had gazed upon him as he had been led up;—saw his eager face; saw his hurried, agitated manner; saw his sightless eyeballs, showing that there was an utter blank there; heard the colloquy: and gazing as if their whole souls were in their intensified look, saw these balls take clearness and expression of intelligence; saw the astonishment and joy in the man's face; and involuntarily they burst out, too, in loud acclamations of praise to God.

The restored man joined them most gladly in following Christ.[1]

---

[1] Mark x. 46–52; Luke xviii. 35–43; Matt. xx. 30–34. Matthew speaks of two as being healed. Mark and Luke of but one. It is probable

CHAPTER XXXVII.

JERUSALEM.

THE interest of this history now concentrates at Jerusalem; and the events which transpired there make it necessary to give a detailed description of the city itself. Jerusalem with its surroundings was unique, picturesque, and in many parts beautiful, a place well worthy of our minute attention, even apart from the sacred associations which it must always have in our minds.

The reader will imagine a valley running nearly north and south, (more accurately N. 5° E.)—the valley of Jehoshaphat, at the bottom of which, in the wet season, flowed the brook Kedron; it was perhaps then as now, a dry watercourse in the summer months. On the west side of this valley, we reach, by a steep ascent, at the height of 190 feet, the present surface of Moriah, which is 318 yards across. This has for its western boundary, the valley of Tyropœon (also formerly "the valley of Cheesemongers,") about half the depth of that of Jehoshaphat, and 117 yards in width. Crossing this valley westwardly, and again ascending to an elevation about equal to that of Moriah, we find ourselves on Mount Zion, "beautiful for situation, the joy of the whole earth." This mountain (or rather hill) is 600 yards across and three-fifths of a mile in length. On the west

---

that Bartimeus was the more noted of the two; and it is a maxim among critics *qui plura narrat pauciora complectitur ; qui pauciora memorat pluro non negat; he who describes the larger number embraces in it the fewer: he who notices the fewer, does not deny the larger.* A similar case occurs in Matt. viii. 28–31; Mark v. 1–21; and Luke viii. 26–40. There may have been a healing also, before entering Jericho. See Luke xviii. 35–43.

and south of it passes the valley of Hinnom, shallow at first, but deepening as it goes southwardly, till at the southwest bend of Zion, it has a depth of 150 feet; and finally where, after curving around Zion on the south, and then taking an easterly course, it unites with the valley of Jehoshaphat, it is 300 feet deep. The Tyropeon, nearly at the point of their junction, opens into both, and has in it at its opening, the Pool of Siloam, placed by Milton (by poetic license) though 700 yards distant, "fast by the oracles of God." Our imaginary journey, as the reader perceives, was from east to west; it passed just at the southern edge of the temple enclosure, which enclosure was opposite the northeast corner of Zion, a high stone bridge across the Tyropeon uniting the two. The portion of Mount Moriah south of the temple-enclosure was called Ophel, and was occupied by the Nethenim or servants dedicated to the use of the temple (Nehemiah iii. 26): it terminates in a bluff forty feet high, just above the fountain of Siloam.

The city wall, on the west and south, kept along the edge of the almost precipitous descent to the valley of Hinnom, until the Tyropeon was reached, when stretching across this, and then over the lower end of Ophel, it thence skirted the valley of Jehoshaphat, till it reached the southeastern angle of the great wall supporting the temple platform. On the north side of Zion, the wall also skirted the edge of the mountain, on the verge of a descent of thirty cubits,[1] and finally crossed the Tyropeon to the western wall of the temple enclosure.

In the course of time, a larger space was needed for the city; and a hill, called Acra, adjoining Zion on the northward, and like that "surrounded by deep valleys,"[2] was also enclosed by a wall carried along on the edge of its precipices, except where this crossed the lower ground to be

---

[1] Jos. Bell. v. 4, § 4.   [2] Ib. v. § 1.

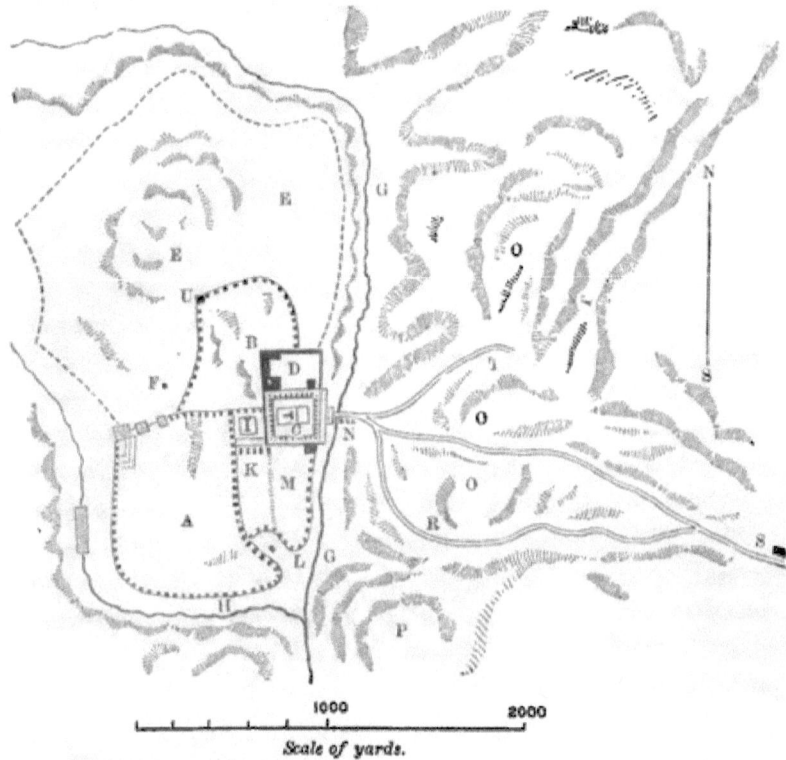

Map of Jerusalem and its environs, **as they were in the time of Christ.**

A. Mount Zion.

B. Acra, or Lower City.

C. Temple Enclosure.

D. Tower of Antonia.

E. E. Bezetha, at that time built upon; **not enclosed till A. D. 40. The dotted lines show** the probable course of these subsequent walls.

F. The reputed place of the crucifixion.

G. G. Valley of Jehoshaphat and Brook Kedron.

H. Valley of Hinnom; the Lower Pool of Gihon is marked in it.

I. Probable site of the Xystus, or place for public assemblies.

K. Bridge across the Tyropeon. This valley extended down to

L. The Pool of Siloam.

M. Ophel.

N. Double-arched bridge over the valley of Jehoshaphat; (on authority of the ancient Rabbins).

O. O. O. The Mount of Olives.

P. Mount of Offence. See 1 Kings xi. 7; 2 Kings xxiii. 13.

R. Camel road to Bethany and Jericho.

S. Bethany.

T. T. Probable route of David when **escaping from Absalom. 2 Sam. xv., xvi.**

U. Present Damascus Gate.

united with the wall of Zion, at a gate called Gennath: on the east, this wall of Acra, joined the tower of Antonia situated at the north of the temple enclosure.[1]

The city, however, grew finally even beyond Acra, and a large space of ground, north and east of that hill, reaching to the valley of Jehoshaphat, was covered with houses; but this, called Bezetha, was not inclosed in our Saviour's time; the wall afterwards bounding it on three sides, having been built by Agrippa at a period shortly subsequent to the crucifixion.

Zion, Moriah, and Acra, although called mountains, in historical descriptions, did not rise above the general level of the country adjacent, and could be termed such only in consequence of being isolated by the surrounding valleys: but all this region had a considerable elevation above the Mediterranean, Zion being 2610, and the Mount of Olives 2797 feet above the level of that sea.

Let a spectator be supposed then in those ancient times to be seated on the Mount of Olives, and gazing down over Jerusalem. He would perceive that the general level of the city inclined to the eastward, and that every object was thus brought distinctly into view. The whole was like a map at his feet. Prominent over all, as well as nearest to him,

---

[1] No subject connected with the topography of Jerusalem has given rise to such warm discussions as the course of this wall. The author after a most patient and thorough examination of the opposing authorities, has placed Acra in the northern extension of Moriah, (there wider than further south;) this being apparently the only spot that would admit of Josephus's description of its walls. Such a position also corresponds best to all the facts in his description of the siege and destruction of Jerusalem. What is now called "the Damascus gate," was undoubtedly connected with that wall; and the author has placed it at the northwestern angle in his map of Acra, in this book.

The difficulty in topographical researches is enhanced by the fact that the present city is built upon about twenty feet of *debris* of the old one, which help to fill up valleys and to make outlines obscure.

would be the "Mountain of the House," that huge mass of masonry composed of large stones with rebated faces and rising to a height that overtopped every thing else, as if jealous respecting its pre-eminence. In fact, the summit of Acra, which was originally higher, had been cut down in order that "the temple might be superior to it."[1]   From his elevation on the Mount of Olives the spectator would be able to look over the ramparts of the exterior wall of the temple enclosure, and to see within it parts of the long cloisters with their marble columns in triple or quadruple rows, and the great marble-paved court; he would see then rising on this platform the more sacred courts reached by great ranges of marble steps, and by huge doors glittering with gold and silver; and finally the temple itself, its front 150 feet wide and as many in height, "covered all over with plates of gold." The great altar would be sending up the smoke from its sacrifices, and even at his elevation he might hear the chanting from the many voices of worshippers, or the trumpets and other instruments sounded from the steps of the temple by the altar.

Then below on the high stone bridge connecting Moriah with Zion would be multitudes passing between the temple and the city.

The picturesque outline of the city walls would next perhaps attract the notice of the spectator, for as they were erected mostly on the edges of the precipices, their battlemented outline, and the numerous towers built to strengthen them, would all stand out distinctly before his eye. Some of these towers had a singular combination of solidity below with an airy and delicate architecture above. The solid impenetrable substructure of one of them, Hippicus, at the northwest corner of Zion, still remains, the rebated work on its stones giving a good architectural effect to the solid unbroken wall.

---

[1] Jos. Bel. v. 4, § 1; Ibid. v. 5, § 6.

Jerusalem as it was in the time of Christ; viewed from the south-east: the summit of the Mount of Olives in the foreground.

Just eastward of Hippicus, and forming part of the defences at the northern end of Zion, were two other principal towers, one of which we will allow Josephus to describe: "The second tower which he [Herod the Great] named from his brother Phasaelus, had its breadth and its height equal, each of them forty cubits, over which was its solid height of forty cubits, over which a cloister went round about whose height was ten cubits, and it was covered from enemies by breast-works and bulwarks. There was also built over that cloister another tower, parted into magnificent rooms and a place for bathing, so that this tower wanted nothing that might make it appear to be a royal palace. It was also adorned with battlements and turrets, more than was the foregoing, and the entire altitude was about ninety cubits."[1] It will be remembered that it stood on the edge of a descent of thirty cubits. Hippicus was smaller, but similarly ornamented, and just eastward of Phasaelus and in the same wall was the tower Mariamne, named after Herod's late wife, smaller also than the latter, but "its upper buildings were more magnificent and had greater variety than the other towers had." "Now as these towers," says Josephus, "were tall they appeared taller by the place on which they stood, for that very old wall wherein they were was built on a high hill, and was itself a kind of elevation that was still thirty cubits taller, over which the towers were situated, and thereby were made much higher to appearance." The other towers in the line of walls were inferior in ornament, but "the niceness of the joints and the beauty of the stones were in no way inferior to those of the holy house itself." These towers were twenty cubits wide, and as many in height, and above this solid substructure were rooms "of great magnifi-cence," and cisterns for rain-water; Acra had forty and Zion sixty of such towers attached to their walls. "The whole

---

[1] Jos. Bel. v. 4, § 3.

compass of the city [including Bezetha] was thirty-three furlongs," or about four miles and a quarter of our measure, the dimensions not large, but we must remember that the cities of that region are compactly built, the streets being frequently only four or five feet in width. The population at the time of our Saviour is supposed to have been 200,000. Tacitus estimated it at much more than that.

The palace of Herod the Great and its grounds were among the most striking features of the city, and for these, lest any other description may seem extravagant, we will again resort to Josephus. He had just been describing the towers Mariamne and Phasaelus in the northern wall of Zion, and he adds : "Now as these towers were themselves at the north side of the wall the king had a palace inwardly thereto adjoined, which exceeds all my ability to describe it, for it was so curious as to want no cost or skill in its construction, but was entirely walled about to the height of thirty cubits, and was adorned with towers at equal distances, and with large bed-chambers that would contain beds for a hundred guests a-piece, in which the variety of the stones is not to be expressed, for a large quantity of those that were rare of the kind was collected together. Their roofs were also wonderful, both for the length of the beams and the splendor of their ornaments. The number of the rooms was also very great, and the variety of the figures that were about them was prodigious; their furniture was complete, and the greatest part of the vessels that were put in them was of silver and gold. There were besides many porticos one beyond another, round about, and in each of these porticos curious pillars, yet were all the courts that were exposed to the air everywhere green. There were moreover several groves of trees, and long walks throughout them, with deep canals and cisterns, that in several parts were filled with brazen statues through which the water ran." [1]

---

[1] Jos. Bel. v 4, § 4.

There was also a palace on Acra, of which however we have no definite account. The castle of Antonia, joined to the northern side of the temple enclosure, was also a conspicuous object, both on account of its situation with one turret overtopping the temple precincts and looking directly down into its courts, and also for its vastness and magnificence; " for the inward parts had the largeness and form of a palace, it being parted into all kinds of rooms and other conveniences with a court and places for bathing and broad spaces for camps, insomuch that by having all conveniences that cities wanted it might seem to be composed of several cities, but by its magnificence it seemed a palace." [1]

The walls and towers were constructed with the white limestone, (Josephus calls it white marble), of that region; a large portion of which was probably taken from beneath the city itself. Some curious persons, lately observing a small hole just outside the present northern city-wall, not unlike a burrow in the banks of a rabbit warren, enlarged it a little; and through it they presently slid down into a subterranean chamber, about seven hundred feet long from north to south, and from three to four hundred feet in width, the height from ten to fifty feet. It has all been cut in the solid rock, with rude pillars at intervals to support the roof. A recent explorer says, " It was evidently a quarry, and I could see that the stones were all hewn and polished on the spot. On every side were immense piles of chippings, still bearing, like the rocky walls, the marks of the chisel. At the extreme end several huge blocks remain, not completely dislodged. From hence down to Moriah is an easy slope, along which they could easily have been rolled;" and the floor of the chamber is descending, and in several places is hewn smooth. This quarry is underneath what in our map is represented as Acra. Doubtless there are many chambers and passages under Jerusalem, yet unknown.

---

[1] Jos. Bel. v. 5, § 8.

26 *

The grounds beyond the walls were covered over with gardens, among the enclosures of which the Roman soldiers, in the first assaults by Titus, became entangled and suffered bloody defeats. On the south of the city were the "king's gardens;" and where the valleys of Hinnom and Jehoshaphat unite is still the well called after Nehemiah, which often overflows and refreshes the flat surface adjoining.

Many an individual in those days lingered on the heights of Olivet, to gaze long on that scene below;— on the city, like a hive of human beings, many of its common structures, doubtless, giving evidence of the wealth which the whole world poured toward Jerusalem ;—on the battlemented walls and the numerous towers, all, from their position, brought into strong relief ;—on the castles and palaces, and the long, high bridge between Moriah and Zion, with its numerous passengers in full view ;—on the beautiful green frame-work of gardens surrounding the city ;—and most especially on the Mountain of the House, lifting its crowning splendor of the temple high in the air; the glitter of its gold partly hid by the smoke from the sacrificial altar curling upward, while were heard the sounds from the worshippers there, now sinking into low notes of music, and now rising to loud strains in the hallelujahs, and filling the air with their melody.

CHAPTER XXXVIII.

THE PUBLIC ENTRY.

THE Messiah was now on his way to Jerusalem for the celebration of the Passover festival; and proceeding onward, after the cure of Bartimeus, he arrived in the evening at Bethany, where he was to spend the night.

On the morrow, it quickly became evident that the public enthusiasm respecting him was going to break through all bounds, and to make a demonstration of itself, such as had never yet been seen. The rumor, " *that the kingdom of God should immediately* **appear,**" was still spreading, and people were wrought up **to a state of the** highest **expectancy;** ——the excitement all the **greater in consequence of the vague-** ness of their surmisings, in **which both curiosity** and imagination had **the** widest scope. **He was now** in Bethany, where he had raised the dead: what could not power such as that effect? Bartimeus and his companion **had followed** him, full of enthusiasm and ready to testify to every one whom they met, what had been done for them: many of those around Christ, had themselves witnessed this wonderful act. The excited company at Bethany was soon increased in consequence of the circulation of this new and stirring rumor circulating in Jerusalem itself and among the throngs already come up **to** the festival. For, although it wanted yet four days to the Passover, large numbers[1] had assembled, some of them from distant lands.[2] Strangers and citizens were full **of excitement; and the feeling re-** specting Christ, **which had been kept hushed through fear of the rulers, and had dared to show itself only in whispers, was now beginning to take an outspoken and decisive char-** acter. **" How was this new kingdom to** be established?" The bitter hostility of the rulers toward him was well known: their plots for his death were also surmised. His denunciations of the hypocrisy of most of them had been public. " Would vengeance now overwhelm them, and make clear the way for his supremacy?" "What would **this new kingdom** be?" We **may** well imagine what an **excitement such surmisings would occasion** amid a demonstrative people, such **as they** were; and that amid it, enthu-

---

[1] John xii. 12.   [2] Ib. verse 20.

siasm for the Messiah would be constantly on the increase.

Early in the morning he sent two of his disciples to a spot in the neighborhood of Bethany, where he said they would find an ass and her colt tied: these they were to bring to him. The owner, when informed who needed them, gave his immediate consent. There was an old prophecy by Zechariah, whose favorite theme had been the coming of the Messiah, and whose words were therefore greatly treasured by the Jews: "Rejoice greatly, O daughter of Zion; shout, O daughter of Jerusalem: behold thy king cometh unto thee: he is just and having salvation; lowly and sitting upon an ass, and upon a colt, the foal of an ass."[1] Even the triumphs of Christ were not to contribute to human pride. Kings advancing towards their capitals in triumphal processions, choose all the pomp and circumstance that can dazzle men's eyes; and whatever glory earth can afford is put in requisition, amid which the recipient of honors advances with a heart swelling in gratified ambition. What a contrast was there here, where even the triumph carried with it lessons to pride and pomp; where humility ruled; and where the emotion most manifest was to be in tears over approaching human woes.

The principal road from Jericho through Bethany to Jerusalem has now doubtless exactly the course that it had in those ancient times. After leaving Bethany it passes by curves and gentle ascents along the offshoots of the eastern side of Olivet, until about half way to the city, it crosses, at considerable elevation, over the southern shoulder of the mountain, and by a gap among some cliffs emerges on its western side. There the city and temple burst suddenly upon the sight; and as the ground on which they stand has a slight inclination toward the east, the full extent, and all

---

[1] Zech. ix. 9.

the picturesque beauty and grandeur of Jerusalem and its surroundings are placed fully before the eye. The slanting descent thence to the Kedron is nearly a mile in length, and most of it is in full view from any part of the city and from the cloisters of the temple.

The numbers attending Christ had multiplied; and as they advanced along the roads toward the city the excitement constantly increased. They had an indefinable idea that something extraordinary was to occur;—the kingdom of heaven *immediately* to appear; and the accordance of the present scene with their ancient prophecy,—this unusual manner of the Messiah's approach to the city,—roused their expectations into the strongest enthusiasm. "Tell ye the daughters of Zion, Behold thy king cometh;" and truly he was there! His kingdom mistaken, but the mistake adapted only to increase the powerful sensation. The enthusiasm presently broke through all the bounds that had been imposed by the fear of their rulers; the people from other parts of the country being indeed less fettered by this than the residents in Jerusalem. The multitudes, as they hurried out in great numbers to meet the procession, gathered up palm branches[1] such as they were accustomed to wave in their Hallels to Jehovah at the Feast of Tabernacles: and soon the cry arose, both among those preceding and those following the Messiah, "Hosanna," (that is, "Save, Lord, we beseech thee"), "Hosanna in the highest," "Blessed is the King that cometh in the name of the Lord: peace in heaven and glory in the highest." It was as if the temple service had been transferred to the heights of Olivet, the open mountain serving as God's grandest of sanctuaries, with spontaneous worship poured out there from overflowing hearts. Christ's enemies had quickly taken the alarm; and Pharisees mixing with the crowd, cried out to him,—

---

[1] John xii. 12, 13.

" Master, rebuke thy disciples."

But, far from disclaiming this worship paid to him as God, he replied,—

" If they should hold their peace, the stones would immediately cry out."   Their worship received no rebuke.

In the city and on the cloisters of the temple people gathered in groups to gaze with extreme wonder at the sight. Fresh multitudes were hurrying up the mountain, attracted by the flying rumors, and as the enthusiasm was contagious were equally joining in the hosannas.   " Blessed is the King that cometh in the name of the Lord," was repeated among the cries : and the throngs were now cutting branches from the trees, and strewing them, as also their garments, in the way[1] before the Messiah, tokens of honor usually shown to eastern kings in those days.[2]

It had become a triumphal procession ; and the shouts of " Hosanna in the highest," " Blessed is the kingdom of our Father David that cometh in the name of the Lord," " Hosanna to the Son of David," " Save, Lord, we beseech thee," floated over Moriah and over Zion ;—a worship, the sponta-

---

[1] Matt. xxi. 8.

[2] Tholuck, *in loco.* The Targum on Esther, x. 15, says, "when Mordecai went forth from the gate of the king's house, the streets were covered with myrtle and the porches with purple."   See also 2 Kings ix. 13.

The following singular incident is from Robinson's Researches, Vol. ii. p. 162: "At that time [just after the rebellion in 1834, against the Egyptian conscription] when some of the inhabitants [of Bethlehem] were already imprisoned, and all were in deep distress, Mr. Farran, then English consul at Damascus, was on a visit to Jerusalem, and had ridden out with Mr. Nicolayson to Solomon's pool.   On their return, as they rose the ascent to enter Bethlehem, hundreds of the people, male and female, met them, imploring the consul to interfere in their behalf, and afford them his protection ; and all at once, by a sort of simultaneous movement, they 'spread their garments in the way' before the horses. The consul was affected to tears, but had, of course, no power to interfere."

THE MOUNT OF OLIVES AND PORTIONS OF THE TEMPLE AND COURTS AND OF THE CASTLE OF ANTONIA.

The view supposed to be from the south-west angle of Antonia, at the time of Christ's Public Entry into Jerusalem.

neity and heartiness of which were manifest to every one
who heard.

But suddenly the noises ceased; and all turned to look
in new wonder at him, who was the centre and the object of
the demonstration.

He was weeping.

Had they been Pharisees and scribes around him, using
taunts and threatenings, he could have met their insults
with unruffled feelings; but these rejoicings of friends and
these strong demonstrations of affection melted his heart
into tenderness, as he thought of the doom gathering over
the city there spread out, and so fair to look upon, and
which would soon leave scarcely a vestige behind; its people, and the hundreds of thousands who gathered there from
all countries, after indescribable sufferings massacred, or
tortured to death, or carried into slavery in distant lands.
His prescient eye saw the Roman legions encircling the
place; saw the rush of combatants; his ear heard the shouts
of rage or despair; he saw the dying and dead covering
mountain-sides and valleys, after the fierce sorties. He saw
the Roman lines of circumvallation; and the sickening
scenes within them throughout the city, as famine was
doing its horrible work, till even a mother could feed on
her own child; saw the madness of sectaries among the
people, till Jew was murdering Jew, and the streets were
running with blood and were covered with corpses in
the fratricidal combats;—saw finally the assault, the last
struggles of the people, not for life, but in the madness of
death, as the foreign hordes filled the streets and houses;
saw the temple on fire and people throwing themselves by
hundreds from its battlements to the great depths below,
resistance over—only death now left.

He was weeping; and the crowds so lately filling the air
with their joyful cries and their hymns of hosannas, stood
now silent, looking on with curiosity and wonder. He said:

27

"If thou hadst known, even thou, at least in this thy day, the things which belong unto thy **peace** ! but now they are hid from thine eyes. For the days shall come upon thee that thine enemies shall cast a **trench** about thee, and compass thee round, and keep thee in on every side : and shall lay thee even with the ground and thy children within thee ; and they shall not leave in thee one stone upon another ; because thou knewest not the time of thy visitation."

The multitudes heard him with very deep sadness ; but their reverence and demonstrations of affection were unabated as the procession moved on, and so continued down the mountain and across the Kedron, and as they ascended by the eastern gate into the corridors of the temple.

The whole city was by this time in a state of excitement; and people were hurrying about with the inquiry, what could it mean ? When they found at last that the noises,— the hosannas, and exclamations were ascending now from the temple courts, thither streamed the vast city population, —Pharisees, Scribes, Rabbis, the common multitudes,—all in confusion hastening there with the hurried question :

" Who is this ?" The crowds there answered :

" This is Jesus, the prophet of Nazareth of Galilee."[1]

Immediately some left the crowd, hurrying back to their homes. In those homes and along the streets were the decrepid, the diseased, and the blind ; and friends hastened now to them, with the thrilling intelligence that Jesus, with his miraculous healing powers, was in the temple. What news to them! With outstretched arms, and appealing voices, they begged to be carried or led : and very soon the throngs about Christ were pushed asunder by eager men forcing openings amongst their dense masses and carrying the diseased; or by blind men, with objurgations and entreaties in the same breath, making their eager way, disregardful

---

[1] Matt. xxi. 10, 11.

alike of priest, or Rabbi, or commoner; only one thought filling their whole soul—that wild, strange hope that they might receive sight and be cured;—their hope forcing every thing aside so that they might be quickly before Christ.

The throngs yielded **readily** when they saw the cause; for the expectation of witnessing miracles became immediately as intense **almost as was** the **hope of the** infirm themselves. **The lame were before** him : they were healed. The blind pressed into his presence, and stood **there for a** moment or two, with faces showing the wrought-up feelings within, and with their sightless eye-balls so drearily blank and sadly disfiguring. But only for a moment: for **at** the word from Christ, those eye-balls changed; a perceptive power had shot in them : the intensely earnest and entreating countenance was suddenly brightened with an expression of wildness of delight; the spectators saw how perfect the cure was; and all mingled with the joyful cry of the relieved men, their shouts of praises and of glorifying God. No wonder that there rang through **all those courts** of the temple such spontaneous, heartfelt **strains of thanksgiving as had** never been heard there before; and could **never have been** known in the formal hymns **and ceremonies of the priests. No** wonder that **the hosannas rose up louder and louder, shout** after shout, as **new** and still more extraordinary cases of curing occurred; and **that the** children **who had** crowded there with the rest, and are always in their warm fresh hearts, quick in sympathies with sorrow and joy, and quick for open demonstrations, joined readily in the cry,

" Hosanna to the Son of David ! Hosanna to the Son of David !" which was repeated everywhere in the courts.

But there were also intensely angry faces among the crowds; and presently men rushed up to the Messiah,—chief-priests and scribes they were,—with the exclamation :

" Hearest thou **what** they say ?"

Indeed the cry, " Hosanna to the **Son of David,"** was a

full acknowledgment of his Messiahship; and unchecked as it was by him, it filled up the measure of these men's indignation and rage. They had witnessed the miracles just performed; but in them sympathy with distress was extinguished by malice, and by seeing how the crowds were carried away by his merciful deeds. They gnashed their teeth at the hosannas so broadly expressive, and broke in with the inquiry above:

"Hearest thou what they say?"[1] referring to the children.

"Yea: have ye never read, Out of the mouths of babes and sucklings thou hast perfected praise?"[2]

It was a favorite method with the Messiah to parry their malicious assaults with some question which they could not answer, or which threw them into confusion, in which they lost their power to hurt.

The Pharisees said among themselves, as they retired, discomfited from the scene,

"Perceive ye that ye prevail nothing? Behold the world is gone after him."[3]

CHAPTER XXXIX.

AT THE TEMPLE.—WOES DENOUNCED.

THE Messiah returned that evening to the quiet of Bethany, leaving behind him however in Jerusalem an agitated people, full of emotions of various kinds. The hosannas, long after night had spread its silence over the city, seemed to the rulers to be still ringing in their ears; and the scenes on the side of Olivet, and in the temple,—

---

[1] Matt. xxi. 15, 16.   [2] Ps. viii. 2.   [3] John xii. 19.

the outburst of enthusiasm among the populace—the miraculous cures and consequent rejoicings were still haunting them, long after they had retired to their homes.

Their chagrin was not allayed the next morning by rumors of fresh occurrences; namely, that Christ was again in the temple, and was a second time cleansing it of the abominations which notwithstanding his former expulsion of the *Colbonists* and the sellers of oxen and birds, had been renewed in the temple courts. " It is written," he said, "My house is the house of prayer, but ye have made it a den of thieves." Many of the people had suffered from the haughtiness and extortions of the Colbonists, and were glad now to see severity used upon them; and the convictions of all were with him as regarded the desecration of the temple, where chaffering had once more taken the place of prayer, where the lowing of cattle was mingling with the sounds of people's devotions, and the spirit engendered was that of greedy gain.

When the place had been cleansed and order restored, the Messiah proceeded to teach in the cloisters; the multitudes still retaining the enthusiasm of the previous day, and listening with the deepest earnestness to his doctrines. But among them were men now fully bent on his destruction, provoked to still greater wrath by the events of the morning, and by seeing how in every act whether of gentleness and healing, or of force, he was carrying with him and from these rulers, the affections of the people. They "feared him because all the people were astonished at his doctrine."[1] In the evening he returned to Bethany.

On the next day he came again to the temple, and recommenced his teaching, when the chief priests and elders irritated beyond endurance, made an effort to overpower him by an official demand respecting his power to teach.

---

[1] Mark xi. 15–18.

27 *

" By what authority doest thou these things? and who gave thee this authority ?"

Their object was doubtless to bring him into discredit with the people by making it evident that he had received no scholastic training, and had no diploma from the Rabbis: but it was defeated in a very simple manner. Indeed, the simplicity of means by which, often, their chicanery was foiled, is one of the most striking things in his encounters with these men. He said,

" I will also ask you one thing; and answer me. The baptism of John, was it from heaven, or of men ?" They saw the drift of the question, and hesitated. If they should say from heaven, he would ask, why then do ye not believe him? If of men—so they murmured to each other,—" all the people will stone us: for they be persuaded that John was a prophet." They answered :

" We cannot tell."

" Neither do I tell you by what authority I do these things."[1]

We must frequently observe the great skill combined with very simple means with which Christ either parried or rebutted the attacks upon him by the rulers. They tried every method for bringing him into a dilemma, some contradiction of himself, or some position of danger before the people or before the government. Lengthy discussions with such men would have been unwise, yet it was necessary to answer them. His new doctrines—that for instance of the kingdom where all men loving God would be equal before Jehovah—were often adapted to produce a revulsion of feeling in any Jewish audience, yet still they were truths which had to be uttered. The cunning of his adversaries was of the sharpest kind, and ready to take advantage of every prejudice among the people, and to use it as a means of as-

---

[1] Mark xi. 27-33.

sault: and so they came with questions, often frivolous ones which yet required attention; or others adapted to entangle him in a variety of ways. Sometimes he relieved himself, as in this instance, by simply putting a counter-question: very often by a parable containing simply an answer, or a refutation, or perhaps a very startling doctrine couched in a manner not to give offence to the listening multitudes, of whom he was evidently more hopeful than of the leaders. Sometimes however he broke through all trammels, at the risk of giving deadly offence to both. Indeed if we consider what the universal prejudices of the Jewish people were, we must believe that there was a wonderful attractiveness in Christ to keep the multitudes from discarding him entirely, after some of his bold declarations. Once, as we know, all did leave him except the twelve, and he said to them, " Will ye also go away?"

He gave now in the temple-courts, while the people and rulers were about him, an instance of this boldness by uttering some parables exceedingly sharp in their tenor and application: for the conclusion was, " Therefore I say unto you, The kingdom of God shall be taken from you, and given to a nation bringing forth the fruits thereof."[1]

It was a prophecy of a most frightful nature to them. The chief priests and Pharisees were aware that the application bore chiefly on them as the rulers, " but when they sought to lay hands on him, they feared the multitudes:" for the people, even with such a terrible warning sounding in their ears, had still the glow in their hearts toward him occasioned by the incidents of that day. If the leaders had attempted violence on him, the multitudes would have resisted and a tumult ensued, with a consequent vengeful interference by the Roman government: for through all these scenes the guards were keeping a careful watch from that tower in the southeast corner of Antonia.

---

[1] Matt. xxi. 28–32, and 33–46; xxii. 1–14.

But a crisis was evidently approaching. The rulers, in connection with their intended violence toward him, were consulting "that they might put Lazarus also to death; because by reason of him many of the Jews went away and believed on Jesus."[1]

At present, uniting once more in a strange fellowship with their opponents, the Herodians, they sent some of their disciples with the latter; and both having made their way up to the Messiah, they began in a suspiciously-complimentary address:

"Master, we know that thou art true, and teachest the way of God in truth, neither carest thou for any man; for thou regardest not the persons of men. Tell us, therefore, what thinkest thou? Is it lawful to give tribute unto Cæsar, or not?"

If he should answer in the negative, the Herodians were there to accuse him of hostile feeling toward the Roman government; if in the affirmative, he must excite the hostility of the Jews, to whom the tribute was hateful in its nature, and burdensome from its excess.

He saw their cunning, and the wickedness in their apparent compliment that he cared for no man, nor regarded the persons of men.

"Why tempt ye me, ye hypocrites?" he said. "Show me the tribute money."

A penny (a *Roman denarius*) was brought.

"Whose is this image and superscription?" They told him it was Cæsar's.

A Denarius of the time of Tiberius Cæsar.

---

[1] John xii. 10, 11.

" Render therefore unto Cæsar the things which are Cæsar's; and unto God the things that are God's."

They gained nothing by this attempt; and another was now made by the Sadducees, unbelievers respecting any future state. They came to him propounding a certain case, intended to perplex any opponent to their doctrine; and they were answered: and then came a lawyer, "tempting him."

" Master, which is the great commandment in the law?" He answered:

" Thou shalt love the Lord thy God with all thy heart, and with all thy soul, and with all thy mind. This is the first and great commandment. And the second is like unto it, Thou shalt love thy neighbor as thyself. On these two commandments hang all the law and the prophets."

He himself became interrogator now.

" What think ye of Christ? Whose son is he?"

The Pharisees answered, "The son of David;" and some questions on this subject finished the colloquy, and the public effort of his enemies on this day.

But it did not finish the exciting scenes in those temple-courts. It was a mixed assemblage there; the rulers, Scribes and Pharisees; the disciples; the vast multitude which had been increasing every day at Jerusalem for the Passover, and which had gathered up here to hear the words of this Wonderful Person. He turned now to these last and to his disciples, and cautioned them against the Scribes and Pharisees, showing how the precepts of these men were belied by their conduct; and denouncing their hypocrisy and vain-gloriousness, their impositions on the people, and their assumptions. Of persons wishing to be his own followers, he said,

" But he that is greatest among you shall be your servant. And whosoever shall exalt himself shall be abased; and he that shall humble himself shall be exalted."

He turned then to the Scribes and Pharisees themselves.
His words recently spoken had excited the astonishment of
the multitudes, for they were not accustomed to hear their
religionists publicly addressed in his bold, denunciatory style,
and the leaders themselves had winced repeatedly as with
many a scowling look and many a vow of vengeance they
had listened to what they dared not dispute with one who
seemed to penetrate their hearts, and who knew their lives
so well. They saw also the looks of the people evidencing
even through the marks of astonishment their approval
and assent to what he said, and witnessed with horrified
forebodings the enthusiasm he was lighting up in the hearts
of the multitudes, who were evidently fast sliding away
from the Pharisaic rule. But there was little time for their
observation of others, for he turned now directly to themselves, and their blood curdled with rage at words which
now fell on their ears.

"Woe unto you, Scribes and Pharisees, hypocrites! for
ye shut up the kingdom of heaven against men; for ye
neither go in yourselves, neither suffer ye them that are entering, to go in.

"Woe unto you, Scribes and Pharisees, hypocrites! for
ye devour widows' houses, and for a pretence make long
prayer; therefore ye shall receive the greater damnation.

"Woe unto you, Scribes and Pharisees, hypocrites! for
ye compass sea and land to make one proselyte; and when
he is made, ye make him twofold more the child of hell than
yourselves.

"Woe unto you, ye blind guides, who say, Whosoever
shall swear by the temple, it is nothing; but whosoever
shall swear by the gold of the temple, he is a debtor. Ye
fools and blind. * * *

"Woe unto you, Scribes and Pharisees, hypocrites! for
ye pay tithes of mint and anise and cummin, and have
omitted the weightier matters of the law, judgment, mercy,

and faith; these ought ye to have done, and not to leave the other undone. Ye blind guides, which strain at a gnat,[1] and swallow a camel.

" Woe unto you, Scribes and Pharisees, hypocrites! for ye make clean the outside of the cup and of the platter, but within they are full of extortion and excess. * * *

" Woe unto you, Scribes and Pharisees, hypocrites! for ye are like unto whited sepulchres, which indeed appear beautiful outward, but are within full of dead men's bones and all uncleanness. Even so ye also outwardly appear righteous unto men, but within ye are full of hypocrisy and iniquity.

" Woe unto you, Scribes and Pharisees, hypocrites! because ye build the tombs of the prophets, and garnish the sepulchres of the righteous. * * * Wherefore be ye witnesses unto yourselves, that ye are the children of them which killed the prophets.

" Fill ye up then the measure of your fathers.

" Ye serpents, ye generation of vipers, how can ye escape the damnation of hell?" * * *

It was terrible, and the people stood in silent astonishment and awe, wondering to hear denunciations poured out in this burning, lava-like stream, on the sanctimonious-looking men lately so lordly and pretentious, now standing mute in self-conviction or in rage. It must have been a strange thing too to see those features of Christ, usually marked with such gentleness, mingled with grandeur, now worked up into an expression awful in its power, as if the terribleness of the final judgment-seat were here being anticipated and exhibited on Moriah's temple heights. They gazed with wonder on that face, lighted up as they had never seen it before; they trembled at words so terrible, the more

---

[1] In a former page was noticed that they strained the water for drinking, lest they might inadvertently swallow unclean animals; the camel was also an unclean animal.

terrible because the multitudes felt their justice upon men whom their better feelings had long taught them to doubt, though fear had kept them in restraint. There was a mighty eloquence in the language, a singular force in the manner of delivery, and a horror of doom in the terrible climax, that held the people in breathless wonder, and filled them with awe. If to any one now the words seem to be too terrible, we must remember that these were men who, thoroughly wicked at heart, were making the highest claims for sanctity, and were exercising the largest power over the nation, giving tone to society and character to the country, both at home and abroad. They were, above all, the authors and conservators of that mysterious, terrible, unwritten law, which might be moulded into any form, and in every form was claiming a power greater than God's own Word. He shows in this address some of the uses to which it could be applied, but doubtless we have exhibited to us only a small portion of the evils of which it was the origin. The people had always succumbed to these men; it was desirable that the nation should be aroused, as if by a peal of thunder, and if it were yet possible should be disenthralled.

But presently the language changed. The speaker turned from the woes to a rapid sketch of the murderous persecutions these men would soon instigate and carry into execution on "prophets and wise men and scribes" coming after him, and to notice the terrific visitations gathering over the city in consequence of their iniquitous rule, and then carried away by his knowledge of the horrible scenes which he knew these rulers were bringing on the city, and by his sympathies he broke out in that lamentation over it which has never been equalled for pathetic force of language:

"O Jerusalem, Jerusalem, thou that killest the prophets and stonest them which are sent unto thee, how often would I have gathered thy children together, even as a hen gathereth her chickens under her wings, and ye would not! Behold your house is left unto you desolate. For I say unto you, Ye shall not see me henceforth, till ye shall say, Blessed is he that cometh in the name of the Lord."[1]

Doubtless it was this lament which when these exciting scenes were all over, and he was preparing toward evening to leave the courts, led the disciples to say, as **they pointed to** the temple and its **"goodly stones and gifts :"**

"Master, **see what manner of stones and what buildings** are here !"

They thought perhaps that the sacredness of the **spot and** the costliness of the work and offerings, a hearty tribute of the nation to God, might produce an exception for it in the foretold doom, but there was to be none.

"Seest thou these great buildings ?" he answered; "there shall not be left one stone upon another that shall not be thrown down."[2]

A quiet evening after so exciting a day, fell on the Messiah and his disciples as they were ascending Olivet on their way to Bethany once more; the last night, it was to be, which the Master was to spend in that house of kind and hospitable friends.

On the ascending slope **of the mountain he sat down for a while** by the road-side over **against the** temple,[3] and against **all that fair scene of city and country below :** temple, palaces, battlements, **towers, and the great hives of** human habitations, all distinctly in sight. The smoke of the evening sacrifices was ascending; the evening sounds of a large city (sounds never noisy as with us, no rattling of carriages, but more gentle) filled the air; it was such a quiet and calm and fair scene that it might seem as if to last forever; so little **there** appeared outwardly to court danger, and so much of peace and innocent enjoyment and repose.

But within the walls there were **fierce and** hellish passions

---

[1] Matt. xxiii. 1–39.   [2] Mark xiii. 1, 2.   [3] Mark xiii. 3.

28

at work in the hearts of rulers, and secretly and with silent steps the ruin of Jerusalem was now drawing near.

As the Messiah sat there by the road-side gazing down with eyes in which such anticipations might be read, the disciples came to him and said privately:

"Master, but when shall these things be? and what sign will there be when these things shall come to pass?" He replied:

"Take heed that ye be not deceived,"[1] and he gave them signs by which they might know of the approach of the final catastrophe to Jerusalem;[2] by observing which afterward it doubtless was that so many of the Christians taking refuge in other cities were then saved. But the scene which he sketched there to the disciples of their own future must have been appalling to them, even with the dimness of comprehension and the mistakes which still affected their minds. He said:

"They shall deliver you up to councils, and in the synagogues ye shall be beaten, and ye shall be brought before rulers and kings for my sake for a testimony against them."[3] "They shall lay their hands on you, and persecute you, delivering you up to the synagogues and into prisons, being brought before kings and rulers for my name's sake." "Ye shall be betrayed both by parents, and brethren, and kinsfolks, and friends, and some of you shall they cause to be put to death. And ye shall be hated of all men for my name's sake. But there shall not a hair of your head perish. In your patience possess ye your souls."[4]

He promised them supernatural help, which at that time could be but imperfectly understood by them; but he called them to meet dangers of which they did have a clear comprehension—the hatred of all men, betrayals, insults, violent death.

---

[1] Luke xxi. 7.   [2] Matt. xxiv. 15–28; Luke xxi. 20–37.
[3] Mark xiii. 9.   [4] Luke xxi. 12–19.

The world has never yet appreciated the heroism of Christianity, perhaps never will appreciate it. The milder qualities of that religion — gentleness, peacefulness, and other traits, meekness and forgiveness of injuries — considered mean-spirited by the world — are so much oftener dwelt upon in men's minds with sensations of shrinking from them, that the great, noble heroism of Christianity is not well **understood.** This itself is **also not an impressive heroism except on pecu-liar and rare occasions,** for its acts lie in *self-conquest deep in our hearts,* in a fixedness of endurance which insults cannot shake, and in a preparedness for death itself in the Master's cause, if that should be required. Persecutions to this last extent do not often occur now, but the heroism *to meet* them, if they should come, must be received into every man's heart before he can be a Christian in truth. The Master led the way in this, knowing all the horror of such an end, and feeling it, yet meeting it still. He called his disciples to it here on the mountain-side, not disguising any part, but showing clearly what they had to encounter; he requires it of his followers now — *the highest and noblest feeling in man, courage unto death for a principle and through love.* Such is Christianity if received **into** the **soul; such** in its incipiency, in its constant staying **there, and to the** last gasp of life.

CHAPTER XL.

THE PLOT.

WHILE the events **just narrated were** transpiring on the side of Olivet **the** Sanhedrim were in session in the **house** of Caiaphas, the high-priest, with the determined purpose to take Jesus *by subtilty* and to kill him,[1] and the seizure in order to be successful they believed must be effected by night not by day. For the popularity of the Messiah among the multitudes was now so great that an open, public attempt would only recoil upon themselves.

They believed that it was necessary now for something decisive to be done, and that their action must be prompt. The scenes of that day in the temple showed that there could be no circumventing him, or bearing him down by the weight of authority, and that by no cunning could he be made to commit himself in the eyes of the government or the people. In all such plots they had met with worse than defeat. And the closing events at the temple, the warnings against them and those woes had stung them into a rage which they felt demanded only one result.

But even among themselves there were men now secretly favoring Christ; kept from avowing it through fear of their compeers, and of the decree that any one acknowledging him should be excommunicated. "They loved the praise of men more than the praise of God,"[2] and perhaps no better example of the crushing weight of the Pharisaic power could be given than this awe felt by part of the rulers themselves, sealing the mouth and preventing any outward demonstration, although in their secret conscience believing in Christ. We are soon to have in events to be detailed an exemplification of the subtility and unscrupulousness of the Sanhedrim exhibited in their ready violation of all their own laws and usages, and of the political pretensions of their whole lives.

They met this time, for the sake of secrecy, not in their chamber at the temple, but in the house of Caiaphas; and there they laid their plans.

There were several very serious difficulties in their way. In the first place, they had not the power to put any man to

---

[1] Matt. xxvi. 3-5.   [2] John xii. 42, 43.

death. Three years previously, the Roman government had taken this privilege from the Sanhedrim : and, although, not long after the crucifixion, Stephen was stoned to death just outside of Jerusalem without authority from the governor, it was done by a sudden rush, and an irregular act of violence, not by formal vote of the Sanhedrim, although doubtless they were pleased with the result. In the case of so great a personage, and so beloved by the people as the Messiah, any such deed could not be attempted; especially at the Passover, when the governor himself was at Jerusalem.

In addition to this, "the whole criminal proceeding prescribed in the Pentateuch rests upon three principles, which may be thus expressed : publicity of the trial ; entire liberty of defence allowed to the accused, and a guaranty against the dangers of testimony. One witness was not sufficient."[1] The Hebrew lawyers, in relation to cases where life was at stake, maintained that, "A tribunal which condemns to death once in seven years may be called sanguinary." "It deserves this appellation," said Dr. Eliezur, "when it pronounces like sentence in seventy years :"[2] moreover, according to the Talmudists, it was not lawful to try causes of a capital nature in the night, and it was equally unlawful to examine a cause, pass sentence and put it in execution the same day. The last was very strenuously insisted on.[3] The proper and constant time for the sitting of the Sanhedrim was from the end of the morning service to the beginning of the evening service; sometimes the sessions were prolonged till night, and then they might determine what they had been deliberating on by day : but they might not begin any new business by night.[4]

The forms of trial also, allowed to the accused every opportunity for defence ; and placed the greatest restrictions

---

[1] Olshausen.   [2] Olshausen.   [3] Jahn's Arch.
[4] Lightfoot—*Courts of the Temple.*

28 *

upon judges against haste in action. Says an eminent French advocate who has written on this subject:

"On the day of trial, the executive officer of justice caused the accused person to make his appearance. At the feet of the elders were placed men who, under the name of *auditors* or *candidates*, followed regularly the sittings of the council. The papers in the case were read, and the witnesses called in succession. The President addressed this exhortation to each of them: 'It is not conjectures, or whatever public rumor has brought to thee, that we ask of thee: that we are not occupied by an affair, like a case of pecuniary interest, in which the injury may be repaired. If thou causest the condemnation of a person unjustly accused, his blood, and the blood of all the posterity of him, of whom thou wilt have deprived the earth, will fall upon thee: God will demand of thee an account, as he demanded of Cain an account of the blood of Abel. Speak.' * * * The witnesses were to attest to the identity of the party, and to depose to the month, day, hour, and circumstances of the crime. After an examination of the proofs, those judges who believed the party innocent stated their reasons: those who believed him guilty spoke afterwards, and *with the greatest moderation*. If one of the *auditors* or *candidates* was entrusted by the accused with his defence; or if he wished, in his own name, to present any elucidations in favor of innocence, he was admitted to the seat, from which he addressed the judges and the people. But this liberty was not granted to him if his opinion was in favor of condemning. Lastly; when the accused person himself wished to speak, they gave most profound attention. When the discussion was finished, one of the judges recapitulated the case. They removed all the spectators; two scribes took down the votes of the judges; one of them noted those that were in favor of the accused, and the other, those who condemned him. Eleven votes out of twenty-three were sufficient to acquit;

but it required thirteen to convict. * * If a majority of the votes acquitted, the accused was discharged *instantly;* if he was to be punished, the judges postponed pronouncing sentence till the third day: during the intermediate day, they could not be occupied with anything but the cause; and they abstained from eating freely, and from wine, liquors, and everything which might render their minds less capable of reflection.

"On the morning of the third day they returned to the judgment-seat. Each judge who had not changed his opinion said, *I continue of the same opinion and condemn.* Any one who at first condemned might, at this sitting, acquit; but he who had once acquitted was not allowed to condemn. If a majority condemned, two magistrates immediately accompanied the condemned person to the place of punishment. The Elders did not descend from their seats; they placed at the entrance of the judgment-hall an officer of justice, with a small flag in his hand; a second officer on horseback, followed the prisoner, and constantly kept looking back to the place of departure. During this interval, if any person came to announce to the elders any new evidence favorable to the prisoner, the first officer waved his flag, and the second one, as soon as he perceived it, brought back the prisoner. If the prisoner declared to the *magistrates* that he recollected some reasons which had escaped him, they brought him before the *judges* no less than five times. If no incident occurred, the procession advanced slowly, preceded by a herald, who, in a loud voice, addressed the people thus: 'This man (stating his name and surname) is led to punishment for such a crime; the witnesses who have sworn against him are such and such persons: if any one has evidence to give in his favor, let him come forth quickly.' "[1]

---

[1] "Trial of Jesus," by Dupin, Advocate and Doctor of Laws. Translated from the French by J. Pickering, LL. D.

Such were the restrictions which the chief-priests and scribes and elders—chiefly Pharisees—should have felt in their deliberations "to take Jesus by subtilty and kill him;" but they had now determined, in order to accomplish their purpose, to disregard all restrictions of usages and law. If they could seize him by night,—well into the night,—when the multitudes would be asleep, they might avoid an uproar among the people: if they could, by a night conclave, establish charges against him and condemn him, he would then, when the people would awake in the morning, be in an attitude of an already convicted criminal; and the multitudes would be stupefied, or at least kept in a state of wonder, and thus in check: moreover, if they could condemn him on a charge of blasphemy, the most hideous of all charges in the eyes of the Jewish nation, the people not knowing how the trial had been conducted, but only of the condemnation under it, might be led, by a sudden revulsion of feeling to swerve from favor to the opposite extreme of hatred, and might themselves join in the condemnation. The rulers might also work on the intense popular feeling of pride in their temple, by charging him with a wish to destroy that temple; and could enter this also in their condemnation. Then there would be but another step to be taken; and the way for that would now be prepared. The Sanhedrim could not order an execution; but, they might, on the charge of treason against the Roman government, induce the governor to give such an order: and this ruler was now in Jerusalem, ready to their hand. His residence was at Cæsarea; but he was always in this city on the great festivals, for the double purpose of guarding against insurrections, and of holding court for the trial of great criminals; the inferior one being left to the Jewish elders themselves. The Sanhedrim wanted, in this case, to have a punishment inflicted that would not only gratify their revenge, but would stamp the sufferer with infamy, and annihilate respect and hope in his adherents; and this could be brought about most readily by charging Christ with attempting to put down the Roman authority, and to elevate himself, as king, instead; a crime sure to bring on him the severest punishment that the Roman power could inflict. If the governor would not listen to this charge, they might then take one step further, and one pretty sure to be successful, by insinuating that charges against his own loyalty could be sent on to Rome, and be laid at the feet of Tiberias, whose keen jealousy of power and unscrupulous despotism were fully known to all.

Such was clearly their arranged plan: for it is evident that, through the whole trial, they proceeded according to a settled scheme of action; and the suborned witnesses, previously prepared, knew, when brought forward, exactly what they were to say.

The meetings of the Sanhedrim were properly in their own room by the temple or in their larger council house below; but in case of emergency, they might be held in the palace of the high priest; and this was to be now their place of consultation, as there it would have less publicity than in their usual places of assemblage.

We have seen on a former occasion the kind of men, of which their law required the Sanhedrim to be composed. The high priest was president; and in order that the reader may have some knowledge of the High Priests and their title to respectability in the Jewish nation, the subjoined list from Lightfoot is furnished, beginning with the 23d from the Babylonish captivity; we will remember, here, what the Jewish writer, Jost, says on a former page, "that a priest-hood, which the king [Herod] conferred on whom he pleased, and of whose incumbents he had killed two and deposed four, &c., could by no means satisfy the requisitions of God's government, and of the Judaism resulting from it." The list is as follows:—

23. Hyrcanus; his mother, Alexandra, an ambitious woman and the equally ambitious **Pharisees**, rule the nation.

24. Aristobulus, **younger brother of Hyrcanus**, after the death of their mother, **makes** war upon his brother, drives him from his kingdom to a private life, and takes both his priesthood and his kingdom to himself. They both **desire help** from the Romans, Scaurus and Pompey: Aristobulus, **provoking Pompey**, causes **the sacking of** Jerusalem and the subjugation **of the** Jews to the Roman yoke, **from under** which **they were never relieved.** Pompey restores the high-priesthood to Hyrcanus and carries Aristobulus and his son Antigonus to Rome.

25. Alexander, son of Aristobulus, escaping from Pompey on the way to Rome, is made high-priest; tries to subvert the government, and his effort is twice suppressed by the Roman Gabinius.

26. Antigonus, son of **Aristobulus**, escapes from Rome, and gets the high-priesthood. Hyrcanus (23d **high-priest**), delivered into his hands by the **Parthians, kneels before** Antigonus, who bites off his uncle's **ears, so that the latter might** no longer aspire to the high-priesthood.[1] Antigonus is taken by Antony, whipped, crucified, and decapitated.

27. Ananelus, an inferior priest, sent **for** out of Babylon, is made high-priest by Herod. Alexandra, daughter of Hyrcanus, combining with Mariam, Herod's wife, had him deposed, and caused him to be succeeded by

28. Aristobulus, **fifteen years** of age, **of rare** beauty. After one year's enjoyment of it, he is drowned by Herod's order, and Ananelus (No. 27) is restored.

29. Jesus son of Farans. Herod deposes him.

30. Simon son of Boethius. Herod married his daughter, **and** made him high-priest.

31. Matthias, **son of Theophilus. Deposed by Herod.**

32. Jozarus, son of Simon (No. 30). Herod deposes him.

33. Eleazur; made high-priest by Archelaus.

34. Jesus, son of Sie; gets Eleazur removed, and has his place.

35. Jozarus (No. 32) again. Was high-priest at the birth of Christ. Removed.

36. Ananus; **made high-priest** by Cyrenius. Removed.

37. Ismael; appointed by Valerius Gratus, governor of Judea. Removed by Gratus at the end of one year.[2]

---

[1] Jos. Bel. i. 13, § 9.   [2] Jos. Ant. xviii. 2, § 2.

38. Eleazur, son of Ananus; appointed by Gratus; held it one year; removed by the same.
39. Simon; appointed by Gratus; held it one year.
40. Caiaphas, also called Josephus.   He was Gratus's creature also.
    These four changes were made by Gratus in eleven years. Annas, or Ananus, who **had been** high-priest, four changes before him, is said to be high-priest with him, (Luke iii. 2).   Caiphas was [afterwards] removed **by** Vitellius.[1]

This will **help us to form an idea of the tribunal plotting the** death **of the Messiah by subtilty, and before which he was to** appear **for** judgment—a body **of seventy** men, almost entirely Pharisees—chiefly such characters as he had **delineated** in his temple address; some believing on him, but too timid to acknowledge their belief; at their head a high-priest, at a time when that office was given or taken away at the caprice of the Roman governor, and was little respected; the Sanhedrim, sufficiently full of hate itself, and stimulated still more by the other Scribes and Pharisees. The recklessness with which this body proceeded in the trial to tread under foot all former laws and usages and went forward to the end, shows the strength **of the venom** in their hearts.

CHAPTER XLI.

THE SUPPER AT BETHANY.—JUDAS.

THE means which the Sanhedrim desired for effecting their purposes were speedily found.   There was a traitor among the disciples **themselves.**

Events have just been multiplying so fast, that an effort

---

[1] Lightfoot.

will be necessary, in order to keep them clearly in our minds. We therefore recapitulate and observe that,

The 9th of the Jewish month, Nisan, corresponding to our *Saturday*, (the Jewish Sabbath), the Messiah spent at Jericho.

10th.—He came to Bethany.

11th.—His public entry into Jerusalem; returns for the night to Bethany.

12th.—Comes again to Jericho. Cleanses the temple; teaches; returns to Bethany.

13th. *Wednesday.*—Again in Jerusalem; discourses in the temple. The woes denounced. The Sanhedrim have their consultation and form their plans.

On the evening of this last day, after those denunciations in the temple, and the quiet scene on Olivet where the disciples, in the anticipation of common danger, drew nearer in heart to their Master than ever before, he and they proceeded to Bethany, where they were now entertained at supper in the house of "Simon the leper," Lazarus being one of the guests at the feast.[1] Among the Jews, a slight dinner, chiefly of fruits, milk, cheese, etc., was eaten at eleven o'clock of our time, their principal meal being at six or seven in the evening. Their feasts were always at this latter time. Hands were washed before eating, and the feet of the guests or travellers also, sometimes by servants, or by members of the family, where particular honor was intended,[2] as is done indeed at the present day.

This time was one when all the tender sensibilities of Christ's friends were deeply aroused; for there was in all of them a sense of some impending danger to him—of probably some fearful calamity; his own words, the known

---

[1] Matt. xxvi. 6; John xii. 2.

[2] See 1 Sam. xxv. 41; Gen. xviii. 4, and xix. 2; also "Robinson's Researches," Vol. iii. p. 25, describing the manner in which the feet of his party were washed at Ramleh.

fierce and cunning wrath of his enemies, and the scenes of the day, all going to show that a crisis must be drawing nigh. Every person knew that those woes hurled so thickly on the rulers would not be forgotten: these men had never been so reprobated, exposed, and in effect defied, before; and all this now by one individual, without resources in governmental help or powerful friends. Only a miracle could save him; and that exercise of power although within his reach, he had intimated he would not exert. He had said that he would submit, and had declared that his death by violence was near: and the prophet long before had said that he should be "led as a sheep to the slaughter," that "the chastisement of our peace was [to be] upon him," that "with his stripes we should be healed," and that the Lord had "laid on him the iniquity of us all."[1] He himself knew that this would be his last supper at Bethany among these friends; for his hour would now soon come.

While they were at this meal, Mary, the sister of Lazarus came in, and opening a vessel of very costly perfume, she poured some of it on his head,[2] and with it also washed his feet, after which she wiped them with the hair of her head; the scent of the opo-balsam filling all the house. There was a secret indignation among some of the disciples at this waste, when they thought how the money might have been spent among the poor, and Judas spake out his thoughts, "Why was not this ointment sold for three hundred pence[3] [equal to $45 of our money] and given to the poor?" not that he felt uncommon sympathy for the poor, but "because he was a thief and had the bag and bore what was put therein." The Messiah said, "Let her alone: against the day of my burying hath she kept this. For the poor always ye have with you; but me ye have not always."[4]

---

[1] Is. liii. 5, 6.   [2] Matt. xxvi. 7.
[3] A penny, or Denarius, was a day's wages for a laboring man: See Matt. xx. 2.   [4] John xii. 3.

29

What momentous events seem at times to hang on little things:—seem to us; but in the inscrutable counsels of God, where, and where only his purposes and our free agency can be reconciled, they do not seem so to depend; all being foreknown to him. From this time Judas was a traitor, the worst that the world has ever known.

When he had been selected to be among the twelve, he was probably a man in character and disposition much like the others, but of financial capabilities better than theirs. They were all dark in mind and self-seeking; but still with varieties of dispositions and intellect, which in their peculiar position became every day more developed and marked. Christ exerted no miraculous power over their wills, but left their affections and wills free to act; trying to influence them by his own great example and teachings;—still leaving them to choose. With Christ himself before him day by day, for about three years, Judas still chose the wrong. What a wonderful history his would be if we knew it;—those transitions from bad to worse, and still worse in his heart; the struggles there,—for there were doubtless such, early in his case; the admiration for Christ gradually lessened by base passions rising in him and taking its place: the affection always weak perhaps, but sometimes lighted up to greater strength, then flickering and dying away, and at last dead: and then all the soul's life in him dead.

Doubtless Judas endeavored in his own mind to justify himself;—as what man in his case does not?—and probably with a result half satisfactory to himself. He might try to consider himself an injured man, led on for three years with expectations of great final triumph and reward; but thwarted just at the very time when the reward seemed to be within reach. On Monday the multitudes had saluted his Master in terms of reverence and worship. Once before they had endeavored to put him in the seat of royalty, but he had withdrawn himself from them; and now the outburst of enthusiasm had broken through every restraint and the shouts of their hosannas had rung over Jerusalem and through the temple cloisters. How easy would it have been for Jesus, sustained by his miraculous powers, to have made himself the mighty earthly ruler so long expected and hoped for; and to have aggrandized and made glorious the whole Jewish nation! And in refusing this, (the traitor might argue) he had done a wrong to all the Jewish people; and especially to Judas, who might in that new kingdom have become so wealthy. Worse than that, he had offended all the rulers and insulted them (still, Judas arguing) with woes heaped on them, and insulted the nation by declaring that God was withdrawing his favor from it, soon to give it to another people. So all hopes of aggrandizement and wealth from this source had perished from the mind of Judas, who had hoped to be treasurer in that great earthly kingdom which all were expecting to see established.

One other bitter ingredient had just been put into that cup, where every drop seemed to him now to be turning into gall. It was when the Messiah on their way from Jerusalem had told his disciples that they should be everywhere persecuted, betrayed by father and brother; should be hated, and some of them put to death. He had spoken of the Comforter that should be with them and of their inward peace and their final rewards in heaven; but an avaricious man could see nothing in all this except the suffering and the persecution and the losses; no requital to a heart like his.

Here now at the supper when his indignation about the waste showed itself, he was met with a reproof, gentle in its tone and very mild, but in his state of feeling all the more provoking to him from its very mildness. It manifested such a want of an appreciation of money and of him, the treasurer; he felt also now, from Christ's insight into his character, that his hypocrisy was to him unmasked, his motive known and his thieving revealed.

So Satan entered into him now,[1] unresisted, and had the full possession.

One thought more, and that was quickly supplied by the Tempter.   If Christ must die, why then might not he, Judas, *have a pecuniary benefit from the event?*

The love of money is declared in Scripture to be the root of *all* evil; and on the very next day Judas went to the Jewish rulers to bargain for betraying his Master, with whom he could still remain, and of whose movements he could inform them, and also the most fitting time for their purposes. All was soon agreed upon.   He asked them, "What will ye give me and I will deliver him unto you?   And they covenanted with him for thirty pieces of silver," the price of a slave according to the old Jewish law.[2]

CHAPTER XLII.

THE PASSOVER FEAST.

A GREAT festival commemorative of the most remarkable event in the Jewish history had come down to them from the day when they first properly began to be a nation.   Their forefathers had been slaves in Egypt.   One night, after a series of miracles designed to set them free, but resisted by the Egyptian monarch, a visitation the most appalling possible to their bond-masters was to effect their deliverance.   The first-born in every family was to be that night slain by a divine judgment throughout that whole

----

[1] Luke xxii. 3.

[2] Exodus xxi. 32.   If this money was in shekels, thirty pieces would amount to $15 05 of our money; if the Roman *stater*, to $22 50.

country, the houses of the Israelites alone being excepted. It was a momentous time; on the one side seemingly their last hope of deliverance from slavery; on the other a visitation made that raised a universal cry of anguish, wailing for the Egyptian dead over all the land, and those dead the favored ones, the first-born, in every house. In the morning the Jews were sent off—deliverance had come.

The Feast of the Passover in commemoration of this *passing by* the Israelitish houses when all others were visited by the vengeful messenger, was the greatest of all the Jewish festivals, and brought to Jerusalem the whole Jewish people from their own region and from distant lands. This immense assemblage had on their arrival to divide themselves into companies of not less than ten or more than twenty,[1] and each company had to prepare a lamb, or if no lamb could be found, a kid to be eaten on this occasion. It was to be a male of that year without blemish, and was to be brought on the day before the commencement of the festival to the great altar of the temple, and killed there between the hours of three and six in the afternoon. This was to be on the 14th of the month Abib, (afterward called Nisan), the first month of their sacred year. The blood was sprinkled at the foot of the altar, the fat taken out and thrown into the fire on the altar, the body carried home for the supper and roasted whole, the skin given to the owner of the house. All houses in Jerusalem were on this occasion open indiscriminately to the public, and might be used by common right during the feast. The flesh not eaten at the supper was to be burned together with the bones. There was also other meat, called the peace-offering, placed on the table to take off the edge of their appetites, so that they might not eat voraciously of the Paschal lamb, also in case it might not be sufficient for a large company.

---

[1] Tholuck.

At or before noon of the 14th all leaven was to be carefully removed from the houses, and during eight days they were to eat only unleavened bread, in commemoration of the haste with which their ancestors had left their place of bondage. Bitter herbs[1] were also to be provided for this Paschal supper, and they had also a sauce, called *charoseth*, composed of things sweet and bitter pounded together in memory of the clay in which their forefathers labored when making bricks in the land of Egypt.

After sunset (now the beginning of the 15th, by the Jewish reckoning, their day beginning at sunset), the company assembled and took their places around the table, reclining on couches, (the posture of freemen), to show that they had got out of servitude into freedom. On other occasions the Jews might choose their posture, and they often sat at table, but at the Paschal supper their rulers prescribed that "a man is bound to eat and to drink and to sit in a posture of freedom," that is to recline.

That was the usual posture among the Greeks and Romans at their feasts. They leaned on the left arm, a cushion or bolster under the shoulder assisting to ease the posture; and if there were several at table, the chief person occupied the middle place, the others in front or back of him, or similarly arranged at other tables placed at right angles with this. As they reclined slantingly to the table, so as to bring each man's head before the chest of the one next behind him, if the former wished to speak to the latter, especially if it was anything secret, he leaned his head back on the bosom of the other (*in sinus recumbere*, Plin. Epist. iv. 22). The Gemara says of the Persians that, "when they could not discourse because of their way of leaning at meals, they talked by signs either with their hands or upon their fin-

---

[1] Ex. xii. 8.

gers:" and the Jews had probably adopted the same custom
during their captivity in Persia.

On the morning of the 14th of Nisan (our Thursday) the
Messiah sent two disciples, Peter and John, from Bethany to
Jerusalem, to prepare for the Passover supper: in the evening he and the remainder of them followed to that city.
We may easily imagine the traitor, in this to him uncon-
genial, but for the present necessary, companionship; for he
was watching for the best time and place in which to execute
his contract with the Sanhedrim. He had that day bar-
gained with them; had returned and joined the party of the
disciples; and was now accompanying them to unite in the
Paschal supper. What a thoroughly depraved wretch he
must have felt himself to be, in spite of every effort of
justification in his own mind! We can imagine him, sometimes afraid to look his Master or companions in the face;
sometimes trying to be brazen and composed, but failing
continually in the effort; sometimes shrinking away and
wishing to be apart from the company; and again mingling
with them in order to prevent suspicion, and because he
hated to be alone with his own thoughts. We can see his
eye cowering before the looks of others; or assuming an
impudent, or affectedly-composed, or defiant expression;
sometimes startled by words from them which were innocent
of any particular meaning, but yet, in his convictions, seeming to be pointed at him; often wondering whether his own
changed tones of voice, or his unaccounted-for absence, in
the morning, or his present manner, might not have betrayed
him. He followed on, thus, over Olivet, and into the city;
feeling, as he entered it, that he was bound by a hellish
compact with the rulers there; and that men so determined
in malice as they had showed themselves to be, held him
now in their power, in a kind of triumph through his
weakness and baseness. He had seen that triumph in their
gladness and the glistening of their eyes that day, as the

compact was made; and he knew that they despised him, while they were thankful and glad. Of his Master, and of that long-continued kindness to him, and gentleness, and Divine goodness, he dared not think at all, to-day; for every such thought was a dagger, and made him shrink with pain.

They proceeded to the room selected for this meal, and soon afterwards took their places at the table; John being in front of the Messiah, as they reclined on their couches. But, alas! even in this time of deep distress when, as they had been informed, the hour of agony and death was close at hand, the old feeling of ambition and strife revived.[1] Perhaps it was on the question, who should have the second place of honor at the table, which was always the one just in front of the Master; perhaps it had originated from some other matter even more discreditable than that; but the Saviour,—how merciful, how gentle, how Godlike in this mercy and gentleness!—said to them, "The kings of the Gentiles exercise lordship over them; and they that exercise authority upon them are called benefactors. But ye shall not be so: but he that is greatest among you, let him be as the younger; and he that is chief as he that doth serve. For whether is greater, he that sitteth at meat, or he that serveth? Is not he that sitteth at meat? but I am among you as one that serveth,"[2] &c. So, in order to impress this injunction, he arose from table and, laying aside his upper garment, took a basin and towel, and entered on a very menial office, that of washing their feet. By the usages of that country, this was never done by a superior to an inferior; and when he came to Peter, that impetuous disciple drew back:

"Lord, dost thou wash my feet?" and declared that it should never be done.

---

[1] Luke xxii. 24.   [2] Ib. 25–27.

"If I wash thee not, thou hast no part with me," was the reply; and the startled disciple cried out:

"Lord, not my feet only, but also my hands and my head."[1]

Judas was amongst them, and Christ, doubtless, washed his feet also. How the conscious traitor must have shrunk at his touch!

The company, however, was not long troubled with the presence of this man. Soon after their reclining at table, the rest of the disciples, for the first time, became aware that there was such a traitor among them. The Saviour said:

"Verily I say unto you, One of you which eateth with me shall betray me."

A shudder must have gone through them, with a deep gloom on the heart; and there must have been a quivering of the lip, as they all asked,

"Lord, is it I?"

No consciousness among the eleven, but a query by each whether he was suspected, and a wish, by the expected answer, to stand acquitted before the company. They turned upon each other inquisitive and doubting glances;—those men who had been with him so long, so attached, erring often, always dark in apprehensions, grieving him by their mistakes;—but traitor! who was the miscreant? Their glances went around the table; their feelings were warm with indignation; they were ready to shrink from each other:—after all this fellowship, and these pleasant communings, a traitor! Who was he? Peter could bear it no longer; but gave John a secret sign to question further; and this disciple, leaning back so as to bring his head on the Saviour's breast, asked, in a whisper, who it was. The

---

[1] John xiii. 6–9. "Among the duties required from a wife towards her husband, there was one, that she should wash his face, his hands, and his feet. This was expected by a father from his son; the same from a servant toward his master."—*Lightfoot.*

answer was a certain signal by which John could know and could communicate to Peter who was the individual.[1] To Judas he said:

"That thou doest, do quickly;" an expression enigmatical to the rest, but the traitor, excited and thrown off his guard, asked—

"Master, is it I?" The answer was—

"Thou hast said,"[2] equivalent to, "It is thou." He left the room unmasked, a fugitive from their company and from his Lord—lost.

One of the disciples gone, and he a traitor!

There was a vacant place at the table. What of the rest? A gloomy feeling fell on the company, such as there always is from desertion. A vacancy sometimes has connected with it remembrances of worth and nobleness, but there was none in the present case. Baseness, hypocrisy, treachery were the remembrances that Judas left behind, and there was no wickedness that now they might not expect from him, directed probably against themselves. Contempt for his conduct could scarcely buoy them up, for he had been one of them, and they felt that the baseness had been directly from among their own company. They were prostrated in spirit by the discovery, felt disgraced, dishonored by the recent companionship—what suspicions might not the Master have now about them? They looked toward the vacant place with a deep sinking in their hearts, toward the Master so long the beloved, the admired, the venerated, in their inmost soul. His face was very sad. Could he doubt *them?* Nay, why might he not doubt them now? Eyes were turned again upon him, trying to read in his face expressions of confidence and trust in them. He spoke by-and-by, and the words were even more dark and gloomy than their saddest thoughts. "*All ye shall be offended because of me this night,*

---

[1] John xiii. 23-28.   [2] Matt. xxvi. 25.

for it is written, I will smite the shepherd and the sheep shall be scattered abroad." Even on the back of this assertion there was no censure of them, but simply the promise, "But after that I am risen, I will go before you into Galilee."[1] Indeed there was almost too much prostration of feeling among the company generally for any sentiment except grief; yet even then hope was given to them. But Peter spake up, for his heart recoiled at the thought of the general desertion, and he knew not yet how weak he himself was. His voice was confident: "Though all should be offended of thee yet will I not be offended." And he looked for an approval of his bravery. It came not, but the answer, "Verily I say unto thee that this day, even in this night, before the cock crow twice, thou shalt deny me thrice."[2] The tones of the Saviour's voice must have been even sadder than the words, and both drew from Peter with still greater vehemence the assertion, "If I should die with thee, I will not deny thee in anywise." And the others said the same.[3] They had been roused up by Peter's vehemence; their feelings rallied around their Lord, and they broke through the gloom consequent on Judas's desertion to make bold protestations of their fidelity. It was not kept.

The whole procedure at this meal was specially prescribed, and according to the account of the Talmud it was as follows :—

1. The guests being placed around the table they mingled a cup of wine with water over which the master of the family (or if two or more families were united a person deputed for the purpose) gave thanks and drank it off. The thanksgiving for the wine was to this effect: "Blessed be thou, O Lord, who hast created the fruit of the vine," and for the day as follows: "Blessed be thou for this good day, and for this holy convocation which thou hast given us for

---

[1] Mark xiv. 30, 31,   [2] Matt. xxvi. 31, 32.   [3] Ibid. 32-35.

joy and rejoicing. Blessed be thou, O Lord, who hast sanctified Israel and the **times.**"

2. They then washed their hands, after which the table was furnished with the Paschal lamb roasted whole, with bitter herbs and with two cakes of unleavened bread, together with the flesh of the peace-offering and the *charoseth* or thick sauce above mentioned.

3. The officiator, or person presiding, then took a small piece of the salad, and having blessed God for creating the fruit of the ground he ate it, the other guests following his example, after which all the dishes were removed from the table that the children might inquire and be instructed in the nature of the feast. (Ex. xii. 25, 26). The text on which they generally discoursed was Deut. xxvi. 5–11.

4. Then replacing the supper they explained the import of the bitter herbs and Paschal lamb, and over a second cup of wine repeated Psalms cxiii. and cxiv., with an eucharistic prayer.

5. The hands were again washed, accompanied by an ejaculatory prayer, after which the master of the house proceeded to break and bless a cake of the unleavened bread, half of which he distributed among the guests, reserving half beneath a napkin if necessary for the *aphicomas* or last morsel, for the rule was to conclude with eating a small piece of the Paschal lamb.

6. They then ate the rest of the cake with the bitter herbs, dipping the bread in the charoseth or sauce.

7. Next they ate the flesh of the peace-offering, and then the flesh of the Paschal lamb, which was followed by returning thanks to God and a second washing of the hands.

8. A third cup of wine was then filled, over which they blessed God or said grace after meat, (whence it was called the cup of blessing),[1] and the wine was drank.

---

[1] See 1 Cor. x. 16.

9. Lastly, a fourth cup of wine was filled, called the cup of the Hallel, over that they completed the supper either by singing or reciting the great Hallel, a hymn of praise consisting of Psalms cxv. to cxviii., inclusive, and also with a prayer.[1]

If the Messiah followed **this order** it was doubtless in **the** fifth and eighth **parts of it that the eucharistic feast of the** Christian church was instituted : "**Take, eat, this is** *my body,* which **is given for you ; this do in remembrance of me.**" "**This cup is the new testament in** *my blood,* which is shed for you."

" My blood of the *new covenant ;*" for that is here the meaning of the word. A covenant is an agreement between two individuals to do or forbear some act or thing ; *a contract :* and it was here a contract by the Messiah on one side to be sealed with his own life-blood.

There was once, long before this time, a scene of great solemnity at the foot of Sinai, just after God had given to Moses on **the** top **of** the mountain **the** written covenant : and that scene was when that **covenant was** ratified by **the** people of Israel, with the shedding **of the** blood of victims, —burnt-offerings and **peace-offerings to God. There had** just then **been the most imposing event that our world has** ever **witnessed : for on Sinai there were "thunders and** lightnings, and a **thick black cloud upon the mount, and the** voice of the trumpet sounding loud : so that all the people that were in the camp trembled. And Moses brought forth the people out of the camp to meet with God : and they stood at the nether part of the mount. And Mount Sina¹ **was** altogether on a smoke, because the Lord descended upon it **on fire : and** the smoke thereof **ascended as** the smoke of a furnace, **and the whole mount quaked greatly.** * * * And **all the people saw the** thunderings and the lightnings,

---

[1] Horne's " Introduction," originally from Lightfoot.

and the voice of the trumpet and the mountain smoking, and when the people saw it they removed and stood afar off. And they said unto Moses, Speak thou with us and we will hear: but let not God speak with us lest we die."[1]

Their leader had now come down from the mountain top, and from the cloud shrouding that Majesty which none might see clearly and live; and he told to the people "all the words of the Lord, and all the judgments: and all the people answered with one voice and said, All the words which the Lord hath said will we do." He wrote down the words; and built an altar, and erected twelve pillars to represent the tribes. Then on this altar, they offered burnt-offerings and sacrificed peace-offerings of oxen unto the Lord. And Moses took half of the blood, and put it in basins; and half of the blood he sprinkled on the altar. And he took the *book of the covenant*, and read it in the audience of the people; and they said,

"All that the Lord hath said will we do, and be obedient."

"And Moses took the blood, and *sprinkled it on the people*, and said, *Behold the blood of the covenant, which the Lord hath made with you concerning all these words.*"[2]

It was a grand and most solemn and imposing spectacle. How different from it in all the outward seeming, was this spectacle in the private room at Jerusalem, where Christ who had just before laid aside his upper garments to wash his disciples' feet, now brake the bread to them, and gave them the cup to drink. But there was a moral grandeur in this simple scene, which no cloud enveloping a mountain, and thunder and lightning there, could ever reach: for he said respecting this new covenant, "This cup is the new testament in my blood, which is shed for you."[3] *His own*

---

[1] Exodus xix. 10–18; xx. 18, 19.   [2] Exodus xxiv. 3–8.
[3] Luke xxii. 20.

blood it was which was to be sprinkled on all nations; he the sacrifice for all the world!

The Israelites moved off from Sinai, awed and frightened by the earthquakes and the signs on the mountain's brow; and they said to Moses, "Speak thou with us and we will hear; but let not God speak with us, lest we die;" but the words of Christ draw us toward him and toward heaven, through the fullness of love to all men which they display.

Having finished the Passover meal, they sang their hymn: and then before leaving the room, there was an address from the Messiah to his disciples, and afterwards a prayer, to both of which angels might well have been listeners; for the words seem to blend together both heaven and earth. They were the last of the teachings of the greatest Teacher earth has known or ever will know.

We perceive in the words of this address, shades of thought never seen but in the truest and deepest affection, which always has promptings of its own peculiar kind. "In my Father's house are many mansions: if it were not so I would have told you. I go to prepare a place for you. And if I go and prepare a place for you, I will come again and receive you unto myself; that where I am there ye may be also." That was a most tender as well as true regard, which, when he should get into possession of the kingdom in heaven, would not be contented till it had brought him to take them up to himself. Yet they were frail men, full of darkness and errors.

How tender and beautiful is the love of Christ! He had now almost completed his mission on the earth. He had been our Example and our Teacher: one act remained,—*to die for us.* The cross was to be raised up before all the world as evidence of God's hatred of sin, and of the unyielding nature of his law against unrighteousness;— Christ to be there, the expiation, the voluntary sacrifice offered for all mankind. "As Moses lifted up the serpent in the wilderness, even so must the Son of man be lifted up; that whosoever believeth in him should not perish, but have eternal life."[1]   He had often looked forward to this event with shudderings of his human nature at its horrors; yet he turned not aside, but said, "For this cause came I unto this hour."   The hour was now close at hand.

CHAPTER XLIII.

GETHSEMANE.

THE traitor in the meanwhile was busy in his work. He knew the habits and resorts of the Messiah; and was forwarding preparations for the seizure, which the Sanhedrim intended to make this night. Their plans were laid: they had now a ready instrument for the first act, bought with their gold.   A company was formed, subordinates of the Sanhedrim and temple,[2] armed and sufficient in number to bear down opposition: but strong as it was, the chief priests and captains and elders also attended,[3] to see that their work was surely done.   The traitor had given as a signal, the act of kindest friendship in salutation, "Whomsoever I shall kiss, that same is he; hold him fast."[4]

Silently their preparations were made; the traitor sometimes looking to see that the company was sufficiently large and of the right spirit; sometimes sending his thoughts back to that supper-table, to the agitating question put around, "Is it I?" and to the sadness on the Saviour's face in that scene; and, most of all, to the words respecting himself by

---

[1] John iii. 14, 15.   [2] Mark xiv. 43.   [3] Luke xxii. 52.   [4] Matt. xxvi. 48.

Christ, "It had been good for that man if he had not been born :"[1] and sometimes, perhaps, he queried, whether Christ would not, when this party should appear, disperse, or over-awe them by his miraculous powers; or pass unharmed from among them, as he had often done before. Perhaps Judas expected this last : and thought with a high degree of satis-faction that in such a case he would still have his pay secured.

Thus they were prepared, and were awaiting in Jerusalem the order to move.

It was the time of the full moon; and a mellow light was shed on the streets of the city and the hills about it, as the Messiah and his disciples left their supper-room, and, pass-ing the eastern gate, descended the slope leading down toward the Kedron. They went along in sadness; their minds filled with the solemn events at that Passover meal, and with the sense of the fierce trials close at hand ; and as they met, or passed, company after company on the way, the festive gladness of the latter came jarring on their hearts. How easily could a few words from the Messiah, then, have aroused all those multitudes,—more than two millions—in and about the city, and have made them the quick executors of his will and power: for the general enthusiasm toward him needed but a spark to make it, to all opposers a consu-ming flame; and his miraculous powers could also have called even angels down, if need should be. But he passed on in silence: he did not desire observation, but retirement and a few hours for prayer : and he would then be ready for the self-sacrifice which was to drain his life-blood. His hour had come : and the deed he knew, was necessary for the redemption of our race.

But still the trial to his human nature would be horrible; and he felt it already with a shrinking and a quivering

---

[1] Matt. xxvi. 24.

through all his frame; the death convulsions foreshadowing themselves during the silent anticipations of that night.

We cannot understand the mysteries of the divine and human natures in Christ. All we know is that the human nature was such as ours, with all its capacity for suffering pain; and that, having lived our life here, God knows, from his own sufferings, to pity man:—also, that the Divinity was in him there with its greatness and power; and doubtless too, with such a keenness in all the intellectual and emotional sensations in this suffering, as our minds can never comprehend, and our hearts can never know. It was so in all the life of Christ; his intellect, his emotions, not simply ours but ours *sublimed* and passing off to those of the God, though still having their home here on earth. How far all this might work concentrated horrors—infinite in extent, —into these few hours of time at Gethsemane, and into these anticipations, and into the sufferings when they really came, who can tell? "The spirit of a man may bear his infirmities, but a *wounded spirit,* who can *bear it?*" If so with man, how was it with Christ!

Across the valley of Jehoshaphat, and somewhere on the slopes of Olivet, was a garden, Gethsemane[1] by name, which he had been in the habit of frequenting with his disciples;[2] and to this place they now ascended; the hushed noises of the city, and of those of the multitudes who had not yet gone to repose, scarcely reaching that retired spot. The Messiah felt the need of prayer—of communion with the Father, and of strengthening for the coming hours, in which his human nature would be so fearfully tried. Having reached Gethsemane, he said to the disciples, "Pray that ye enter not into temptation;" and then, taking Peter, and James, and John, he went with them further into the garden apart from the rest. Here, also, he left these three, saying,

---

[1] Meaning "place of olive presses."   [2] John xviii. 2.

as he did so, "My soul is exceeding sorrowful, even unto death:" and he went then further, alone, for prayer. He fell on his face; and it was a time of anguish such as no human thought can ever reach. We know it but in part from his words of prayer, "O my Father, *if it be possible*, let this cup pass from me;" "take away this cup from me;"[1] yet, with the addition, "nevertheless, not what I will, but what thou wilt." The fearfulness of the struggle in him is only shadowed to us; for the reality cannot be reached by words. "Sorrowful, *even unto death*," and that in Christ! in him who had come to suffer, and to redeem the world by suffering this death, and had predicted it frequently, and had advanced steadily toward it, but was now involved in horror so great that, for a moment, this had the mastery. What must the agony in that prayer have been; even the Divine nature borne down, as if dissolution were near! What a depth of horror was there! Yet, "not as I will, but as thou wilt;" and with those words the fierceness of that almost mortal anguish passed away.

The prayer was brief; for such sensations could not be endured by any human nature long; and he came back to where the three disciples had been left. They were asleep. How different their quiet rest, their unconsciousness, the relaxed limbs and the breathing in their deep repose, from the agony that had just been almost crushing him, and which still made itself felt in all his system! The night, also, so mellow and so calm! The light of the full moon over the hushed landscape; and the soft music of the nightingales harmonizing with all else made it a scene of perfect midnight beauty; but all this—the mellowness, the beauty, the nightingales' song,—all jarred terribly on a nature so distressed and just now so wildly tossed with horror,—almost so abandoned, seemingly, of heaven and earth.

---

[1] Matt. xxvi. 39; Mark xiv. 36.

He awoke the disciples with words of half reproach, but which, in his gentle nature, were qualified immediately with an apology for them: "What! could ye not watch with me one hour? Watch and pray that ye enter not into temptation: the spirit indeed is willing, but the flesh is weak."[1]

He left them a second time, retiring once more for prayer, and the convulsion of anguish again passed over him, but modified by an entire resignation to the will of God. "O my Father, if this cup may not pass away from me, except I drink it, thy will be done." The convulsions that seemed as of a divinity perishing, "my soul sorrowful unto death," must have been indeed frightful beyond any but infinite power to understand.

He came back again to the three disciples, and found them as before in deep and quiet sleep, for it was late now and "their eyes were heavy." Again, in strong contrast to his own feelings was that hush in all the scene, as if nature might be almost in mockery of its Master; the world in its perfectness of repose appearing to have shut him out and to be closed against him abandoned in his agony; and yet it was to ransom its millions and bring them to salvation that he was about to suffer. He spoke to the disciples again, but they answered him confusedly and only half aroused, and he left them once more for his retirement and prayer. There was a strange restlessness in the Messiah that night, a part of the terrible nervous strain upon his system, and of the agitations of his internal being—how different from his former long seasons of quiet communion with God on the mountains of Galilee! These were briefer, broken times of prayer, with an agitation that could not long admit of quiet even in such communion. FOR THE PRAYER ITSELF WAS A CONVULSION; and during this third one a sweat of blood broke out upon him, the bloody perspiration falling in great

---

[1] Matt. xxvi. 41.

drops to the ground.[1] In that anguish, which brought the blood thus oozing from his face and body, an angel came to his side to sustain and comfort him.

Mortal man may never fathom the depth of that agony in Gethsemane!

He came a third time to his disciples, and told them that the hour was now at hand.

This was indeed soon apparent even to their half-aroused consciousness; for torches and lanterns were now seen gleaming amid the garden-alleys on Olivet, and voices coming nearer were heard, and very soon the company in Gethsemane were all surrounded by a rude multitude armed with swords and staves. Judas came forward:

"Hail, Master!" and he kissed him.

The others pressed around.

"Whom seek ye?" the Messiah asked.

"Jesus of Nazareth."

"I am he," he said, and faced them calmly, and as he did so the company shrank down before him, for there was a strange power in that Presence even there, although his greatest humiliations were begun. Urged on, however, by their leaders the armed men seized him, and a scene of confusion for a little while ensued. Peter made resistance, and a servant of the high-priest was maimed, but Christ healed the man adding a reproof to his follower for the act: "Put up thy sword into the sheath; the cup which my Father

---

[1] Luke xxii. 44. Dr. Mead from Galen, observes: Contingere interdum poros, ex multo aut fervido spiritu adeo dilatari, ut etiam exeat sanguis per eos, fiatque sudor sanguineus: *It happens sometimes that by great or deep mental agitation the pores are so much dilated that blood issues from them and there is a bloody sweat.* (Quoted from Clarke's Commentary.) "An interesting example of a sweat of blood, under circumstances of terror, accompanied by loss of speech is given in an article by Dr. Schneider in Casper's Wochenschrift for 1848, and cited in the Medical Gazette for that year."—*Alford.*

hath given me, shall I not drink it?"[1] He said also to Peter, "Thinkest thou that I cannot now pray to my Father, and he shall presently give me more than twelve legions of angels? But how then shall the Scriptures be fulfilled that thus it must be."[2] He spoke further to the leaders, asking why they had come as against a thief with swords and staves? He asked no favors of them for himself, but for his disciples that they might be allowed to depart uninjured. They proceeded immediately to bind him,[3] and then led him away. The disciples fled.[4]

CHAPTER XLIV.

HALL OF CAIAPHAS.

THE Pharisees and chief priests and rulers had so far succeeded. It was night, and the millions at the pass-over having eaten the paschal supper were now asleep. A comparative quiet reigned in Jerusalem and through its suburbs and on Olivet, as the armed men having the Messiah now bound in their charge passed back in the city and threaded its streets. They were conducted first to the house of Annas. This individual, called also Ananus, had been high-priest himself, and was yet styled such as a token of respect; he was father-in-law to Caiaphas, at present in the high priesthood, and father also of Eleazar, late high-priest, and was moreover at this time Sagan or prefect to the priests, an office of which there is frequent mention among the Rab-bins.[5] His age and his former and present offices gave his

---

[1] John xviii. 11.
[2] John xviii. 8, 12.
[5] Lightfoot, *in loco.*

[3] Matt. xxvi. 53, 54.
[4] Mark xiv. 50.

opinions weight; and the proceedings of this night, all so irregular in their character, needed every extraneous aid that could be procured in order to shield the perpetrators. For in the morning when the multitudes would wake up and receive information of these acts during the night, there would be a great excitment and many inquiries would be started tending to a tumult, **against all which they desired** to be able immediately to present the highest Jewish **authority.** Annas had no power as a judge, and any meeting at his house **would be an informal one, but it was important** to be able to quote his opinion in **a decided manner before** the populace.

From his house they proceeded very soon to the palace of Caiaphas himself. The Sanhedrim in the meantime had been collecting there, and the Messiah still bound was now in the presence of his judges evidently met not for trial but for condemnation. The case had been already in their minds fully prejudged. This was not, however, a formal sitting of the Sanhedrim; for such according to their laws could not be held by night, and no trial could regularly be commenced at night; and as these judges would in the morning be on **trial** themselves in the **minds of the people, it was necessary to** keep up **the appearance of adhering to the forms of law.** All the while over the **Sanhedrim hung the dread of the** populace **and of tumults, and of thus being** foiled at last. They planned that when their decision should come before the people it should come suddenly, and should be a decision adapted to stamp such black infamy upon the accused as would astound and stupefy the hearers, until the governor's quickly-added judgment should put the whole matter into the hands **of the military, and not only** defy resistance from **the multitudes, but also save the Sanhedrim** from the consequences of possible **tumult by having made it a** governmental affair. Therefore the object **was to have** now a secret examination **in order that all** preparations **might** be made for a quick decision in the formal, regular meeting, which the Sanhedrim would afterwards have at earliest dawn.

The house at Damascus, described in chapter xix. of this book, will afford us a good idea of the plan of this one of Caiaphas; but the latter was probably on a much larger scale, and its raised reception room at the side of the court was of sufficient proportions to accommodate the council now assembled. We may presume that instead of a recess with one arch and divan, as in the former house, this had several arches and columns separating its large hall from the court, but with no other division between it and the spectators in the court. As the high-priest was president of the Sanhedrim, his palace would in all probability have such a place for public trials, where the proceedings both within the hall and without would be open to inspection on either side. The present was however very far from being a public trial, but was a secret conclave as it had need to be. Peter who had followed his Master at a distance found, on presenting himself, that the doors were closed against him, and he was admitted only at the solicitation of John, who was known to the high-priest, and who spoke to the woman doing duty as gate-keeper,[1] that office being sometimes occupied by women in Judea.[2]

The court was now filled with soldiers and attendants; the two gates giving access from the street were shut against intruders; the place was lighted up by torches flaring from the columns or walls; the Sanhedrim, at least such of them as were willing to engage in this secret, hellish work were there, sitting and gloating their eyes on him whom they felt to be at last in their power, and were determined to make their victim; the Messiah stood before them bound and guarded.

So the examination began.

---

[1] **John xviii. 16.**   [2] **Lightfoot.**

False, suborned witnesses had been provided and were ready for their part of the work.

The high-priest commenced with asking the Messiah about his disciples and his doctrines, hoping to find some admissions made by which he might bring charges of a weighty character, but he could find **none.** There was a sublime dignity in the Saviour as he stood **and answered. His case was** evidently prejudged, his **judges were fixed in purpose, and he** knew it all; **they were** trying to **entangle him by admissions;** there were men there **also ready for personal violence;** and he saw all of this. But he answered calmly and with dignity: "I spake openly to the world, I ever taught in the synagogues and in the temple whither the Jews always resort, and in secret have I said nothing. Why askest thou me? Ask them which heard me what I have said unto them; behold they know what I said." This challenge to a fair examination by witnesses was met by gross violence from one of **the** officers who struck the Saviour with the palm **of his** hand with the sharp question: "Answerest thou the high-priest so?" **It was calmly** borne. "If I have spoken evil, **bear witness of the evil;** but if well, **why** smitest thou me." [1]

The **Messiah had been asking for only what was customary in Jewish trials, or rather for less than that; for he** asked **but a candid examination of those** who had listened **to** his teachings, while it was customary in these trials to begin with the testimony for the accused, giving the witnesses a fair hearing, and encouraging them to speak for the defence. Instead of that, the Sanhedrim now began with seeking for **false witnesses** against him, but they sought in vain. Many were **offered, but** their evidence was contradictory and none of it of a sufficiently damnatory **kind.** [2] At last came two who **declared that they had heard him say, "I am able to**

---

[1] John xviii. 19–23.   [2] Matt. xxvi. 59–60.

destroy the temple of God, and to build it in three days;"[1] and at their testimony the eyes of the judges glistened, for here was a charge that would work against him before all the people, holding as they did their temple in such reverence, and feeling such pride in its greatness. However, even in this charge the witnesses were not agreed. The Saviour did not reply to them.

At last the high-priest, wearied with the impotence of his efforts so far and out of patience, determined to force a crisis, and to have a decided answer in a matter that he believed would produce condemnation in the minds of all men, people as well as Sanhedrim, and to insure success he commenced with their most solemn form of adjuration or oath.

"*I adjure thee by the living God,*" he said, "that thou tell us whether thou be the Christ, the Son of God,"[2] which was a form of demand that put the adjured person under the curse of the law, unless he should make reply, the answer so returned being considered under oath whose falsity was accounted perjury.[3] The interest of the assembly was wrought up to the highest. Men leaned forward, and a deep silence fell upon that room. The Messiah had hitherto refused to answer the false and frivolous charges brought[4] before judges so resolved to condemn; but he now replied,

"Thou hast said," [a common form, meaning "yes, it is so:"] "nevertheless, I say unto you, Hereafter shall ye see the Son of Man sitting on the right hand of power, and coming in the clouds of heaven."[5]

It was enough. They had succeeded: and a wild scene of triumph, execration, rage and violence quickly ensued. The high priest rent his robes, crying out,

"He hath spoken blasphemy: what further need have we of witnesses? Behold ye have heard his blasphemy: what think ye?"

---

[1] Matt. **xxvi.** 61.   [2] Ibid. 63.   [3] Tholuck *in loco.*
[4] Matt. xxvi. 62.   [5] Ibid. 64.

"He is guilty of death;" was shouted from all parts of the hall: and they now rushed upon him, spit in his face, buffeted **him,** and striking him with the palms of their hands, asked, scornfully and tauntingly, "Prophesy unto us, thou Christ, who is he that smote **thee?**"[1] **Even the ser-**vants joined in these insults and taunts.[2]

Greatness **is never so great as when calmly sustaining** itself amid **insults and** injuries; truth never so **grand as** when it stands unflinchingly, unmoved amid **danger: and so** the Messiah had **stood throughout** this trial;—so **continued to** the last. He had been sublime often in his powerful teachings, and in his omnipotence, when he stayed nature's laws, and bade all diseases relax their hold, and the dead to live; but sublimer still he was in his mildness and forgive-ness among all these his enemies offering him insults and violence and thirsting for his blood.

One thing must come out clearly to our minds in this matter; and that is, the decisive manner in which he asserted his Godship here; and in which he allowed them to act upon that **as** his claim, to the last. The Sanhedrim were condemning him *on such a claim;* yet there was no **retract-**ing or denying, on his **part. They understood him clearly and fully, and charged him with blasphemy, in making** himself **God; and had pronounced him guilty of death for it. If** he meant to **assert no such** title, it was easy to say so, and to disabuse their minds, and, at least, deprive them of all excuse in their meditated deed of death; but he put in not one word to that effect.

Indeed, through all his ministry, that claim had been his **great** offence in their eyes. They had been willing to ac-knowledge him as a prophet; but he had again and again, publicly **and fully asserted for** himself more than that, even the Godship **and its authority** and rights. A claim like

---

[1] Matt. xxvi. 65–68.   [2] Mark xiv. 65.

this, and indeed any remote inclination to it, was, in the eye of the Jewish law, the most awful crime that could be committed,—indeed an unpardonable one. We have seen how Moses and Aaron were shut off by Jehovah himself from entering the Promised Land, simply for arrogating to themselves, in a momentary excitement, divine authority in performing a miracle; and so rigidly and severely was every sin of blasphemy regarded in the Jewish law, that each one hearing words of this nature was bound to rend his clothes on the spot, as a sign of abhorrence. The Talmuds also say, respecting testimony to such language: "When witnesses speak out a blasphemy which they have heard, then all hearing the blasphemy are bound to rend their garments."[1] This law of blasphemy, "as it was understood among the Jews, extended not only to the offence of impiously using the name of the Supreme Being, but to every usurpation of his authority, or arrogation by a created being of the honor and power belonging to him alone. Like the crime of treason among men, its essence consisted in acknowledging or setting up the authority of another sovereign than one's own, or invading the power belonging exclusively to him."[2]

Often had the Messiah startled his audiences by his claims either to the attributes of God or to the Godhead itself; but the majesty and the mightiness of the power clearly inherent in him had borne down opposition; and the clamors raised at his seeming assumptions were lost in the loud shouts by men healed of all diseases, and by their friends; joy, love, gratitude, triumphing at the time. Once, however, they took up stones to stone him, "for blasphemy," they said; "and because that thou being a man makest thyself God."

Here now, before the Sanhedrim; charged with the same thing; condemned to death for it; violence used; that charge

---

[1] Lightfoot.
[2] J. Pickering, LL. D. See also Lev. xxiii. 16; Deut. xiii.

of blasphemy evidently one that was to go out officially from this hall, and to be repeated before the multitudes of the Passover ;—he made no disclaimer, but allowed the record of his claims to the Godhead to stand. And so it remains ; —Jesus condemned for making himself God, and executed for it, he admitting the charge, and, without protest of error on their part, allowing them to proceed.[1]

In the large court adjoining this hall, watching all these proceedings with an agitated, and often sick and failing heart, was a disciple, ardent, quick, and yet weak ;—he who had said impetuously at the supper, "Though all men shall be offended because of thee, yet will I never be offended." "Though I should die with thee, yet will I not deny thee." "I am ready to go with thee, both into prison and to death." The disciples had fled when their Master was seized at Gethsemane, but Peter and John had followed the crowd in their midnight progress along the streets ; and John, having influence at the high priest's house, had been allowed to enter, and as we have seen, had got Peter admitted within the precincts. In the court, at some suitable spot, a fire had been built ; for the night was cold : and, as Peter sat there among the soldiers, peering timidly but anxiously around, he was charged by some one of the female attendants with having been also with Christ. He denied it : "Woman I

---

[1] Jewish writers all say, that, admitting the Gospel historians to be true, this must be the view of the case. Mr. Jos. Salvador, a physician and learned Jew of Paris, in a recent work, "*Histoire des Institutions de Moise et du Peuple Hébréu,*" says, "But Jesus, in presenting new theories, and giving new forms to those already promulgated, speaks of himself as God." In a note he adds : "The expression '*Son of God*' was in common use among the Jews, to designate a man of remarkable wisdom and piety. It was not in this sense that Jesus Christ used it." In another note, respecting the rending of his garments by Caiaphas, he adds, "I repeat that the expression '*Son of God*' includes here the idea of God himself : the fact is already established and all the subsequent events confirm it."

31 *

know him not."[1] It was a terrible fall from the high professions that he had made, and from his vaunted readiness to die with Christ: his impulsiveness wanted the calm and immovable courage of John, which led this loving disciple afterwards to stand by the cross, and to show his affection for his Master even there. Peter was, in after times, one of the boldest of Christian ministers, and fully redeemed himself from the contempt forced on us by this conduct in the court, as we see him cowardly shrinking to one side, false and base. He withdrew from the brightness of the fire; and approached the arched way; but was there recognized by the woman keeping the gate, who said, "This fellow was also with Jesus of Nazareth." One false step; and now another: for he declared, with an oath, "I do not know the man."

The scene in the hall itself, during these denials by the disciple had become as we have seen, tumultuous, with outcries and wrath and violence. Peter saw his Master maltreated: he saw the rush of the crowd in that more elevated place of judgment: he heard their cries of execration and of abhorrence, affected or real; saw that face so glorious even still in its majesty of kindness and its forgiveness, spit upon and buffeted; he witnessed the madness that ruled there; and saw the great triumph that lighted up the faces of the high priest and other leaders, as they felt that their enemy was now securely entangled among their toils, and could not escape. As the torches threw their ruddy light upon all the scene, and portions of the tumultuous crowd were thrown into strong relief, or, retiring into the shadows, were succeeded by others, the faces bore still the same expression of wrath and malignity and triumph bent upon Christ. Peter saw and heard all; too anxious for his Master not to be closely observant, yet shrinking from being himself observed.

---

[1] Luke xxii. 57.

There came at last a lull in the noises; for morning was now approaching, and the rulers having done their deeds of darkness to their satisfaction, were separating, in order to **prepare** for the more formal meeting of the Sanhedrim, which must be held at the earliest hour of the day. Peter lingered still. His heart had failed him in his recent temptation,—that which Christ had cautioned him **to pray against** —and he **despised himself** for the weakness which **he felt** was still on him : **but he could not** bring himself **to leave the place; and he hung about the court with a** strange tumult in his heart, affection, reverence, anxiety, fear. **Probably** his Master, in some of the latter scenes, had noticed the disciple's face filled with affection and yet fright; and had also met Peter's eyes among the crowd. Another temptation **came** to the disciple, and he cowered under **it still** more ; **his** heart entirely giving way, till he seemed to be transformed into another man. A person said to him, "Surely thou art one of them : for thou art a Galilean, and thy speech betrayeth thee ;"—for the Galileans interchanged some sounds in their language so as to make some of their words difficult to be **understood by** the people **of Judea. He** cursed and **swore :—"I know not** the man **of whom ye** speak." **The words caught the ear of the Messiah ; and he** turned **and looked on the wretched culprit;—on that face so** filled **with fright and** shame ;—the eyes of the Saviour expressing compassion mixed with gentle reproach. It was Peter, the boaster that he would die with him ; and the cock now giving warning of approaching day, had not crowed **twice** before he had thrice denied his Lord,—this last time **with oaths.** At this look of Christ, **the** disciple went out, **and wept bitterly.**

The **faint dawn, soon** afterwards struggling through the night, and coming **slowly** over the Mount of Olives, saw in **those** streets, **a man convulsed** with **grief** and shame, humbled and self-accusing, and filled with remorse :—not much, seemingly in that large city, and this tumultuous world; but yet a sight that angels love to look upon; for, in such penitential feelings, souls are purified and saved. How the disciple must have loathed and abhorred himself!

Peter afterwards became strong and brave for his Lord, confessing him boldly before rulers, and amid direst persecutions: and, it is believed, he unflinchingly met a martyr's death in his Master's cause.

———

CHAPTER XLV.

THE TRIAL BEFORE PILATE.

THE day at last broke fully over Jerusalem; and the people in that region being early-risers, the vast multitude in and about the city were soon astir, ignorant yet of the scenes at Caiaphas's house, and thinking with gladness of the occasion before them; for the day succeeding the Passover-meal was always their high festival day. The whole of the Passover season was to be a time of rejoicing,[1] but this day was always given to peculiar ceremonies, and sacrifices for feasting; and, as it was the sixth day of the week, (our Friday), and the morrow would be their Sabbath,—a more solemn time—it seemed to them that an unusual enjoyment of festivity was to be crowded into this day.

On this, the 15th of Nisan, all the males were bound to appear in the court of the temple, bringing with them a burnt-offering for their appearance and a double peace-offering, one for the solemnity, and one for the joy of the times.

---

[1] See Deut. xvi. 10–12.

These offerings were called in their language, *Chagigah,* a word meaning *festivating* or *rejoicing;* and were to be a bullock or sheep, (2 Chron. xxx. 24, and xxxv. 7, 8), quite distinct from the sacrifice for the Passover supper, and for a different purpose. Part of this chagigah offering was given to the priest, and with the remainder "they proceeded to their feastings together with great mirth and rejoicings, according to the manner of that festival."[1] This day was also the one from which the fifty days to Pentecost were to be numbered; and (which usually added greatly to its joyousness), it was the time when the first fruits of their barley harvest were to be presented to God; before which no one was permitted to cut any grain;[2] and so this day was called a sacred day. The cutting of this first fruit was a matter of ceremony. Those who were deputed by the Sanhedrim for the ceremony of reaping it went forth in the evening of the feast (Chagigah) day; and people flocked with them to see the sight, and also that it might be done with the greater pomp. When it grew dusk, he that was about to reap said, "The sun is set?" and all said, "Well." He repeated, "The sun is set?" and the people replied again, "Well:" "With this sickle;" "Well:" "With this sickle;" "Well:" "In this basket;" "Well:" "In this basket;" "Well." And if it happened on the Sabbath-day, he said, "On this Sabbath;" "Well:" "On this Sabbath;" "Well:" "I will Reap;" "Reap:" "I will Reap;" "Reap." And so, as he said this thrice over, they answered to it all, "Well."[3] Their regular Sabbath (as, after sunset, was the case in this instance) did not hinder this ceremony; and on the next day, the sheaf was offered in the temple, after which, and not before, the Jewish people might proceed to their harvesting.

Such in the regular order of things would have been this Chagigah or great festival day, a time of peculiar feasting

---

[1] Lightfoot.   [2] Leviticus xxiii. 9–11.   [3] Lightfoot.

and rejoicing; and now with the feelings suited to it the great multitudes rose on that (Friday) morning in the brightness and freshness of the dawn.

But the Sanhedrim had been yet earlier risers, for their work had to be quickly done. As the earliest morning light crept down into the judgment-hall and the court-yard, and upon the wearied and exhausted individuals there—the Messiah still among them—the members of the Sanhedrim, with the chief-priests and elders and scribes[1] might have been seen gliding toward the house of Caiaphas, where they were soon formed into the regular council prescribed by their law. They could now pronounce a legal judgment, and their action was rapid, the way to it having all been prepared during the night. The Messiah was placed before them.

"Art thou the Christ? tell us," they demanded.

"If I tell you ye will not believe," he replied; "and if I also ask you, ye will not answer me, nor let me go. Hereafter shall the Son of man sit on the right hand of the power of God."

They were impatient, for time was pressing, and all cried out as with one voice,

"Art thou then the Son of God?"

"Ye say that I am:" (the Jewish form, equivalent to, "I am").

"What need we any further witness?" they cried "for we ourselves have heard of his own mouth."

He was immediately condemned.

From this he was taken while it was yet early[2] to Pilate's judgment-hall.

In the meantime, by means of various spreading reports, the multitudes were coming to a consciousness of these transactions, and they stood appalled—their senses almost paralyzed by what they heard. Their enthusiasm toward the

---

[1] Mark xv. 1; Luke xxii. 66. [2] Luke xxii. 66–71. [3] John xviii. 28.

Messiah had been very great. All had taken him to be at least a prophet; many believed him to be much more than that. The rumor of a few days previous, that "the kingdom of heaven was shortly to appear," had turned all eyes toward him in expectation of something wonderful in which he was to be the great and glorious leader, and they had conversed about it among themselves until curiosity, if not enthusiastic, had highest power. They remembered also the scenes in the temple; his majesty of appearance there, his teachings and the force of his words, his countenance so grand in its changing expressions as he hurled the merited woes upon Pharisees and Scribes; they remembered his healings in the temple and the general joy caught from the healed men—the hosannas shouted out and caught up again repeated till the temple courts were filled with the sounds of glorifying him as God; and the scenes just previously on the descent of Olivet, where the throngs were spreading their garments in his way, and hailing him as king and more than king—"Hosanna," "Save, Lord, we beseech thee." Those among the multitudes who had not witnessed these things had heard them repeated in their ears so often, and with so much of the eastern enthusiasm of manner that they had caught the same feeling—and now? Now the rumor went that he *had been condemned at a formal meeting of the Sanhedrim for* BLASPHEMY; that witnesses had sworn to his saying that he would destroy their temple; that he had been sentenced to death, and was at present before the Roman governor, whither their rulers had taken him in order to have the sentence confirmed!

Those of the multitudes who hastened toward the judgment-seat of Pilate found there that the rumor was true, and found the Roman soldiers by the gates and in the judgment-hall. The great Roman power had hemmed him in on every side. A shudder as if their own dissolution were at hand crept through the crowds, among whom however the agents

of the Sanhedrim were now also at work infusing doubts
and uttering anathemas against him whom the rulers had
condemned for blasphemy.

Pilate is described by Philo, a learned Jewish writer[1] of
that age, as a man "with a nature inflexible and implacable
in its arrogance;" he had been appointed Procurator of Judea, A. D., 26, and had made himself odious to the Jews by
his cruelty and savage nature of which we have an example
in his having compelled the Jews to mingle the blood of
some of their own people in their sacrifices at the temple,
(Luke xiii. 1).

Before this man the Messiah still bound now stood for
trial, his accusers who were the Sanhedrim having followed
him and being now there also with their charges and their
fully settled plans.

Judgment among the Romans was always public and *sub
dio*, (in the open air); and in order to make their decrees
more solemn, officers of high rank took with them a tesselated pavement (in Heb. Gabbatha, John xix. 13), which
was placed on an elevated spot; on this pavement was put
the *Bema* or judgment-seat, and on this the judge took his
place when a trial was about to be commenced. This was
in the present case in front of the Governor's palace; and
about it, the Jewish elders were now standing for accusation;
but they refused to enter the palace itself, that being a Gentile's residence, entering which would defile them till evening, and prevent their joining in the Chagigah ceremonies
on that day.[2]   Pilate, however, could take the accused per-

---

[1] Born in Alexandria, where he wrote about the year A. D. 40.

[2] The reader will observe that this removes the seeming difficulty in
John xviii. 28, which has sometimes puzzled commentators. The *passover* mentioned there must have been the *Chagigah* eaten during the day,
and from which any defilement in the morning would have debarred
them. Such defilement continuing only till sunset could not exclude them
from any religious duty after sunset; but they wanted to share the Chagigah feast. The whole seven days' feast of unleavened bread was often

son within the palace for private examination there. The hall back of the judgment-seat had its guard of soldiers and officers, and the Governor had also his officers at the *Bema* where he took his seat.

Pilate, according to the Roman legal usage, demanded of the accusers what charges they **had to** bring : but they tried to evade the question, and to **see what their own authority** could effect.

"**If** he were not a malefactor, we would not have delivered him up unto thee," they said. The Governor rejoined with a sneer,

"Take ye him and judge him according to your law :" and they now showed their object :

"It is not lawful for us to put any man to death."[1]

He saw their purpose : and saw the calm and dignified face before him, the noble expression of features, the grandeur even yet marked upon that brow. How unlike a culprit! How strange that such a person should be brought before him as a malefactor to be put to death! He looked on the countenance of the crowd of accusers, malignant amid all their attempts at **hypocrisy ; fierce,** though under the assumptions of rank **and justice ; wrathful** in their very first **words before him ; and lighted up with•eagerness** for revenge. They **were dark, scowling faces,** though their owners stood **in robes of office around the bound individual** before him, whose features expressed even then only benignity and kindness, mingled with calmness and resignation.

He again demanded of them an accusation, ánd they now brought forward a political charge, "We found this fellow **perverting** the nation, and forbidding to give tribute unto Cæsar, saying **that he himself is Christ, a** king."[2] The Governor **gazed at him, and felt a** wish for a private inter-

called the Passover, (as in Josephus, Bel. ii. 1, § 3, also Ant. xi. 4, § 8) and in 2 Chron. xxxv. 7, 8, bullocks are called the *Passover* offering.

[1] John xviii. 28–31.   [2] Luke xxiii. 2.

32

view: he would not have such a person maligned by those hypocritical men without any means of help. So Pilate withdrew to the hall in the rear, **and** had Christ brought there to him.

"Art thou the King of the Jews?" he asked. The Messiah answered,

"Thou sayest it," (a form of assent): and added,

"Sayest thou this thing thyself, or did others tell it **thee** of me?" The reply to that was indignant,

"Am I a Jew? Thine own nation and the chief priests have delivered **thee unto** me: what hast thou done?" The Messiah replied:

"My kingdom is not of this world: if my kingdom were of this world, then would my servants fight, that I should not be delivered to the Jews:[1] but now is my kingdom not from hence."

"Art thou a king, then?"

"Thou sayest that I am a king [equivalent to Yes, I am a king]. To this end was I born, and for this cause came I into the world, that I should bear witness unto the truth. Every one that is of the truth heareth my voice."

"What is truth?" said Pilate, a skeptic probably as regards all truth, as a Roman courtier might readily be; and still more so, surrounded as he was with such hypocritical faces as were those of the accusers; for he had immediately seen that "for envy" they had delivered Christ.[2]

He did not wait for an answer to this question, but went out before the expectant crowds, who were eager for his return. The Sanhedrim had felt that there was good reason to dread such an interview: and they stood now, with ill-

---

[1] It is observable that here also the distinction is kept up between the people and the rulers, the latter obviously meant by the word Jews, it is well to bear it in mind in the further reading of John respecting the trial and crucifixion.

[2] Matt. xxvii. 18.

disguised anxiety on their faces, and in alarm. Pilate's
words confirmed their fears.

"I find no fault in him at all."[1] Filled now with open
fierceness, they pressed warmly once more the accusation,
which they believed must ultimately alarm the Governor.

"He stirreth **up the people,** teaching throughout **all**
Jewry, beginning from Galilee to this place."[2] From Galilee! thought **Pilate: and he** was glad; **for it would give**
him **an** opportunity **to throw the trouble and the odium that**
might arise from this trial **on Herod, Tetrarch of** Galilee,
who was now in Jerusalem. **He** probably **also** expected
some gratification of spite in the perplexity it would occasion
Herod: for these two governors were at enmity at this time.
He therefore sent the Messiah to Herod, who was pleased;
for now at last, this ruler had an opportunity of seeing one
of whom he had so often heard; and rumors of whose mira-
cles were so astonishing that he had even taken him to be
John risen from the dead. **He** hoped perhaps to see some
miracle performed.

Before this monster of lust and cruelty, the Messiah was
now standing; the accusers having accompanied him there.
They might hope for **better success before** such a mixture **of**
baseness, and weakness **and barbarity, as Herod had shown**
himself to be in **the case of** the Baptist: **and they now urged**
their accusation with new vehemence; **while** the **Tetrarch**
himself put question after question, with greater and greater
bitterness and savage feeling, as he found himself not replied to in any one of them. The Saviour opposed to the
contemptible ruler and his insolent questions, as he had previously done **to his** accusers before Pilate,[3] only the calm
dignity of silence; until the Tetrarch, irritated by receiving
no reply, **turned on him his soldiers, who, with the ruler,**
"set him at naught, **and mocked him, and arrayed him in a**

---

[1] John xvii. 34–38.   [2] Luke xxiii. 5.   [3] Matt. xxvii. 12.

gorgeous robe:" after which he was sent back to Pilate. These missions between the two governors brought about a reconciliation between them, and they now became friends.[1]

The governor of Judea was perplexed; for on the one hand was the Sanhedrim, with the weight of their position, and their official condemnation in this case, with accusations also of a political nature, which, if disregarded, might bring him into trouble; and on the other he believed in the Messiah's innocence, and saw their motive in all this malignant action; and he had been also cautioned by his wife, warned in a dream[2] "to have nothing to do with that just man." He made an effort at extricating himself through an old custom, which was to yield up to the people's clemency on this day, any malefactor whom they might demand; and now, as they were becoming clamorous for this favor, a hope sprang up in the governor that they might be less savage than their rulers, and might designate the accused for this favor. He said to them,

"Will ye that I release unto you the King of the Jews?"[3]

The rulers were startled; but they were not to be readily foiled. They immediately mingled with the multitude,[4] repeating charge after charge against the Messiah; sustaining these with all the authority of their office; appealing to the people's reverence for their temple, there in full view; and using such other devices as their malignity could invent; and soon there were symptoms of disapprobation at Pilate's suggestion. There was in prison a notorious felon, Barabbas by name, put there for robbery and murder, and attempt at sedition; and from those crowds—probably many of them of a base sort, such as could sympathize with that culprit—after a while, arose a demand:

"Away with this man, and release unto us Barabbas."[5]

---

[1] Luke xxiii. 6–12. [2] Matt. xxvii. 19. [3] Mark xv. 9.
[4] Matt. xxvii. 20. [5] Luke xxiii. 18.

"What will ye then that I shall do unto him ye call the King of the **Jews**?" asked the Governor. And they answered with the terrific cry,

" *Crucify* him !"

Pilate was horror-struck, and attempted to remonstrate :

" Why, what evil hath **he** done?" But the cry **was only** vociferated more fiercely,

" Crucify **him !**"[1]

They **were going far** beyond their own **law, which ordered** stoning **to death, as** the severest punishment **for the** greatest crime known among them, namely, blasphemy : **but** this **did not** satisfy them now. They demanded the most cruel and the most painful of all Roman punishments, one exciting such horror among the Romans themselves, that Cicero says of it, **"Ab** *oculis, auribusque et omni cogitatione hominum removendum est :"*[2] *it should be banished from eyes and ears, and even from the very thoughts of men:*—so ignominious also, that it was inflicted, as the last mark of detestation, on the vilest of people,—was the punishment of robbers and murderers, provided that *they were slaves ;* **but it was** thought too infamous a punishment **for freemen, let their crimes** be what they might.[3]

One word **from** the **governor,—an order for acquittal**— would have been decisive; and we may wonder that it was not **given, when** he **heard** their horrible **demand,** especially as he had just said to them, "Behold, I, having examined him before you, have found no fault in this man touching those things whereof ye accuse him: no, nor yet Herod : for **I sent** you to him, and lo nothing worthy of death is done unto him:"[4]—but we must remember, not as an exculpation, but as one of the facts in the case, that Pilate was amenable to Rome, to which their accusations against himself, could

---

[1] Mark **xv.** 12–14.   [2] *In Verrem.*
[3] Adam Clarke.   [4] Luke **xxiii.** 14, 15.

easily be sent. He thought he would try whether their malice might not be satisfied if the object of their vengeance should be degraded and punished before their eyes; his claims of kingship being made the badges of his disgrace. He, therefore, had the Messiah scourged; and delivered him into the hands of his soldiers, who "platted a crown of thorns and put it on his head, and they put on him a purple robe, and said, Hail, King of the Jews! and they smote him with their hands;" "they smote him on the head with a reed, and did spit upon him," and bowed their knees in mock worship:[1] after which Pilate coming out said,

"Behold I bring him forth to you that ye may know that I find no fault in him."

Jesus was led before them wearing the crown of thorns and the purple robe. Mockery it was, but, even still there was a dignity in his manner which they could not tear from him or disguise, and a strange Presence recognized by Pilate even there, as if the kingship thrust forward in mockery was felt to be actual truth. He said to them,

"Behold the Man!"—and there broke out again that fierce demand:

"Crucify him, crucify him." The governor saw that all efforts at conciliation were fruitless; there was now only one shout from them, and that for blood; he looked down on the fierce, and determined faces, and saw no relenting there, only malice, and but half-suppressed rage against himself. He quailed before the possible consequences of this in his own person: it would be the easiest and safest thing for him to yield. But even in yielding, he put in a protest:—"Take ye him and crucify him; for I find no fault in him." In their triumph now at success, and their attempts at justification, they overshot their mark. "We have a law and by our law he ought to die, because he made himself the Son of

---

[1] John xix. 1–3; Mark xv. 18, 19.

God." The governor was startled and amazed; it was a
new aspect in the affair; for hitherto they had been urging
it upon him on political grounds. The strange dignity of
the accused had before impressed him;—his calmness, truly
like that of a God while all were raging around him for his
destruction;—the majesty which no mocking could put
down. He went back to the hall again, and summoned the
Messiah. "Whence art thou?" he said.

There was no reply. Pilate was urgent for an answer,
and tried to bring the terrors of his power to his aid.

"Speakest thou not unto me? Knowest thou not that I
have power to crucify thee and have power to release thee?"
The answer was:

"Thou couldest have no power at all against me, except
it were given thee from above; therefore, he that delivered
me unto thee hath the greater sin."

Outside there was a feeling of impatience becoming
strong among the rulers. They dared not come to the hall,
for that would defile the hypocrites; but these interviews
and colloquies in it were always to them subjects of distrust
and fear. Previously they had found their cause suffer from
such an examination by Pilate; and now, when he appeared
again before them, he made still further efforts for the release of Christ. But they had one powerful means kept in
reserve for extremities, and such an extremity seemed now
to have come. Of all the Roman emperors, Tiberius (then
ruling) was the most jealous and implacable: and, in his
eyes, *majestatis crimen omnium accusationum complementum
est* (Tacitus, Ann. iii. 38); "*the crime of treason is the climax
of all accusations.*" They cried out loudly to Pilate:

"If thou let this man go, thou art not Cæsar's friend;
whosoever maketh himself a king, speaketh against Cæsar.[1]
Thou art not well affected toward Cæsar!

---

[1] John xix. 4–12.

He resisted no more. They had conquered, and they knew now that by this threat of accusing the governor, whose soul crouched with fear before the bloody tyrant, their triumph was secured.

The governor seated himself on the judgment-seat at the tesselated pavement, and the Messiah was brought before them once more. He said,

"Behold your king!" and there arose a storm of wrath with shouts,

"Away with him, away with him, crucify him!"

"Shall I crucify your King?" he asked.

They were now mad with rage, for they cried out—the chief-priests leading in it,

" *We have no king but Cæsar.*"[1]

The rulers must have felt a thrill of horror in their own hearts as the words burst from them; for it had always been their boast that they had no king but God, and would acknowledge no other; and this they had always put forward as their grounds of resistance to the Roman power and its claims. But madness filled them at this time. Their words were blasphemy and treason against God, according to all they had ever professed before; they were making themselves contemptible in their own eyes and abhorrent to all the nation, and faces in the multitude there showed horror at the cry; but there was no open protest, and the blasphemy and treason stand yet against the rulers in the madness of that hour.

Pilate on the judgment-seat called for water, and performed a significant act. He washed his hands publicly so that all might see it, and declared before them,

"I am innocent of the blood of this just person; see ye to it."

An answering cry came from the whole assembly there,

---

[1] John xix. 13-16.

and it contains under the circumstances the most frightful words ever uttered by human lips:

" *His blood be on us and our children!* "[1]

" Pilate gave sentence that it should be as they required."[2] He had Barabbas released then and delivered into their hands.

What were the feelings of the multitudes in Jerusalem all this while? The **people who** had cried their **hosannas, the** admiring throngs that had **gazed on** his **miracles, the men** cured, **the blind men of Siloam and of Jericho, and the halt** and blind healed in the temple, what were their thoughts? Lazarus, the disciples, where were they? Was **there no** voice from any one of them? There must have been a sickening sensation throughout **the** city, a feeling that a dark, hellish deed was being done, and a resistance in men's hearts to the whole proceeding of the Sanhedrim. "Why," the people must have thought, "why the secret stealing upon the party in Gethsemane? why the night-council? why the violation of all precedents and of all Jewish law? why this indecent haste?" The hellish malice of the Pharisees and chief-priests was manifest; **the** instigations to the crowd to release Barabbas a robber and **murderer, and** to demand crucifixion as **regards Jesus; their goadings on of the un-** willing Governor; all th**is was too transparent not to be seen** through **and** understood, **and the hearts of all true men must** have **recoiled from it in** horror and disgust. But what, **to** their apprehension, could they do? It was now but three hours after sunrise,[3] and already Pilate had pronounced the sentence, and Jesus was in the hands of the Roman soldiers; the power of that colossal Roman empire had closed around **him, and** he was hemmed in by it to his death. True it was reported **that the** Sanhedrim had **in** formal conclave con-

---

[1] Matt. xxvii. **24, 25.**

[2] Luke xxiii. 24. **This** governor after having ruled ten years was deposed and banished to Vienne, where he is said **to have committed suicide.**

[3] **See** Mark xv. 25.

demned him for blasphemy, **even** on his own words before **them**; but men through the city still recoiled with a sicken-**ing sensation from** the whole thing as a dark, hellish work. Those who thought of God's **justice,** even if they did not be-**lieve** in Christ, **trembled;** those who believed in him felt crushed to the **earth and** knew the truth of their **Master's** word—that a woe was gathering to burst over **all their land.**

There **was one man** among them almost frenzied. **It was** Judas. **He had** probably hoped that there would **be some** way **of** escape for **the** Messiah, some miracle from him per-haps for his **own** deliverance, and he had scarcely antici-pated such an end. **He** had the money; Christ **he** had hoped would escape. **Thus he** had doubtless reasoned, and the Pharisees he had **thought would** be doubly overmatched. Therefore the most restless man in all Jerusalem in watching the proceedings **of the council, and at** the Prætorium, was doubtless this traitor, in **whose heart** remorse was taking its **everlasting hold. Now** the end had come, and with it came recollections and anticipations, and a fearfulness of horror; **for hell was already lighted up** in his heart. He saw the flashing **of** triumph **in** the Pharisees' eyes; remorse was blazing in a frenzy from his own. He hurried to their council, which seems to have adjourned from the Prætorium to their council-room, and entered it with the cry,

" I have sinned in **that** I have betrayed the innocent blood." There **was only a cold-blooded,** sneering answer:

" **What is that to us? See thou to that."** He flung down their money and rushed out. **Was the** woe at the Paschal supper pursuing him? Had it not been ringing in his ears all the night and all the morning? " Woe unto the man by whom the Son of man was betrayed; it had been better for that man if he had not been born." [1] Remorse and the woe were upon **him,** and **the wretch** immediately committed suicide by hanging. [2]

---

[1] Matt. **xxvi. 24.**   [2] Matt. xxvii. 5.

The Sanhedrim gathered up the money; it was not lawful they said to put it into the treasury of the temple, as it was the price of blood; so they bought with it a field for burying strangers and called the place "*The Field of Blood.*"

CHAPTER XLVI.

THE CRUCIFIXION.

PILATE had yielded. As soon as he had discovered the motive of the Jewish leaders, "that for envy they had delivered him,"[1] and saw that they proposed making himself the instrument of their malice, and moreover saw the greatness of the Messiah under these trying circumstances he had "determined to let him go;"[2] but his own nature was too pusillanimous to allow him to hold unflinchingly to the right amid dangers to himself, and at that *argumentum ad hominem* at the last he had withered and lost his manhood. We can almost see. him as in the symbolical act he was washing his hands, ashamed of himself, trying thus but unsatisfactorily to his own heart to shake off the responsibility of the condemnation, warm in admiration of the wonderful being whom he had delivered to the leaders to be crucified, and despising and hating them. What a contempt he must have felt for men, who while they were so instigated by deadly malice and were urging him to crucify an innocent person, had yet refused to enter his hall lest they should be defiled by crossing the threshold of a Gentile, and so should be unfitted for the religious ceremonies of the day.

---

[1] Matt. xxvii. 18.   [2] Acts iii. 13.

He was glad to see them go at last and vacate his premises, but as he turned from them it must have been with many compunctions as to his own conduct, and a sense of meanness and degradation in himself. He felt however that he had obtained one great triumph over these base men, and that was when they had given the lie to all their former pretensions, and had lowered their pride and had abjured all that they had ever declared sacred and inviolable, in that mad cry from them, " We have no king but Cæsar."

There was usually before crucifixion a scene of horrible suffering and indignity, from which the outrages already inflicted by the soldiers on the person of Christ may perhaps have saved him on this occasion. It was the scourging by the *flagellum*, an instrument so frightfully severe that people sometimes died under the infliction.[1] Horace calls it *horribile flagellum*. It consisted of a handle with thongs " knotted with bones or heavy indented circles of bronze, or terminated with hooks, in which case it was aptly denominated scorpion." It was used solely in the case of slaves who were as already stated, the only persons who could be executed by crucifixion, the punishment for theft and murder. Luke[2] says that Pilate proposed to scourge Jesus, and John[3] speaks of a scourging during the trial. Matthew's record[4] is " Then released he Barabbas unto them, and when he had scourged Jesus he delivered him to be crucified;" and similar to this is the account by Mark.[5] Commentators are divided on the question whether there was but one scourging, that is during the trial, or in addition the customary one after sentence had been pronounced. The soldiers, of whose barbarity we have proofs during the trial, would be ready for any subsequent cruelties; and such a scourging may have produced the ex-

---

[1] Jahn's Archæology.   [2] xxiii. 16 and 22.
[3] xix. 1.   [4] xxvii. 26.   [5] xv. 15.

haustion which led them to compel Simon the Cyrenian to assist in bearing the cross.[1]

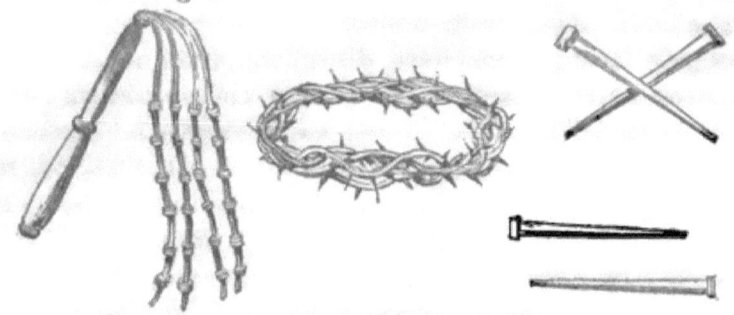

It was against all Jewish law to examine a cause, pass sentence, and put it in execution on the same day,[2] but law and usage were nothing to their leaders on this occasion. They wanted the life-blood no matter at what cost or how procured.

The movement from the judgment-hall was onward toward the place of crucifixion, the Saviour as was customary on such occasions bearing his cross; though soon owing to his exhaustion the soldiers compelled a man coming from the country to assist in supporting its weight. The crowds had gathered in large numbers, some of them stupefied, amazed, stunned, but helpless now; for any resistance, if they felt so disposed, would be insurrectionary, and would only bring on them the quick vengeance of Rome; some were exultant and noisy in their demonstrations of triumph and joy. As the company moved onward to the place of crucifixion, weeping was heard in the crowd, and the Saviour turned

---

[1] The cross was usually about ten feet in length. Hasselquist, a Swedish naturalist, supposes that the crown of thorns was made from the *naba* or *nabka* (so called by the Arabs) very common in that country. It has numerous small and sharp spines and leaves much resembling ivy; the latter circumstance adding to their mockery, as it seemed to represent a victor's wreath.

[2] Jahn.

33

toward the sounds. Sympathy, kindness, commiseration at last and in that company; people wailing and lamenting aloud! They were women, and their voices sounded strangely among those mixed, discordant noises, where tauntings and revilings and rejoicings were the general manifestations of feeling. He turned sadly toward the women; exhaustion and pain showed themselves in his tones, but he thought even then more of these mourners than of himself.

"Daughters of Jerusalem," he said, "weep not for me, but weep for yourselves and for your children. For behold the days are coming in the which they shall say, Blessed are the barren, and the wombs that never bare, and the paps which never gave suck. Then shall they begin to say to the mountains, Fall on us; and to the hills, Cover us. For if they do these things in a green tree, what shall be done in the dry?"[1]

Once more onward toward the place of execution; the crowds half-awed by the solemn words, and by the indefinite danger foreshadowed in the language of one always so prophet-like, but the leaders were there applying fresh stimulants to rage and to tauntings and obloquy. A Roman officer; Roman soldiers; Jesus with his burden; two malefactors also with their crosses bearing him company as if an additional degradation was attempted to be forced upon him by their companionship; the rulers of the Jews still unwearied and determined to see the end fully accomplished; the crowds, some awed and silent, some vociferous and insulting; the women, their voices of wailing mingling with the harsh sounds of bold, fierce men—such was the company that advanced along the thoroughfares of Jerusalem from the Governor's palace to Calvary.

A spot called Golgotha, signifying "the place of a skull," being a slight elevation with its summit in full view was to

---

[1] Luke xxiii. 27–30.

be the scene of the crucifixion, and they soon arrived there; for it was not far from the Prætorium, and just outside the city walls. There the preparations were quickly made. The garments of the person to be executed were always the perquisites of the Roman guards, and those of our Saviour were now divided among the quaternion or four soldiers, the outer one falling to one of them by lot. The preparations for nailing him to the cross were soon completed. It was customary, in respect to the very horrible pains suffered in this first act, to give previously to the individual a stupefying potion; and such an one was now handed to the Messiah, but after tasting it he refused to drink.[1]

He was then nailed to the cross.

"Father, forgive them," he said, as they did this, "for they know not what they do."[2]

The company had been painfully attentive, even the most hardened and cruel; a deep horror, a solemnity, a shrinking in their nerves as they heard the grating sounds of the nails in his limbs; a shuddering through the crowd; sobs and sounds of weeping here and there, and then a shout of derision and scorn, with bitter tauntings, drowning all other sounds; such was the scene. What fiends men can be when they are under wicked leaders, and are stimulated by hellish passions! and devils seemed to have a terrible power there in that hour of the crucifixion of Christ. The cross now had been put in its place and elevated, and it stood there with its burden bloody from the stripes and the nailing, and with its inscription in Greek and Latin and Hebrew:

"JESUS OF NAZARETH THE KING OF THE JEWS."[3]

The Jewish leaders had requested Pilate to change it to a different form, containing a pretension to be king; but he

---

[1] Matt. xxvii. 34. [2] Luke xxiii. 34.

[3] Latin was the official language; Greek was the one usually spoken in that country by the learned; and Hebrew, or rather its cognate, Aramaic by the common people.

refused. The chief priests and scribes and elders were there leading on the tauntings: "He saved others, himself he cannot **save.** If he be the King **of Israel,** let him now come down from the cross, **and we will believe him.** He trusted in God; let him deliver him now if **he will** have him; for he said, I am the Son of God." Their action, their language, their feelings were hellish; there seemed to be nothing **human** left **in them, and** yet these men were the rulers of the nation.

The crowds joined mostly in these cries, and in their own peculiar way. They had followed, some engaged in the interest of **the rulers** and their agents, some from idle curiosity, **some from better motives; but** there had doubtless been in many, the expectation of some **great** phenomena,—a great **miracle, perhaps some supernatural** effort at release, some **struggle by that strange power in him** for deliverance; and **now that there had been none they were** angered, and would feel that there was some revenge **due** them for their disappointment. They tried to have it, led too, as they were by men in authority; the soldiers **also, and** even the two crucified malefactors, or at least one of them, joined in their mockings and taunting cries. The shouts of the people showed how the cunning device of the priests in suborning witnesses to say that they had heard him threaten to destroy their **temple, had succeeded in** revolutionizing their feelings; **for their cry was, "Ah, thou that** destroyest the temple, and **buildest it in three days, save thyself, and** come down from **the cross."**[1] The priests sneered at him, in their own peculiar way,—"He saved others; himself he cannot save." One of the malefactors by and by, struck to the heart by the strange scene,—the revilings cast on one so innocent, the **gentleness and forgivingness** of the sufferer in his greatest pains,—the **contrast between the** raging, venomous people

---

[1] Mark xv. 29.

and Christ,—rebuked his companion as he was saying, "If thou be Christ, save thyself and us."

"Dost thou not fear God," he said, "seeing that thou art in the same condemnation? And we indeed justly; for we receive the due reward of our deeds, but this man hath done nothing amiss." He added to Jesus himself,

"Lord, remember me when thou comest into thy kingdom."

It was but a simple prayer: it was the first appeal ever made to the Cross of Christ; and it was answered in kindness:

"Verily I say unto thee, To-day shalt thou be with me in Paradise."[1]

There stood near to the cross a group,—a singular one it was amid that scene of scoffing, and malice, and triumph at Christ's sufferings;—for the faces and actions of these persons gave demonstration how deeply they sympathized with the sufferer. They were his mother; her sister, wife of Cleophas; Mary Magdalene; and the faithful John. Best love is ever bravest; and these loved the most. They stood there, true to him, their souls writhing under those tauntings and those scornful insulting cries. They looked toward the cross; and they there saw the marks of agony; the anguish apparent in his face, and in the spasms and convulsions of his body;—that face so gentle and calm, and so God-like always, but now clouded with the pain which expressed itself in every line and feature;—the eyes now bloodshot;—the brow and form wounded and bloody;—the languor of exhaustion stealing over the limbs and frame. Not one word, however, of complaint from him; his eyes still showed love to them and to all. His voice and tone when he spoke, were now as always, in kindness and love.

---

[1] Luke xxiii. 39–43.

33 *

He addressed them; but his words were few, in consequence of his spasms of agony:

" Woman, behold **thy son !**" **and to** John,

" Behold, thy mother :"

Those tones had the marks of pain in them; but yet how true they were to his strong, undying love ! John took her from that hour as his own mother, to his home.[1]

The hours dragged on; and the anguish increased. In one of our best authorities we have the following account of the effects of crucifixion :

" **1. The** position of the body is unnatural, the arms being extended back and almost immovable. In case of the *least motion* **an extremely painful sensation** is experienced **in** the hands and **feet,**[2] which are pierced with nails, and the **back, which is lacerated with stripes.** 2. The nails being driven through the parts of the hands and feet which abound **in nerves and tendons, create the most** exquisite anguish. **3. The exposure of his many** wounds to the open air brings **on an inflammation which** every moment increases the poig-**nancy of the** suffering. 4. In those parts of the body which are distended or pressed, more blood flows through the arteries than can be carried back into the veins. The consequence is that a greater quantity of blood finds its way from the aorta into the head and stomach than would be carried there by a natural and undisturbed circulation. The blood-**vessels of the head become pressed and** swollen, which of **course, causes pain and redness of the** face. The circumstance of the blood being impelled in more than ordinary quantities into the stomach, is an unfavorable one also, be-

---

[1] John **xix.** 25–27.

[2] Gregory of Nazianzen **has** asserted that one nail only was driven through them; **but** Cyprian, (De passione), who had been a personal witness to crucifixions, and is consequently, **in this** case, a better authority, states on the contrary, that two nails or spikes were driven, one through each foot.—*Jahn's Archæology.*

cause it is that part of the system which not only admits **of** the blood being stationary, but is peculiarly exposed to mortification. The aorta not being at liberty to empty, in a free and undisturbed way as formerly, the blood which it receives from the left ventricle of the heart, is unable to receive its usual quantity. The blood of the lungs is therefore, unable to find a free circulation. **This** general obstruction extends its effects likewise to **the right ventricle, and the con**-sequence is an **internal excitement and exertion and** anxiety, which are more intolerable than the anguish **of** death itself. All the large vessels about the heart, and all the veins and arteries in that part of the system, on account of the accumulation and pressure of blood, are a source of inexpressible misery. 5. The degree of anguish is gradual in its increase, and the person crucified is able to live under it, commonly till the third, and sometimes even till the seventh day."[1]

The group of friends felt all the bitterness of those still continued gibes and tauntings, and the wagging of heads at him, by the passers by ; for the spot was at some thorough-fare, probably **near the angle where the walls** of Acra **and** of Zion met, **and by the gate Gennath, in the latter.** They were themselves a marked object, with **their deep sympathy** depicted in their **faces; and many a look** of contempt was directed at them ; but no violence dared to be offered in the presence of the Roman officer and his soldiers: and the elders and rabble felt too much engrossed with their tauntings of Christ to give much time to others of less note. Was there not one sentiment of compassion in the revilers? **no feeling for the anguish shown** on that brow and in the convulsed limbs? Their **words show only** malignity, and spite, **and triumph.**

But after a while, as this was **going on, every one in**

---

[1] Jahn's Archæology.

Jerusalem and in the region about it became conscious of a singular gloom darkening the air and settling down over all objects; becoming deeper and deeper; coming silently and enwrapping everything,—the city, and temple, and mountains around. People stopped, and looked at each other in wonder; and presently in alarm: for it was becoming night, although the time was at full mid-day. The crucifixion had been at nine o'clock:[1] it was now twelve; but soon there was no sun to be seen in the sky, only the blackness of darkness everywhere. Men groped along in uncertainty of motion, deep horror now in every heart. The Chagigah ceremonies had been going on in the city, and at the temple, and the great altar fires were blazing on Moriah with the sacrifices there. Very many of the people, it is true, had, from early morning, felt no heart for the festivities of this, their great day of rejoicing: for they had been stunned by the announcement of the seizure and binding and condemnation of Christ, and by the scenes at the Prætorium; and a sickening sensation had crept through them, when they heard of the crucifixion: but others, deceived by the artful proceedings of the Sanhedrim, or callous, or fickle, or unwilling to lose the rejoicings that had always made this day so cheerful, were proceeding with the Chagigah festivity, when this darkness came settling down over their mirth, and substituted for it, horror and alarm. They left their feasts untouched; they sat in silence, or whispered to each other, or hastened to secret places, as if fearful that, in this blackening gloom, some mighty Avenger was coming through the air ready to strike,—they could not tell where, or whom, or how. Some ascended rapidly to the sacred

---

[1] Third hour, (nine o'clock), according to Mark xv. 25, which agrees with Matthew and Luke. The Gospel of John says at the sixth hour, (or noon), which is evidently an error by transcribers; the Greek letter representing six being very similar to that for three. In some of the best ancient Greek readings, we find the third hour, also in John.

precincts of the temple, thinking that perhaps there might be more safety or less alarm in that place; and found the priests, with pallid faces, looking in their white dresses about the altar lighted by the strong glare from its fires, more like unwilling spirits of doom aghast at their work, than like pacificators between God and man, and the ministers of joy on this festive day. There was universal horror, and a momentarily increasing fear amid these millions congregated at Jerusalem. The words of Christ to the women, on the way to Golgotha, were spreading among the crowds, "Daughters of **Jerusalem,** weep not for me, but for yourselves and for your children," &c.: and people also remembered his frequent prophecies respecting the city and its terrible approaching end. "Had the **time now come?" they** thought. "Was this the beginning?" Men sat down, covering their faces in the horror that was chilling them through; or stood like statues, as if turned to marble in this fear that was paralyzing every faculty: women clasped their children to their hearts, and shed over them their silent **tears,** or broke into wailings at what seemed **to** be the doom already arrived.

All nature was mourning as at some horrible event; and all thoughts were turned towards the scenes at Golgotha,— the cross, the victim, the deepening agonies there. That spot was involved in the darkness, as if heaven would not look upon it, and was shrouding it from all sight;—or, as if heaven was sympathizing with the sufferings there, and veiling itself in gloom.

So the hours passed on, in this unnatural and frightful darkness, until the ninth hour (three o'clock) was near at hand. The anguish of Christ had been increasing, with all the peculiar mental as well as bodily distress belonging to that mode of suffering. Death was approaching, a death in which all the powers are strained into the fullest agony before they finally give way. The mind is fearfully affected; and the writhings and distortions of the higher, intellectual nature form the greatest of the horrors which precede the dissolution.

Such a spasm came now. There was a cry, extorted by its anguish.

"Eli! Eli! lama Sabacthani," meaning, "My God, my God, why hast thou forsaken me?"

Men with hearts steeled against all sympathy, and full of malignity, were still about the cross; and they said,—mistaking the words—

"Let be: let us see whether Elias will come to save him."

The mental spasm, however, was soon over; and the Godlike nature in him had again the supremacy; but what a horrible darkening there had been to bring forth that desponding cry!

During these pains, the body is parched by a burning sensation; and to his complaint of thirst now, the soldiers filled a sponge with their vinegar, or sour wine (their common drink), and it was handed to him on the extremity of a hyssop stalk.

The end had come. He said,

"It is finished."[1]—"Father, into thy hands I commend my spirit."[2]

One cry, a piercing, anguished cry, drawn from him by the death agony, and it was over.[3] The sufferings had ceased.

Nature, as if in sympathy, was convulsed. The earth shook as if it were in terror; the rocks were rent in sunder; the veil of the temple, hiding the holy of holies from the eyes of all but the high priest, was rent in twain from top to bottom, as by unseen hands; graves opened of their own accord, and bodies of the dead appeared moving about, as though the grave were resigning its power,—its dominion gone. The centurion who had been superintending the ex-

---

[1] John xix. 30.   [2] Luke xxiii. 46.   [3] Matt. xxvii. 50.

ecution exclaimed, "Truly this was the Son of God."[1] A **fear** had come on all who were watching there, and others joined the officer in the exclamation: they smote on their breasts,[2] and returned to the city, fear, sadness, remorse fill-**ing** their hearts. The physical darkness had now passed away, and light was restored to the earth once more.[3]

The group of friends by the cross had not been the only sympathizers watching these sad events. There were others further off—people true to Christ still in their hearts, some of whom had followed him from Galilee,[4] but powerless to help. To them the former group had retired toward the last of these scenes. In addition to their sympathies, there were many very sad thoughts among his friends on that day, understanding very imperfectly as they did the nature of the kingdom which he had come to establish among men. Their love for him had given rise to many hopes of seeing him aggrandized in the world; some hopes there had also been for themselves: all such hopes were quenched now.

Life in the malefactors still lingered on: and it was cus-tomary with the Romans, when this was the case longer

---

[1] Matt. xxvii. 54. [2] Luke xxiii. 49.

[3] This darkness was undoubtedly miraculous; but there was a singular case of darkness, from natural, though still unexplained causes, on what is called in New England "The Dark Day," which occurred on the 19th of May, 1780. President Dwight, in speaking of it, says: "Candles were lighted in many houses; the birds were silent and disappeared, and the fowls retired to roost. The legislature of Connecticut was then in session at Hartford. A very general opinion prevailed that the day of judgment was at hand. The House of Representatives being unable to transact their business adjourned. A proposal to adjourn the Council was under consideration. When the opinion of Col. Davenport was asked, he answered, 'I am against an adjournment. The day of judg-ment is either approaching, or it is not. If it is not, there is no cause for an adjournment; if it is, I choose to be found doing my duty; I wish therefore that candles may be lighted.'" This darkness, like that at Jeru-salem, seems to have been local.

[4] Luke xxiii. 49.

than they wished in any sufferer on the cross, to hasten death by breaking the bones of the legs with a mallet; or, by plunging a spear into the heart; or, by kindling a fire below, thus to hasten the end by suffocation. The day following this would be the Jewish Sabbath; and it was important to have the bodies removed before sunset, when their holy day would commence: so the soldiers came and broke the bones of the malefactors, but there was no necessity for this violence on the Saviour's body, and it was spared: one of them however, to try whether there might not still be life, thrust a spear into his side, and there came out blood and water, decisive evidence that death had taken place.[1]

Silence had fallen gradually upon this scene; the leaders fully sated in their revenge, had left, and most of the people had dropped off toward their homes in fear and remorse. A few remained, watchers from affection; and the Roman guard was still on duty there.

We turn to gaze on that spectacle;—the cross, the body, the bloody marks on brow and limbs, the stamp of death on the victim slain;—*slain for us.*

"Behold the Lamb of God, which taketh away the sin of the World."

---

[1] *Serum and blood*, showing that the blood had resolved itself into its constituent principles, as it always does after death.

"The researches of modern surgery have established the fact that an effusion of blood would have taken place in any case, being the natural consequences of such a wound, and is, under the circumstances, decisive evidence of the actual death of Christ."—*Bloomfield, in loco.*

"In order to ascertain whether Christ was really dead or not, or whether he had merely fallen into a swoon, a soldier thrust his lance into his side (undoubtedly his left side), but no signs of life appeared. If he had not been previously dead, a wound of this kind in his side would have put a period to his life, as has been shown by the physician Eschenbach and by Gruner. The part pierced was the *pericardium;* hence lymph and blood flowed out."—*Jahn's Archæology.*

CHAPTER XLVII.

THE BURIAL.

THE supernatural **darkness had passed; but the hearts** of the multitudes were still **palpitating** with **the fear** and awe which the recent **events had produced;**—**the pall** over all nature, the earthquake, the significant rending **of** the veil of the Holy of Holies, the dead moved from their graves. They felt that a horrible deed had been done, for which they might look for some avenging hand: and, when the people who had been to the crucifixion, and had joined in the derision there, now returned smiting their breasts in horror and remorse and reporting the words of the Centurion and others who had witnessed the end, "Certainly this was a righteous man," "Truly this was the Son of God," a deep dejection fell **on the city,** a gloom of the **soul** darker than that which **had** just **before** been **filling their sky.**

Sunset was approaching. **After that they were bound to** go out and **cut the first fruits with festivity:**—**they had no** heart for it now.

As the morrow would be the Sabbath, the time from three till sunset was called "the preparation;" being given to cooking and preparing their food for the holy day: sometimes the whole of Friday was called the day of preparation. The Jewish law also directed that the bodies of persons ex- **ecuted** should be buried before **sunset of** the day of execu- **tion; and those at Calvary must now be removed.**

There were members of the Sanhedrim believing on Jesus; but that **horrible punishment** of excommunication, decreed, a year before, **on** any one who might confess him, and the rancorous spirit of that body, had kept them in a

34

craven fear; but two of their number now broke through thi.. feeling;—Joseph of Arimathea; and also Nicodemus, who had, three years previously, come to Jesus by night. They had taken no part in the deliberations and the condemnation at the house of Caiaphas; and the Sanhedrim had, probably, used the precaution to keep all doubtful persons from the councils on these occasions. Joseph had been, at heart, a disciple: and is spoken of as a good man and just, waiting for the kingdom of God: and although it would have been more creditable to him to have shown his discipleship earlier, we must remember that the heroic spirit of Christianity had not yet taken a decided form, except in the Lord himself; and, also, how dark and cramped the minds of the Jews were, respecting the Messiah. The eleven themselves had all fled, when their Master was seized at Gethsemane.

Joseph now went boldly to Pilate, and asked that the body of Christ might be delivered up to him. The governor sent for the centurion having it in charge, to inquire whether death had taken place so soon; and, being satisfied of this, gave orders that it should be given to the applicant; who now, assisted by Nicodemus, took it from the cross. The former was a wealthy man, and possessor of a garden having in it a new tomb, in which no one had ever yet been laid.[1] Thither they transported the body of the Messiah; having wrapped with it in the clean linen of its shroud, a very large quantity of spices, (aloes and myrrh),[2] which would absorb the juices, and keep it in preservation for embalmment when the Sabbath should have passed. They laid it thus in the new tomb, and rolled a very large stone against the mouth of the sepulchre.[3] The faithful women from Galilee, had, never, through all this day, deserted their

---

[1] It was an ancient custom for families to have burial places in their garden. See 2 Kings xxi. 18–26.

[2] John xix. 38–42.   [3] Matt. xxvii. 60.

Lord: they had now followed the body to the sepulchre; and when it had been removed from all human eyes, they still sat down opposite the spot, gazing there tearfully; still faithful to him in death.[1]

It was, however, only fidelity to the strong affection produced by the past; for all **hopes in** them respecting **Christ** on this earth were now **extinct.** **He** had often spoken **of** his resurrection from **the tomb on** the third day ; but, **what** is now familiar to **us, through history, was, at that time, to** them an unknown future, with foretellings concerning **it so** strange and foreign to their ideas **as to** bring to the mind no comprehension of their meaning; and all his followers had believed, when he foretold his rising again, that he spoke of the final resurrection at the end of the world. Nicodemus and Joseph had so little expectation of a near rising again that they had enveloped the body in spices, so as to preserve it for embalmment after their Sabbath; these women themselves, when they afterwards came to the sepulchre, on the resurrection morning, had **with** them spices[2] for the embalming: and even the eleven, **on that** third **day,** when they heard that he had arisen, **treated the report as an idle tale.**

So, at this **time, in all the followers of the Messiah** hope **was** dead, **except what there might be in a far distant day,** when **the end of all things should come.** The world was **a** blank to those who had trusted in him as the Messiah that was to do so much for the nation and for himself, and, perhaps, for them. Crucified; dead; what was there to hope for now? How longingly had friends, how tremblingly had enemies, all through that day, been in a half-expectation **as of some** miracle for his own deliverance! but none had come. It was **ended now: the closed** sepulchre, and the huge stone[3] **rolled against its** mouth, seemed to these watch-

---

[1] Luke xxiii. 55; Matt. xxvii. 61.   [2] Luke xxiv. 1.
[3] Mark xvi. 4.

ers an obliteration of all the hopes which they had entertained. So they believed; but affection still remained; and
they sat there, tearfully by the sepulchre as the sun went
down and the evening shadows began to gather around.

But they were startled **soon by** the martial tread of armed
men, and by numerous irregular footsteps of others, advancing along the alleys of the garden. On these came; **and**
presently a company of soldiers filed up, and stood in array
before the sepulchre; while chief priests and Pharisees
busied themselves to make sure that the body was still safe
within the tomb.

Hatred had been more keenly observant than affection,
respecting Christ's words; **and was now more** attentively
revolving them; and the fears of these rulers had pictured
to them a possible surreptitious disposal of the body: and
especially were they **alarmed when they** found that two of
the Sanhedrim **itself, one of them a** man of large pecuniary
resources,—were the leaders in taking the body from the
**cross, and depositing it in a sepulchre belonging to one of
these now acknowledged disciples,—men of rank.** They
had hoped that in the death of Christ their troubles would
cease; but a worse possible one had suddenly started up.
The body in the tomb and garden belonging to Joseph, now
courageous, as he had just shown himself to be in going to
Pilate for it, and a man of means sufficient to enable him to
hire **men for any purpose;—he and** Nicodemus also able to
give the protection of their rank to subordinates; while in
the Sanhedrim were others, also, secretly favorable;—how
easy, they thought, would it be, **and** under these circumstances—(judging others by themselves)—how likely, to
steal the body away, and to start then the report of an actual
resurrection! So, when they heard the particulars of the
burial, they hastened **to** Pilate.

"Sir," they said, "we remember that that deceiver said,
while he was yet **alive,** After three **days I** will rise again.

Command, therefore, that the sepulchre be made sure until the third day, lest his disciples come by night, and steal him away, and say unto the people, He is risen from the dead: so the last error shall be worse than the first."—Pilate answered curtly,

"Ye have a watch : go your way, make it as sure as ye can."[1]

The Roman garrison in Antonia could easily furnish men, with officers to take command :[2] and, with this power from the Governor, they found themselves immediately provided with what they needed : and a sufficient guard,[3] with **the**

---

[1] Matt. xxvii. 63–65. Pilate's words, 'Εχετε κουστωδίαν, may mean either *ye have* or *have ye,* the word, 'Εχετε being both in the indicative present and imperative.

[2] It is obvious, from Matt. xxviii. 12–15, that the guard was composed of Roman soldiers ; for, had they been Jewish watchmen from the temple there would have been no occasion to bribe them to secresy, or to offer to stand between them and Pilate, if their unfaithfulness should reach his ears.

[3] Bishop Porteus, **in his lectures on Matthew, gives sixty as the** number of men composing **this guard. He says: "The** chief priests **went** to Pilate as soon as the sun **was set on Friday, the day** of the **preparation and crucifixion ; for then began the following day or Saturday, as the Jews always began to reckon their day from** the **preceding evening. They had a guard as soon as they possibly could after the** body was **de**posited in the sepulchre ; **and one cannot** help admiring **the** goodness of Providence in so disposing events, that the extreme anxiety of these men, to prevent collusion, should be the means of adding SIXTY *unexceptionable witnesses* (the number of Roman soldiers on guard), to the truth of the resurrection, and of establishing the reality of it beyond all power of contradiction." The writer of the present work united with a friend,—a **professor** in a theological seminary, himself a library of erudition,—in a **search among** numerous ancient folios and quartos for the Bishop's authority for **stating so large a number ; and we** both were surprised to find how little, on **this subject, could be found** among commentators and other writers. All **that we could discover was a** quotation in Poole's Synopsis, from Theophylact (**tenth century**), κουστωδία εξήκοντα 'εστι στρατιώτων, *a guard consists of sixty soldiers.* **The** rulers **would take** care that, on this occasion, the guard should be a large one.

34 *

Pharisees and chief priests in company, were quickly on their way to the sepulchre. The number of their watch was large, but these leaders were resolved that no precautions should be wanting; and that all secret plottings by the disciples, or violence from any revulsion of feeling among the populace should be equally guarded against. They took care to see at the sepulchre, that the body was yet there safe; and then, drawing a cord across the stone which filled the entrance, and sealing the ends of this cord with their seals to the rock on either side, they felt now satisfied, that, with the soldiers in addition stationed about the place, they had made all secure. They thought, as they retired from the garden to their homes, that they might now have rest.

But with such remembrances as were theirs men cannot calmly and quietly rest. Night came down silently over the city, stealing on so imperceptibly that it might seem as if trying as it always does to soothe and to invite to quiet and repose, but there was a seething of many feelings all through Jerusalem, and through the country around that was hostile to rest.

The rulers themselves felt that the day's acts had written up against them a terrible record which they had some time or other to meet. The excitement of the previous night and of the day was over, and they could now reflect; the strong tension on the nervous system was past, and left them exhausted. They sat down to think. Tired and worn as they were, many thoughts in them, enemies to peace were harassing them, and were to harass them forever. Conscience is never dead, and it now came stinging like a viper, and telling them that their earnest zeal in all this was but masked revenge? Why their night assemblage, if truth and justice only were required? Why the suborning of witnesses? Why their actual breaking through all the old rules for trial although preserving the forms? Why their untiring persistence? Why the forcing of things to this terrible end?

Was not all this course a tacit acknowledgment in themselves that their cause was not good? that they were fighting against **truth and** right? Suppose moreover that this wonderful be-**ing** should be the Messiah after all? and should be their future judge?

Whatever doubts there might be on that subject **there was** one which had **in it a terrible certainty; for to gain** their ends this day they **had humiliated** themselves before **the** Roman governor, a **Gentile as they had never done before.** Their own cry, **"We have** no king but **Cæsar,"** was still ringing in their ears. It was to ring there **forever.** **It had** always been their proud boast before **their** countrymen and the world, that they did not and would not bow to the Ro-man yoke. Had they not bowed their necks and themselves put the yoke on this day before Pilate and before the pub-lic? But far worse than that—*they had forsworn God.* Their opposition to Rome had always been on the ground that God was their King, and that they could have no other. But the mad cry, "We have no king but Cæsar," was cast-ing **off God** and **was** swearing fealty to the bloody, despica-ble monster at Rome **in** place of Jehovah; *was blasphemy; was shutting themselves* **out from God.** And **was not the very fact that they could be induced to do this in that persecution to death, a proof that their cause was the devil's cause, and** that they were only his dupes? So their consciences whis-pered as they laid down to rest.

But they slept at last. Nature wearied out and exhausted gave way at length, and they dropped into repose wrapped in such dreams as proud men utterly humiliated, and men feeling **that** they had just publicly abjured God, and substituted for **him the vilest of all** earthly tyrants may have; so they slept, —to **wake again to a** frightful consciousness on the morrow.

The night **settling** down found the disciples crushed in heart, and with no consciousness of noble, heroic conduct as a relief. They knew and felt how pusillanimous their course had been. John only had possessed courage enough to stand near the cross an acknowledged follower of Christ. Their hopes of earthly glory were now gone; their Master had met a felon's death; they themselves might soon be seized by the same relentless Sanhedrim and dragged to punishment; what a vista had Christ's oft repeated predictions as to themselves opened to their view! Yet their recollections of him were precious. Faithless as they had been, one of them false, they clung the more pertinaciously to the memories of his kindnesses, his counsels, his gentleness in their mistakes and waywardness, his constant love to them; and their affection to his memory still constituted a bond among themselves saddened, and borne down by a consciousness of their baseness in deserting him in his hour of need. Humbled they truly were, but unconsciously to themselves they had in this humility and this feeling of self-accusation, and in their affection to the memory of Christ, the elements which would yet be worked into greatness of life. They slept at last, worn out with long agitation—slept such a sleep as the sorrowing and despondent have.

As twilight spread over the vast throngs in the city and on the hills around, these talked uneasily and gloomily of what they had that day seen and heard. A great many of them remembered the Crucified as he had moved among their hills and valleys in Galilee and Perea, the crowds following and shouting their gratitude at his healings; the whole world there glorifying God for what their eyes beheld of his wonderful greatness and goodness. Some of these multitudes had cried Hosanna to him here at Jerusalem only a few days before, and they recollected how full their hearts had then been of admiration and love. They remembered his stopping amid the joy of the shouting train to weep over Jerusalem, and his spoken lamentation then and on the following day over the city. Many in their hearts' deep convictions still hailed him with Hosannas as the Messiah. But if he were the Messiah then what must be thought of their country's sin that day ! So they queried sadly and anxiously as night sank down upon them and they retired to their rest.

The city and country slept ;—the rulers from the exhaustion of the previous night and day ; **the** disciples worn out with sorrow and self-reproach ; **the people** weighed down with gloomy thoughts. They slept : and, penetrating **with** its fangs deeper and deeper **in the** nation's **vitals, so as to** hold, with a sure and unrelenting grasp ; and beginning **already** its devourings, to be continued till the life of that people should all be like a quivering nerve, wherever they might be found,—*was the doom intensified by that hideous prayer,*

" His blood be on us and on our children."

Jesus had prayed that they might be forgiven; but forgiveness is not forced on those who do not ask for it themselves, and who persist in wrong ; and the Jews still insist on the justice of that condemnation.

That prayer has never yet been cancelled.

CHAPTER XLVIII.

THE RESURRECTION.

THE hours passed heavily by, over those guards at the sepulchre ; and morning **came, the Jewish** Sabbath with its **long hours of** entire **rest; only the most** necessary duties of **life being** allowed on their holy day. But people through these **hours rested** uneasily ; for their thoughts were ever turning towards that body lying in the sepulchre, **and** to the events of the preceding day ; and many discussions now took place; often renewed, always unsatisfactory; some-times greatly exciting, generally of a gloomy kind. Sunset came again at last, closing their wearisome Sabbath, to which day even the temple solemnities could give no relief; for the voices of the multitude raised in their sacred melodies were dulled by an undefined dread. For, had not a mysterious power on the previous day, rent from top to bottom the veil shutting the Holy of Holies from common eyes?—a fact of portentous significance, especially combined as it was with the numerous other terrors and unnatural events. Even their Most Holy Place had not escaped.

The night came down again on Jerusalem; the moon was near the full, and a mild light was shed on every object,—the city, the garden, the sepulchre, and the guards pacing back and forth in their watch in front of its sealed door. At the previous sunset had been according to the Jewish reckoning the beginning of the third day since the cruci-fixion; and twenty-four hours from this period would re-lieve the guard from their duty, and the Sanhedrim from their fears; for the specified time for his rising would then be past. The grave had not yet been invaded; the seals had not been broken; the guard were cautioned to particu-lar vigilance in the short remaining time; though, indeed, scarcely was caution necessary; for the Roman discipline was the severest ever known, and was particularly and pro-perly so respecting the *vigiliæ* or watches at night.

Hour after hour passed on in quietude; the pleasant, mel-low moonlight lying on the sleeping city, on the crests of Moriah and temple pinnacles, on battlemented walls and castles, on the garden, on the helmets and breast-plates, and spears of the guards, giving a charm to the scene, height-ened by the entire silence around, which was broken only by the pace of the watch in front of the tomb. It had got at last to be near morning; in a little while the dawn would begin to creep upward in the eastern sky.

Suddenly the earth shook, and the whole garden was illuminated by an unnatural light, so dazzling as almost to blind the beholder;—and the guards stood paralyzed and trembling at what they beheld. An angel was there; "his countenance like lightning, his raiment white as snow." He had descended suddenly and was among them in the overwhelming glory of the heavenly world, compared with which all earthly beauty in the scene around was blank and drear;—except the glory of the tomb, by which he now stood, and which reflected back the dazzling brightness from his face. The glare lighted up all objects around, and made distinct to the eye everything which now occurred.

The angel rolled away the stone from the mouth of the tomb.

JESUS CAME FORTH ALIVE.

The resurrection had come.

There was no mistaking that form standing in the blaze of the heavenly light:—the hands and feet pierced by the nails of the crucifixion; the wounded side; the brow marked by the thorns; that majesty of countenance, each feature and mark clear and easily recognized; and all manifest to the returning senses of the guard.

Christ, the crucified unto death, was before them; and had come out from the sealed and carefully guarded tomb.

The guard recovered from their stupor of amazement and fear: it was in vain to contend with the supernatural, and with power such as was before their eyes: their work of guarding was indeed over, and it was manifest had all been in vain. No seal, no bars, the millions of the world to guard such a place and to keep the dead there, would not have availed.

Early on that morning, a hasty admission was demanded into the houses of some of the chief priests; and these men were astonished to see several of the soldiers before them, showing marks of great alarm. They brought the news that Christ had risen, and described the circumstances attending his coming forth among the living, himself alive again.

The intelligence **was astounding.** The **rulers** had provided against the surreptitious taking **of the** body by the disciples; but here was an account which, if **it** should spread abroad, would bring the whole Jewish people upon them **in** a tempest of excited and angry feeling, demanding punishment on the abettors of the crucifixion: and the numerous guard which they had placed there in order to make sure that there should be no fabricated story of a resurrection, would now **every** one of them, be evidence that a resurrection had actually **occurred.**

The danger of that terrible reaction among the vast multitudes **was imminent; and to** prevent it, the guards must **at once be bought over** if possible; no matter what the cost might be. **They** were all quickly sent for; **and in** the mean time, swift messengers through **the city brought the** Sanhedrim **together, to** an exciting consultation about this amazing news. The soldiers were brought before them: and the ample pecuniary means at the command of the rulers were turned to account.

" Say ye,"—this was the injunction—" Say ye, His disciples came by night, and stole him away while we slept. **And** if this come **to** the governor's ears, we will persuade him and secure you."

The soldiers knew that the same golden means could **be made effectual with the governor likewise;** and consequently **little danger** would accrue to them; so they took the bribe, **and spread** abroad the prescribed report,[1] which the Sanhedrim took care to have repeated by their special messengers sent out for that purpose through the city and country around.[2]

---

[1] Matt. xxviii. 11–15.

[2] The authority for this last is **Justin Martyr, a** cotemporary with the apostle **John.**

The story was a bold one: for every person knew that the punishment to any Roman soldier sleeping on his post was death; and these guards were circulating a report, which showed on the face of it, a gross infidelity to their trust and a clear violation of all military law; and therefore stamped the authors of the story as unworthy of belief. Every one, too, would ask, how could it be possible for the number of persons necessary to such a stealing as this, to come and re-move the heavy stone and carry away the body, without waking such sleepers by the noise which they must neces-sarily make;—the guard being so numerous as it was? But the report, though carrying such improbabilities on its front, had its intended effect upon many of the people, backed as it was by the emissaries of the Sanhedrim; and took a per-manent hold on the public mind.

We will here anticipate history a little, in order to re-mark that the Sanhedrim never dared to join issue with the apostles on this subject; although, soon after this event, the latter were preaching the doctrine of the resurrection in Jerusalem itself, and making thousands of converts by this preaching. These eleven men, so timid lately, **after they had undergone** the **wonderful change** produced by **the de-scent of the Holy** Ghost on them on **the day of Pentecost,** preached boldly and publicly *the resurrection,* of which they offered themselves as evidence. Peter and John proclaimed this at the temple, in Solomon's Porch, before the multitudes and priests: charging on them that they "killed the Prince of Life, *whom God hath raised from the dead; whereof we are witnesses."*[1] The rulers heard them, and were "grieved that they taught the people and preached through **Jesus, the resurrection of the dead;"** but although they laid hands on them **and** confined them till the next day, they dared not dispute the fact itself, and bring to issue the ques-

---

[1] Acts iii. 15.

tion, on which friends and enemies all saw that the whole fabric of their new religion was resting.[1] Why did they not for consistency's sake, and for their own cause, prosecute the disciples; and have an official investigation before the Sanhedrim, if they had dared to do so; especially now when their own story of the stealing had the lie publicly given to it in the very temple precincts, the apostles offering themselves as witnesses? On the next day after this seizing of Peter and John, "the rulers and elders and Scribes, and Annas the high priest, and Caiaphas, and John, and Alexander, and as many as were of the kindred of the high priest," assembled; and the two disciples, Peter and John, were brought out and placed before them, a determined and formidable assembly indeed. But there was no charge made there of preaching falsehood; simply the question asked;

"By what power, or by what name, have ye done this?" Peter replied to them, and said it was through

"Jesus Christ of Nazareth, whom ye crucified, whom God raised from the dead:" and the rulers dared not there dispute the fact of the resurrection. They only, after the apostles had been removed to give opportunity for consultation, decided,—"But that it spread no further among the people, let us straitly threaten them, that they speak henceforth to no man in this name:"[2] and this was done; but still there was no attempt to make any issue *on the question of the resurrection.*

Again, soon after this threat and charge to the apostles, a large number of the latter were in the temple preaching as before. They had been in prison, but were released by supernatural interposition: in the morning the prison door was found open and the room empty; and the apostles were obeying the words of their delivering angel, "Go stand and speak in the temple to the people all the words of this life."

---

[1] 1 Cor. xv. 14–17. [2] Acts iv. 17.

The multitudes were around them in this preaching, captivated by their words; and the messengers of the Sanhedrim,
sent to bring the teachers again before that body, had to do
it without violence, lest the crowd should stone the messengers themselves. The Sanhedrim were almost humble in
their appeal: "Did not we straitly command you, that ye
should not teach in this name? and behold ye have filled
Jerusalem with your doctrine, and intend to bring this man's
blood upon us."

But there was no denial by these leaders of the resurrection, which, in every contest with the apostles, the rulers felt
must be conceded as an admitted fact.

CHAPTER XLIX.

AFTER THE RESURRECTION—THE ASCENSION.

THE hearts of the disciples and of the followers of
Christ had, through that Jewish Sabbath, been burdened
with a heavy load. They had all mistaken his prediction
concerning his rising again, a circumstance that seems strange
to us, looking as we do at this event through the light of
history; but to their minds it was a truth too great to be
fully comprehended, and was mingled with visions of a general resurrection at the end of the world. Any dim idea
that they might have received from the plainness of his
words was swept away by the horrors at Calvary where
their Master might have seemed to them to be deserted of
God and man.

Consequently on this night they had not been watching,
but Christ's enemies for other purposes had watched. The

disciples did not see the glory of the resurrection, but strangers did. The former were left to sleep, though the Lord had risen from the dead.

The assembling of the Sanhedrim and the calling of the matter before that council had all been very early; for when some women came to the sepulchre at dawn[1] they found no one there. On the way these followers of Christ had been querying how they should get the great stone removed from the entrance; for they were bringing spices with the intention of having the body embalmed. No thought in them of his rising again as the object of their errand very clearly proves.

These women were the ones who had at the crucifixion stood watching the scene, some near, some further off, and who had afterward followed the body to the tomb; Mary Magdalene and Joanna and Mary the mother of James[2] and other followers from Galilee.

They came into the garden with their burden of spices. They found that the stone had been rolled away; the tomb was open! They ran to look in; it was empty!

Amazement was their first feeling; then alarm. "Who had taken the body? For what purpose? Where was it? There had been such hate shown by the ruling powers during the last three days that nothing was too dark for them, no act that they might not perpetrate: or had friends taken the body from some mistaken motive?" Thought at such moments is far quicker than words, and these queries were flashing through their minds, only however creating perplexities. Mary Magdalene, having given a glance to assure herself that the sepulchre was empty, turned and ran back to

---

[1] Matthew says, "as it began to dawn;" Mark, "very early;" "at the rising of the sun;" Luke, "very early;" John, "when it was yet dark." For such metonomy of sun-light, see Judges ix. 33; Ps. civ. 12; 2 Kings iii. 22.

[2] Luke xxiv. 10.

the city to the lodging-place of Peter and John whom, on seeing them she saluted with the lamentation:

"They have taken away the Lord out of the sepulchre, and we know not where they have laid him." These two disciples started immediately for the tomb.[1]

In the meantime the women left behind had entered the sepulchre. Two men suddenly appeared now beside them; angelic messengers they were quickly seen to **be; and the women, trembling with fear, bowed down their faces before** them.[2] One of the angels said,

"Fear not ye, for I know that ye seek Jesus which was crucified. He is not here; for he is risen, as he said. Come, see the place where the Lord lay. And go quickly and tell his disciples that he is risen from the dead, and behold he goeth before you into Galilee; there shall ye see him; lo, I have told you."[3]

They hurried off, trembling still at the thought of what they had just seen and heard, but filled with an ecstatic joy. What glorious tidings **were** these of which they were the messengers! *Risen, alive again, soon to meet them once more; they should see him again, now far more glorious* **and more** *wonderful even* **than before!** They stopped not, but were **hurrying back to the city full of eagerness to communicate the news when, on the way, they met the Saviour** himself!

He stood before them! What was he like? The same to all outward senses as previously, except that he now bore in his hands and feet the marks never, never, we may believe, in the glorified body to be erased;—the marks from **that** sacrifice of himself made for the redemption of the world.

They knew him at once, and at his salutation, " All hail!"

---

[1] John xx. 1–3. [2] Luke xxiv. 4, 5.

[3] Matthew xxviii. 5–7. **Matthew and** Mark speak of one angel; Luke of two. The same criticism applies here as in a former case, *Qui plura narrat pauciora complectitur.*

35 *

they fell at his feet embracing them and worshipping him. He said:

"Be not afraid; go tell my brethren that they go into Galilee, and there shall they see me."

He left them, and hurrying on their mission they soon reached the house where all except Peter and John were staying, but here they received a terrible check to their eagerness and joy. The disciples treated their story as an idle tale![1]

The nine listened to their earnest words, which were almost incoherent through their haste and agitation, looked at them, saw how they trembled still from excitement, and how pale their looks; heard their confused voices in the earnestness of their asseverations, the tones of joy and earnestness and disappointment intermixed; and concluded that some strange phantom in their confused senses had bewildered them. The disciples were never disposed to credulity, and throughout this day they showed an amount of the opposite feeling which seems strange to us with our present means of judging of these things. But the resurrection was to them a new thought; even to us now it is an amazing one though familiar to our minds. They had been weeping[2] at their loss; the other feeling was too great a joy to suddenly find admittance amid such gloom.

Peter and John, on the report of Mary Magdalene, had started from their home in another part of the city, and John's warm affection brought him the first to the sepulchre, where he stooped and looked reverently in not venturing to enter. Peter arriving soon had greater boldness and went in, and John also entered now. The empty tomb betrayed no signs of a rapid and confused departure, for the linen clothes used for enveloping the body were folded, and the napkin for the head had been wrapped up and laid by itself.[3]

---

[1] Luke xxiv. 11.   [2] Mark xvi. 10.   [3] John xx. 4–7.

They queried as they stood there, now joined by Mary Magdalene who had followed them, and were perplexed by what they saw. Thieves had not taken the body, for the spices were there, and in that case would not have been left behind; friends had not done it, for they would have taken the grave-clothes also. No account of a resurrection had yet reached these two, and "they knew not the Scripture" about his rising.[1] Their eyes confirmed what they had heard concerning the removal of the body; but the rest was still to them a dark perplexing mystery. They returned to the city leaving Mary Magdalene still at the tomb.

She was left there alone, weeping, outside the sepulchre; but presently stooping down, she looked in to see the spot where the body had just been lying. She was startled at seeing two angels sitting there, one at each end of the tomb; the heavenly visitants, their robes of white, and their meditative posture, harmonizing with the sacred place. They addressed her:

"Woman, why weepest thou?"

"Because they have taken away my Lord, and I know not where they have laid him," was the reply; her simple language evidence of the full strength of her grief.

She turned as she said this;—some other person was standing near her; but her eyes,—holden, as was afterwards the case with the two disciples going to Emmaus, or overflowing with grief,—failed to recognize who it was. A voice, also unrecognized said,

"Woman, why weepest thou? whom seekest thou?" Her mind was full of the one thought of the abstraction of the body; seemingly with scarcely a glance at the questioner, whom she supposed to be the gardener, she replied.

"Sir, if thou have borne him hence, tell me, where thou hast laid him, and I will take him away."

---

[1] John xx. verses 9, 10.

There was but one word in reply to this; but it was in that tone so well known to her—

"Mary!"—She turned :—

"Rabboni!" (Master): **and** she fell **at** his feet.—It was Jesus himself.

Her joy, and love, and reverence were making demonstration in the act of worship, as she lay there, her heart overflowing with gladness. Alive! restored to them! The marks in the feet showed that it was no phantom, but the same! Not a spirit, but himself! In her reverence and joy, **she would** have clung to these feet, but there was not time for such demonstrations now. He said,

"Touch me **not; for I** am not yet ascended to my Father; **but** go to my brethren, and say unto them, I ascend unto my Father, and your Father; and to my God, and your God."[1]

She went to deliver the message; her soul all full of gladness, **and of that one thought that the** Lord was among them **again, living, speaking; that** face, so grand always, glorious still in its benignity and kindness; that voice, still full of its old intonations of mercy and goodness: Jesus was alive again! her thoughts gave swiftness to her movements; and she was soon before the apostles in their city home. But the manner in which they received her message **grated** on all her sensibilities. They refused to believe that **it could be so;**[2] **the very enthusiasm of** her feelings was to **them a proof that an excited imagination** had deceived her. The announcement, they thought, was too astounding to be believed: they wanted the evidence of their own senses; indeed, they argued, could they even then believe?

Our knowledge of the Saviour, after his resurrection, is **but** fragmentary. In the history of the Gospels he comes **before us suddenly, and without** preparation of circum-

---

[1] John xx. 11–17.   [2] Mark xvi. 9–11.

stances; and then disappears; to be revealed again, without explanation or cause given : his earthly ministrations always so mysterious to us, must indeed be doubly so in that space **lying** between earth and heaven; the interval between the resurrection and his ascension.

At this place, however, the inquiry may suggest itself to the reader, what was the nature of the body **in which he** now appeared? There have been three opinions **started by** learned and good men : 1st—That it was a spiritual body, such as the dead shall have after the resurrection ;[1] 2d—That it was the same body as before, but glorified, or as the earlier writers express it, changed in its qualities and attributes : and 3d—That it was the same body as before, but which was to be spiritualized and glorified at the ascension. It will **be** best only to remark here, that the last of these opinions seems to be the correct one. The body of Elijah was also spiritualized at the moment of its ascension from the earth. As respects the sudden transportation from place to place, or a sudden appearance or disappearance, all difficulties in any of the above views cease in comparison with the resurrection itself. We are among **the** supernatural agencies ; and admitting **the power of the resurrection, we** must admit power for **the rest.**

Christ thought it best to remain, **after the resurrection,** forty days[2] on earth. It was important to give full proof of his having risen again ; not only immediately after that event, but at subsequent times and different places ; and these to be occasions, when men's minds would be recovered from the first surprise, and a cooler judgment be exercising itself. **It was** important also that the disciples, whose mission was **to be so extensive** and dangerous, should not have a feeling of sudden and entire desertion ; but should have a sense of

---

[1] 1 Cor. xv. 43, 44.   [2] Acts i. 3.

a nearness to them, a care and affectionate regard, all open to their outward senses, and giving an assurance to their mind and heart that their Lord had not forsaken them, would not forsake them, in this new relative condition between him and themselves. Being with them, as he was, for forty days; not continuously, in which case familiarity might have lessened reverence; but at intervals, and under circumstances to give assurance of his identity, his deep affection, and his continued supernatural powers, and also, with these powers, of a greatness in his Presence more wonderful even than before, he could thus make them have a fulness of faith in his final parting words—"Behold I am with you alway, even unto the end of the world." They would, indeed, need the consciousness of that presence in many a scene of their after life,—the arena with the wild beasts ready to tear them to pieces, and the rage of men more savage than beasts;—and they could have it all the stronger, from the feeling that he had, in his affection, lingered with them, these forty days, to afford them proof of his care and attachment in his new state, and to give words of kindness and love, uttered in their ears;—manifestations of his closeness with them which they could fully understand. With such a feeling, not of forsakenness, but of *the Presence* derived from the forty days, and the demonstration to their senses that they were not, and to their hearts that they never could be, forsaken, they could go forth into the world, as they did, to meet all its rage, and, amid that rage, to persevere.

On this day of the resurrection, two disciples were going to Emmaus, a village seven-and-a-half miles northwest from Jerusalem; and were talking sadly as they went about what they had recently seen and heard. They were joined on the way by the Saviour himself, who inquired the cause of their sadness and the subject of their conversation.

"Their eyes were *holden* that they should not know him."[1]
One of them asked him in surprise,—

"Art thou only a stranger in Jerusalem, and hast not
known the things which are come to pass there in these
days?" And in answer to a question from him, they spoke
of the Messiah as "a prophet mighty in deed and word before God and the people," and gave a statement of the trial
and crucifixion. "But we trusted," they said, "that it had
been he which should have redeemed Israel;" and added
that they had been astonished by the reports of the women:
and that the sepulchre was certainly empty, as some of their
own number had seen. He replied to this:

"O fools [unintelligent] and slow of heart to believe all
that the prophets have spoken:" and proceeded then to explain the prophecies relating to himself.

Coming to the village, he was invited to go with them to
their home: where now at table, assuming the office of host
instead of guest, he took bread and blessed it, and brake
and gave to them to eat. They knew him then, for the re-
striction was taken from their sight: but he vanished, as
they became aware who he was. They said,

"Did not our heart burn within us, while he talked with
us by the way, and while he opened to us the Scriptures?"

They returned to the city immediately, and hastened to
the room where the apostles (except Thomas,[2]) with others
were assembled;—the doors carefully closed through fear
of their Jewish enemies;[3]—but as they entered, full of the
joyful news, they were met at once by the no less joyful
annunciation that he had appeared to Peter that day.[4] These

---

[1] Luke xxiv. 16.

[2] Luke calls them "the eleven," (though Thomas was absent), just as
Paul in 1 Cor. xv. 5, says, "he was seen of the twelve," though Judas
was then dead.

[3] John xx. 19.

[4] Luke xxiv. 34; 1 Cor. xv. 5. The circumstances of this appearing
are no where described.

two described their meeting with him; but, while they were yet speaking, **Christ** himself stood in the midst of the assembly, with the salutation,

"**Peace be unto you.**"

The suddenness of his appearance overcame all who were present. How could any but a spirit enter through that closed door, and stand so suddenly in their midst? **They** shrank, terrified before so dreaded an object, a spirit of unknown nature, as he seemed to them to be; but he hastened to re-assure them.

"Why are ye troubled? and why do thoughts arise in your hearts? **Behold my** hands and my feet, that it is I **myself; handle me and see; for** a spirit hath not flesh and bones as ye see me have:"—**and** he showed them his hands and feet.

There was a whirl of sensations in their hearts, a joy that longed to be full,—for it **was mixed** with doubts;—a belief **struggling for ascendency—and yet the** truth seemed to be **too great for belief; hope, mixed with** doubts; love, that longed to clasp the feet of **the Master,** and yet fear; a full recognition of the features with their grand and gentle, and now pitying expression;—and yet how could it be that he was the same? The crucified, the dead, how could it be?

How different from this doubtfulness in the strong yet shrinking natures of these men, was the quick and full belief of the weaker, and yet more courageous because more **loving natures of the women, as shown** that day!

The company had been at supper when he entered. To **assure them fully** he asked for meat, and he ate before them; and afterwards he gave explanations of the prophecies, and counsel respecting themselves after he should have left the earth;[1] and also a symbol of the future descent of the Holy

---

[1] Luke xxiv. 36–48.

Ghost on them, after which they would have the power of knowing hearts, and of forgiving sins.[1]

Eight days subsequently he showed himself again to the disciples in their room in Jerusalem, Thomas on this occasion, being present; and to this doubter, who had openly expressed his requirements of clearer demonstrations before he would believe, he gave tangible evidences of his identity.

"Reach hither thy finger, and behold my hands; and reach hither thy hand, and thrust it into my side; and be not faithless, but believe." Thomas exclaimed on this—

"My Lord and my God!" The Saviour replied,

"Thomas, because thou hast seen me, thou hast believed: blessed are they who have not seen, and yet have believed."[2]

There was to be a great occasion in Galilee, to which the Saviour, in the meeting with the women on the morning of his resurrection, had adverted, with directions to tell the disciples to proceed to that region, the number of his followers being greatest there.

There, it was intended, should be the most impressive manifestation of himself and to the largest number, and there also the grand commission to preach the Gospel *to all the world.*

First, however, there was a more private interview with his disciples on the borders of its lake. Some of these had again resorted to their former means of livelihood, and while they were employed in fishing the Saviour appeared on the shore and invited them to a meal already there prepared. They were Simon Peter, Thomas, Nathaniel, James and John, with two others not specified by name.

Could Peter ever see the Saviour now without thinking of the scene in the house of Caiaphas, and of his own sin and shame? The dawn after that night had beheld him in the streets bowed down with remorse and convulsed with

---

[1] John xx. 22.　　　　[2] John xx. 26-29.

grief, but no tears and no remorse could ever efface from his memory the terrible sin of that denial of his Lord. But his bitter repentance had brought forgiveness. The Saviour had through all that sin seen a warm-hearted, generous nature, whose very impulsiveness might under the great influences of the Spirit yet bring out the best results. Christ pitied the weak and loved the good that he saw in him.

On this occasion he must have shrunk from his Lord almost with a hatred of himself, ashamed to look into the face of one so beloved and revered, whom yet he had so basely denied with an oath. After the meal the Saviour, as if to lift up this fallen disciple from that despairing consciousness of his degradation, and to reinstate the penitent in the eyes of his companions, turned to him especially:

"Simon, son of Jonas, lovest thou me more than these?"

The language employed on this occasion was doubtless Aramaic, but the singular distinctive power of certain words in both question and answer, as given in John's record, must have had its equivalent in what was said, or it would not have been so carefully preserved as it is in the Greek of the Gospel. We follow the history as in John:

"Simon, son of Jonas, lovest thou me more than these?"

The word used is $\dot{\alpha}\gamma\alpha\pi\tilde{\alpha}\varsigma$ (*agapas*), which signifies *a strict union of affection, a feeling of strong love;* and Peter on hearing Christ seems to have shrunk into a horror at his unworthiness to respond in the same expressive terms. There is another word, $\varphi\iota\lambda\tilde{\omega}$ (*philō*), signifying an affection of less endearment, a warm friendship, and the convicted and now modest though still ardent disciple resorted to it. He answered, "Yea, Lord, thou knowest that $\varphi\iota\lambda\tilde{\omega}$ $\sigma\varepsilon$ (*philo se*) I have affection for thee." "Feed my lambs," was now the injunction of Christ by which Peter was publicly reinstated in his apostleship.

But there was such a hiatus between the Saviour's expressive word and that of the apostle, that Christ wishing in his great tenderness and kindness to place the fallen man, even in the language of his regard, on the same level as the others tried to draw him to it, and he asked once more,

" Simon, son of Jonas, lovest thou me (*agapas me*)?"

" Yea, Lord," said the remorseful, diffident man again, " φιλῶ σε (*philo se*), I have affection for thee."

" Be a shepherd to my sheep," was the injunction now.

Christ then as if unwilling to distress the sad and shrinking disciple by such contrast of terms used the same one as Peter :

" Simon, son of Jonas, φιλεῖς (*phileis*) me? Hast thou affection for me?"

The disciple grieved because he asked him this third time *phileis me?* answered warmly,

" Lord, thou knowest all things, thou knowest *philo se*, I have affection for thee." Christ gave the injunction,

" Feed my sheep."

What a history in Peter's heart there is caught by glimpses in this dialogue; the long remorse, the prostration from his former confidence in himself; affection ardent yet all enveloped in shame; days and nights of mourning; a heart now chastened by his grief!

What a tenderness and depth of love in Christ is also here made manifest!

The Saviour addressed some further remarks to him, signifying the trial before him, and what death he should die, adding then to him, " Follow me." [1]

Peter turned and saw John close by. These two, the affec-

---

[1] John xxi. 15–23. For this difference in phraseology see Alford *in loco*. It is all lost in our version, where the repetitions in the questioning seem to want force. Alford says *agapan* is more used for "that reverential love grounded on high graces of character;" *philein* for "personal love, human affection."

In the first and last of Christ's injunctions to Peter are Βόσκε, *feed ;* the second one is Ποίμαινε, *be a shepherd.* See Bloomfield *in loco*.

tionate, gentle, brave man, and the rash, impetuous, but
really timid one, had by the magnetism of opposites which
we often see in life formed a mutual attachment, and Peter
said in his old, impulsive manner:

"Lord, and what shall this man do?"

"If I will that he tarry till I come, what is that to thee?
follow thou me;" and these words being mistaken a report
was spread from that time that John was not to die, confirmed seemingly, for a while, in after periods by the very advanced age to which that apostle lived.

The mountains of Galilee had ever been the favorite resort of Christ, and through all that region he had left the
chief marks of his goodness and love and of his divine
power; and therefore we might have expected here something peculiar in these last manifestations of himself. It
was so. He had directed the eleven to meet him here; and
on this occasion doubtless we must place the meeting with
the five hundred brethren alluded to in another part of the
Scriptures.[1] Here was the great mission for an universal
Gospel given to his followers. Some of those present at this
meeting doubted their own senses, so amazing was the fact
of the resurrection; but others worshipped, their hearts full
of mingled sentiments, awe, reverence, wonder, tenderness,
and deep and clinging love. For there were in him the
marks of the wounds at Calvary, and all remembered his
words about the meaning of the sacrifice of himself there
made.

Standing among them on the mountain-top where they had
met, he said:

"All power is given unto me in heaven and in earth.
Go ye therefore and teach all nations, baptizing them in the
name of the Father, and of the Son, and of the Holy
Ghost; teaching them to observe all things whatsoever I

---

[1] 1 Cor. xv. 6.

have commanded you ; and lo, I am with you alway, even unto the end of the world." [1]

The eleven then returned to Jerusalem ; and he met them, now, on the Mount of Olives, and went with them along on the road to Bethany, by spots to them full of recollections of recent, stirring events. Was it the memory of the late triumphal passage across that mountain, and the loud *Hallels* of the people, which started the query by them,

"Lord, wilt thou, at this time, restore again the kingdom to Israel ?"

It was indeed necessary that these men, so persistent in the old Jewish errors, should have supernatural enlightenment before going on their wide mission to the world ; and he now again promised it to them. He directed them to remain at Jerusalem till it should come. "For John truly baptized with water; but ye shall be baptized with the Holy Ghost not many days hence." [2]

The party were now approaching Bethany. He knew that in a few minutes that last separation would take place. In his presence they had felt confidence, strength, comfort. Very soon they would be left; and what a fight there was before them in the world! and what a duty to be performed! But they were to be strengthened for it, as, indeed, all men are for duty. He said to them, "Ye shall receive power, after that the Holy Ghost is come upon you ; and ye shall be witnesses unto me both in Jerusalem, and in Judea, and in Samaria, and unto the uttermost part of the earth."

He now lifted up his hands and blessed them.

—They must have trembled at the significancy of the act.— There might well be a rush of all tender emotions as he finished the blessing, *for they were losing him.* He was ascending—floating upward, and heaven was drawing its own to itself. It was at a season when the sky of Palestine is

---

[1] Matt. xxviii. 16–20.   [2] Acts i. 5 and 6.

usually cloudless; but as the disciples with uplifted eyes, gazed intently, a cloud formed, and gathered around him, and shut him from their sight.

Two angels stood beside them.

"Ye men of Galilee," they said, "why stand ye gazing up into heaven? This same Jesus, which is taken up from you into heaven shall come again in like manner as ye have seen him go into heaven."[1]

They felt that they were left alone: but they knew that they were not deserted by their Lord. His presence is with all who love him, and will be so, evermore.

CHAPTER L.

"*WHAT THINK YE OF CHRIST?*"

WE have been able in this book to see him only in part; for such a work as this could not attempt to embrace all his life on earth. Many acts and nearly all his teachings had to be omitted; and, far more than that, there was a great purpose in both his life and death—the humiliation and sacrifice of a Divine being for the sin of the world,— which in its fulness must be beyond the comprehension of any human mind. He comes before us strangely in the Gospels; we gaze upon him for a while, and our highest wonder and warmest affections are enlisted as they never can be in any one else: but as we try to comprehend, he passes from us, as he did from the disciples of old when near to Bethany, and a cloud receives him out of our sight. Our intellect and our heart however both know that there has

---

[1] See Luke xxiv. 50–53; Acts ii. 4–11.

been present with them, ONE, before whom they gladly bow, saying with the apostle "My Lord and my God!"

The world, ever since his appearance, has acknowledged a perfectness both in his life and teachings, to which nothing can be added, from which men can take nothing away. He stands alone before us. No one can be compared to him. He is so far above all else that no similitude can be imagined: and yet, very strangely, we do not feel that he is very far removed. There was such a lovingness in him for all men that, although he is infinitely above all, we have a consciousness that he is not very far away, but is near to us. What a Lord and God we have in this Christ!—one felt to be Infinite, and whom we worship with all reverence, yet whom our hearts can cling to with all the fulness of their love, for we know that he has shown infinite love to us.

In reading the Gospels, we must be fully convinced, that the writers of them drew their materials from an actual life. No man or set of men could have invented such a character and such teachings and exemplifications of teachings: least of all could Jews have done it: and especially at such a time. He was entirely at variance with all the expectations and longings of the nation: his precepts and foretellings went for the extinction of Jewish hopes, the most extravagant that any country ever cherished: the people were the most bigoted in the world and had the attendants of bigotry, a watchful jealousy and selfishness: they were vain and proud: they persistently and strictly declined all social intercourse with other people: yet here, in these writings, is exhibited to us, as the promised Messiah and the great hope of the nation, an individual breaking through exclusiveness and teaching universal charity, universal brotherhood, universal love: advocating a kingdom in the heart, in lieu of their expected external dominion and glory, and saying "Whosoever of you will be the chiefest, shall be the servant of all." Now, the writers of these memoirs (the Gospels) were not capable of inventing a character and teachings such as these. If any one wishes to see the *beau ideal* of Jewish teachers and their sayings, let him look at Shammai and Hillel their most distinguished men in those times, as shown in the Jewish history quoted in this book. Where indeed has been the philosophic or the imaginative thinker of any time or country who could have invented such a character as that of Christ, and could have delineated it so consistently in varied action as is done in these books? The writers of them could, evidently have drawn their materials only from actual life.

It would have been most in regular order to notice at the beginning of the present work the evidence respecting the authority of the Gospels; but the author thought it would be best to leave this to the conclusion, as the reader might then feel more interested in the examination of that subject. We give the evidence in the reverse order of the time of its occurring, beginning at periods when the Christian religion was fully engrafted on national forms and institutions, and became part of the world's widest histories.

We notice first, the evidence from Pagan authorities.

Julian (surnamed the Apostate) wrote, (A. D. 331–363), against Christianity. He bore witness to the authenticity of the four Gospels and referred to the genealogies in Matthew and Luke by name, and recited the sayings of Christ in the very words of the Scriptures. He also bore testimony to the Gospel of John as having been composed at a time when great numbers in Greece and Italy had been converted to the Christian faith. He admitted the miracles of Christ.

Hierocles, president of Bythinia, a learned man and cruel persecutor of Christians, wrote (about A. D. 303) against their religion. His work, or extracts from it, refer to at least six out of the eight writers of the books of the New Testament. Instead of suggesting any suspicion that this book was not written by those to whom it was ascribed, he confined his effort to hunt out flaws and contradictions.

Porphyry wrote (about A. D. 270) a work against Christianity. His learning was extensive. He "possessed every advantage which natural abilities, or political situation could afford to discover whether the New Testament was a genuine work of the apostles and evangelists, or **whether it** was imposed **upon** the world **after the decease of its pretended authors. But no trace of this suspicion is any where to be found; nor did it ever occur to Porphyry to suppose it was spurious."** His writings contain **plain** references to the Gospels of Matthew, Mark and John; **and** speaking of **the** "Christians," he calls Matthew *their* evangelist. He conceded **the** miracles of Christ as real facts.

The Talmuds (about A. D. 230); refer to **the** nativity **of** Christ, and his journey into Egypt, and agree that he performed numerous miracles, which they ascribed to his having acquired the *Shemmaphoresh,* **or the** ineffable name of God, which they say he clandestinely **stole out** of the temple: **or they** impute **his power to magic arts.**

Celsus flourished **A. D. 176, or about seventy-six years** after **the death of Saint John.** His works have about eighty quotations **from the books of the New Testament or references to them.** "Among **these there is** abundant **evidence** that he was acquainted with the Gospels of Matthew, Luke and John. His whole argument proceeds upon the concession that the Christian Scriptures were the works of the authors to whom they are ascribed. Such a thing as a suspicion to the contrary **is** not breathed; **and yet** no man ever **wrote against** Christianity with greater virulence."[1]

The *younger Pliny,* in **a letter to** Trajan, written A. D. **107, (or seventy-four years after the** crucifixion), **from** Bythinia, where **he was pro-consul, says:** "For this super-

---

[1] McIlvain's Lectures.

stition is spread like a contagion, not only into cities and
towns, but into country villages also;" and "that there are
many of every age, of every rank, and of both sexes," adhering to it. He put many to torture, and could learn
from them only "that they were wont, on a stated day, to
meet together before it was light, and to sing a hymn to
Christ, as to a god alternately; and to oblige themselves by
a sacrament not to do anything that was ill; but that they
would commit no theft, or pilfering, or adultery; that they
would not break their promise, or deny what was deposited
with them, when it was required back again; after which it
was their custom to depart and to meet again at a common
but innocent meal,"[1] probably their feast of charity. It
may be as well to quote his account of the manner of treating those brought before him: "I asked them whether they
were Christians or not? If they confessed that they were
Christians, I asked them again, and a third time, intermix-
ing threatening with the questions. If they persevered in
their confession, I ordered them to be executed; for I did
not doubt but, let their confession be of any sort whatsoever,
this positiveness and inflexible obstinacy deserved to be punished." The Christians had already become so numerous
in Bythinia, (a region bordering northwardly on the Black
Sea and Sea of Marmora), that, according to this letter, the
heathen temples had been almost forsaken, and "few pur-
chasers for the sacrifices had of late appeared."[2]

Tacitus, who wrote about the same time as Pliny, speaking of the Christians, says: "The name was derived from
Christ, who in the reign of Tiberius suffered under Pontius
Pilate, the procurator of Judea. By that event, the sect of
which he is the founder, received a blow which for a time
checked the growth of a dangerous superstition; but it revived soon after and spread with recruited vigor, not only

---

[1] Quoted from his letter to the Emperor.   [2] Epist. lib. x. Ca. 97.

in Judea, the soil that gave it birth, but even in the city of Rome; and he then describes the persecutions of the Christians under Nero (thirty-one years after the death of Christ), in a manner which shows that they must then have been very numerous in that city.[1]

We may apparently be allowed to add:

Josephus (born A. D. 37). He says, "Now, there was about this time Jesus, a wise man, if it be lawful to call him a man, for he was a doer of wonderful works, a teacher of such men as receive the truths with pleasure. He drew over to him, both many of the Jews, and many of the Gentiles. He was the Christ;[2] and when Pilate, at the suggestion of the principal men amongst us, had condemned him to the cross, those that loved him at the first did not forsake him, for he appeared to them alive again the third day, as the divine prophets had foretold these and ten thousand other wonderful things concerning him; and the tribe of Christians, so named from him, are not extinct at this day."[3]

Lastly *Acta Pilati*. It was customary for the governors of provinces to send to the emperor an account of remarkable transactions in the places where they resided, which were preserved as the *acts* of their respective governments. Such ACTA PILATI are referred to by the early Christian writers in their controversies with heathen opponents or their appeal to heathen governments, as things well known. Eusebius, bishop of Cæsarea (A. D. 315) says, "Our Saviour's resurrection being much talked of through Palestine, Pilate

---

[1] Annal. lib. xv. § 44.

[2] Literally "Christ was this man," ὁ χριστος ὁυτος ἠν. The genuineness of this section in Josephus's writing has been doubted, mainly because it is thought to be too strong from one still an unbeliever; but it is found in all the copies of his works which are now extant, whether printed or manuscript; in a Hebrew translation preserved in the Vatican library, and in an Arabic version preserved by the Maronites on Mount Lebanon. See the subject discussed in Horne's Introduction, vol. ii.

[3] Antiq. xviii. 3, § 3.

informed the emperor of it as likewise his miracles, of which he had heard; and that being raised up after he had been put to death, he was already believed by many to be a God." Justin Martyr, in his first Apology for the Christians, which was presented to the emperor Antoninus Pius and the senate of Rome, about A. D. 140, having mentioned the crucifixion of Christ and some of its attendant circumstances, adds, "and that these things were so done, you may know from the Acts made in the time of Pontius Pilate." Afterwards, in the same apology, having noticed some of our Lord's miracles, he says, "And that these things were done by him, you may know from the Acts made in the time of Pontius Pilate." Tertullian in his Apology for Christianity, (about A. D. 200), after speaking of the crucifixion, resurrection and ascension, speaks of "an account of all these things relating to Christ" sent by Pilate to Tiberius.[1]

We proceed now to the evidence from Christian writers, of whom we have an unbroken series extending back into the times of the apostles. These are in such numbers that we have room only to glance at them and to give an epitome of what may be gathered from their works. They are as follows: *Jerome*, (about A. D. 378), who wrote many works, and whose catalogue of the New Testament Scriptures is exactly like our own; *Origen*, (A. D. 185 to 253), bears testimony to the authenticity of the New Testament as we now have it; his pupils, *Gregory*, bishop of Neo-Cæsarea, and *Dionysius*, bishop of Alexandria, did the same; *Cyprian*, a martyr, (A. D. 258), quotes largely from our sacred books; *Tertullian*, (A. D. 160–220), recognizes the four Gospels, as written by the Evangelists to whom we ascribe them, and has large extracts from their works; *Clement of Alexandria*, preceptor of Origen, quotes largely from most of the books of the New Testament; *Athenagoras*, (A. D. 180), indis-

---

[1] Horne's Introduction.

putably quotes from Matthew and John; *Irenæus*, (A. D. 170), wrote treatises from which we learn that he received as authentic and canonical Scripture the four Gospels, the authors of which he describes, and the occasions on which they were written; *Melito*, bishop of Sardis, *Hegesippus* and *Tatian*, all of about the same period, have left us similar testimony; *Justin*, (born about A. D. 89, suffered martyrdom about 164), who studied first the Grecian philosophies, and then embraced Christianity, has left us numerous quotations from the four Gospels, which he uniformly represents as containing the genuine and authentic accounts of Jesus Christ and of his doctrine, and says that these memoirs were read and expounded in the Christian assemblies for public worship; *Papias*, bishop of Hierapolis, (about A. D. 110), bears express testimony to the Gospels of Matthew and Mark, which he ascribes to these evangelists; *Polycarp*, an immediate disciple of St. John and bishop of Smyrna, (suffered martyrdom about A. D. 166), has, in the very small portion of his writings now remaining, about forty allusions to the different books of the New Testament; *Ignatius*, (bishop of Antioch, A. D. 70, suffered martyrdom about 110), distinctly quotes the Gospels of Matthew and John, and cites or alludes to the Acts and most of the Epistles; *Hermas*, cotemporary with St. Paul, (see Epistle to the Romans xvi. 14), has left a work in three books which contains numerous allusions to the New Testament; *Clement*, bishop of Rome and fellow-laborer of Paul, (see Philippians iv. 3), wrote an epistle, several passages in which exhibit the words of Christ as they stand in the Gospels, and cites most of the Epistles; *Barnabas*, fellow-laborer with Paul, (Acts xiii. 2, 3, &c.), is the author of an epistle still extant, in which are expressions identically the same as some occurring in the Gospel of Matthew, and one in particular which is introduced with the formula *it is written*, which was used by the Jews when they cited their sacred books. He quotes mostly from the Old

37

Testament, as he was arguing chiefly with Jews. But his epistle contains the exact words of several texts in the New Testament, in addition to those noticed above, and allusions to some others, with **many** phrases used by the Apostle Paul.

In the writings of these last five, (called **the** Apostolic Fathers, because cotemporary with the apostles), although their references to the Scriptures are often only fragmentary, there is scarcely a book of the New Testament which one or other of them has not quoted or referred to; and they uniformly speak of them as "Scriptures," "Sacred Scripture," **and** as the "Oracles of God." In quoting from them they most frequently use the same words which are still read **in the New** Testament; **and even when** they appear to have quoted from memory, without intending to confine themselves to the same language, or when they have merely alluded to **the** Scriptures without professing **to** quote them, it is clear that they had precisely the same texts in their view which are still found in the books of the New Testament. In all **the questions which** occurred to them, either in doctrine or morals, they uniformly appealed to the same Scriptures which are in our possession.

We have thus a cumulative evidence from both the enemies and friends of Christianity, making irresistible the conclusion, that at the **time and** in the country as claimed on this **occasion, books were written which** are called the Four Gospels (we omit notice of other parts of the New Testament); and to this conclusion concentrate also the facts of Christian churches and Christian institutions as our own eyes see them: churches and institutions which must have had an origin at some time, and which can be assigned only to that time and that place. These books show in each of them striking individuality of style and manner, and yet with this there is a similarity which proves that they must have a common source of information. Three of them appear to have been written, each independently of any other; for there are notable discrepancies which would not have occurred had they been produced in concert. These differences which are sometimes so great as to puzzle commentators can however be reconciled.

Matthew had been a publican. Tax-gatherers, as we have already noticed, were extremely odious to the Jews. The farmers of the taxes employed *portitores* or inferior officers; and he was apparently **one of** these, having been taken from "the receipt of custom," **as he himself describes.**[1] **His Gos-** pel presupposes in the reader a **knowledge of Jewish cus-** toms and of the country to such a degree as to show that it was written for Jews; and there is some reason to suppose that it was composed in the vernacular, Aramaic; probably however it was both in that language and in Greek, the former about A. D. 38, and designed for Jewish converts at home; the latter, A. D. 61, for such converts abroad. Josephus also wrote his history in both these languages. Greek was in those days the universal language adopted by those who wished their writings to be extensively read. As a collec- tor of customs Matthew would be acquainted with that lan- guage, and Jews **were scattered abroad over** the world; his Gospel **seems however to be mainly designed for converts** at home, and to be **suited to a time of severe trials in the** Christian church there, probably those **conducted by Saul.**

Mark (probably the same as John, Acts xii. 12), was not an apostle. He was son of a sister of Barnabas, and was with him and Paul in their first mission, from which he withdrew in a manner to displease the latter. He after- wards, however, reinstated himself in Paul's favor, and was with him in his imprisonment at Rome;[2] thence, it is be- lieved, he went into Asia where he joined Peter, whom he accompanied to Rome. It was during this last period in

---

[1] ix. 9. See also Mark ii. 14 **and Luke v. 27.**

[2] See Col. iv. 10 and Philemon 24.

the imperial city, while with this apostle, that Mark's Gospel is supposed to have been written, from materials supplied by Peter, whose amanuensis he indeed seems to have been. The humility of that apostle is conspicuous in every part of it, where anything is related of him, his weakness and fall being fully exposed to view, while the things which redound to his honor are either slightly touched or wholly concealed. If so written, it was about A. D. 60 or 63. The frequent *Latinisms* in this Gospel indicate a Roman origin, while the Hebraisms in its Greek show that the author was a Jew. It was evidently designed for Gentile believers, as is evident by his explanations of Hebrew customs. Robinson in his Harmony of the Gospels remarks that Mark and John " follow, with few exceptions,[1] the regular and true sequence of the events and transactions recorded by them." Matthew and Luke " manifestly have sometimes not so much regard to the regular order of time as they have been guided by the principle of association," transactions having certain relations to each other, being often grouped together, though they may have happened at different times and various places.

Luke "the beloved physician" as Paul styles him, appears to have been of Gentile parentage but to have embraced Judaism in early life; we infer the former from a distinction made by Paul (Col. iv. 11 and 14) between him and three others "who are of the circumcision;" while also his Judaism may be inferred from his intimate knowledge of the Jewish religion, rites, ceremonies and usages, and also from the fact that when Paul was assaulted at Jerusalem on the charge of bringing Gentiles into the temple, Luke is not mentioned, although he was the companion of this apostle in that city. He appears, on the authority of the ancient Christian writers to have been born at Antioch in Syria,

---

[1] The exceptions are Mark ii. 15–22; vi. 17–20; xiv. 27–31; xiv. 66–72; in John xii. 2–8; xviii. 25–27; xx. 30, 31.

where, as well as at Alexandria in Egypt, was a school for medicine. A knowledge of medicine did not always imply, in those days, great progress in general learning; but the style in Luke's writings, although showing many Hebraisms is more polished than that of the other Gospels, and the classic idioms and Greek compound words are numerous. He comes before us, first as Paul's companion (probably physician) in Galatia, whence he accompanied that apostle to Philippi. There they separated, but they were reunited at Troas in Paul's journey to Jerusalem, to which Luke accompanied him, whence he also followed him to Cæsarea. It was doubtless during Paul's confinement of two years in this last city, that Luke wrote his Gospel, that is during the years 58 and 60. Philip the evangelist was a resident there; and between this city and Jerusalem there was constant communication: and thus Luke from his very frequent opportunities of intercourse with the immediate followers of the Messiah, could draw ample authentic materials for his history. There is clear evidence all through his Gospel that it was written for the benefit of Gentile converts.

John during the early times of the Christian church remained in Jerusalem, where he assisted in the council held A. D. 49 or 50. We learn from the early Christian writers that he afterwards removed to Asia Minor, where he founded and presided over seven Christian churches, making his residence chiefly at Ephesus, which after Jerusalem had been destroyed, became the chief centre of Christian labors. It is believed that he wrote his Gospel in that city, at a date long after the others: for the efforts in it to explain Jewish usages indicate that he was writing for a people little acquainted with such matters. Opinions as to the precise time of his writing vary from the year 68 to 97. He appears studiously to omit notice of those passages in Christ's history and teachings which are given in the other Gospels, or if he mentions them at all it is in a cursory

37 *

manner. This has led to a general belief that he wrote in order to supply deficiencies in **their** accounts; but probably his more **immediate** object was to counteract some heresies then growing up in the **Christian Church.**

These are the writers of the **four books** purporting to give a history of the ministry of **Christ on** earth. They do not delineate him: they simply describe events. They **tell** in a plain **manner** what they, or others with whom they were conversant, saw and heard; often giving us only hints of facts, sometimes great masses of miraculous or other facts, but without attempts at analyzing or drawing conclusions, or at side remarks of their own. **Simply a** history, told in a plain direct **manner and** in lucid style.

We must remember the **character of the** period when those histories were written, and **mark the** aggressive nature **of the religion which they presented to** the world. **It** was **a religion** aggressive against all others. It admitted no compromise **with** opposing doctrines and no hesitancy in preaching **its own; it** was to be proclaimed in **the face of** hostile governments and rulers; it made war on heathenism and Judaism; it was subversive of all religions but itself, and demanded activity in such subversion. Its friends were warned that they would be seized upon, imprisoned, betrayed by nearest kinsmen, and put to death for it: but they were **to persevere and still to make war on all** other religions. **Now, such a condition of things would of** course provoke **every species of hostility; and the claims** of such a system **would have** the keenest scrutiny respecting every one of its **items.** Rage, jealousy, indignation, scorn, hatred, vengeful power,—all this would be let loose upon the advocates of Christianity, who, if smitten on one cheek were to turn the other to the smiter, but were still to persevere, still to preach. **We** have a striking exhibition of **such** things in Pliny's letter to Trajan quoted above; and that is an exhibition only in Bythinia of **what was universal.** Such were the times when the Gospels were produced and first read; surely not times when untruths could be foisted upon the world, and cast in the teeth of such enemies as Christianity encountered, or could produce advocates ready to die for them. *Truths*, such as the Gospels present could do this, but only *truths:* nothing else could safely meet investigations such as these accounts challenge and would assuredly receive, or could have such results as were theirs.

But, with all these conclusive facts from history before us, the *internal* evidence of the Gospels is yet the most satisfactory; for it comes without intervening authorities, directly and clearly to our minds. Christ is there before us, and we can see for ourselves. The simple fact of himself thus before us is better proof,—a greater miracle it may be called —because appealing to our intellect,—than the restoring to life of the dead was to the outward senses of the believers at Bethany or Nain. There is such a *singleness* in him, such an *aloneness* in qualities, such a well-defined exception from . everything ever before or since seen or conceived of, that, as he is placed before us, he is the best evidence for himself and for all his claims.

We have been following him through many scenes, sometimes of applauses, where he was glorified of all, sometimes of humiliations and pain, even to buffeting and a most agonizing death. How *equal* he is in all! In his intercourse with the humble and despised of the earth,—publicans and sinners,—in his commonness among men, the Divinity in him is never lowered in our eyes; and on the other hand, we feel that the shoutings of Hosanna to him, hailing him as God, do not rise up to the height of his elevation, and that no earthly honors could do so. He was perfect man and perfect God. He gave love like a God, for he died in it; and he demanded love like a God—love greater than we may have to father or mother or brother or sister and a readiness to die in it for him. " He that loveth father or mother **more** than **me is** not worthy of me," is the language of one feeling himself to be above parents and nearer to us than parents and all of earth. His demands on us are the largest : no two masters—he the only one. Yet he died for us : died that, through the strangest of all mysteries, we might have life through his death. What a bond there is between him and **us**! We may believe also that in heaven, where that only is great which is good, these scenes on our humble earth had infinite greatness, for they may solve an enigma even in omnipotent power—showing the Divine love to exist in the highest type of this affection, that is a *self-sacrificing love.*

We can see Jesus in some respects better than those twelve apostles could see him; for we behold him through an atmosphere purified for more than eighteen centuries by his example and teachings : and as he thus appears before us we find it difficult to recognize his human form, for to our cleared vision this is *transfigured* as it was on the heights of Hermon and we see heaven in communion with him. We know how the experiences of many nations, through many generations, have borne testimony to the life-giving nature of his doctrines and of his appearance on our earth ; we know how through him as years have rolled on, millions constantly have felt comforted cheered and blest, have been made happy in life and more than conquerors in death : and as we gaze at him we hear the accumulations of Hallels through all time since the scene at Calvary,—the Hallels of mortals brought into a glorious soul-life by his death : we hear shouts and see throngs, very far greater than on the side of Olivet ; and in their cry we gladly join,—" HOSANNA TO OUR LORD AND GOD! HOSANNA IN THE HIGHEST !"

INDEX.